JUMP Math 7.2

Book 7 Part 2 of 2

T0302620

Contents

jump math™

MULTIPLYING POTENTIAL.

JUMP Math
One Yonge Street, Suite 1014
Toronto, Ontario M5E 1E5
Canada
www.jumpmath.org

Writers: Dr. Sohrab Rahbar, Dr. Sindi Sabourin, Kelly Young
Editors: Megan Burns, Liane Tsui, Natalie Francis, Dimitra Chronopoulos, Jackie Dulson, Janice Dyer, Wendy Scavuzzo
Layout and Illustrations: Linh Lam, Fely Guinasao-Fernandes, Sawyer Paul, Marijke Friesen, Gabriella Kerr
Cover Design: Blakeley Words+Pictures
Cover Photograph: © Gary Blakeley, Blakeley Words+Pictures

ISBN 978-1-927457-48-1

Third printing June 2021

Printed and bound in Canada

A note to educators, parents, and everyone who believes that numeracy is as important as literacy for a fully functioning society

Welcome to JUMP Math

Entering the world of JUMP Math means believing that every child has the capacity to be fully numerate and to love math. Founder and mathematician John Mighton has used this premise to develop his innovative teaching method. The resulting resources isolate and describe concepts so clearly and incrementally that everyone can understand them.

JUMP Math is comprised of teacher's guides (which are the heart of our program), interactive whiteboard lessons, student assessment & practice books, evaluation materials, outreach programs, and teacher training. The Common Core Editions of our resources have been carefully designed to cover the Common Core State Standards. All of this is presented on the JUMP Math website: **www.jumpmath.org**.

Teacher's guides are available on the website for free use. Read the introduction to the teacher's guides before you begin using these resources. This will ensure that you understand both the philosophy and the methodology of JUMP Math. The assessment & practice books are designed for use by students, with adult guidance. Each student will have unique needs and it is important to provide the student with the appropriate support and encouragement as he or she works through the material.

Allow students to discover the concepts by themselves as much as possible. Mathematical discoveries can be made in small, incremental steps. The discovery of a new step is like untangling the parts of a puzzle. It is exciting and rewarding.

Students will need to answer the questions marked with a [notebook icon] in a notebook. Grid paper notebooks should always be on hand for answering extra questions or when additional room for calculation is needed.

Contents

PART 1

Unit 1: Ratios and Proportional Relationships: Fractions and Ratios

Unit 2: The Number System: Adding and Subtracting Integers and Fractions

Unit 3: Expressions and Equations: Equivalent Expressions

Unit 7: The Number System: Multiplying and Dividing Integers

Unit 8: Statistics and Probability: Probability Models

PART 2

Unit 1: The Number System: Multiplying and Dividing Rational Numbers

Unit 2: Ratios and Proportional Relationships: Multistep Ratios and Proportions

Unit 3: Expressions and Equations: Equations, Ratios, and Inequalities

Unit 4: Geometry: Angles and Areas

Unit 5: The Number System: Repeating Decimals and Terminating Decimals

Unit 6: Geometry: Volume, Surface Area, and Cross Sections

Unit 7: Statistics and Probability: Statistics

NS7-32 Multiplying Fractions

Here is $\frac{1}{3}$ of a rectangle.

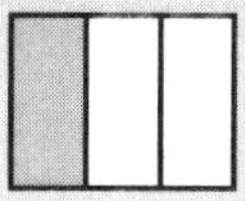

Here is $\frac{1}{4}$ of $\frac{1}{3}$.

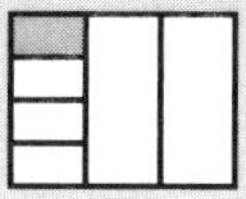

How much is $\frac{1}{4}$ of $\frac{1}{3}$? Extend the lines to find out.

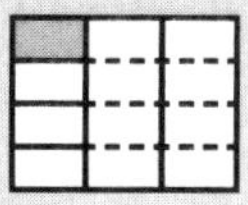

$\frac{1}{4}$ of $\frac{1}{3} = \frac{1}{12}$

1. Extend the horizontal lines in the figure, then write a fraction equation using the word "of."

a) 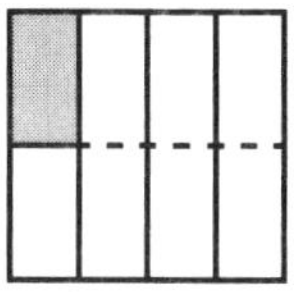

$\frac{1}{2}$ of $\frac{1}{4} = \frac{1}{8}$

b) 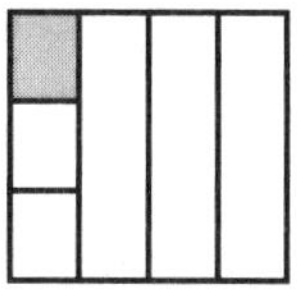

$\frac{1}{3}$ of $\frac{1}{4} =$

c) 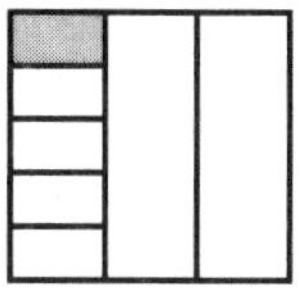

$\frac{1}{5}$ of $\frac{1}{3} =$

d) 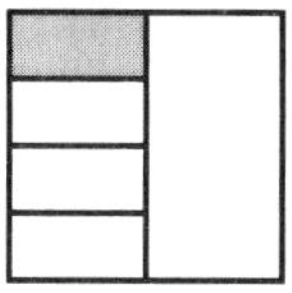

REMINDER: The word "of" can mean "multiply."

2. Rewrite the fraction equations in Question 1 using the multiplication sign instead of the word "of."

a) $\frac{1}{2} \times \frac{1}{4} = \frac{1}{8}$ b) c) d)

$\frac{1}{3} \times \frac{1}{5} = \frac{1}{15}$ ⟵ 3×5

3. Multiply.

a) $\frac{1}{2} \times \frac{1}{7} =$ b) $\frac{1}{4} \times \frac{1}{5} =$ c) $\frac{1}{7} \times \frac{1}{6} =$ d) $\frac{1}{3} \times \frac{1}{3} =$

Here is $\frac{2}{3}$ of a rectangle

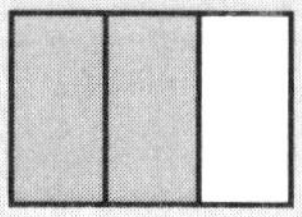

Here is $\frac{4}{5}$ of $\frac{2}{3}$.

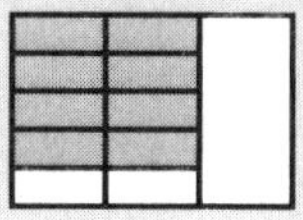

How much is $\frac{4}{5}$ of $\frac{2}{3}$? Extend the lines to find out.

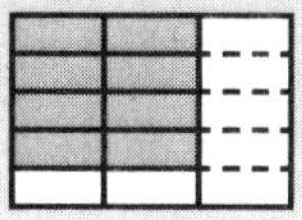

$\frac{4}{5}$ of $\frac{2}{3} = \frac{8}{15}$

4. Write a fraction equation for the figure. Use multiplication instead of the word "of."

a) 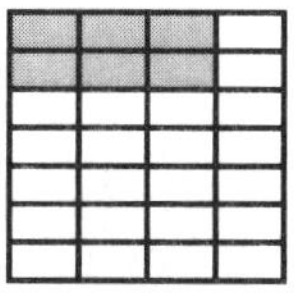

$\frac{2}{7} \times \frac{3}{4} =$

b) 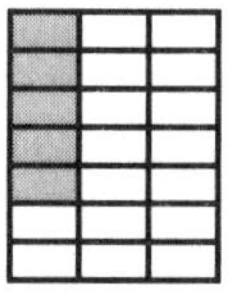

$\frac{5}{7} \times \frac{1}{3} =$

c) 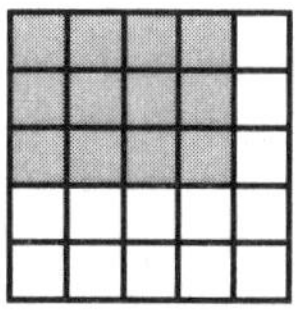

d) 

$\frac{4}{5} \times \frac{2}{3} = \frac{8}{15}$ ← Multiply the numerators: 4 × 2 ← Multiply the denominators: 5 × 3

So $\frac{4}{5} \times \frac{2}{3} = \frac{4 \times 2}{5 \times 3}$

5. Multiply.

a) $\frac{2}{3} \times \frac{4}{7} = \frac{8}{21}$ b) $\frac{1}{3} \times \frac{4}{5} =$ c) $\frac{6}{7} \times \frac{2}{5} =$ d) $\frac{4}{9} \times \frac{5}{7} =$

e) $\frac{2}{3} \times \frac{7}{9} =$ f) $\frac{2}{9} \times \frac{5}{8} =$ **Bonus ▶** $\frac{2}{5} \times \frac{3}{7} \times \frac{6}{7} =$

You can multiply improper fractions and mixed numbers the same way you multiply proper fractions.

$2\frac{1}{2} = \frac{5}{2}$ ← 2 × 2 + 1

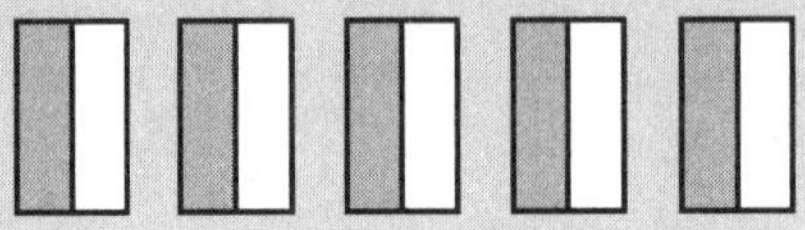

$\frac{3}{4} \times \frac{5}{2} =$

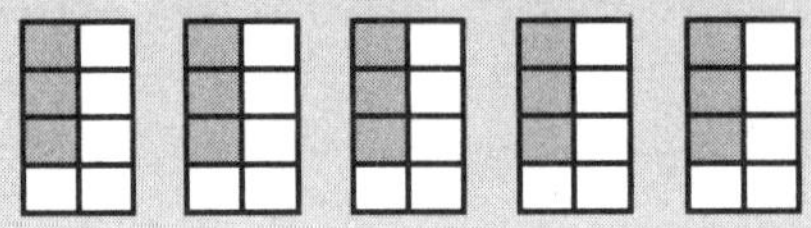

$= \frac{15}{8}$ ← 5 groups of 3 are shaded. ← 2 groups of 4 are in each whole.

6. Multiply. Reduce your answers to lowest terms.

a) $\frac{3}{2} \times \frac{5}{4}$ b) $\frac{2}{3} \times \frac{11}{4}$ c) $1\frac{3}{5} \times \frac{3}{8}$ d) $\frac{13}{9} \times \frac{3}{8}$

e) $\frac{4}{3} \times 3\frac{1}{2}$ f) $\frac{6}{5} \times \frac{11}{4}$ g) $\frac{9}{7} \times \frac{14}{3}$ h) $\frac{8}{9} \times 3\frac{3}{4}$

7. Rob is making $\frac{3}{5}$ of a strawberry cake.

The recipe calls for $\frac{1}{2}$ cup of strawberries.

What fraction of a cup of strawberries does Rob need?

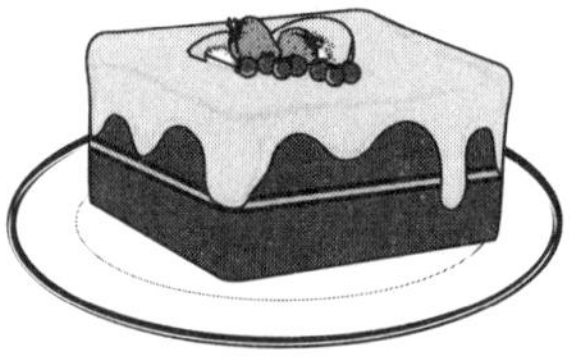

8. There was $\frac{2}{5}$ of a pie left over. May ate $\frac{1}{3}$ of the leftover pie. What fraction of the whole pie did May eat?

9. John spent $\frac{5}{8}$ of his free time playing outside. He spent $\frac{3}{4}$ of his outside time playing basketball. What fraction of his free time did he spend playing basketball?

You can multiply positive fractions with negative fractions, too!

Remember: $(+) \times (-) = -$ $(-) \times (+) = -$

$\frac{4}{5} \times \left(-\frac{2}{3}\right) = -\frac{4 \times 2}{5 \times 3} = -\frac{8}{15}$ and $-\frac{3}{5} \times \frac{1}{4} = -\frac{3 \times 1}{5 \times 4} = -\frac{3}{20}$

10. Multiply.

a) $-\frac{3}{4} \times \frac{5}{7} = -\frac{15}{28}$ b) $\frac{1}{3} \times \left(-\frac{2}{5}\right) =$ c) $\frac{2}{3} \times \left(-\frac{4}{5}\right) =$ d) $-\frac{2}{7} \times \frac{3}{5} =$

e) $\frac{6}{7} \times \left(-\frac{4}{5}\right) =$ f) $-\frac{3}{7} \times \frac{8}{11} =$ **Bonus ▶** $-\frac{1}{3} \times \frac{4}{7} \times \frac{2}{5} =$

REMINDER: $(+) \times (+) = +$ $(-) \times (-) = +$

11. Multiply.

a) $-\frac{1}{3} \times \left(-\frac{2}{5}\right) = \frac{2}{15}$ b) $-\frac{3}{10} \times \left(-\frac{7}{8}\right) =$ **Bonus ▶** $-\frac{2}{5} \times \frac{1}{3} \times \left(-\frac{2}{3}\right) =$

REMINDER: $-\frac{3}{4} = \frac{-3}{4} = \frac{3}{-4}$ $\frac{-3}{-4} = \frac{3}{4}$

12. Multiply.

a) $\frac{-2}{7} \times \frac{4}{5} = -\frac{2}{7} \times \frac{4}{5} = -\frac{8}{35}$ b) $\frac{1}{4} \times \frac{3}{-5} =$ c) $\frac{4}{-9} \times \frac{2}{5} =$

d) $\frac{2}{3} \times \frac{-6}{11} =$ e) $-\frac{2}{9} \times \frac{-4}{5} =$ f) $\frac{-5}{7} \times \frac{2}{-3} =$

g) $\frac{4}{5} \times \frac{-2}{-7} =$ h) $\frac{-3}{-7} \times \frac{-2}{5} =$ **Bonus ▶** $\frac{2}{-3} \times \frac{-4}{5} \times \left(-\frac{8}{5}\right)$

You can multiply negative mixed numbers and negative improper fractions the same way you multiply negative proper fractions.

Examples: $-\frac{3}{4} \times \frac{7}{2} = -\frac{3 \times 7}{4 \times 2} = -\frac{21}{8}$ $\frac{3}{4} \times \left(-3\frac{1}{2}\right) = \frac{3}{4} \times \left(-\frac{7}{2}\right) = -\frac{3 \times 7}{4 \times 2} = -\frac{21}{8}$ (7 = $3 \times 2 + 1$)

13. Multiply. Reduce your answers to lowest terms.

a) $-\frac{2}{3} \times \frac{9}{5}$ b) $\frac{3}{4} \times \left(-1\frac{5}{7}\right)$ c) $\frac{1}{3} \times \frac{6}{-5}$ d) $\frac{3}{-2} \times \frac{-8}{7}$

e) $-\frac{3}{4} \times \frac{6}{-5}$ f) $-\frac{3}{5} \times 1\frac{1}{6}$ g) $\frac{-8}{3} \times \left(-\frac{6}{5}\right)$ h) $-\frac{5}{4} \times \frac{-9}{-5}$

NS7-33 Multiplying Decimals

REMINDER: To show $\frac{2}{10}$ of $\frac{3}{10}$, shade 3 columns to show 3 tenths and shade 2 rows to show 2 tenths.

$\frac{2}{10}$ of $\frac{3}{10}$ is $\frac{6}{100}$, so $\frac{2}{10} \times \frac{3}{10} = \frac{6}{100}$

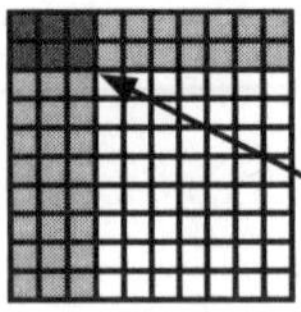

$\frac{6}{100}$

1. Shade squares to show each amount. Find the product.

a) 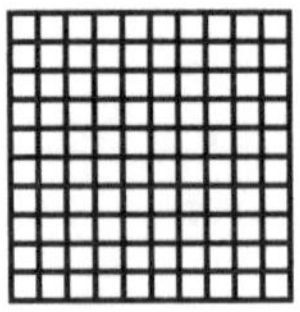

$\frac{2}{10} \times \frac{8}{10} =$

b) 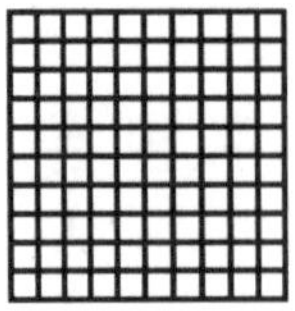

$\frac{5}{10} \times \frac{4}{10} =$

c) 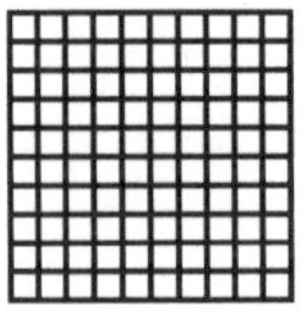

$\frac{3}{10} \times \frac{5}{10} =$

d) 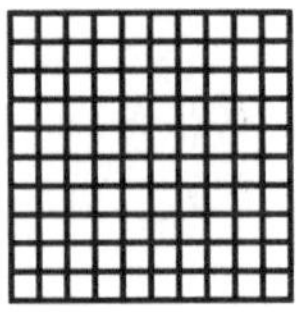

$\frac{6}{10} \times \frac{1}{10} =$

2. Write a multiplication equation for the picture.

a) 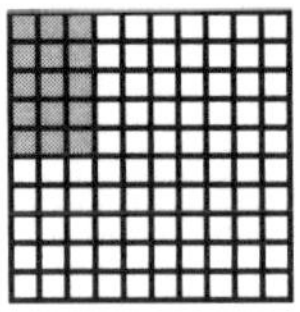

$\frac{5}{10} \times \frac{3}{10} = \frac{15}{100}$

b) 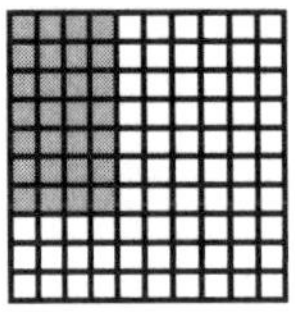

c) 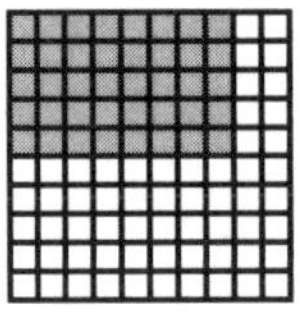

d) 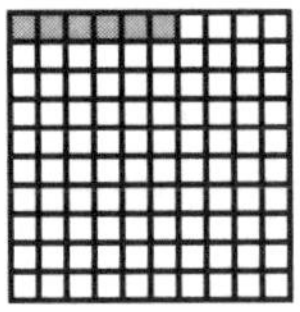

3. Multiply.

a) $\frac{7}{100} \times \frac{3}{10} = \frac{21}{1,000}$

b) $\frac{7}{10} \times \frac{3}{10} =$

c) $\frac{7}{1,000} \times \frac{3}{10} =$

d) $\frac{7}{100} \times \frac{3}{100} =$

e) $\frac{7}{1,000} \times \frac{3}{100} =$

f) $\frac{7}{100} \times \frac{3}{10,000} =$

4. Look at your answers to Question 3. How can you find the number of zeros in the denominator of the product before multiplying?

5. Multiply the decimals as shown in part a).

a) $0.3 \times 0.7 = \frac{3}{10} \times \frac{7}{10} = \frac{21}{100} = 0.21$

b) $0.6 \times 0.3 =$

c) $0.4 \times 0.03 =$

d) $0.006 \times 0.3 =$

e) 0.07×0.04

f) 0.03×0.008

To multiply decimals, follow these steps.

Example: 13.5×0.08

Step 1: Multiply the decimals as if they were whole numbers:

$135 \times 8 = 1{,}080$

Step 2: 13.5 has **1 digit** after the decimal point and 0.08 has **2 digits** after the decimal point. Shift the decimal point **1 + 2 = 3** places left:

1 0 8 0.   So $13.5 \times 0.08 = 1.080$ or 1.08

6. Use Steps 1 and 2 to multiply the decimals.

a) $0.2 \times 0.6 =$ *0.12*

				1	*2* • ← 2 × 6

b) $0.3 \times 0.07 =$ ________

				1	*2* • ← 3 × 7

c) $0.7 \times 0.9 =$ ________

					•

d) $0.02 \times 0.08 =$ ________

					•

e) $0.16 \times 0.003 =$ ________

					•

	1	6
×		3

f) $2.6 \times 0.007 =$ ________

					•

×		

g) 3.7×5.4

h) 9.2×0.65

Bonus ▶ $0.03 \times 0.04 \times 0.0002$

7. Sara bought 7.3 ounces of butter. Each ounce of butter costs $0.38. How much did she pay for the butter?

You can multiply negative decimals the same way you multiply positive decimals.

Remember: $(-) \times (+) = -$ $(+) \times (-) = -$ $(-) \times (-) = +$

Example: $-0.3 \times 0.5 = -0.15$ (15 = 3 × 5)

8. Multiply.

a) $0.4 \times (-0.7) =$ *−0.28*

b) $-0.5 \times 0.4 =$ ________

c) $-0.2 \times (-0.8) =$ ________

d) $0.05 \times (-0.4) =$ ________

e) $-0.05 \times 0.03 =$ ________

f) $-0.02 \times (-0.007) =$ ________

9. Find two numbers that multiply to −0.18. How many solutions can you find?

NS7-34 Dividing Fractions by Integers

1. One half of the rectangle is shaded. What fraction of the rectangle is the striped part?
Hint: How many striped pieces would fit into the whole rectangle?

a) $\frac{1}{6}$ 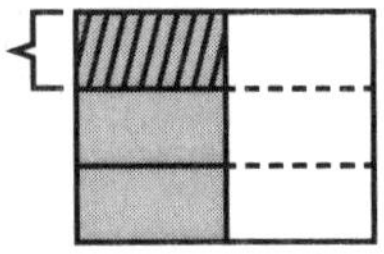

b) ___ 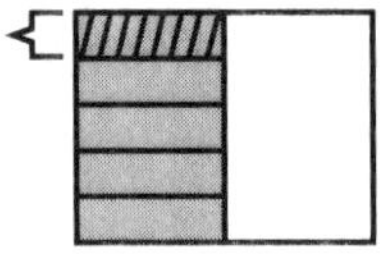

c) ___ 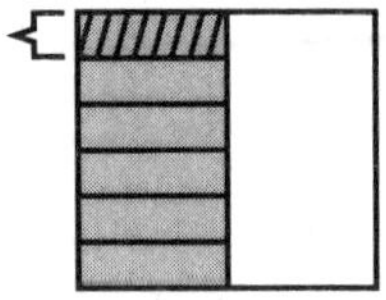

2. What is the area of the striped part? Hint: Extend the lines to divide the rectangle into smaller parts.

a) $\frac{1}{12}$ 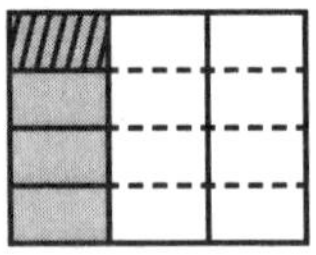

b) ___ 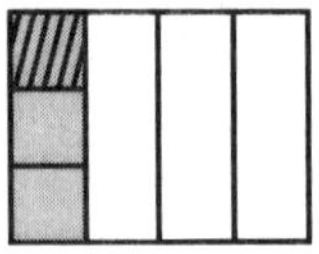

c) ___ 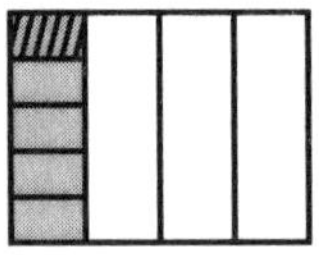

The picture in Question 2.a) shows that $\frac{1}{3} \div 4 = \frac{1}{12}$ because $\frac{1}{3}$ of the whole rectangle is divided into 4 equal parts.

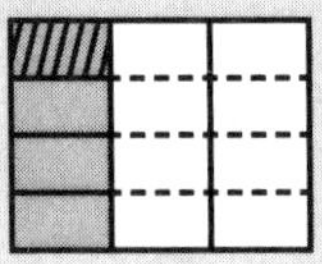

3. Write a division equation for the pictures in Question 2.

a) $\frac{1}{3} \div 4 = \frac{1}{12}$

b)

c)

Five people share $\frac{2}{3}$ of a cake. What fraction of the cake does each person get?
Divide $\frac{2}{3}$ into 5 equal groups. How much is in each group?

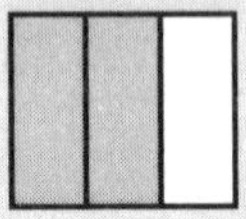 $\div 5 =$ 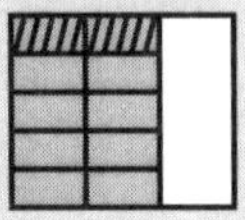 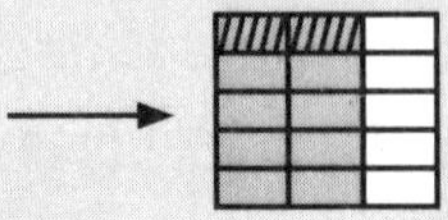 So $\frac{2}{3} \div 5 = \frac{2}{15}$

4. Use the picture to divide the fraction.

a) 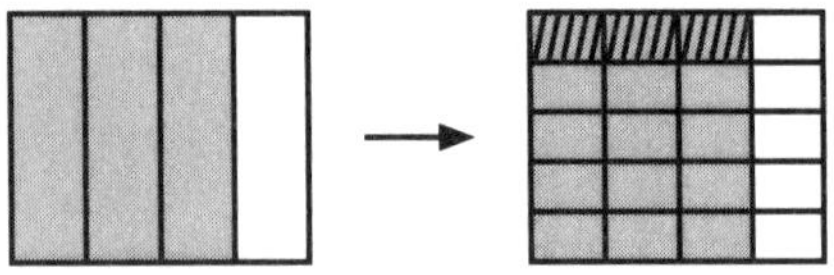

$\frac{3}{4} \div 5 = \frac{3}{20}$

b) 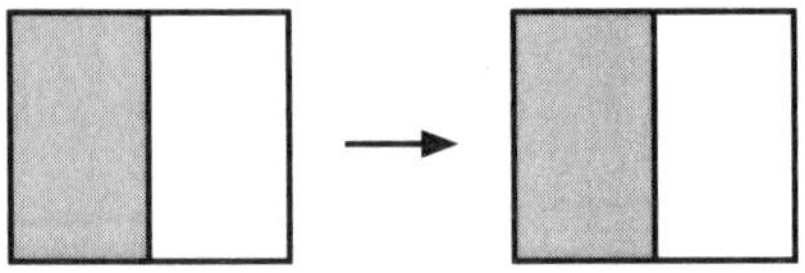

$\frac{1}{2} \div 4 =$

c) 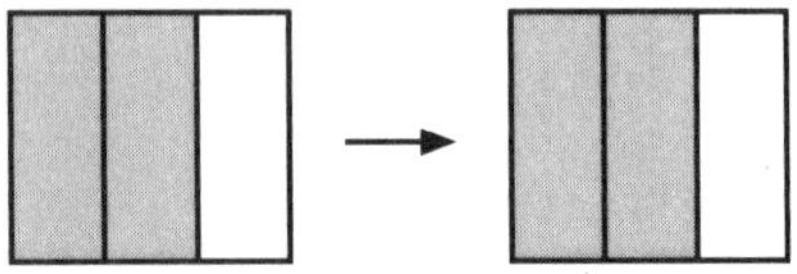

$\frac{2}{3} \div 5 =$

d) 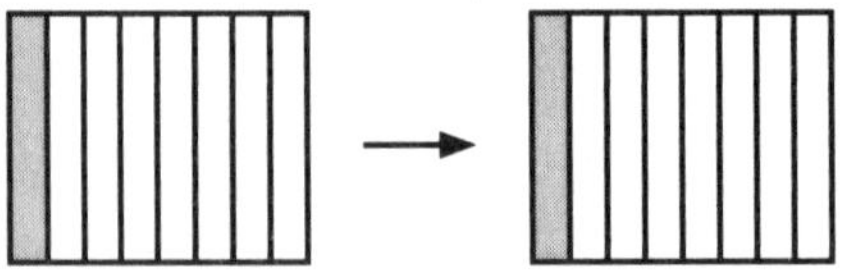

$\frac{1}{8} \div 3 =$

5. Finish the picture to divide.

a) 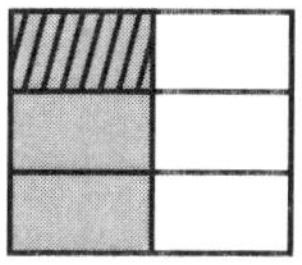

$\frac{1}{2} \div 3 = \frac{1}{6}$

b) 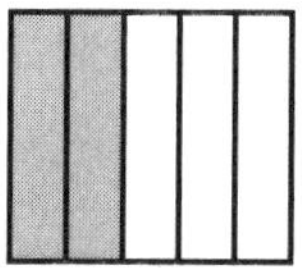

$\frac{2}{5} \div 3 =$

c) 

$\frac{1}{4} \div 6 =$

d) 

$\frac{3}{4} \div 2 =$

> REMINDER: You can check division by using multiplication: $8 \div 2 = 4$ because $4 \times 2 = 8$.
>
> To multiply a whole number by a fraction, multiply the whole number by the numerator. $3 \times \frac{1}{5} = \frac{3}{5}$

6. Check your answers to Question 5 using multiplication. Example: Does $3 \times \frac{1}{6} = \frac{1}{2}$?

> $\frac{2}{3} \div 5 = \frac{2}{3 \times 5} = \frac{2}{15}$

7. Divide.

a) $\frac{3}{4} \div 5 = \frac{3}{4 \times 5} = \frac{3}{20}$

b) $\frac{5}{7} \div 2 =$

c) $\frac{4}{5} \div 3 =$

> You can divide fractions by negative numbers the same way you divide fractions by whole numbers.
>
> Remember: $(-) \div (+) = -$ $\quad (+) \div (-) = -$ $\quad (-) \div (-) = +$
>
> Examples: $\frac{3}{5} \div (-2) = -\left(\frac{3}{5} \div 2\right) = -\frac{3}{10}$ $\qquad -\frac{3}{5} \div (-2) = \frac{3}{5} \div 2 = \frac{3}{10}$

8. Determine the sign of the division and write it in the circle.

a) $\frac{3}{5} \div (-2) = \ominus \left(\frac{3}{5} \div 2\right)$

b) $-\frac{3}{4} \div (-5) = \oplus \left(\frac{3}{4} \div 5\right)$

c) $-\frac{2}{7} \div (-4) = \bigcirc \left(\frac{2}{7} \div 4\right)$

d) $\frac{3}{-4} \div 5 = \bigcirc \left(\frac{3}{4} \div 5\right)$

e) $\frac{-1}{8} \div (-3) = \bigcirc \left(\frac{1}{8} \div 3\right)$

f) $\frac{-5}{-9} \div (-2) = \bigcirc \left(\frac{5}{9} \div 2\right)$

9. Divide. To check your answer, multiply and reduce to lowest terms.

a) $-\frac{2}{3} \div 7 = -\frac{2}{3 \times 7} = -\frac{2}{21}$

Check: $-\frac{2}{21} \times 7 = -\frac{14}{21} = -\frac{2}{3}$ ✓

b) $-\frac{3}{7} \div (-4) =$

Check:

c) $\frac{-2}{3} \div (-5) =$

Check:

d) $-\frac{2}{3} \div (-7)$

e) **Bonus ▸** $-\left(\frac{-4}{9}\right) \div (-5)$

f) **Bonus ▸** $-\left(\frac{-2}{-5}\right) \div (-4)$

NS7-35 Dividing Integers by Unit Fractions

Amit divides a string 6 m long into pieces 2 m long:

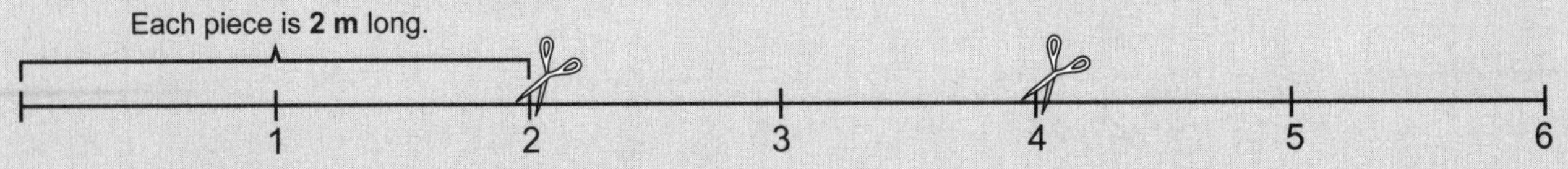

3 pieces of length 2 m fit into 6 m, so $\mathbf{6 \div 2 = 3}$.

Hanna divides a string 3 m long into pieces $\frac{1}{2}$ m long:

2 pieces of length $\frac{1}{2}$ m fit into 1 m, so 6 pieces fit into 3 m ($3 \times 2 = 6$) and $\mathbf{3 \div \frac{1}{2} = 6}$.

1. Answer the questions and complete the division equations.

a) How many pieces of length $\frac{1}{3}$ fit into 1? ___*3*___ $1 \div \frac{1}{3} =$ ___*3*___

How many pieces of length $\frac{1}{3}$ fit into 2? ___$2 \times 3 = 6$___ $2 \div \frac{1}{3} =$ ___*6*___

How many pieces of length $\frac{1}{3}$ fit into 5? ________ $5 \div \frac{1}{3} =$ ______

b) How many pieces of length $\frac{1}{4}$ fit into 1? ________ $1 \div \frac{1}{4} =$ ______

How many pieces of length $\frac{1}{4}$ fit into 3? ________ $3 \div \frac{1}{4} =$ ______

How many pieces of length $\frac{1}{4}$ fit into 7? ________ $7 \div \frac{1}{4} =$ ______

c) How many pieces of length $\frac{1}{5}$ fit into 1? ________ $1 \div \frac{1}{5} =$ ______

How many pieces of length $\frac{1}{5}$ fit into 4? ________ $4 \div \frac{1}{5} =$ ______

How many pieces of length $\frac{1}{5}$ fit into 5? ________ $5 \div \frac{1}{5} =$ ______

2. Find the quotient.

a) $9 \div \frac{1}{5} =$ ___*9*___ $\times$ ___*5*___ $=$ ___*45*___

b) $8 \div \frac{1}{4} =$ ______ $\times$ ______ $=$ ______

c) $8 \div \frac{1}{3} =$ ______ $\times$ ______ $=$ ______

d) $7 \div \frac{1}{7} =$ ______ $\times$ ______ $=$ ______

e) $8 \div \frac{1}{9} =$ ______ $\times$ ______ $=$ ______

f) $9 \div \frac{1}{8} =$ ______ $\times$ ______ $=$ ______

To find $2 \div \frac{1}{4}$, ask: How many $\frac{1}{4}$s fit into 2?

There are 4 quarters in each whole, so there are 8 quarters in 2.

So $2 \div \frac{1}{4} = 8$

1				1			
$\frac{1}{4}$	$\frac{1}{4}$	$\frac{1}{4}$	$\frac{1}{4}$	$\frac{1}{4}$	$\frac{1}{4}$	$\frac{1}{4}$	$\frac{1}{4}$

3. How many fit into 2?

a)

1		1	
$\frac{1}{2}$	$\frac{1}{2}$	$\frac{1}{2}$	$\frac{1}{2}$

$2 \div \frac{1}{2} =$ ______

b)

1			1		
$\frac{1}{3}$	$\frac{1}{3}$	$\frac{1}{3}$	$\frac{1}{3}$	$\frac{1}{3}$	$\frac{1}{3}$

$2 \div \frac{1}{3} =$ ______

c) $2 \div \frac{1}{5} =$ ______

d) $2 \div \frac{1}{10} =$ ______

4. Use the number line to decide how many steps of size $\frac{1}{3}$ fit into 4.

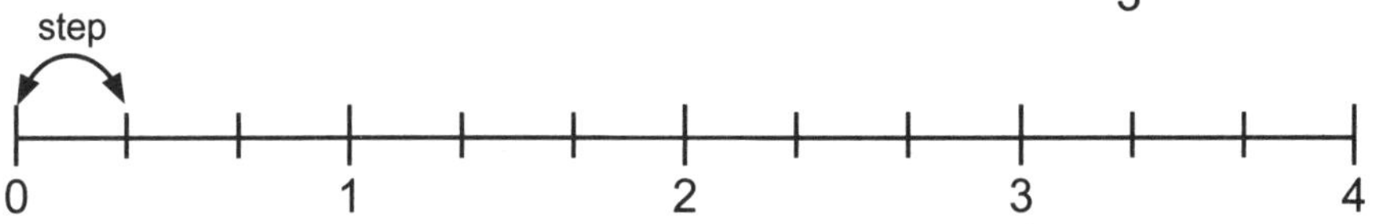

Write the division equation. ______________________________

5. Draw a number line to divide $4 \div \frac{1}{2}$. Then write the division equation.

How many $\frac{1}{3}$s fit into 5? Three $\frac{1}{3}$s fit into 1, so 5 times as many $\frac{1}{3}$s fit into 5. $5 \div \frac{1}{3} = 5 \times 3 = 15$

6. Divide.

a) $3 \div \frac{1}{3} =$ ______ $\times$ ______ $=$ ______

b) $4 \div \frac{1}{3} =$ ______ $\times$ ______ $=$ ______

c) $3 \div \frac{1}{2} =$ ______ $\times$ ______ $=$ ______

d) $5 \div \frac{1}{2} =$ ______ $\times$ ______ $=$ ______

e) $4 \div \frac{1}{5} =$ ______ $\times$ ______ $=$ ______

f) $5 \div \frac{1}{4} =$ ______ $\times$ ______ $=$ ______

REMINDER:	$(-) \div (+) = -$	$(+) \div (-) = -$	$(-) \div (-) = +$

7. Determine the sign of the fraction and write it in the circle.

a) $\frac{-3}{-5} = (+) \frac{3}{5}$ b) $\frac{-4}{5} = \bigcirc \frac{4}{5}$ c) $\frac{2}{-7} = \bigcirc \frac{2}{7}$ d) $-\frac{3}{-4} = \bigcirc \frac{3}{4}$

e) $-\frac{-7}{4} = \bigcirc \frac{7}{4}$ f) $-\frac{-2}{-3} = \bigcirc \frac{2}{3}$ g) $\frac{-9}{-5} = \bigcirc \frac{9}{5}$ h) $-\frac{-4}{-11} = \bigcirc \frac{4}{11}$

You can divide integers by unit fractions the same way you divide whole numbers by unit fractions.

Examples: $-2 \div \frac{1}{5} = -2 \times 5 = -10$ $-2 \div \left(-\frac{1}{5}\right) = 2 \times 5 = 10$

8. Determine if the answer is positive or negative. Then divide.

a) $-2 \div \frac{1}{-3} = (+)$ __2__ $\times$ __3__ $=$ __6__

b) $4 \div \left(-\frac{1}{3}\right) = \bigcirc$ ____ $\times$ ____ $=$ ____

c) $3 \div \frac{-1}{2} = \bigcirc$ ____ $\times$ ____ $=$ ____

d) $5 \div \frac{1}{-2} = \bigcirc$ ____ $\times$ ____ $=$ ____

e) $4 \div \frac{-1}{-5} = \bigcirc$ ____ $\times$ ____ $=$ ____

Bonus ▸ $-5 \div \left(-\frac{-1}{-4}\right) = \bigcirc$ ____ $\times$ ____ $=$ ____

9. Mike has a scoop that measures $\frac{1}{2}$ cup. He needs 3 cups of flour. How many scoops of flour does he need?

10. Megan has 3 chocolate bars. She cuts each chocolate bar into quarters. How many pieces does she have?

NS7-36 Dividing Fractions by Unit Fractions

1. How many $\frac{1}{6}$s fit into the shaded number?

a) 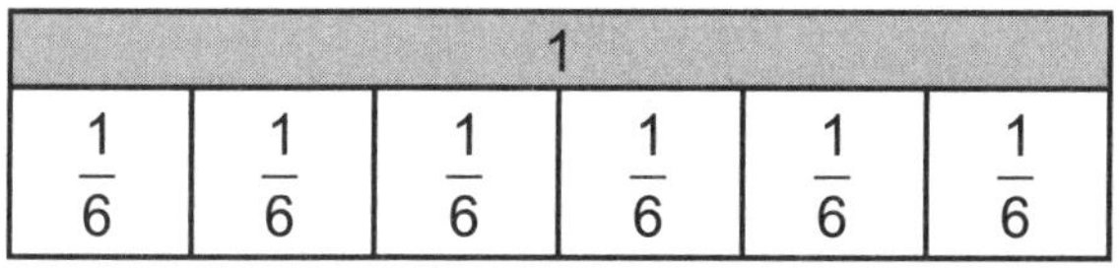

$1 \div \frac{1}{6} =$ ______

b) 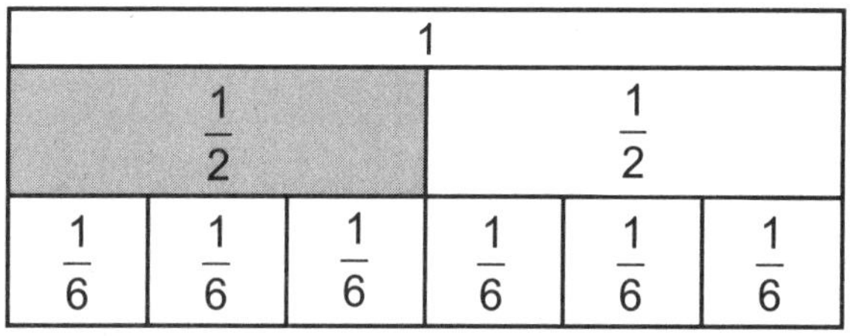

$\frac{1}{2} \div \frac{1}{6} =$ ______

c) 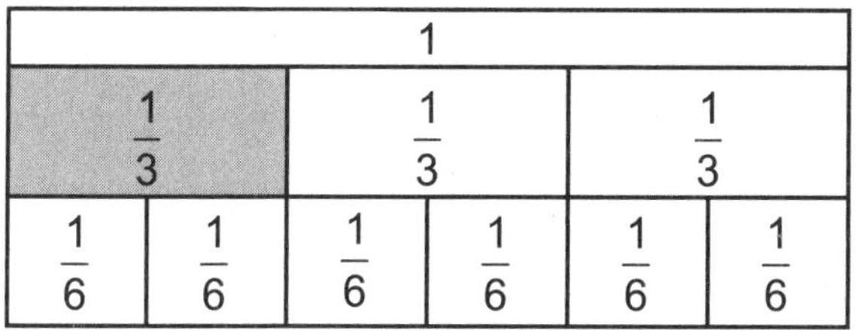

$\frac{1}{3} \div \frac{1}{6} =$ ______

d) 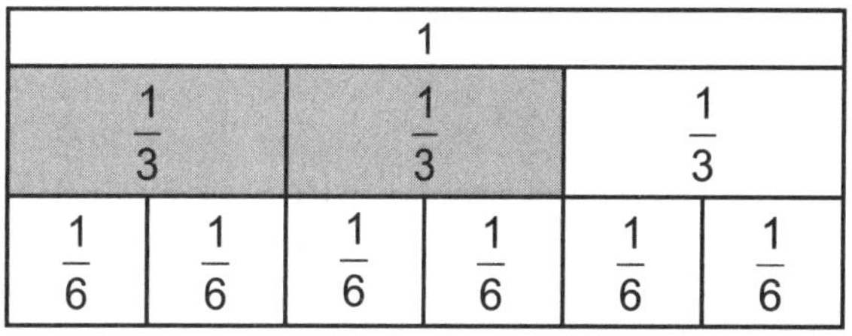

$\frac{2}{3} \div \frac{1}{6} =$ ______

2. How many $\frac{1}{10}$s fit into the shaded number? Write the division equation.

a) 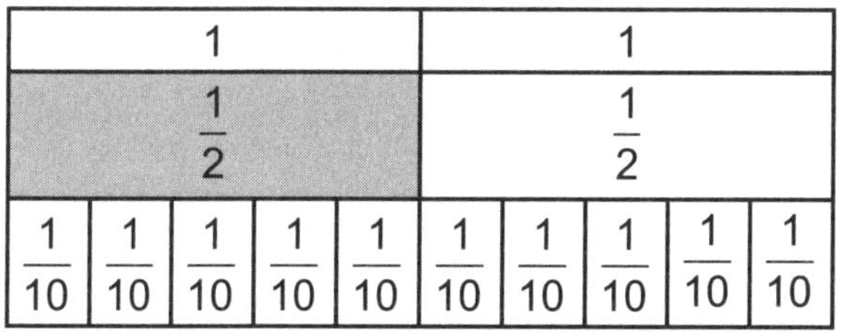

____

b) 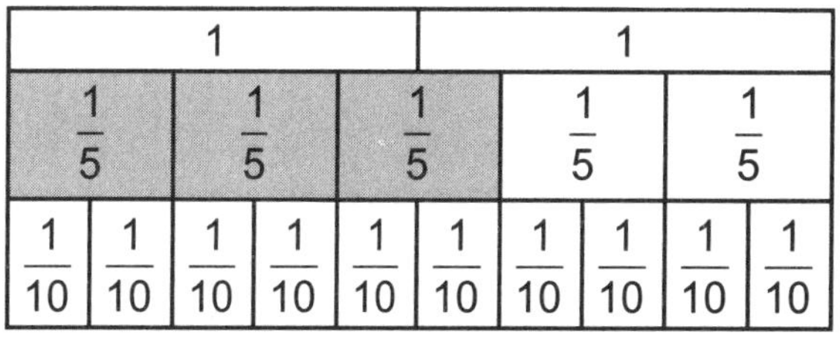

____

To find $\frac{3}{4} \div \frac{1}{8}$, ask: How many eighths fit into $\frac{3}{4}$?

8 eighths fit into 1, so $\frac{3}{4}$ of 8 eighths fit into $\frac{3}{4}$.

$\frac{3}{4} \div \frac{1}{8} = \frac{3}{4}$ of $8 = \frac{3}{4} \times 8 = 6$.

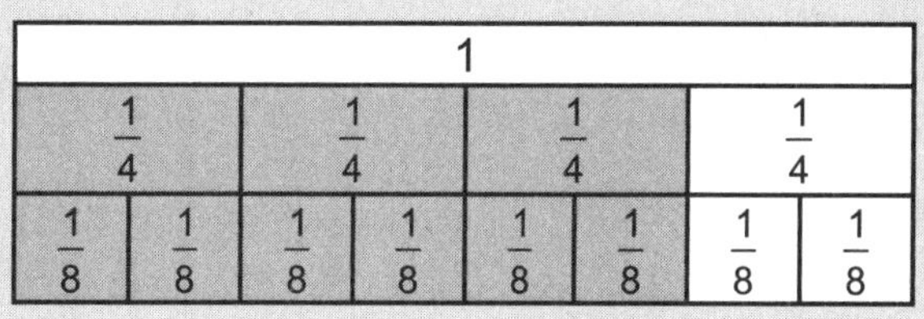

3. Write the division as a multiplication.

a) $\frac{2}{3} \div \frac{1}{6} = \frac{2}{3} \times 6$ b) $\frac{3}{4} \div \frac{1}{12} =$ c) $\frac{3}{2} \div \frac{1}{10} =$ d) $\frac{5}{3} \div \frac{1}{6} =$

REMINDER: $\frac{3}{4} \times 8 = 8 \times \frac{3}{4} = \frac{24}{4}$ ← 8 × 3

$= 6$

4. Multiply the fraction and the whole number.

a) $\frac{3}{5} \times 10 = \frac{30}{5}$ ← 3 × 10
$= 6$

b) $\frac{1}{4} \times 8 =$

c) $\frac{2}{5} \times 15 =$

d) $\frac{3}{4} \times 24 =$

5. Use multiplication to divide.

a) $\frac{2}{3} \div \frac{1}{9} = \frac{2}{3} \times 9$
$= \frac{18}{3}$
$= 6$

b) $\frac{5}{3} \div \frac{1}{6} =$

c) $\frac{9}{5} \div \frac{1}{20} =$

d) $\frac{5}{4} \div \frac{1}{12} =$

You can divide negative fractions by unit fractions the same way you divide positive fractions by unit fractions.

Remember: $(-) \div (+) = -$ $(+) \div (-) = -$ $(-) \div (-) = +$

Examples: $-\frac{3}{4} \div \frac{1}{5} = -\frac{3}{4} \times 5 = -\frac{15}{4}$ $-\frac{3}{4} \div \left(-\frac{1}{8}\right) = \frac{3}{4} \div \frac{1}{8} = \frac{3}{4} \times 8 = \frac{24}{4} = 6$

6. Determine if the answer is positive or negative, then divide.

a) $-\frac{2}{5} \div \frac{1}{3} =$ (−) ______ × ______ = ______

b) $\frac{2}{5} \div \left(-\frac{1}{3}\right) =$ ◯ ______ × ______ = ______

c) $\frac{1}{3} \div \frac{-1}{2} =$ ◯ ______ × ______ = ______

d) $-\frac{3}{4} \div \frac{1}{-3} =$ ◯ ______ × ______ = ______

e) $-\frac{4}{7} \div \left(-\frac{1}{5}\right) =$ ◯ ______ × ______ = ______

Bonus ▶ $\frac{2}{5} \div \left(-\frac{-1}{-4}\right) =$ ◯ ______ × ______ = ______

7. Divide. Start by converting the mixed numbers to improper fractions.

a) $-1\frac{2}{3} \div \frac{1}{4} = -\frac{5}{3} \times 4$
$= -\frac{20}{3} = -6\frac{2}{3}$

b) $1\frac{3}{4} \div \left(-\frac{1}{5}\right) =$

c) $1\frac{5}{7} \div \left(-\frac{1}{2}\right) =$

d) $-3\frac{1}{2} \div \left(-\frac{1}{3}\right)$

e) $1\frac{2}{7} \div \frac{1}{3}$

f) $-1\frac{1}{5} \div \left(-2\frac{1}{3}\right)$

NS7-37 Dividing Integers by Fractions

1. Outline blocks of size $\frac{3}{4}$. How many fit into 3?

1				1				1			
$\frac{1}{4}$	$\frac{1}{4}$	$\frac{1}{4}$	$\frac{1}{4}$	$\frac{1}{4}$	$\frac{1}{4}$	$\frac{1}{4}$	$\frac{1}{4}$	$\frac{1}{4}$	$\frac{1}{4}$	$\frac{1}{4}$	$\frac{1}{4}$

$3 \div \frac{3}{4} =$ _____

2. Outline blocks of size $\frac{2}{3}$. How many fit into 4?

1			1			1			1		
$\frac{1}{3}$	$\frac{1}{3}$	$\frac{1}{3}$	$\frac{1}{3}$	$\frac{1}{3}$	$\frac{1}{3}$	$\frac{1}{3}$	$\frac{1}{3}$	$\frac{1}{3}$	$\frac{1}{3}$	$\frac{1}{3}$	$\frac{1}{3}$

$4 \div \frac{2}{3} =$ _____

How many bars of length $\frac{2}{5}$ m fit along a bar of length 4 m?

Step 1: Calculate how many bars of length $\frac{1}{5}$ m fit along the bar of length 4 m.

1					1					1					1				
$\frac{1}{5}$	$\frac{1}{5}$	$\frac{1}{5}$	$\frac{1}{5}$	$\frac{1}{5}$	$\frac{1}{5}$	$\frac{1}{5}$	$\frac{1}{5}$	$\frac{1}{5}$	$\frac{1}{5}$	$\frac{1}{5}$	$\frac{1}{5}$	$\frac{1}{5}$	$\frac{1}{5}$	$\frac{1}{5}$	$\frac{1}{5}$	$\frac{1}{5}$	$\frac{1}{5}$	$\frac{1}{5}$	$\frac{1}{5}$

$4 \div \frac{1}{5} = 20$

Step 2: Since $\frac{2}{5}$ m is twice as long as $\frac{1}{5}$ m, only half as many bars of length $\frac{2}{5}$ m will fit.

1					1					1					1				
$\frac{1}{5}$	$\frac{1}{5}$	$\frac{1}{5}$	$\frac{1}{5}$	$\frac{1}{5}$	$\frac{1}{5}$	$\frac{1}{5}$	$\frac{1}{5}$	$\frac{1}{5}$	$\frac{1}{5}$	$\frac{1}{5}$	$\frac{1}{5}$	$\frac{1}{5}$	$\frac{1}{5}$	$\frac{1}{5}$	$\frac{1}{5}$	$\frac{1}{5}$	$\frac{1}{5}$	$\frac{1}{5}$	$\frac{1}{5}$

Divide the answer from Step 1 by 2, $20 \div 2 = 10$, so $4 \div \frac{2}{5} = 10$.

3. Determine how many pieces will fit.

a) How many pieces of length $\frac{2}{3}$ fit into 4?

$4 \times 3 = 12$ pieces of length $\frac{1}{3}$ fit into 4, so $12 \div 2 = 6$ pieces of length $\frac{2}{3}$ fit into 4.

b) How many pieces of length $\frac{3}{4}$ fit into 6?

_______________ pieces of length $\frac{1}{4}$ fit into 6, so _______________ pieces of length $\frac{3}{4}$ fit into 6.

c) How many pieces of length $\frac{3}{5}$ fit into 6?

_______________ pieces of length $\frac{1}{5}$ fit into 6, so _______________ pieces of length $\frac{3}{5}$ fit into 6.

4. Write each answer from Question 3 as a division equation.

a) $4 \div \frac{2}{3} = 6$ b) c)

REMINDER: You can use multiplication to check division: $8 \div 2 = 4$ because $2 \times 4 = 8$.

5. To check your answers to Question 4, multiply and reduce to lowest terms.

a) $6 \times \frac{2}{3} = \frac{12}{3} = 4$ ✓ b) c)

6. Divide.

a) $6 \div \frac{2}{3} = (\underline{\ 6\ } \times \underline{\ 3\ }) \div \underline{\ 2\ } = 18 \div 2 = 9$

b) $8 \div \frac{2}{5} = (\underline{\ 8\ } \times \underline{\ 5\ }) \div \underline{\ 2\ } =$

c) $10 \div \frac{2}{5} = (\_\_\_ \times \_\_\_) \div \_\_\_ =$

d) $5 \div \frac{1}{4} = (\_\_\_ \times \_\_\_) \div \_\_\_ =$

e) $6 \div \frac{1}{2} = (\_\_\_ \times \_\_\_) \div \_\_\_ =$

f) $12 \div \frac{3}{4} = (\_\_\_ \times \_\_\_) \div \_\_\_ =$

To find the **inverse** or **reciprocal** of a fraction, turn the fraction upside down.

Examples: The inverse of $\frac{7}{5}$ is $\frac{5}{7}$ and the inverse of $\frac{1}{4}$ is $\frac{4}{1}$ or 4.

The inverse of $-\frac{3}{4}$ is $-\frac{4}{3}$ and the inverse of $\frac{8}{-5}$ is $\frac{-5}{8}$ or $-\frac{5}{8}$.

7. Write the inverse of the number.

a) The inverse of $\frac{3}{2}$ is $\frac{\ }{\ }$

b) The inverse of $\frac{4}{9}$ is $\frac{\ }{\ }$

c) The inverse of $-\frac{2}{5}$ is $\frac{\ }{\ }$

d) The inverse of $\frac{7}{-2}$ is $\frac{\ }{\ }$

e) The inverse of $\frac{1}{8}$ is $\frac{\ }{\ } =$

Bonus ▶ The inverse of -3 is $\frac{\ }{\ }$

Tess uses the **invert-and-multiply** rule to find $8 \div \frac{4}{5}$:

$8 \div \frac{4}{5} = 8 \times \frac{5}{4} = \frac{40}{4} = 10$

She finds the same answer as with the previous method: $8 \div \frac{4}{5} = (8 \times 5) \div 4 = 40 \div 4 = 10$ ✓

8. Use the invert-and-multiply rule to solve the problems in Question 6. Did you get the same answer? If not, find your mistake.

a) $6 \div \frac{2}{3} = 6 \times \frac{3}{2} = \frac{18}{2} = 9$ ✓

b) $8 \div \frac{2}{5} =$

c) $10 \div \frac{2}{5} =$

d) $5 \div \frac{1}{4} =$

e) $6 \div \frac{1}{2} =$

f) $12 \div \frac{3}{4} =$

You can divide integers by fractions the same way you divide whole numbers by fractions.

Remember: $(+) \div (-) = -$ $(-) \div (-) = +$ $(-) \div (+) = -$

Example: $-8 \div \frac{2}{5} = -(8 \times 5) \div 2 = -40 \div 2 = -20$

Or you can use the invert-and-multiply rule: $-8 \div \frac{2}{5} = -\left(8 \times \frac{5}{2}\right) = -\frac{40}{2} = -20$ ✓

9. Use the invert-and-multiply rule to divide.

a) $2 \div \left(-\frac{2}{3}\right) = -\left(2 \times \frac{3}{2}\right) = -\frac{6}{2} = -3$

b) $-8 \div \left(-\frac{4}{5}\right) =$

c) $15 \div \frac{5}{-2} =$

d) $12 \div \left(-\frac{4}{-5}\right) =$

10. Use the invert-and-multiply rule to divide. Reduce your answer to lowest terms.

a) $6 \div \left(-\frac{4}{5}\right) = -\left(6 \times \frac{5}{4}\right) = -\frac{30}{4} = -\frac{15}{2}$

b) $2 \div \frac{-6}{5} =$

c) $-9 \div \frac{6}{5} =$

d) $-15 \div \frac{9}{-2} =$

e) $12 \div \left(-\frac{8}{-3}\right) =$

Bonus ▶ $30 \div \left(-\frac{-15}{-4}\right) =$

REMINDER: You can check division by using multiplication: $-8 \div 2 = -4$ because $-4 \times 2 = -8$.

11. To check your answers to Question 10, multiply and reduce to lowest terms.

a) $-\frac{15}{2} \times \left(-\frac{4}{5}\right) = \frac{60}{10} = 6$ ✓

b)

c)

d)

e)

Bonus ▶

12. Divide. Start by converting the mixed numbers to improper fractions.

a) $-3 \div 1\frac{3}{4} = -3 \div \frac{7}{4} = -3 \times \frac{4}{7}$

$= -\frac{12}{7} = -1\frac{5}{7}$

b) $2 \div \left(-1\frac{4}{5}\right) =$

c) $-5 \div \left(-1\frac{1}{3}\right)$

d) $-2 \div \left(-2\frac{1}{3}\right)$

e) $-4 \div \left(-1\frac{2}{3}\right)$

f) $6 \div \left(-3\frac{3}{4}\right)$

NS7-38 Dividing by Fractions

1. Use the invert-and-multiply rule to divide.

a) $1 \div \frac{4}{5} = 1 \times \frac{5}{4} = \frac{5}{4}$

b) $1 \div \left(-\frac{5}{8}\right) =$

c) $1 \div \frac{3}{-5} =$

REMINDER: You can check division by using multiplication: $-8 \div 2 = -4$ because $-4 \times 2 = -8$.

To multiply fractions, multiply the numerators and the denominators: $\frac{2}{5} \times \frac{3}{7} = \frac{2 \times 3}{5 \times 7} = \frac{6}{35}$

2. Find the inverse to divide. Use multiplication to check your answer.

a) $1 \div \left(-\frac{8}{3}\right) = -\frac{3}{8}$

Check: $-\frac{3}{8} \times \left(-\frac{8}{3}\right) = \frac{24}{24} = 1$ ✓

b) $1 \div \frac{7}{5} =$

Check:

c) $1 \div \frac{5}{9} =$

Check:

3. How many $\frac{2}{5}$ cup servings are in 1 cup of cottage cheese? Between which two whole numbers does your answer lie?

4. A rectangular field with area 1 square kilometer is $\frac{2}{3}$ of a kilometer wide. How long is it?

Megan finds $\frac{4}{5} \div \frac{2}{3}$ in two steps.

Step 1: She finds how many $\frac{2}{3}$s fit into 1.

$1 \div \frac{2}{3} = \frac{3}{2}$

Step 2: She finds $\frac{4}{5}$ of $\frac{3}{2}$.

$\frac{4}{5}$ of $\frac{3}{2} = \frac{4}{5} \times \frac{3}{2}$

$= \frac{12}{10} = \frac{6}{5}$

5. Write the division as a multiplication.

a) $\frac{3}{4} \div \frac{5}{7} = \frac{3}{4} \times$ ——

b) $\frac{2}{5} \div \frac{3}{4} = \frac{2}{5} \times$ ——

c) $\frac{7}{8} \div \frac{1}{3} = \frac{7}{8} \times$ ——

6. Use the invert-and-multiply rule to divide. Reduce your answer to lowest terms.

a) $\frac{3}{4} \div \frac{5}{2} = \frac{3}{4} \times \frac{2}{5}$

$= \frac{6}{20}$

$= \frac{3}{10}$

b) $\frac{4}{7} \div \frac{3}{5} =$

c) $\frac{7}{9} \div \frac{9}{12} =$

7. Use multiplication to check your answers to Question 6.

a) $\frac{3}{10} \times \frac{5}{2} = \frac{15}{20}$

$= \frac{3}{4}$

b)

c)

8. Divide. Start by converting the mixed numbers to improper fractions.

a) $4\frac{2}{3} \div \frac{3}{5} = \frac{14}{3} \times \frac{5}{3}$

$= \frac{70}{9} = 7\frac{7}{9}$

b) $2\frac{3}{5} \div \frac{4}{7} =$

c) $\frac{2}{5} \div 2\frac{1}{3} =$

d) $3\frac{2}{5} \div \frac{3}{4}$

e) $1\frac{3}{4} \div 2\frac{1}{2}$

f) $4\frac{1}{5} \div 1\frac{1}{4}$

> You can divide negative fractions by fractions the same way you divide positive fractions.
>
> Remember: $(-) \div (+) = -$ $(+) \div (-) = -$ $(-) \div (-) = +$
>
> Example: $-\frac{3}{4} \div \frac{2}{5} = -\frac{3}{4} \times \frac{5}{2} = -\frac{15}{8}$

9. Divide. Hint: Determine if the answer is positive or negative first.

a) $-\frac{2}{5} \div \frac{3}{2} = -\frac{2}{5} \times \frac{2}{3}$

$= -\frac{4}{15}$

b) $-\frac{7}{5} \div \left(-\frac{3}{4}\right) =$

c) $\frac{3}{4} \div \left(-\frac{6}{5}\right) =$

10. Divide. Hint: Convert the mixed numbers to improper fractions.

a) $-2\frac{1}{3} \div \frac{3}{4} = -\frac{7}{3} \times \frac{4}{3}$

$= -\frac{28}{9} = -3\frac{1}{9}$

b) $2\frac{3}{4} \div \left(-\frac{3}{5}\right) =$

c) $-1\frac{3}{5} \div \left(-1\frac{1}{2}\right) =$

11. Alex makes a cake using $1\frac{1}{3}$ cups of sugar. The cake is divided into 12 pieces. How much sugar is in each piece?

12. Ivan bought $\frac{4}{5}$ kg of dry lasagna. Each person needs $\frac{2}{35}$ kg. How many people can he feed?

13. A string of length $2\frac{2}{5}$ m is divided into pieces of length 40 cm. How many pieces are there?
Hint: Convert 40 cm to a fraction of a meter.

NS7-39 Word Problems—Fractions

Answer all problems in your notebook.

1. A foot is 12 inches. A yard is 3 feet. What fraction of a yard is 8 inches?
   Hint: First, find how many inches are in a yard.

2. A year has 12 months. A decade has 10 years.
   What fraction of a decade is 8 months?

3. What fraction of a day is 45 minutes?

4. If a year has 52 weeks, what fraction of a century is 13 weeks?

5. What fraction of a day is 40 seconds?

6. Three people share $\frac{4}{5}$ of a lasagna. What fraction of the lasagna does each person eat?

7. Kate bought $\frac{8}{3}$ cups of sugar. She used $\frac{1}{4}$ of it to bake a cake. She then ate $\frac{3}{10}$ of the cake. How much sugar did she eat?

8. Five people share $\frac{1}{2}$ lb of almonds equally. How much does each person get?

9. A string of length $3\frac{1}{2}$ m is divided into 5 equal parts. How long is each piece?
   Hint: Convert the mixed number to an improper fraction.

10. How many $\frac{1}{2}$ cup servings are in $\frac{3}{4}$ of a cup of yogurt?

11. How wide is a rectangular strip of land with length $1\frac{3}{4}$ km and area $\frac{1}{2}$ square km?

12. Ted needs $1\frac{1}{3}$ cups of flour for a cake. He only has a scoop that measures $\frac{1}{4}$ cup. How many scoops does he need?

13. Sam biked $\frac{2}{3}$ km in 4 minutes. How far did he bike in 1 minute?

14. Letter-size paper is $8\frac{1}{2}$ in by 11 in and legal-size paper is $8\frac{1}{2}$ in by 14 in. How much smaller is the area of letter-size paper than legal-size paper?

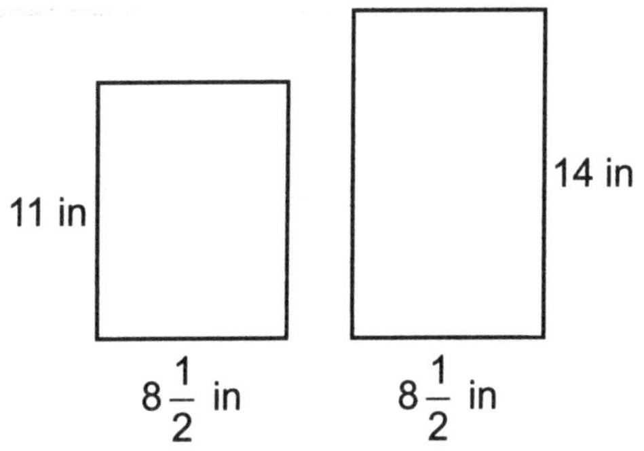

15. The temperature is currently 0°F. The temperature increases $2\frac{1}{2}$ °F each hour.

Write an equation that shows what the temperature was or will be …

a) 3 hours ago $(-3) \times \left(2\frac{1}{2}\right) = \left(-7\frac{1}{2}\right)$

b) 3 hours from now ____________________

c) 5 hours ago ____________________

d) 5 hours from now ____________________

16. The temperature is currently 0°F. The temperature decreases $1\frac{1}{2}$ °F each hour.

Write an equation that shows what the temperature was or will be …

a) 3 hours ago $(-3) \times \left(-1\frac{1}{2}\right) = \left(+4\frac{1}{2}\right)$

b) 3 hours from now ____________________

c) 5 hours ago ____________________

d) 5 hours from now ____________________

17. The temperature is currently 0°F. Write an equation to show your answer.

a) The temperature decreases an average of $3\frac{1}{4}$ °F every hour. What will the temperature be in 8 hours? ____________________

b) The temperature increases an average of $1\frac{3}{4}$ °F every day. What will the temperature be in a week? ____________________

c) The temperature increases $3\frac{1}{2}$ °F every week. What was the temperature 6 weeks ago?

____

d) The temperature decreases $\frac{1}{2}$ °F every minute. What was the temperature $3\frac{1}{2}$ minutes ago?

____

NS7-40 Dividing Decimals by Integers

REMINDER: To divide by 10, 100, or 1,000, move the decimal point 1, 2, or 3 places left.

Example: 85 = 85.0, so

$85 \div 10 = 8.5$ $85 \div 100 = 0.85$ $85 \div 1{,}000 = 0.085$

1. Divide.

a) $7 \div 100 =$ ______ b) $26 \div 10 =$ ______ c) $51 \div 100 =$ ______

d) $923 \div 1{,}000 =$ ______ e) $923 \div 100 =$ ______ f) $923 \div 10 =$ ______

2. Count how many places you would shift the decimal point to make a whole number. Then write a division statement.

a) | | 0. | 0 | 6 |

_2_ places (two zeros)

$0.06 = 6 \div$ _100_

b) | 0. | 0 | 3 | 2 |

______ places

$0.032 = 32 \div$ ______

c) | | 7 | 0. | 1 |

______ places

$70.1 = 701 \div$ ______

d) | 0. | 2 | 0 | 7 |

$0.207 =$ ______

e) | 0. | 0 | 1 | 9 |

$0.019 =$ ______

f) | 1. | 0 | 0 | 3 |

$1.003 =$ ______

3. Rewrite the division statement so that you are dividing a whole number by 10, 100 or 1,000.

a) $2.4 \div 4$

$= (\underline{24} \div \underline{10}) \div \underline{4}$

$= (\underline{24} \div \underline{4}) \div \underline{10}$

b) $0.35 \div 7$

= (____ ÷ ____) ÷ ____

= (____ ÷ ____) ÷ ____

c) $0.42 \div 6$

= ______________

= ______________

d) $5.6 \div 7$ e) $0.016 \div 8$ f) $14.08 \div 2$

4. Rewrite the division statement in one step, and then divide.

a) $3.2 \div 4$

= _(32 ÷ 4) ÷ 10_

= _8 ÷ 10 = 0.8_

b) $0.15 \div 5$

= ______________

= ______________

c) $0.054 \div 9$

= ______________

= ______________

d) $5.6 \div 7$ e) $8.46 \div 2$ f) $0.00015 \div 5$

5. Liz cycles 0.63 miles in 7 minutes. How far does she cycle in 1 minute?

To find 5.12 ÷ 2 using long division:

Step 1: Divide as though the decimal is a whole number.

Step 2: Put the decimal point in the quotient directly above the decimal point in the dividend.

So 5.12 ÷ 2 = 2.56

	2	5	6
2)	5	1	2
−	4	↓	↓
	1	1	
−	1	0	↓
		1	2
−		1	2
			0

→

	2.	5	6
2)	5.	1	2
−	4	↓	↓
	1	1	
−	1	0	↓
		1	2
−		1	2
			0

6. Use 438 ÷ 3 = 146. Place the decimal point in the correct place. Add any zeros you need.

a) 3)4.38 (quotient digits 1 4 6)

b) 3)43.8 (quotient digits 1 4 6)

c) 3)0.438 (quotient digits 1 4 6)

d) 3)0438. (quotient digits 1 4 6)

7. Divide as though the decimal is a whole number. Then put the decimal point in the correct place.

a) 3)2.55

b) 4)71.6

c) 9)93.6

d) 6)3.54

e) 7)8.4

f) 8)1.28

g) 4)35.6

h) 2)10.4

8. Four tangerines cost $2.60. How much does each tangerine cost?

You can use two methods to write $\frac{3}{5}$ as a decimal:

Method 1: Use equivalent fractions

$$\frac{3}{5} = \frac{3 \times 2}{5 \times 2} = \frac{6}{10} = 0.6$$

Method 2: Use long division

Write 3 as 3.0, then find 3.0 ÷ 5

$$\frac{3}{5} = 0.6$$

	0.	6
5)	3.	0
−	3	0
	0	0

9. Use long division to write the fraction as a decimal.

a) $\frac{1}{2}$ b) $\frac{4}{5}$ c) $\frac{2}{4}$ d) $\frac{2}{5}$

Ken uses long division to write $\frac{3}{4}$ as a decimal:

He writes 3 as 3.00, then finds 3.00 ÷ 4.

$\frac{3}{4} = 0.75$

	0.	7	5
4)	3.	0	0
−	2	8	↓
	0	2	0
−	0	2	0
	0	0	0

10. Use long division to write the fraction as a decimal.

a) $\frac{1}{4} =$

	0.		
4)	1.	0	0
−			
−			

b) $\frac{5}{4} =$

	1		
4)	5.	0	0
−	4		
−			
−			

c) $\frac{1}{8} =$

	0			
8)	1.	0	0	0
−				
−				
−				

d) $\frac{5}{8} =$

	0			
8)	5.	0	0	0
−				
−				
−				

11. Use long division to write the fraction as a decimal.
Remember: (−) ÷ (+) = −, (+) ÷ (−) = −, (−) ÷ (−) = +

a) $-\frac{1}{5} =$

	0.	
5)	1.	0
−		
−		

b) $-\frac{7}{4} =$

	1.		
4)	7.	0	0
−			
−			
−			

c) $\frac{7}{-8} =$

	0.			
8)	7.	0	0	0
−				
−				
−				

d) $\frac{-3}{-8} =$

	0.			
8)	3.	0	0	0
−				
−				
−				

12. Five friends earn a total of $33.75 shovelling snow. How much does each friend earn?

13. The fastest result for the men's 4 × 100 m relay at the 2012 London Olympics was 36.84 s. What was the average time for each runner?

14. Which is a better deal: 3 stickers for $1.35 or 7 stickers for $2.73?

NS7-41 Dividing by Decimals

1. a) Show how many 4s fit into 8.

0 1 2 3 4 5 6 7 8 9 10

$8 \div 4 =$ ______

b) Show how many 0.4s fit into 0.8.

0 0.1 0.2 0.3 0.4 0.5 0.6 0.7 0.8 0.9 1.0

$0.8 \div 0.4 =$ ______

2. a) Show how many 2s fit into 6.

0 1 2 3 4 5 6 7 8 9 10

$6 \div 2 =$ ______

b) Show how many 0.2s fit into 0.6.

0 0.1 0.2 0.3 0.4 0.5 0.6 0.7 0.8 0.9 1.0

$0.6 \div 0.2 =$ ______

REMINDER: $(-) \div (+) = -$ $(+) \div (-) = -$ $(-) \div (-) = +$

3. Write an integer division that has the same answer. Then divide.

a) $-0.8 \div 0.4$
= *$-8 \div 4$*
= ______

b) $0.4 \div (-0.2)$
= ______
= ______

c) $-0.6 \div (-0.3)$
= ______
= ______

d) $1 \div (-0.5)$
= ______
= ______

REMINDER: To multiply an integer by 10, add a 0.
To multiply a decimal by 10, move the decimal point one place right.
Examples: $-23 \times 10 = -230$ $-2.04 \times 10 = -20.4$

4. Multiply by 10.

a) -34×10
= *-340*

b) 0.005×10
= ______

c) -0.26×10
= ______

d) -0.009×10
= ______

To find $-1.4 \div 0.2$, multiply both numbers by 10: $-1.4 \div 0.2 = -(1.4 \div 0.2)$
$= -(14 \div 02) = -7$

5. Multiply both numbers by 10 or 100 to make the divisor a whole number. Then divide.

a) $0.12 \div (-0.4)$
= *$1.2 \div (-4)$*
= *-0.3*

b) $-2.4 \div 0.6$
= ______
= ______

c) $-35 \div 0.5$
= ______
= ______

d) $0.45 \div (-0.9)$
= ______
= ______

e) $-24 \div 0.06$

f) $56 \div (-0.07)$

g) $-0.3 \div 0.02$

h) $-2.1 \div (-0.03)$

To divide by a decimal, make the divisor a whole number by multiplying the dividend and the divisor by the same power of 10.

Examples: $0.6\overline{)2.4}$ → $6\overline{)24.}$ $\quad$ $0.6\overline{)0.24}$ → $6\overline{)2.4}$ $\quad$ $0.06\overline{)24.}$ → $6\overline{)2400.}$

Then divide by the whole number using long division.

6. Use $238 \div 14 = 17$ to divide. Put the decimal point in the correct place in the answer.

a) $1.4\overline{)23.8}$ (quotient digits: 1 7) $\quad$ b) $1.4\overline{)2.38}$ (quotient digits: 17) $\quad$ c) $14\overline{)2.38}$ (quotient digits: 17)

You may need to add zeros.

d) $0.14\overline{)23.80}$ (quotient digits: 1 7 0) $\quad$ e) $1.4\overline{)238}$ (quotient digits: 17) $\quad$ f) $0.014\overline{)23.8}$ (quotient digits: 1 7)

Bonus ▶ $0.000014\overline{)2.38}$ (quotient digits: 1 7)

7. Use long division to divide.

a) $0.9\overline{)3.33}$ → $9\overline{)33.3}$ $\quad$ b) $0.06\overline{)31.2}$ → $6\overline{)3120.}$

c) $-24.51 \div 0.03$ $\quad$ d) $0.243 \div (-0.09)$ $\quad$ e) $31.65 \div (-0.5)$ $\quad$ f) $-114.72 \div (-0.004)$

8. Tony has 1.44 lb of cheese. He needs 0.08 lb of cheese for one sandwich. How many sandwiches can he make?

9. Nina has \$2.85. How many \$0.05 candies can she buy?

NS7-42 Order of Operations with Fractions and Decimals

1. Evaluate the expression. Do the operation in brackets first.

a) $\frac{2}{3}+\left(\frac{1}{5}\times 4\right)$　　b) $\left(\frac{2}{3}+\frac{1}{5}\right)\times 4$　　c) $\frac{1}{5}+\left(\frac{4}{3}\div 2\right)$　　d) $\left(\frac{1}{5}+\frac{4}{3}\right)\div 2$

e) $\frac{4}{3}-\left(\frac{2}{5}\times 3\right)$　　f) $\left(\frac{4}{3}-\frac{2}{5}\right)\times 3$　　g) $\left(\frac{4}{3}-\frac{2}{5}\right)\div 2$　　h) $\frac{4}{3}-\left(\frac{2}{5}\div 2\right)$

2. Compare the expressions that are similar in Question 1. Does the order you do the operations in affect the answer? _______

REMINDER: Mathematicians have ordered the operations to avoid writing brackets all the time.

Do operations in this order:
1. Operations in brackets
2. Multiplication and division, from left to right
3. Addition and subtraction, from left to right

Examples: $10-5\times\frac{2}{5}+4=10-2+4$ $=8+4=12$　　but　　$(10-5)\times\left(\frac{2}{5}+4\right)=5\times\frac{22}{5}$ $=22$

3. Evaluate.

a) $\frac{2}{3}-\frac{1}{4}+\frac{1}{2}$　　b) $\frac{2}{3}+\frac{1}{2}\times\frac{1}{4}$　　c) $\frac{3}{2}+\frac{1}{4}\times\frac{3}{4}$　　d) $\frac{3}{2}\times\left(8\div\frac{3}{4}\right)$

$=\frac{8}{12}-\frac{3}{12}+\frac{6}{12}$

$=\frac{8-3+6}{12}=\frac{11}{12}$

e) $\frac{5}{2}\div 5\times\frac{4}{5}$　　f) $\frac{5}{2}\div\left(5\times\frac{4}{5}\right)$　　g) $\frac{2}{3}+\frac{1}{2}-\frac{1}{4}$　　h) $\frac{2}{3}+\left(\frac{1}{2}-\frac{1}{4}\right)$

4. Remove any brackets that are not necessary.
Hint: In some expressions, all brackets will be necessary.

a) $\frac{2}{3}+\left(\frac{1}{2}-\frac{1}{3}\right)=$　　b) $\frac{2}{3}\times\left(\frac{1}{2}-\frac{1}{3}\right)=$

c) $\left(\frac{1}{2}\times\frac{1}{3}\right)+\left(\frac{1}{3}-\frac{1}{4}\right)=$　　d) $\left(\frac{1}{2}-\left(\frac{1}{3}+\frac{1}{4}\right)\right)\times\frac{1}{5}=$

REMINDER: Repeated multiplication is written as a power.

Examples: $3^4 = 3 \times 3 \times 3 \times 3$ and $\left(\frac{2}{3}\right)^4 = \frac{2}{3} \times \frac{2}{3} \times \frac{2}{3} \times \frac{2}{3} = \frac{2 \times 2 \times 2 \times 2}{3 \times 3 \times 3 \times 3} = \frac{16}{81}$ ← 2^4 ← 3^4

5. Write the power as a product.

a) $\left(\frac{2}{3}\right)^3 = \frac{2}{3} \times \frac{2}{3} \times \frac{2}{3}$ b) $\left(\frac{1}{3}\right)^2 =$ c) $\left(\frac{3}{2}\right)^5 =$

6. Evaluate the power.

a) $\left(\frac{1}{3}\right)^4 =$ b) $\left(\frac{3}{2}\right)^3 =$ c) $\left(\frac{2}{3}\right)^4 =$

Be careful when evaluating expressions that look similar. Examples: $\frac{3}{5^2} = \frac{3}{25}$ $\frac{3^2}{5} = \frac{9}{5}$ $\left(\frac{3}{5}\right)^2 = \frac{9}{25}$

7. Evaluate the expression. Circle the answer that is equal to $\left(\frac{5}{3}\right)^2$.

a) $\frac{5}{3^2} =$ b) $\frac{5^2}{3} =$ c) $\frac{5^2}{3^2} =$

REMINDER: The correct order of operations is:

1. Operations in brackets
2. Powers
3. Multiplication and division, from left to right
4. Addition and subtraction, from left to right

8. Use the correct order of operations to evaluate.

a) $4 + \frac{2^3}{5} =$ b) $4 + \left(\frac{2}{5}\right)^3 =$ c) $4 \times \frac{9}{10^3} =$

d) $4 \times \left(\frac{9}{10}\right)^3 =$ e) $\left(\frac{3}{10} \div 5\right)^2 =$ f) $\frac{3}{10} \div 5^2 =$

REMINDER: To multiply decimals, multiply the whole numbers first, then shift the decimal point in the answer by the total number of decimal digits in the numbers being multiplied.

Example: $12 \times 12 = 144$ so $1.2 \times 1.2 = 1.44$
1 + 1 2

9. a) Evaluate $0.6^2 = 0.6 \times 0.6$.

b) Evaluate $\left(\frac{3}{5}\right)^2$. Change your answer to a decimal.

c) Compare your answers from parts a) and b). What do you notice? Why is this the case?

Do operations with negative decimals and fractions in the same order as before.
Repeated multiplication is written as a power for negative numbers, too!

Examples: $(-3)^4 = -3 \times (-3) \times (-3) \times (-3) = 81$ and $\left(-\frac{3}{5}\right)^3 = -\frac{3}{5} \times \left(-\frac{3}{5}\right) \times \left(-\frac{3}{5}\right) = -\frac{3 \times 3 \times 3}{5 \times 5 \times 5} = -\frac{27}{125}$

10. Write the power as a product.

a) $\left(-\frac{2}{3}\right)^3 = -\frac{2}{3} \times \left(-\frac{2}{3}\right) \times \left(-\frac{2}{3}\right)$

b) $\left(\frac{-1}{3}\right)^4 =$

c) $1.3^5 =$

d) $\left(\frac{-2}{-7}\right)^5 =$

11. Evaluate the power.

a) $\left(-\frac{1}{3}\right)^5 =$

b) $\left(-\frac{3}{2}\right)^3 =$

c) $(-0.3)^4 =$

d) $\left(\frac{-2}{-5}\right)^2 =$

12. Evaluate. Reduce your answer to lowest terms.

a) $\left(\frac{1}{2} - \frac{1}{3} + \frac{1}{6}\right) \times \left(-\frac{1}{4}\right) =$

b) $2\frac{3}{4} \times \left(\frac{1}{3} - \frac{1}{5}\right) \div \left(-2\frac{1}{3}\right) =$

c) $-\frac{4}{9} \times \left(-\frac{9}{8}\right) + \left(-\frac{7}{8}\right) \times \frac{2}{14} =$

d) $\left(-\frac{1}{2} - \frac{1}{3}\right) \times \left(-\frac{1}{3} + \frac{1}{4}\right) =$

e) $\left(-\frac{3}{4}\right)^2 \times \left(-\frac{5}{2}\right) + \left(-\frac{1}{2}\right)^3 \times \frac{5}{4} =$

f) $\left(-\frac{3}{4} - \left(-\frac{5}{6}\right)\right) \div \left(\frac{2}{3} + \left(-\frac{1}{2}\right)\right) =$

NS7-43 Expressions with Fractions and Decimals

1. Replace the variable with the given number, then evaluate.

a) $t+2\frac{1}{5},\ t=\frac{3}{5}$

$=\frac{3}{5}+2\frac{1}{5}$

$=2\frac{4}{5}$

b) $n+1\frac{2}{10},\ n=\frac{3}{10}$

c) $t-\frac{2}{7},\ t=3\frac{4}{7}$

d) $1\frac{5}{6}-z,\ z=\frac{1}{6}$

e) $3x+2,\ x=\frac{5}{8}$

f) $n-1\frac{1}{10},\ n=3\frac{2}{5}$

REMINDER: To simplify an expression like the one below, you can combine like terms.

Example: $3x - 6 - 4x + 4 + 5x - x = 3x - 2$

$3x - 4x + 5x - x$ → $3x$ $-6 + 4$ → -2

2. Combine like terms to simplify the expression.

a) $4x - 1 - 3x$

b) $2 - 4x + 5$

c) $-5x + 3 + 3x - 8$

d) $3x + 4 + 7 + 6x$

e) $2x + 1 + 4 + 3x + 5$

f) $3x + 2 + 5x + 4 + 7 + x$

You can simplify expressions with fractional terms the same way.

Example: $\frac{3}{7}x - \frac{1}{5} - \frac{1}{7}x + \frac{4}{5} = \frac{2}{7}x + \frac{3}{5}$

$\frac{3}{7}x - \frac{1}{7}x$ → $\frac{2}{7}x$ $-\frac{1}{5} + \frac{4}{5}$ → $\frac{3}{5}$

3. Simplify the expression. Reduce your answer to lowest terms.

a) $\frac{2}{3}x - \frac{4}{5} - \frac{1}{3}x$

b) $\frac{7}{9} - \frac{1}{9}x - \frac{4}{9}$

c) $-\frac{4}{7}x + \frac{1}{6} - \frac{2}{3} + \frac{3}{7}x$

d) $-\frac{1}{2}x + \frac{1}{3} + \frac{3}{4}x - \frac{2}{3}$

e) $\frac{3}{4} - \frac{1}{2}x + \frac{4}{5} + \frac{1}{3}x - \frac{3}{5}$

f) $-\frac{3}{5}x - \frac{2}{3} + \frac{1}{6}x - \frac{4}{9} + \frac{2}{3}x$

4. Fill in the table. Is $-(x + 5)$ equivalent to $-x + 5$ or $-x - 5$? ________

x	$-(x + 5)$	$-x + 5$	$-x - 5$
0	$-(0 + 5) = -5$	$-0 + 5 =$	$-0 - 5 =$
1	$-(1 + 5) =$		
2			
−1			
−3			

REMINDER: $-(+) = -$ $-(-) = +$

The negative sign changes the sign of **every term** in the brackets.

Example: $-(x + 5) = -x - 5$ and $-(x - 5) = -x + 5$

5. Combine like terms to subtract the expressions.

a) $(7x + 5) - (3x + 4)$

$= 7x + 5 - 3x - 4$

$= 7x - 3x + 5 - 4$

$= 4x + 1$

b) $(8x + 3) - (2x - 2)$

c) $(3x + 8) - (x + 5)$

d) $(9x + 7) - (3x - 4)$

Bonus ▶ $(-4x + 7 - 3x) - (5 - 2x - 3)$

You can add or subtract like terms with fractional and decimal coefficients in a similar way.

Example: $2.5x + 0.6 + 1.3x - 1.4 = 3.8x - 0.8$

$3.8x$ ← $2.5x + 1.3x$ 0.8 ← $0.6 - 1.4$

6. Combine like terms to add or subtract.

a) $0.4x + (2.5x - 3)$

b) $2.1x - (1.6x - 1.2)$

c) $\left(\frac{3}{5} - \frac{1}{7}x\right) + \left(\frac{1}{5} - \frac{4}{7}x\right)$

d) $\left(\frac{4}{9}x - \frac{3}{10}\right) + \left(\frac{1}{5} - \frac{4}{9}x\right)$

7. Sandwiches cost \$3.50 each and drinks cost \$1.50 each. The cost of s sandwiches and d drinks is $3.50s + 1.50d$. Find the cost of …

a) 5 sandwiches and 4 drinks

$3.50s + 1.50d$

$= 3.50(5) + 1.50(4)$

$= 17.50 + 6.00 = 23.50$

The cost is $23.50.

b) 6 sandwiches and 6 drinks

The cost is ____________.

c) 2 sandwiches and 7 drinks

The cost is ____________.

NS7-44 Complex Fractions

REMINDER: You can write division as a fraction.

$(+) \div (-) = -$ $(-) \div (-) = +$ $(-) \div (+) = -$

Examples: $3 \div 4 = \frac{3}{4}$ $-10 \div 5 = \frac{-10}{5} = -2$ $-8 \div (-2) = \frac{-8}{-2} = \frac{8}{2} = 4$

1. Write a fraction for the division statement. Reduce your answer to lowest terms.

a) $-2 \div 8 = -\frac{2}{8} = -\frac{1}{4}$ b) $4 \div 10 =$ c) $18 \div (-12) =$

d) $21 \div (-3) =$ e) $(-12) \div (-8) =$ f) $-27 \div 24 =$

g) $(4+3) \div 10 = \frac{4+3}{10} = \frac{7}{10}$ h) $8 \div (3-1) =$ **Bonus ▸** $(4+5) \div (7-1) =$

2. Write a division statement for the fraction, then divide.

a) $\frac{-6}{3} = -6 \div 3 = -2$ b) $\frac{15}{-5} =$ c) $\frac{-12}{-4} =$

d) $-\frac{-21}{7} = -(-21) \div 7 = 3$ e) $-\frac{24}{-3} =$ f) $\frac{-15}{3} =$

g) $-\frac{-77}{11} =$ h) $\frac{-39}{13} =$ i) $-\frac{-18}{-6} =$

$\frac{\frac{3}{4}}{\frac{5}{7}}$ is a **complex fraction.**

In a complex fraction, the numerator or denominator (or both) contains a fraction. You can write a division statement for a complex fraction the same way you do for fractions.

Examples: $\frac{\frac{3}{4}}{\frac{5}{7}} = \frac{3}{4} \div \frac{5}{7}$ $\frac{\frac{3}{4}}{5} = \frac{3}{4} \div 5$ $\frac{-\frac{2}{3}}{\frac{5}{8}} = -\frac{2}{3} \div \frac{5}{8}$

3. Write a division statement for the complex fraction.

a) $\frac{\frac{2}{3}}{-5} = \frac{2}{3} \div (-5)$ b) $\frac{\frac{1}{4}}{\frac{5}{7}} =$ c) $\frac{-\frac{2}{5}}{-\frac{3}{4}} =$

d) $\frac{-4}{\frac{1}{3}} =$ e) $-\frac{\frac{3}{7}}{\frac{1}{3}} =$ f) $-\frac{\frac{5}{3}}{-4} =$

You can use a division statement to evaluate a complex fraction.

Examples: $\dfrac{\frac{3}{5}}{-2} = \dfrac{3}{5} \div (-2) = -\dfrac{3}{5\times 2} = -\dfrac{3}{10}$ $\dfrac{-\frac{2}{3}}{\frac{5}{8}} = -\dfrac{2}{3} \div \dfrac{5}{8} = -\dfrac{2}{3} \times \dfrac{8}{5} = -\dfrac{16}{15}$

4. Evaluate the complex fractions in Question 3.

a) $\dfrac{\frac{2}{3}}{-5} = \dfrac{2}{3} \div (-5) = -\dfrac{2}{3\times 5} = -\dfrac{2}{15}$

b) $\dfrac{\frac{1}{4}}{\frac{5}{7}} =$

c) $\dfrac{-\frac{2}{5}}{-\frac{3}{4}} =$

d) $\dfrac{-4}{\frac{1}{3}} =$

e) $-\dfrac{\frac{3}{7}}{\frac{1}{3}} =$

f) $-\dfrac{\frac{5}{3}}{-4} =$

The numerator or denominator of a complex fraction can be an expression.

Examples: $\dfrac{\frac{3}{5}+\frac{1}{5}}{2}$ $\dfrac{\frac{2}{7}\times\frac{1}{5}}{\frac{1}{6}-\frac{3}{4}}$

5. Evaluate. Reduce your answer to lowest terms.

a) $\dfrac{\frac{2}{3}\div 2}{-5\times\frac{1}{3}} = \dfrac{\frac{2}{3\times 2}}{-\frac{5}{3}} = \dfrac{\frac{2}{6}}{-\frac{5}{3}} = \dfrac{\frac{1}{3}}{-\frac{5}{3}} = \dfrac{1}{3} \div \left(-\dfrac{5}{3}\right) = -\left(\dfrac{1}{3}\times\dfrac{3}{5}\right) = -\dfrac{3}{15} = -\dfrac{1}{5}$

b) $\dfrac{\frac{7}{8}\div\left(-2\frac{3}{4}\right)}{\frac{1}{11}-\frac{5}{22}} =$

c) $\dfrac{-\frac{2}{5}\times 1\frac{1}{2}}{-\frac{3}{4}\div\frac{3}{5}} =$

d) $\dfrac{-\frac{4}{3}\div 8}{3\frac{1}{3}-2\frac{1}{2}} =$

Problem Bank—Rational Numbers

Answer all problems in your notebook.

1. Andy had $48 dollars. He spent $\frac{1}{4}$ of his money on a book and $\frac{3}{8}$ on a pair of gloves.

a) How much money did Andy spend on the gloves?

b) How much money does he have left over?

2. Yu, Peter, and Cathy painted a whole wall.

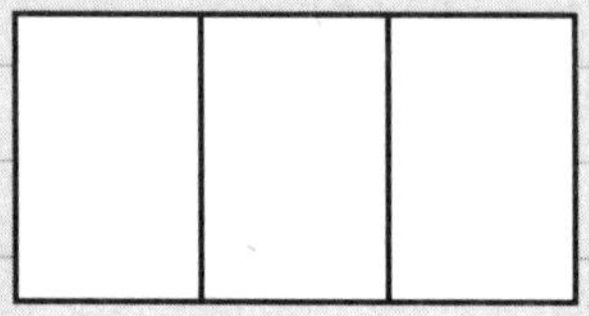

Yu painted $\frac{2}{5}$ of the wall and Peter painted $\frac{1}{3}$.

a) What fraction of the wall did Cathy paint?

b) Each person painted a rectangular section. The wall is 30 m long. How wide was each person's section?

3. Zack stretches for $\frac{1}{2}$ an hour, walks for $\frac{2}{3}$ of an hour, and jogs for $\frac{2}{5}$ of an hour.

Use both methods below to calculate how many minutes he exercised.

Method 1: Add the fractions, and then convert to minutes.

Method 2: Convert the fractions to minutes, and then add.

Did you get the same answer both ways?

4. Jane talked on the phone for $\frac{1}{5}$ of an hour. Ethan talked on the phone for $\frac{1}{100}$ of a day. Who talked on the phone longer?

5. Mindy can do one jumping jack in $\frac{3}{4}$ of a second. How many jumping jacks can she do in $\frac{7}{10}$ of a minute? Circle the correct formula and explain your choice.

$\frac{7}{10}\times\frac{3}{4}$ $\frac{7}{10}\div\frac{3}{4}$ $\frac{3}{4}\div\frac{7}{10}$ $42\div\frac{3}{4}$ $\frac{7}{10}\div 45$ $45\div\frac{7}{10}$ $42\times\frac{3}{4}$

6. Make up a word problem that requires evaluating the expression.

a) $\frac{4}{5}+\frac{1}{3}$ b) $\frac{4}{5}-\frac{1}{3}$ c) $\frac{1}{3}\times\frac{2}{5}$ d) $\frac{10}{3}\div\frac{2}{5}$

7. Scientists recommend that we sleep for around $\frac{3}{8}$ of each day. How many hours should we spend sleeping in a week? What fraction is that of a whole week?

8. Marco spent $\frac{3}{4}$ of an hour doing math homework, $\frac{2}{5}$ of an hour doing geography homework, and $\frac{5}{6}$ of an hour doing science homework.

a) Compare fractions to answer the question.

i) Did Marco spend more or less than half an hour on geography?

ii) Did he spend more time on math or on science?

b) Decide whether the problem requires addition, subtraction, multiplication, or division. Then solve the problem.

i) Marco spent $\frac{1}{3}$ of his math time working on word problems. What fraction of an hour did he spend working on word problems?

ii) How many hours did Marco spend on homework altogether?

iii) How many more hours did Marco spend on science than on geography?

iv) Marco divided his geography time evenly between reading the textbook and answering questions. What fraction of an hour did he spend reading the textbook?

c) Solve the problem.

i) Marco had two hours to do his homework before he had to leave to meet a friend. How many minutes before he had to leave did Marco finish his homework?

ii) Marco spent $\frac{1}{3}$ of his science time reading the textbook. He spent $\frac{1}{5}$ of his remaining science time doing calculations. How many hours did he spend on calculations?

iii) Marco's sister Eva spent $\frac{1}{3}$ of the amount of time on math as Marco, but twice the amount of time on geography and $1\frac{1}{2}$ times as much time on science. Who spent more time doing homework, Marco or Eva?

iv) Marco's brother Sal spent the same total amount of time on homework as Eva did. Sal spent the same amount of time on all 3 subjects. How much time did Sal spend on each subject? Write your answer as a fraction of an hour.

v) Eva spent $\frac{1}{5}$ of her science time reading the textbook. Who spent more time reading their science textbook, Marco or Eva?

9. Write a decimal that is ... (Hint: There may be more than one answer.)

a) between 5.63 and 5.68

b) between −2.70 and −2.80

c) between 21.75 and 21.8

d) between −0.6 and −0.7

e) one tenth greater than −4.54

f) one hundredth less than −6.00

10. Which is the better deal, 3 pens for $2.88 or 5 pens for $4.65?

11. The wind speed in New York City was 26.7 kph (kilometers per hour) on Monday, 16.0 kph on Tuesday, and 2.4 kph on Wednesday. What was the average wind speed over the 3 days?

12. Jacob walks 0.05 km per minute. At that speed, how long would it take him to walk 15 km?

13. Encke's Comet appears in our sky every 3.3 years. It was first seen in 1786. When was the last time the comet was seen before 1800? Show your work.

14. Our ecological footprint is the area of land required to provide us with food, clothing, and other resources, and to absorb our waste (for example, pollution).

a) In the United States, the average ecological footprint is 7.9 global hectares of land per person. In Canada, the ecological footprint is 7.01 global hectares per person. How much greater is the average ecological footprint in the United States than in Canada?

b) The average ecological footprint worldwide is 2.6 global hectares per person. How much greater is the average American's ecological footprint than the world average?

c) There are 317 million American citizens. What is the total ecological footprint of the population of the United States in millions of global hectares?

15. The temperature is currently 0°C. The temperature increases 2.5°C each hour. Write an equation that shows what the temperature was or will be …

a) 3 hours ago $(-3) \times (+2.5) = (-7.5)$ b) 3 hours from now

c) 5 hours ago d) 5 hours from now

16. The temperature is currently 0°C. The temperature decreases 1.5°C each hour. Write an equation that shows what the temperature was or will be …

a) 3 hours ago $(-3) \times (-1.5) = (+4.5)$ b) 3 hours from now

c) 5 hours ago d) 5 hours from now

17. The temperature is currently 0°C. Write an equation to answer the question.

a) The temperature decreases an average of 3.25°C every hour. What will the temperature be in 8 hours?

b) The temperature increases an average of 1.75°C every day. What will the temperature be in a week?

c) The temperature increases 3.5°C every week. What was the temperature 6 weeks ago?

d) The temperature decreases 0.5°C every minute. What was the temperature 3.5 minutes ago?

RP7-26 Canceling Through Multiplication

1. Write the number that makes the equation true.

a) $8 \div 4 \times \square = 8$ b) $8 \times 3 \div \square = 8$ c) $8 \div 2 \times \square = 8$

d) $13 \times 6 \div \square = 13$ e) $-12 \div 3 \times \square = -12$ f) $7 \times (-2) \div \square = 7$

g) $2.5 \times 10 \div \square = 2.5$ h) $3 \div 1.5 \times \square = 3$ i) $-8 \div (-4) \times \square = -8$

> REMINDER: A fraction is reduced to lowest terms when you can't divide the numerator and denominator by a number greater than 1.
>
> For example, $\frac{2}{3}$ is in lowest terms but $\frac{4}{6}$ is not.

2. Reduce the fraction by dividing the numerator and denominator by the same number.

a) $\frac{6 \div 3}{15 \div 3} = \frac{2}{5}$ b) $\frac{6}{9} =$ c) $\frac{5}{10} =$ d) $\frac{8}{14} =$

e) $\frac{-6 \div 3}{15 \div 3} = \frac{-2}{5}$ f) $\frac{6}{-9} =$ g) $\frac{-4}{18} =$ h) $\frac{-5}{-20} =$

3. Reduce the fraction by dividing the numerator and denominator by the same number.

a) $\frac{2 \times 3 \div 3}{5 \times 3 \div 3} = \frac{2}{5}$ b) $\frac{2 \times 3}{3 \times 3} =$ c) $\frac{1 \times 5}{2 \times 5} =$ d) $\frac{4 \times 2}{7 \times 2} =$

e) $\frac{-2 \times 3 \div 3}{5 \times 3 \div 3} = \frac{-2}{5}$ f) $\frac{2 \times 3}{-3 \times 3} =$ g) $\frac{-2 \times 2}{9 \times 2} =$ h) $\frac{-1 \times 5}{-4 \times 5} =$

> Crossing out the common factor from the numerator and denominator of a fraction is called **canceling**.
>
> Examples: $\frac{2 \times \cancel{3}}{5 \times \cancel{3}} = \frac{2}{5}$ $\frac{4 \times \cancel{2}}{7 \times \cancel{2}} = \frac{4}{7}$ $\frac{-5 \times \cancel{4}}{6 \times \cancel{4}} = -\frac{5}{6}$

4. Multiply fractions as shown, then reduce to lowest terms by canceling.

a) $\frac{3}{4} \times \frac{4}{5} = \frac{3 \times \cancel{4}}{\cancel{4} \times 5} = \frac{3}{5}$ b) $\frac{2}{7} \times \frac{5}{2} = \_\_\_ = \_\_\_$ c) $\frac{11}{3} \times \frac{3}{8} = \_\_\_ = \_\_\_$

d) $\frac{5}{9} \times \frac{-2}{5} = -\frac{\cancel{5} \times 2}{9 \times \cancel{5}} = -\frac{2}{9}$ e) $\frac{6}{-11} \times \frac{5}{6} = -\_\_\_ = -\_\_\_$ f) $\frac{-7}{9} \times \frac{9}{-8} = \_\_\_ = \_\_\_$

g) $\frac{3}{-7} \times \frac{-7}{5} = \_\_\_ = \_\_\_$ h) $\frac{-5}{8} \times \frac{3}{5} = -\_\_\_ = -\_\_\_$ **Bonus ▶** $\frac{7}{2} \times \frac{2}{9} \times \frac{5}{7}$

To reduce to lowest terms, you can find the common factor and then cross it out.

Examples: $\frac{5}{10} = \frac{1 \times \cancel{5}}{2 \times \cancel{5}} = \frac{1}{2}$ and $\frac{6}{2} = \frac{3 \times \cancel{2}}{1 \times \cancel{2}} = \frac{3}{1} = 3$

5. Reduce to lowest terms by canceling.

a) $\frac{7}{21} = \frac{\quad}{\quad} = \frac{\quad}{\quad}$

b) $\frac{5}{20} = \frac{\quad}{\quad} = \frac{\quad}{\quad}$

c) $\frac{15}{3} = \frac{\quad}{\quad} = \frac{\quad}{\quad}$

d) $\frac{-3}{6} = -\frac{1 \times \cancel{3}}{2 \times \cancel{3}} = -\frac{1}{2}$

e) $\frac{-2}{10} = -\frac{\quad}{\quad} = -\frac{\quad}{\quad}$

f) $\frac{-3}{-12} = \frac{\quad}{\quad} = \frac{\quad}{\quad}$

Remember: $\frac{3}{5} \times 5 = (3 \div 5) \times 5 = 3$

You can use canceling when you multiply a fraction by an integer.

Examples: $\frac{3}{\cancel{4}} \times \cancel{4} = 3$ $\quad \frac{-5}{\cancel{8}} \times \cancel{8} = -5$ $\quad \frac{2}{-\cancel{5}} \times (-\cancel{5}) = 2$

6. Multiply.

a) $\frac{3}{4} \times 4 =$

b) $\frac{5}{7} \times 7 =$

c) $8 \times \frac{3}{8} =$

d) $\frac{-3}{4} \times 4 =$

e) $\frac{1}{-8} \times (-8) =$

f) $\frac{-6}{-5} \times (-5) =$

7. Reduce to lowest terms by canceling.

a) $\frac{3}{4} \times \frac{4}{9} \times \frac{9}{11} = \frac{3 \times \cancel{4} \times \cancel{9}}{\cancel{4} \times \cancel{9} \times 11} = \frac{3}{11}$

b) $\frac{2}{5} \times \frac{5}{3} \times \frac{3}{7} = \frac{\quad}{\quad} = \frac{\quad}{\quad}$

c) $\frac{-5}{7} \times \frac{2}{3} \times \frac{3}{5} =$

Bonus ▶ $\frac{3}{4} \times \frac{-4}{5} \times 5 =$

Remember: 3 and 5 are a factor pair of 15 because $3 \times 5 = 15$.

You can rewrite the numerator and denominator using factor pairs, and then cancel.

Examples: $\frac{2 \times 15}{5 \times 4} = \frac{\cancel{2} \times 3 \times \cancel{5}}{\cancel{5} \times \cancel{2} \times 2} = \frac{3}{2}$ $\quad \frac{-20 \times 3}{12 \times 7} = \frac{-\cancel{4} \times 5 \times \cancel{3}}{\cancel{3} \times \cancel{4} \times 7} = -\frac{5}{7}$

8. Reduce to lowest terms by canceling.

a) $\frac{6 \times 8}{4 \times 9} =$

b) $\frac{12 \times 5}{15 \times 3} =$

c) **Bonus ▶** $\frac{2}{5} \times \frac{10}{3} \times \frac{9}{6} =$

d) **Bonus ▶** $\frac{-24 \times 6}{5 \times 12 \times (-3)} =$

e) $\frac{12 \times 5}{4 \times 15}$

f) $\frac{5 \times 21}{14 \times 10}$

g) $\frac{8 \times 6 \times 10}{25 \times 9 \times 4}$

h) $\frac{(-4) \times 12 \times (-5)}{10 \times 18 \times (-2)}$

RP7-27 Ratios and Rates with Fractional Terms

1. Find the number that makes the equation true and write it in the box.

a) $\square \times \frac{1}{3} = 1$ b) $\square \times \frac{4}{5} = 4$ c) $\square \times \frac{3}{6} = 3$

d) $\frac{5}{8} \times \square = 5$ e) $\square \times \frac{3}{2} = 3$ f) $\frac{7}{11} \times \square = 7$

1 : 6 and $\frac{1}{2}$: 3 are **equivalent ratios** because they show the same ratio.

For example, if there are 6 slices in a pizza, then half a pizza has 3 slices.

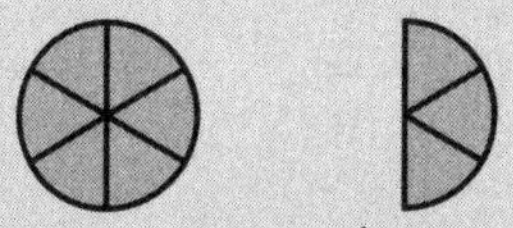

1 : 6 $\frac{1}{2}$: 3

You can make an equivalent ratio that has whole number terms by multiplying both terms by the denominator of the fractional term: $\mathbf{\frac{1}{2}} : 3 = \left(\frac{1}{2} \times \mathbf{2}\right) : (3 \times \mathbf{2}) = 1 : 6$

2. Write an equivalent ratio with terms that are whole numbers.

a) $\frac{2}{3} : 5 = \left(\frac{2}{3} \times 3\right) : (5 \times 3) =$ ___*2*___ : ___*15*___

b) $3 : \frac{4}{5} = (3 \times \quad) : \left(\frac{4}{5} \times \quad\right) =$ ______ : ______

c) $\frac{1}{4} : 3 =$

d) $5 : \frac{5}{6} =$

e) $\frac{7}{11} : 4 =$

f) $4 : \frac{173}{5} =$

3. Write both terms as whole numbers without changing the ratio.

a) 5 mi run in $\frac{1}{2}$ hour

5 : $\frac{1}{2}$

×2 ×2

___*10*___ : ___*1*___

______ mi run in 1 hour

b) 4 mi rowed in $\frac{1}{3}$ hour

4 : $\frac{1}{3}$

______ : ______

______ mi rowed in 1 hour

c) $\frac{3}{4}$ cup of oats for 2 cups of raisins

$\frac{3}{4}$: 2

______ : ______

___*3*___ cups of oats for ______ cups of raisins

d) 19 mi per $\frac{2}{3}$ gal of gas

19 : $\frac{2}{3}$

______ : ______

______ mi per ___*2*___ gal of gas

When both terms of a ratio are fractions, you multiply by a multiple of both denominators to make both terms whole numbers. Use the lowest common multiple (LCM) of the denominators.

Example: $\frac{2}{3} : \frac{5}{4} = \left(\frac{2}{3} \times 12\right) : \left(\frac{5}{4} \times 12\right) = 8 : 15$

4. Multiply by the LCM of the denominators to make an equivalent ratio.

a) $\frac{1}{3} : \frac{1}{2} = \left(\frac{1}{3} \times \quad\right) : \left(\frac{1}{2} \times \quad\right)$

$= \_\_\_\_ : \_\_\_\_$

b) $\frac{1}{2} : \frac{1}{5} = \left(\frac{1}{2} \times \quad\right) : \left(\frac{1}{5} \times \quad\right)$

$= \_\_\_\_ : \_\_\_\_$

c) $\frac{1}{3} : \frac{1}{4} =$

$= \_\_\_\_ : \_\_\_\_$

d) $\frac{5}{6} : \frac{1}{2} =$

$= \_\_\_\_ : \_\_\_\_$

e) $\frac{3}{8} : \frac{7}{12} =$

$= \_\_\_\_ : \_\_\_\_$

f) $\frac{4}{9} : \frac{1}{6} =$

$= \_\_\_\_ : \_\_\_\_$

REMINDER: To complete a ratio table, multiply the numbers in one row by the same number to get the numbers in another row.

5. Find the equivalent ratio using a ratio table by multiplying by the LCM of the denominators. Hint: The arrow may point from bottom to top.

a) (×6 from top row to bottom row)

$\frac{1}{3}$	$\frac{1}{2}$
2	*3*

So $\frac{1}{3} : \frac{1}{2} =$ *2* : *3*

b)

$\frac{1}{3}$	$\frac{1}{4}$

So $\frac{1}{3} : \frac{1}{4} = \_\_\_ : \_\_\_$

c)

$\frac{1}{5}$	$\frac{3}{4}$
	15

So $\frac{1}{5} : \frac{3}{4} = \_\_\_ :$ *15*

d)

$\frac{2}{7}$	$\frac{5}{6}$
12	

So $\frac{2}{7} : \frac{5}{6} =$ *12* $: \_\_\_$

e)

$\frac{2}{3}$	$\frac{1}{2}$

So $\frac{2}{3} : \frac{1}{2} = \_\_\_ : \_\_\_$

f)

$\frac{3}{4}$	$\frac{2}{5}$

So $\frac{3}{4} : \frac{2}{5} = \_\_\_ : \_\_\_$

g)

$\frac{4}{5}$	$\frac{5}{6}$

So $\frac{4}{5} : \frac{5}{6} = \_\_\_ : \_\_\_$

h)

$\frac{5}{11}$	$\frac{2}{9}$

So $\frac{5}{11} : \frac{2}{9} = \_\_\_ : \_\_\_$

i) (×15 from bottom row to top row)

5	
$\frac{1}{3}$	$\frac{1}{5}$

So *5* $: \_\_\_ = \frac{1}{3} : \frac{1}{5}$

j)

$\frac{1}{2}$	$\frac{2}{3}$

So $\_\_\_ : \_\_\_ = \frac{1}{2} : \frac{2}{3}$

k)

$\frac{4}{3}$	$\frac{1}{10}$

So $\_\_\_ : \_\_\_ = \frac{4}{3} : \frac{1}{10}$

l)

$\frac{7}{12}$	$\frac{3}{4}$

So $\_\_\_ : \_\_\_ = \frac{7}{12} : \frac{3}{4}$

RP7-28 Ratio Word Problems with Fractional Terms

A granola recipe uses $\frac{1}{2}$ cup of raisins for every $\frac{1}{3}$ cup of oats. Raj wants to know how many cups of oats are needed for 6 cups of raisins. He finds an equivalent ratio using a ratio table.

Step 1: Raj makes a ratio table showing the cups of raisins for cups of oats.

Step 2: He finds the number he multiplies by in the first column, $6 \div \frac{1}{2} = 12$.

Step 3: He multiplies by that number in the second column.

So $\frac{1}{2} : \frac{1}{3} = 6 : 4$. Raj needs 4 cups of oats.

	Cups of Raisins	Cups of Oats	
	$\frac{1}{2}$	$\frac{1}{3}$	
$\times 12$	6	4	$\times 12$

1. Solve by finding the equivalent ratio.

a) A plant grows $\frac{1}{3}$ cm in $\frac{1}{2}$ day. How many days will it take to grow 6 cm?

cm	Days
$\frac{1}{3}$	$\frac{1}{2}$
6	

b) Sally can ride her bike $1\frac{1}{2}$ miles in $\frac{1}{4}$ hour. How far can she ride in 1 hour?

Miles	Hours
$1\frac{1}{2}$	$\frac{1}{4}$

c) On a map, $\frac{1}{5}$ cm equals $\frac{1}{2}$ km. How many meters does 1 cm on the map represent?

d) A recipe uses $\frac{1}{3}$ cup of milk to $\frac{2}{3}$ cup of flour. How much milk do you need if you use 4 cups of flour?

2. Find the numbers that make the equation true.

a) $2 \times \frac{7}{2} = 7$

b) $6 \times \frac{\square}{\square} = 7$

c) $5 \times \frac{\square}{\square} = 4$

d) $8 \times \frac{\square}{\square} = 13$

e) $5 \times \frac{\square}{\square} = 8$

f) $3 \times \frac{\square}{\square} = 11$

g) $7 \times \frac{\square}{\square} = 20$

h) $15 \times \frac{\square}{\square} = 31$

3. Find the missing term. You will need to multiply by a fraction.

a)

	2	3	
$\times \frac{7}{2}$	7	$\frac{21}{2}$	$\times \frac{7}{2}$

b)

	5	8	
$\times \frac{3}{5}$	3		$\times \frac{3}{5}$

c)

4	8
9	

d)

7	10
11	

e)

$\times \frac{8}{3}$	8		$\times \frac{8}{3}$
	3	5	

f)

9	
4	7

g)

5	
7	3

Bonus ▶

	9
5	6

To make punch, you need 2 cups of cranberry juice for every 3 cups of ginger ale. How many cups of ginger ale are needed for 5 cups of cranberry juice?

Step 1: Make a ratio table showing the cranberry juice for ginger ale.

Step 2: Find the fraction you multiply by in the first column,

$5 \div 2 = \frac{5}{2}$.

Step 3: Multiply by that number in the second column.

$2 : 3 = 5 : \frac{15}{2}$, so you need $\frac{15}{2}$ (or $7\frac{1}{2}$) cups of ginger ale.

Cups cranberry juice	Cups ginger ale
2	3
5	$\mathbf{\frac{15}{2}}$

($\times\frac{5}{2}$ on both sides)

4. Solve by finding the equivalent ratio.

a) If 6 apples cost $5, how much do 9 apples cost?

Apples	Cost ($)
6	*5*
9	

b) Zack can walk 200 m in 3 minutes. How long will it take him to walk 1,500 m?

Distance (m)	Time (min)
200	*3*

c) Two out of every 6 people in a room are seniors. There are 9 seniors in the room. How many people are in the room?

d) Ava has 4 red marbles for every 6 blue marbles in her bag. She has 15 blue marbles. How many red marbles does Ava have?

To make purple paint, mix $\frac{1}{2}$ cup of blue paint with $\frac{1}{3}$ cup of red paint. How much of each color do you need to make 20 cups of purple paint?

Step 1: The ratio is blue : red $= \frac{1}{2} : \frac{1}{3}$, so an equivalent ratio with both terms in whole numbers is 3 : 2.

Step 2: Use a ratio table to find the number you multiply by in the "Total" column, $20 \div 5 = 4$.

Step 3: Multiply by that number in both columns.

You need 12 cups of blue paint and 8 cups of red paint.

Blue	Red	Total
3	2	**5**
12	8	**20**

($\times 4$ on both sides)

5. A cake recipe calls for butter and sugar in the ratio $\frac{1}{2} : \frac{2}{3}$. If Sam used 7 cups of sugar and butter altogether, how many cups of sugar did he use?

6. Anna makes orange paint by mixing $\frac{1}{3}$ cup of red paint with $\frac{3}{4}$ cup of yellow paint. If Anna wants to make 26 cups of orange paint, how many cups of each paint color will she need?

Bonus ▶ How many cups of each paint color will Anna need to make $9\frac{3}{4}$ cups of orange paint?

RP7-29 Unit Rates

1. Divide to find the missing information.

   a) 4 tickets cost \$20
   $\div 4$
   1 ticket costs ______

   b) 3 jackets cost \$135
   1 jacket costs ______

   c) 144 miles per 6 gallons gas
   ______ miles per 1 gallon gas

2. Find the unit rate.

   a) 3 kg rice for 15 L water
   1 kg rice for ______ L water

   b) \$112 for 7 hours
   ______ per hour

   c) 456 miles in 8 hours
   ______ miles in 1 hour

> Ross paid \$24 for 3 shirts. He wants to know how much 1 shirt cost.
>
> **Step 1:** Ross writes the ratios for the situation. He writes a question mark (?) for the missing quantity. $24 : 3 = ? : 1$
>
> **Step 2:** Ross finds the number he divides by in the second term. Then he divides the first term by that number to find the missing number. $24 : 3 = 8 : 1$ ($\div 3$, $\div 3$)
>
> Ross finds that 1 shirt costs \$8.

3. Write a ratio using the description, find the unit rate, then answer the question.

   a) Five sandwiches cost \$15. How much does each sandwich cost?

   ______ : ______ = ______ : ______

   Each sandwich costs __________.

   b) There are 3 jazz CDs for every 12 rock CDs. How many rock CDs are there per jazz CD?

   ______ : ______ = ______ : ______

   For every jazz CD, there are __________ rock CDs.

   c) Seven tickets cost \$28. How much does each ticket cost?

   ______ : ______ = ______ : ______

   Each ticket costs __________.

4. a) Jen earns \$54 cutting lawns for 6 hours. How much does she earn for 1 hour?

   b) Marco earns \$28 babysitting for 4 hours. How much does he earn for 1 hour?

5. Which is the best deal for renting bicycles?

   A. \$15 for 2 hours **B.** \$20 for 3 hours **C.** \$25 for 4 hours

6. Divide to find the missing information. Write your answer as a mixed number.

a) 5 mangoes cost \$16

$\div 5$

1 mango costs $\$\frac{16}{5} = \$3\frac{1}{5}$

b) 4 cakes cost \$13

1 cake costs ____________

c) 5 pencils cost \$9

1 pencil costs ____________

d) 10 shirts cost \$75

1 shirt costs ____________

7. Convert each fraction in Question 6 to a decimal fraction. Then write the answer as a decimal.

a) $3\frac{1}{5} = 3\frac{20}{100} = \$3.20$

b)

c)

d)

8. Use division to find the unit rate.

a) ($\div 3$ on both sides)

3	5
1	$\frac{5}{3}$

So 3 : 5 = 1 : $\frac{5}{3}$

b)

3	5
	1

So 3 : 5 = ☐ : 1

c)

9	4
1	

So 9 : 4 = 1 : ☐

d)

9	4
	1

So 9 : 4 = ☐ : 1

e) ($\div 4$ on both sides)

4	1
1	$\frac{1}{4}$

So 4 : 1 = 1 : $\frac{1}{4}$

f)

7	2
1	

So 7 : 2 = 1 : ☐

g)

5	6
1	

So 5 : 6 = 1 : ☐

h)

1	2
	1

So 1 : 2 = ☐ : 1

i) ($\div 9$ on both sides)

1	
9	10

So 1 : ☐ = 9 : 10

j)

1	
5	3

So 1 : ☐ = 5 : 3

k)

	1
7	5

So ☐ : 1 = 7 : 5

Bonus ▸

1	
2	$\frac{2}{3}$

So 1 : ☐ = 2 : $\frac{2}{3}$

9. Write the fraction to complete the unit rate.

a) 4 hours to walk 10 miles

$4 : 10 = 1 : \boxed{\frac{10}{4}}$

b) 2 wins for every 5 games played

$2 : 5 = \boxed{} : 1$

c) 4 cups of raisins for 9 cups of flour

$4 : 9 = 1 : \boxed{}$

d) 27 minutes to answer 6 questions

$27 : 6 = \boxed{} : 1$

10. Convert each fraction in Question 9 to a decimal fraction. Then write the answer as a decimal.

a) $\frac{10}{4} \xrightarrow{\times 25} \frac{250}{100} = 2.5$ (numerator and denominator × 25)

So $4 : 10 = 1 : \boxed{2.5}$

b) $\frac{}{} = \frac{}{} =$

So $2 : 5 = \boxed{} : 1$

c) $\frac{}{} = \frac{}{} =$

So $4 : 9 = 1 : \boxed{}$

d) $\frac{}{} = \frac{}{} =$

So $27 : 6 = \boxed{} : 1$

11. What would you multiply the rate by to make the fraction equal to 1?

	Rate	Rough Work	Answer
a)	2 km in $\frac{1}{3}$ hr	$= 2$ km $\times \boxed{3} : \frac{1}{3}$ hr $\times \boxed{3}$	2 km : $\frac{1}{3}$ hr = 6 km : 1 h
b)	5 mi in $\frac{1}{4}$ hr	$= 5$ mi $\times \boxed{} : \frac{1}{4}$ hr $\times \boxed{}$	5 mi : $\frac{1}{4}$ hr =
c)	$\frac{1}{2}$ cup of flour for 3 eggs	$= \frac{1}{2}$ cup $\times \boxed{}$: 3 eggs $\times \boxed{}$	$\frac{1}{2}$ cups : 3 eggs =
d)	$\frac{1}{3}$ hr for 4 tasks	$= \frac{1}{3}$ hr $\times \boxed{}$: 4 tasks $\times \boxed{}$	$\frac{1}{3}$ hr : 4 tasks =

12. Alex makes punch by mixing $2\frac{1}{2}$ cups of cranberry juice for every 4 cups of ginger ale.

How many cups of ginger ale does he need for 5 cups of cranberry juice?

Bonus ▶ How many cups of ginger ale and cranberry juice does Alex need to make 26 cups of punch?

RP7-30 Unit Rates and Complex Fractions

REMINDER: If you divide any number (except zero) by itself, the result is 1.

Examples: $\frac{5}{5} = 1$ $\quad \frac{-4}{-4} = 1$ $\quad \frac{1.7}{1.7} = 1$ $\quad \frac{\frac{2}{3}}{\frac{2}{3}} = 1$

1. Find the number to divide by to make 1 in each position. Then write the equivalent ratio.

a) First position

5 : 3

$\div 5$ → 1 : $\boxed{\frac{3}{5}}$ ← $\div 5$

So 5 : 3 = *1* : $\frac{3}{5}$

Second position

5 : 3

$\div 3$ → $\boxed{\frac{5}{3}}$: 1 ← $\div 3$

So 5 : 3 = $\frac{5}{3}$: *1*

b) First position

2 : 7

$\div 2$ → 1 : $\square$ ← $\div 2$

So 2 : 7 = *1* :

Second position

2 : 7

$\div 7$ → $\square$: 1 ← $\div 7$

So 2 : 7 =   : *1*

c) First position

4 : 5

$\div$ → 1 : $\square$ ← $\div$

So 4 : 5 = *1* :

Second position

4 : 5

$\div$ → $\square$: 1 ← $\div$

So 4 : 5 =   : *1*

d) First position

6 : 11

→ 1 : $\square$ ←

So 6 : 11 =   :

Second position

6 : 11

→ $\square$: 1 ←

So 6 : 11 =   :

2. Every 2 lb of rice cost \$5. What's the price of rice per pound? How much rice can you buy with \$1?

In a ratio with a fractional term, you can divide both terms by the fraction.

This will result in a complex fraction. Examples:

$\frac{3}{4}$: 2

$\div \frac{3}{4}$ → 1 : $\boxed{\frac{2}{\frac{3}{4}}}$ ← $\div \frac{3}{4}$

5 : $\frac{2}{3}$

$\div \frac{2}{3}$ → $\boxed{\frac{5}{\frac{2}{3}}}$: 1 ← $\div \frac{2}{3}$

3. Write a complex fraction to find the unit rate.

a) $\frac{1}{2}$: 3

$\div \frac{1}{2}$ → 1 : $\boxed{\frac{3}{\frac{1}{2}}}$ ← $\div \frac{1}{2}$

b) 2 : $\frac{3}{5}$

$\square$: 1

c) $\frac{3}{4}$: 7

1 : $\square$

d) $\frac{7}{9}$: 4

1 : $\square$

4. Write a division statement for the complex fraction, then evaluate.

a) $\frac{\frac{2}{3}}{5} = \frac{2}{3} \div 5 = \frac{2}{3 \times 5} = \frac{2}{15}$

b) $\frac{\frac{1}{4}}{\frac{5}{7}}$

c) $\frac{\frac{2}{5}}{\frac{3}{4}}$

d) $\frac{4}{\frac{1}{3}}$

5. Write a complex fraction to show the unit rate.

a) $\frac{1}{2}$ hour to run 3 miles

$\frac{1}{2} : 3 = 1 : \boxed{\frac{3}{\frac{1}{2}}}$

b) 2 goals per period (third) of a hockey game

$2 : \frac{1}{3} = \boxed{} : 1$

c) $\frac{2}{5}$ cup of raisins for 3 cups of flour

$\frac{2}{5} : 3 = 1 : \boxed{}$

d) $\frac{3}{5}$ hour to answer 4 questions

$\frac{3}{5} : 4 = \boxed{} : 1$

6. Evaluate each complex fraction in Question 5, then find the unit rate.

a) $\frac{3}{\frac{1}{2}} = 3 \div \frac{1}{2} = 3 \times 2 = 6$

So $\frac{1}{2} : 3 = 1 : \underline{\ 6\ }$

b)

So $2 : \frac{1}{3} = \_\_\_\_\_ : 1$

c)

So $\frac{2}{5} : 3 = 1 : \_\_\_\_\_$

d)

So $\frac{3}{5} : 4 = \_\_\_\_\_ : 1$

Nancy runs 8 km every $\frac{2}{3}$ of an hour.

To find her running rate per hour, she uses a complex fraction:

$\frac{8}{\frac{2}{3}} = 8 \div \frac{2}{3} = 8 \times \frac{3}{2} = \frac{24}{2} = 12$, so Nancy runs 12 km in 1 hour.

$\frac{2}{3} : 8$ $\xrightarrow{\div \frac{2}{3}}$ $1 : \boxed{\frac{8}{\frac{2}{3}}}$

7. a) Kyle walks $\frac{1}{2}$ mi in each $\frac{1}{4}$ of an hour. Use a complex fraction to find how many miles he walks per hour.

b) Find the answer to part a) by multiplying by the LCM of the denominators. Did you get the same answer? If not, find your mistake.

8. A dozen muffins is 12 muffins. A recipe calls for $\frac{3}{4}$ cup of almonds to make half a dozen muffins. Use a complex fraction to find how many cups of almonds are needed to make a dozen muffins.

RP7-31 Using Proportions to Solve Percentage Problems I

These are equivalent statements:

$\frac{6}{9}$ of the circles are shaded.

$\frac{2}{3}$ of the circles are shaded.

6 is $\frac{2}{3}$ of 9.

6 : 9 = 2 : 3
part ↑ ↑ whole

1. Write four equivalent statements for the picture.

a) 

$\frac{4}{6}$ are shaded ________

$\frac{2}{3}$ are shaded ________

4 is $\frac{2}{3}$ of 6 ________

4 : 6 = 2 : 3 ________

b) 

____

____

____

____

c) 

d) 

2. Write a pair of equivalent ratios for the picture.

a) 

4 is $\frac{1}{2}$ of 8

4 : *8* = *1* : *2*
part whole

b) 

6 is $\frac{3}{4}$ of 8

____ : ____ = ____ : ____
part whole

c) 

2 is $\frac{1}{5}$ of 10

____ : ____ = ____ : ____
part whole

3. For the statement, write a pair of equivalent ratios and equivalent fractions.

a) 14 is $\frac{2}{3}$ of 21 ____ : ____ = ____ : ____ (part, whole) $\frac{\text{part}}{\text{whole}}$ ____ = ____

b) 12 is $\frac{3}{4}$ of 16 ____ : ____ = ____ : ____ (part, whole) $\frac{\text{part}}{\text{whole}}$ ____ = ____

4. Write a question mark where you are missing a piece of information.

a) 12 is $\frac{4}{5}$ of what number? $\underset{\text{part}}{\underline{12}} : \underset{\text{whole}}{\underline{?}} = \underline{4} : \underline{5}$ $\frac{\text{part}}{\text{whole}}$ $\frac{12}{?} = \frac{4}{5}$

b) 6 is how many quarters of 8? $\underset{\text{part}}{\underline{6}} : \underset{\text{whole}}{\underline{8}} = \underline{?} : \underline{4}$ $\frac{\text{part}}{\text{whole}}$ $\frac{6}{8} = \frac{?}{4}$

c) What is $\frac{2}{3}$ of 12? ____ : ____ = ____ : ____ (part, whole) $\frac{\text{part}}{\text{whole}}$ ____ = ____

d) 27 is how many fifths of 45? ____ : ____ = ____ : ____ (part, whole) $\frac{\text{part}}{\text{whole}}$ ____ = ____

5. Write a pair of equivalent ratios and a pair of equivalent fractions.

a) 15 is what percent of 20? $\underset{\text{part}}{\underline{15}} : \underset{\text{whole}}{\underline{20}} = \underline{?} : \underline{100}$ $\frac{\text{part}}{\text{whole}}$ $\frac{15}{20} = \frac{?}{100}$

b) What is 20% of 50? ____ : ____ = ____ : ____ (part, whole) $\frac{\text{part}}{\text{whole}}$ ____ = ____

c) 21 is what percent of 28? ____ : ____ = ____ : ____ (part, whole) $\frac{\text{part}}{\text{whole}}$ ____ = ____

d) 36 is 9% of what number? ____ : ____ = ____ : ____ (part, whole) $\frac{\text{part}}{\text{whole}}$ ____ = ____

6. Write the two pieces of information you are given and what you need to find (?).
Then write an equation for the problem.

a) What percent of 30 is 5? part 5 whole 30 percent ? $\frac{5}{30} = \frac{?}{100}$

b) If 11 is 50%, what is 100%? part ____ whole ? percent ____ $\frac{\_\_}{?} = \frac{\_\_}{100}$

c) What is 6% of 24? part ? whole ____ percent ____ $\frac{?}{\_\_} = \frac{\_\_}{100}$

d) If 4 is 16%, what is 100%? part ____ whole ____ percent ____ $\frac{\_\_}{\_\_} = \frac{\_\_}{100}$

e) What percent of 90 is 4? part ____ whole ____ percent ____ $\frac{\_\_}{\_\_} = \frac{\_\_}{100}$

f) What is 52% of 18? part ____ whole ____ percent ____ $\frac{\_\_}{\_\_} = \frac{\_\_}{100}$

g) 7 is what percent of 25? part ____ whole ____ percent ____ $\frac{\_\_}{\_\_} = \frac{\_\_}{100}$

If 5 subway tickets cost \$4, how much do 20 tickets cost? Write the ratio of dollars to tickets as a fraction, then find an equivalent fraction by multiplying:

Step 1:

$$\frac{\text{Dollars}}{\text{Tickets}} = \frac{4}{5} = \frac{?}{20}$$

Step 2:

$$\frac{4}{5} \xrightarrow[\times 4]{\times 4} \frac{\quad}{20}$$

Step 3:

$$\frac{4}{5} \xrightarrow[\times 4]{\times 4} \frac{16}{20}$$, so 20 tickets cost \$16.

7. Solve the proportion. Draw arrows and show what number you multiply by.

a) $\frac{3}{4} \xrightarrow[\times 5]{\times 5} \frac{\quad}{20}$ b) $\frac{1}{5} = \frac{\quad}{15}$ c) $\frac{3}{5} = \frac{\quad}{35}$ d) $\frac{4}{7} = \frac{\quad}{49}$

e) $\frac{3}{8} = \frac{\quad}{24}$ f) $\frac{2}{3} = \frac{\quad}{18}$ g) $\frac{13}{20} = \frac{\quad}{100}$ h) $\frac{5}{9} = \frac{\quad}{72}$

8. Solve the proportion the way you did in Question 7. Hint: The arrow will point from right to left.

a) $\frac{15}{\quad} = \frac{3}{4}$ b) $\frac{12}{\quad} = \frac{2}{5}$ c) $\frac{15}{\quad} = \frac{3}{7}$ d) $\frac{12}{18} = \frac{\quad}{3}$

9. Complete the equivalent fraction. Start by reducing the given fraction. The first one has been started for you.

a) $\frac{8}{10} = \frac{4}{5} = \frac{\quad}{15}$ b) $\frac{4}{6} = \frac{\quad}{\quad} = \frac{\quad}{15}$ c) $\frac{40}{100} = \frac{\quad}{\quad} = \frac{\quad}{45}$

d) $\frac{15}{18} = \frac{\quad}{\quad} = \frac{\quad}{30}$ e) $\frac{70}{100} = \frac{\quad}{\quad} = \frac{\quad}{90}$ f) $\frac{50}{75} = \frac{\quad}{\quad} = \frac{\quad}{36}$

10. Tanya is paid \$25 for 3 hours of work. How much would she be paid for 6 hours of work?

11. Three centimeters on a map represent 10 km in real life. If a lake is 9 cm long on the map, what is its actual length?

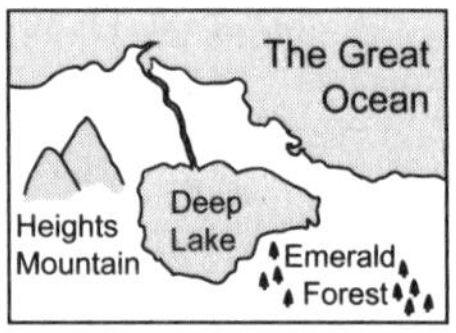

12. A goalie stopped 13 out of every 14 shots. There were 42 shots. How many goals were scored?

RP7-32 Using Proportions to Solve Percentage Problems II

1. Write a proportion to represent the percentage problem. Solve the proportion.

   a) What percent of 20 is 4? part ____ whole ____ percent ____ $\frac{\_\_\_}{\_\_\_} = \frac{\_\_\_}{100}$

   b) If 6 is 25%, what is 100%? part ____ whole ____ percent ____ $\frac{\_\_\_}{\_\_\_} = \frac{\_\_\_}{100}$

   c) What is 17% of 10? part ____ whole ____ percent ____ $\frac{\_\_\_}{\_\_\_} = \frac{\_\_\_}{100}$

   d) What is 17% of 50? part ____ whole ____ percent ____ $\frac{\_\_\_}{\_\_\_} = \frac{\_\_\_}{100}$

   e) 4 is what percent of 5? f) 6 is 25% of what number? g) 24 is 80% of what number?

2. Explain why the proportion $\frac{3}{25} = \frac{x}{100}$ will be easy to solve.

3. Write a proportion $\frac{a}{b} = \frac{x}{100}$ to represent the problem. Solve by first writing $\frac{a}{b}$ in lowest terms.

   a) What percent of 15 is 3? b) What percent of 24 is 6? c) What percent of 30 is 12?

4. Write a proportion to represent the percentage problem. Find an equivalent ratio to rewrite the proportion. Solve the new proportion.

   a) If 6 is 40%, what is 100%?

   part *6* whole *x* percent *40* $\frac{6}{x} = \frac{40}{100}$

   Hint: Start by writing 40% as an equivalent ratio with numerator 2. $\frac{40}{100} = \frac{2}{5}$

   b) What is 75% of 48? Hint: Start by writing 75% as an equivalent ratio with denominator 4.

   part ____ whole ____ percent ____ $\frac{\_\_\_}{\_\_\_} = \frac{\_\_\_}{100}$

   c) What percent of 60 is 45?

   part ____ whole ____ percent ____ $\frac{\_\_\_}{\_\_\_} = \frac{\_\_\_}{100}$

   d) What is 60% of 15?

   part ____ whole ____ percent ____ $\frac{\_\_\_}{\_\_\_} = \frac{\_\_\_}{100}$

5. Solve.

   a) 9 is 60% of what number? b) What is 75% of 24?

   c) 16 is 80% of what number? d) What percent of 360 is 72?

6. If 35% of 120 students use an MP3 player, how many students use an MP3 player?

7. Ten students in a class (40% of the class) bike to school. How many students are in the class?

REMINDER: $\frac{2}{3}$ of a number is 100. What is the number?

$\frac{2}{3} = \frac{100}{?}$ $\begin{matrix}\text{part}\\ \text{whole}\end{matrix}$ $\frac{2}{3} \xrightarrow[\times 50]{\times 50} \frac{100}{?}$ $\frac{2}{3} = \frac{100}{150}$ The number is 150.

8. What is the number?

a) $\frac{2}{5}$ of a number is 4
b) $\frac{3}{7}$ of a number is 9
c) $\frac{5}{11}$ of a number is 25

9. A box holds red and blue beads. Find the total number of beads in the box.

a) $\frac{3}{4}$ of the beads are red. Six beads are red.
b) $\frac{3}{5}$ of the beads are blue. Twelve beads are blue.
c) 60% of the beads are red. Fifteen beads are red.
d) The ratio of red beads to blue beads is 4 : 5. There are 20 red beads. Hint: What fraction of the beads are red?

10. Emma and Sun share a sum of money. Emma receives $\frac{2}{5}$ of the money. Sun receives \$24.

a) What fraction of the sum did Sun receive?
b) How much money did Emma and Sun share?

11. At Franklin Middle School, $\frac{3}{8}$ of the students take a bus to school, $\frac{3}{5}$ walk, and the rest bike. There are 20 students who bike to school. How many students are in the school?

12. In a fish tank, $\frac{2}{3}$ of the fish are red, $\frac{1}{4}$ are yellow, and the rest are green. There are 42 more red fish than green fish.

a) What fraction of the fish are green?
b) What fraction of the total number of fish does 42 represent? Hint: 42 is the difference between the number of red and green fish.
c) How many fish are in the tank?

13. In Carl's stamp collection, 70% of the stamps are American and the rest are international. Carl has 500 more American stamps than international stamps. How many stamps does he have?

14. On an LED sign, $\frac{1}{5}$ of the lights are yellow and the rest are blue and red. There are twice as many blue lights as yellow lights, and there are 200 red lights on the sign. How many LED lights of all colors are on the sign?

RP7-33 Solving Equations (Introduction)

1. Each bag contains the same number of apples. Let x be the number of apples in one bag. Write an expression for the total number of apples.

a) 

____

b) 

____

c) 

____

2. Write the total number of apples two ways to make an equation.

a) There are 9 apples in total.

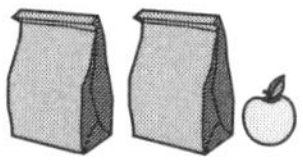

____

b) There are 11 apples in total.

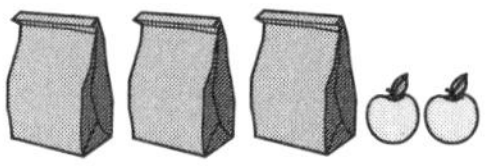

____

c) There are 20 apples in total.

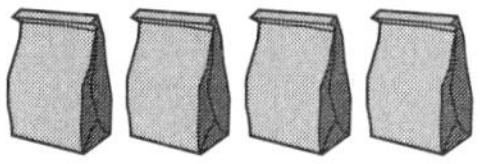

____

3. a) The scales are balanced. Write an equation to show this.

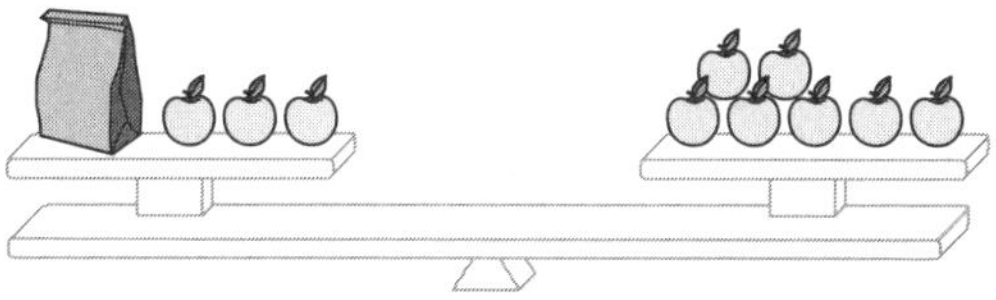

____

b) Remove the same number of apples from each side to keep the scales balanced. Leave the bag by itself on one side. Write the new equation.

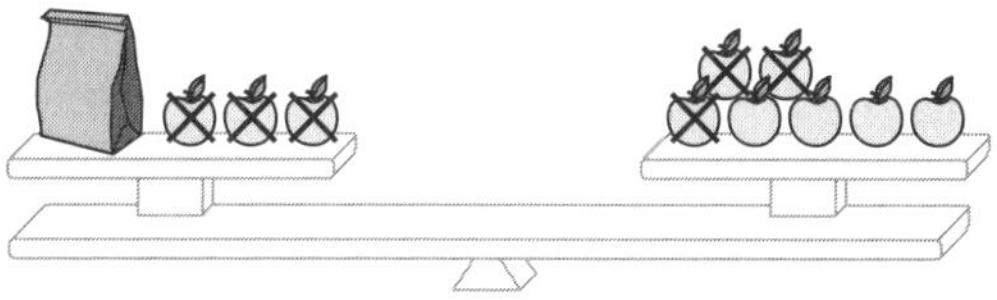

____

c) How many apples are in the bag? ________

Finding the value of a variable in an equation is called **solving for** the variable.

To solve $x + 4 = 10$, subtract 4 from both sides of the equation so that one side has only x.

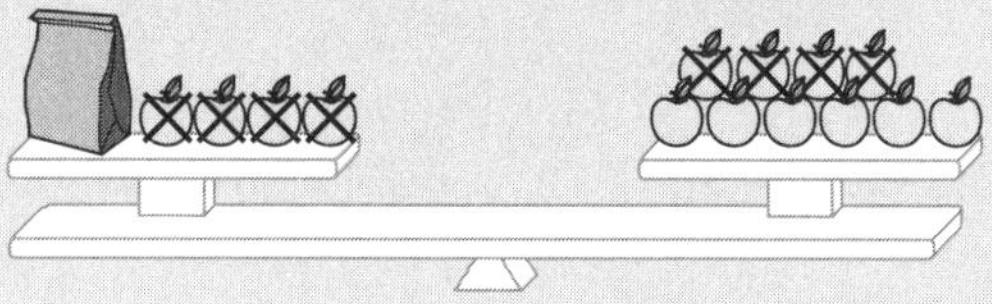

$$\begin{array}{rcr} x + 4 & = & 10 \\ \mathbf{-\,4} & & \mathbf{-\,4} \\ \hline x & = & 6 \end{array}$$

4. Subtract 5 from both sides of the equation.

a) $\begin{array}{rcr} x + 5 & = & 8 \\ \mathbf{-\,5} & & \mathbf{-\,5} \\ \hline x & = & 3 \end{array}$

b) $\begin{array}{rcr} 5 + x & = & 9 \\ \mathbf{-\,5} & & \mathbf{-\,5} \\ \hline \end{array}$

c) $\begin{array}{rcr} 3 & = & 5 + x \\ \mathbf{-\,5} & & \mathbf{-\,5} \\ \hline \end{array}$

d) $\begin{array}{rcr} 0 & = & x + 5 \\ \mathbf{-\,5} & & \mathbf{-\,5} \\ \hline \end{array}$

5. Subtract the same number from both sides of the equation so that x is by itself.

a) $\begin{array}{rcr} x + 2 & = & 8 \\ -\,2 & & -\,2 \\ \hline \end{array}$

b) $\begin{array}{rcr} 7 + x & = & 12 \\ -\,7 & & -\,7 \\ \hline \end{array}$

c) $\begin{array}{rcr} 11 & = & 6 + x \\ -\,6 & & -\,6 \\ \hline \end{array}$

d) $\begin{array}{rcr} 9 & = & 4 + x \\ -\,4 & & -\,4 \\ \hline \end{array}$

6. Solve the equation by subtracting the same number from both sides.

a) $x + 11 = 20$ b) $9 + x = 15$ c) $65 = x + 28$ d) $43 = x + 15$

7. a) The scales are balanced. Write an equation to show this.

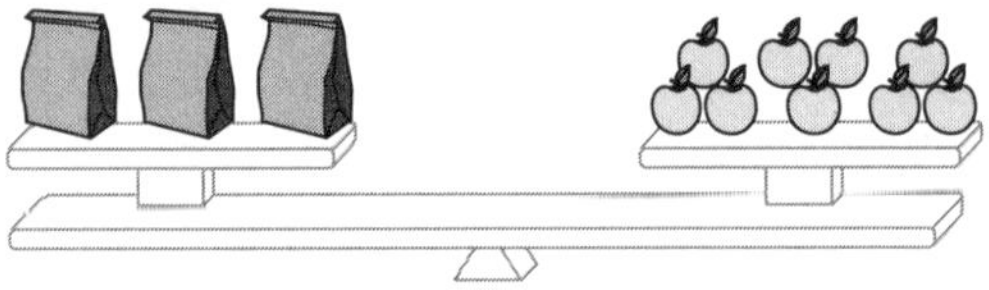

____

b) Divide the quantities on both sides into the same number of equal groups. Leave one group on each side. Write an equation.

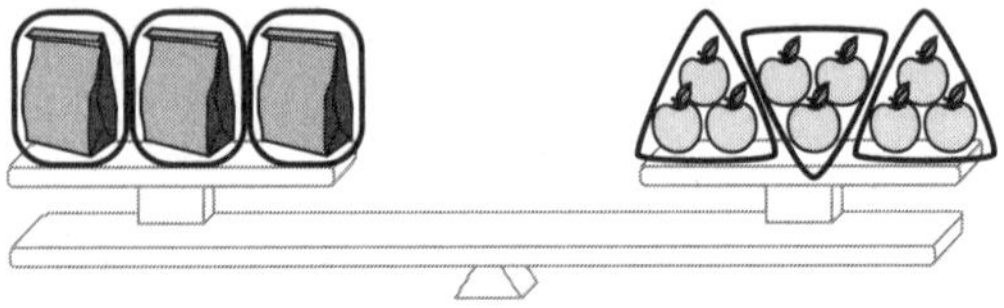

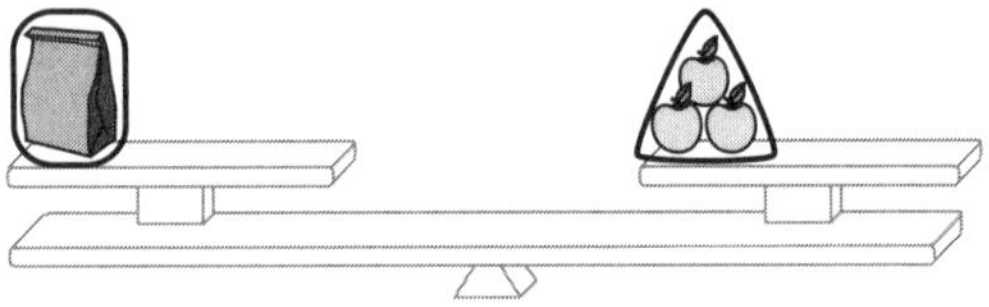

____

c) How many apples are in each bag? _______

8. Divide both sides of the equation by the same number so that x is by itself.

a) $3x = 12$, $\div 3$ $\div 3$

b) $8x = 32$, $\div 8$ $\div 8$

c) $12 = 6x$, $\div 6$ $\div 6$

d) $24 = 4x$, $\div 4$ $\div 4$

9. Solve the equation by dividing both sides of the equation by the same number.

a) $5x = 30$

$5x \div 5 = 30 \div 5$

$x = 6$

b) $3x = 18$ c) $9x = 54$ d) $7x = 56$

e) $3x = 12{,}000$ f) $4x = 680$ g) $8x = 128$ h) $5x = 135$

10. Solve the equation by doing the same thing to both sides of the equation.

a) $x + 4 = 12$ b) $4x = 12$ c) $5 + x = 35$ d) $5x = 35$

e) $5 + x = 11$ f) $39 = 13x$ g) $x + 14 = 27$ h) $3x = 42$

REMINDER: You can subtract a negative number by adding its opposite.

Example: $7 - (-4) = 7 + 4 = 11$

You can add a negative number by subtracting its opposite.

Example: $7 + (-4) = 7 - 4 = 3$

11. Solve the equation by subtracting the same number from both sides.

a) $x + (-4) = 9$

$x = 9 - (-4)$

$x = 9 + 4$

$x = 13$

b) $x + (-8) = 15$

c) $x + 5 = 13$

d) $x + 5 = -13$

e) $x + 3 = -8$

f) $x + (-3) = -8$

g) $x + 3 = 8$

h) $x + (-3) = 8$

REMINDER: You can multiply and divide positive and negative numbers by multiplying their absolute values and using the rules for signs:

$(+) \times (+) = +$ $(+) \times (-) = -$ $(-) \times (+) = -$ $(-) \times (-) = +$

$(+) \div (+) = +$ $(+) \div (-) = -$ $(-) \div (+) = -$ $(-) \div (-) = +$

12. Solve the equation by dividing both sides of the equation by the same number.

a) $4x = -12$

b) $-4x = 12$

c) $x \times (-4) = 12$

d) $-4x = -12$

e) $-42 = x \times (-6)$

f) $-39 = -13x$

g) $5 = \frac{1}{2}x$

h) $-\frac{1}{3}x = 6$

RP7-34 Cross Multiplication (Introduction)

$\frac{3}{4} = 0.75$ means the same thing as $3 \div 4 = 0.75$, so $3 = 0.75 \times 4$.

1. Change the equation to a division statement, then to a multiplication statement.

a) $\frac{10}{5} = 2$ b) $7 = \frac{28}{4}$ c) $\frac{33}{3} = 11$ d) $3 = \frac{21}{7}$

$10 \div 5 = 2$ ______ ______ ______

$10 = 2 \times 5$ ______ ______ ______

2. Change the equation to a multiplication statement.

a) $\frac{7}{2} = 3.5$ b) $1.2 = \frac{12}{10}$ c) $\frac{-24}{6} = -4$ d) $3 = \frac{21}{x}$

$7 = 3.5 \times 2$ ______ ______ ______

e) $\frac{5}{4} = 1.25$ f) $2.75 = \frac{11}{4}$ g) $\frac{-12}{10} = -1.2$ h) $3 = \frac{21}{t}$

You can turn equivalent fractions into equivalent products. Multiply both fractions by the product of their denominators.

Example: $\frac{3}{4} = \frac{9}{12}$. Multiply both fractions by **4** × **12**, the product of their denominators.

$$\frac{3}{\cancel{4}} \times \cancel{\mathbf{4}} \times \mathbf{12} = \frac{9}{\cancel{12}} \times \mathbf{4} \times \cancel{\mathbf{12}}$$

$$3 \times 12 = 9 \times 4$$

Rewriting $\frac{3}{4} = \frac{9}{12}$ as $3 \times 12 = 9 \times 4$ is called **cross multiplying** because the products are obtained by multiplying the numbers in an X shape:

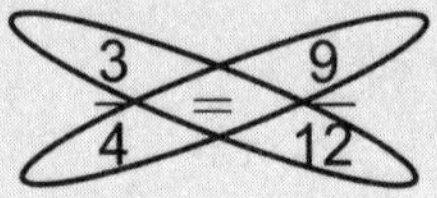

3. Check that cross multiplying works for the equivalent fractions.

a) $\frac{2}{5} = \frac{6}{15}$ b) $\frac{3}{4} = \frac{6}{8}$ c) $\frac{1}{2} = \frac{5}{10}$ d) $\frac{2}{3} = \frac{8}{12}$

$2 \times 15 = 6 \times 5$

$30 = 30$ ✓

e) $\frac{2.5}{3} = \frac{5}{6}$ f) $\frac{-2}{3} = \frac{-8}{12}$ g) $\frac{3}{-5} = \frac{-9}{15}$ h) $\frac{4}{-1.5} = \frac{8}{-3}$

$2.5 \times 6 = 5 \times 3$

$15 = 15$ ✓

4. Cross multiply and write = (equal) or ≠ (not equal) in the box. Are the fractions equivalent?

a) $\frac{3}{4}$ and $\frac{10}{13}$

3 × 13 ☐ 10 × 4

Are $\frac{3}{4}$ and $\frac{10}{13}$ equivalent? ________

b) $\frac{2}{5}$ and $\frac{10}{25}$

____ × ____ ☐ ____ × ____

Are $\frac{2}{5}$ and $\frac{10}{25}$ equivalent? ________

c) $\frac{9}{10}$ and $\frac{81}{100}$

____ × ____ ☐ ____ × ____

Are $\frac{9}{10}$ and $\frac{81}{100}$ equivalent? ________

d) $\frac{5}{7}$ and $\frac{28}{35}$

____ × ____ ☐ ____ × ____

Are $\frac{5}{7}$ and $\frac{28}{35}$ and equivalent? ________

e) $\frac{3}{4}$ and $\frac{15}{20}$ f) $\frac{5}{6}$ and $\frac{35}{42}$ g) $\frac{91}{105}$ and $\frac{104}{120}$ h) $\frac{14}{21}$ and $\frac{30}{48}$

You can cross multiply if you have equivalent complex fractions, too.

Example: $\frac{\frac{3}{4}}{\frac{3}{7}}$ and $\frac{\frac{7}{5}}{\frac{4}{5}}$ $\frac{3}{4}\times\frac{4}{5}=\frac{3\times\cancel{4}}{\cancel{4}\times 5}=\frac{3}{5}$ and $\frac{7}{5}\times\frac{3}{7}=\frac{\cancel{7}\times 3}{5\times\cancel{7}}=\frac{3}{5}$, so $\frac{\frac{3}{4}}{\frac{3}{7}}$ and $\frac{\frac{7}{5}}{\frac{4}{5}}$ are equivalent.

5. Are the complex fractions equivalent? Cross multiply to check.

a) $\frac{\frac{2}{5}}{\frac{7}{3}}$ and $\frac{\frac{2}{7}}{\frac{5}{3}}$

b) $\frac{\frac{3}{4}}{\frac{5}{2}}$ and $\frac{\frac{3}{2}}{\frac{4}{5}}$ c) **Bonus ▶** $\frac{-\frac{3}{4}}{\frac{2}{5}}$ and $\frac{\frac{3}{2}}{-\frac{4}{5}}$ d) **Bonus ▶** $\frac{\frac{3}{4}}{\frac{2}{5}}$ and $\frac{\frac{9}{2}}{\frac{12}{5}}$

6. a) Complete the equivalent fraction. Start by reducing the given fraction.

i) $\frac{8}{10}=\frac{4}{5}=\frac{}{15}$ ii) $\frac{4}{6}=\frac{}{}=\frac{}{15}$ iii) $\frac{70}{100}=\frac{}{}=\frac{}{90}$

b) Use cross multiplication to solve the problems in part a).

c) How would you solve the problem: mentally (by reducing the fraction) or with cross multiplication? Find the missing number.

i) $\frac{40}{100}=\frac{18}{}$ ii) $\frac{19}{20}=\frac{}{7}$ iii) $\frac{50}{75}=\frac{}{24}$

RP7-35 Using Equations to Solve Proportions

You can solve a proportion by cross multiplying and solving an equation.

$\frac{6}{x} = \frac{9}{6}$ ⟶

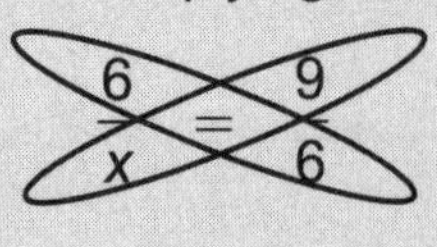

⟶ $9x = 6 \times 6$

$9x = 36$

$x = 36 \div 9$

$x = 4$

1. Cross multiply to write an equation for x. (Do not solve.)

a) $\frac{7}{x} = \frac{3}{5}$ $7 \times 5 = 3x$

b) $\frac{x}{9} = \frac{2}{5}$ $5x = 2 \times 9$

c) $\frac{11}{x} = \frac{5}{2}$ ____

d) $\frac{4}{9} = \frac{x}{3}$ ____

e) $\frac{5}{21} = \frac{3}{x}$ ____

f) $\frac{x}{52} = \frac{4}{8}$ ____

g) $\frac{20}{x} = \frac{12}{25}$ ____

h) $\frac{12}{x} = \frac{3}{10}$ ____

2. Solve for x.

a) $\frac{9}{6} = \frac{x}{3}$

b) $\frac{4}{x} = \frac{2}{3}$

c) $\frac{3}{4} = \frac{6}{x}$

d) $\frac{100}{7} = \frac{9}{x}$

e) $\frac{2}{x} = \frac{10}{4}$

f) $\frac{-5}{x} = \frac{1}{6}$

g) $\frac{2}{-3} = \frac{8}{x}$

Bonus ▶ $\frac{10}{5} = \frac{-x}{9}$

You can solve percentage problems by writing a proportion and then cross multiplying.

Example: What is 70% of 9? $\frac{x}{9} = \frac{70}{100}$ so $100x = 70 \times 9$

$100x = 630$

$x = \frac{630}{100}$

$x = 6.3$

3. Solve by first writing a proportion.

a) What is 90% of 6?

b) 9 is 2% of what number?

c) 3 is what percent of 15?

Bonus ▶ 5 is what percent of 8?

Answer all problems in your notebook.

Write an equation for each problem and solve the equation.
Use a calculator when you need it.

4. a) What percent of 32 is 8?
b) What percent of 125 is 5?
c) What percent of 128 is 32?
d) What percent of 15 is 0.6?

5. Round the solution to the nearest one.
a) 5 is about what percent of 24?
b) About what percent of 17 is 9?
c) 4 is about what percent of 9?
d) About what percent of 7,560 is 3,000?
e) 1.3 is about what percent of 27?

6. If Grace has read 54 of the 297 pages in her library book, about what percent of the book has she read so far?

7. Find the amount. Include units in your answers.
a) 26% of 130 g
b) 11% of 407 m
c) 32% of 11 mL
d) 99% of 8 m^2
e) 40% of 2,222 min

8. About 3% of 592 students are vegans. About how many students are vegans?

9. A basketball team won 60% of the 25 games it played this year.
a) What percent of the games played did the team lose?
b) How many games did the team lose?

10. What is 100% if …
a) 25% is 30?
b) 15% is 30?
c) 3% is 12?

11. About what is 100%? Round the solution to the nearest one.
a) 10 is 7%
b) 74 is 32%
c) 2 is 9%

12. In a Grade 7 class, 6 of the students, or about 27%, were on the honor roll. How many students are in the class?

Bonus ▶ Ben bought a new computer at a 15% discount. He paid $1,020.
a) What percent of the original price did he pay?
b) What was the original price?
c) How much money did Ben save by buying the computer at a discount?

RP7-36 Recognizing Proportional Relationships

You can recognize when to use proportions by looking for words like "for every," "for each," or "per."

1. Underline the key words that tell you to solve proportions. Then solve the problem.

   a) There are 3 tablespoons of sugar in each cup of cola. How many tablespoons of sugar are in 5 cups of cola?

   b) Ted rides his bike at a rate of 15 km per hour. How far can he ride in 3 hours?

   c) Kathy needs to buy 4 ounces of cheese per guest to make a fondue. How much cheese does she need for 12 people?

   d) To make glue, Ravi needs 3 cups of flour for every 2 cups of water. How much flour does Ravi need for 10 cups of water?

For every 3 red marbles, there are 2 blue marbles.

For twice as many red marbles, there are also twice as many blue marbles.

2. Does the statement contain words meaning "for every"? Circle "yes" or "no."

   a) Each pizza costs \$5. yes no

   b) Three people take two hours to paint a fence. yes no

   c) Sharon learns 300 new words every 2 months. yes no

   d) Advertising costs 30¢ per letter. yes no

   e) In 3 years, Mark will be twice his age now. yes no

> To check if a relationship is proportional, double one quantity. If the other quantity doubles, too, then the relationship is proportional.

3. Is there a proportional relationship between the quantities? Write "yes" or "no."

a) When 3 people help to paint the fence, their lunch will cost $10. ________
Hint: When there are 6 people helping, will their lunch cost $20?

b) When 3 people help to paint the fence, the job will take 2 hours. ________
Hint: When there are 6 people helping, will the job take 4 hours?

c) When Sue is 3 years old, Jack is 5 years old. ________
Hint: When Sue is 6, will Jack be 10?

d) For every 2 months that Sindi gets older, she learns 300 new words. ________

e) Mix 2 cups blue paint with 3 cups yellow paint to make green paint. ________

f) When 5 people help to set up the tent, 1 hour is needed. ________

4. a) Match the table to the problem.

A. Two people can do a job in 6 hours.
How long will it take 4 people to do the same job?

B. Tim is 2 years old and Randi is 6.
How old will Randi be when Tim is 4 years old?

C. A recipe calls for 2 cups of flour for every 6 teaspoons of sugar.
How many teaspoons of sugar are needed for 4 cups of flour?

2	6
4	12

____

2	6
4	3

____

2	6
4	8

____

b) Which table(s) from part a) are ratio tables? ________

5. a) Solve the problem.

i) Three people can paint a room in four hours. How long would it take six people to paint the room? ______________

ii) Jon can paint a wall in one hour. How long would it take him to paint four walls? ______________

iii) Blanca is 7 years old. Roy is 12 years old. When Blanca is 13 years old, how old will Roy be? ______________

b) For which problem(s) in part a) did you use ratios? ______________

Ratio and Percentage Problems—Tape Diagrams, Discounts, and Markups

1. a) After a 20% discount, the price of skates is \$60. What was the original price?

100% = \$ ______

%	20	20	20	20	20
\$					

\$60

b) After a 25% discount, the price of a skateboard is \$60. What was the original price?

100% = \$ ______

%	25	25	25	25
\$				

\$60

c) After a 30% discount, the price of a can of juice is 49¢. What was the original price?

100% = ______ ¢

%	10	10	10	10	10	10	10	10	10	10
¢										

49¢

d) After a 60% discount, the price of a pair of gloves is \$12. What was the original price?

%	20	20	20	20	20
\$					

e) After a 40% discount, the price of a sweater is \$45. What was the original price?

Stores often make money by selling products at a higher price than they paid for them. The extra amount is called a **markup**.

Example: A store buys ice skates for \$50 and marks up the price by 20%.
20% of \$50 is \$10, so the price increases by \$10.
The store sells the ice skates for \$50 + \$10 = \$60.

2. a) After a 20% markup, the price of running shoes is \$84. What was the price before the markup?

100% = \$ ______ (first 5 boxes)

%	20	20	20	20	20	20
\$						

\$84 (all boxes)

b) After a 25% markup, the price of inline skates is \$100. What was the price before the markup?

100% = \$ ______ (first 4 boxes)

%	25	25	25	25	25
\$					

\$100 (all boxes)

c) After a 60% markup, the price of skis is \$88. What was the price before the markup?

100% = \$ ______ (first 5 boxes)

%	20	20	20	20	20	20	20	20
\$								

\$88 (all boxes)

d) After a 75% markup, the price of a T-shirt is \$21. What was the price before the markup?

RP7-38 Multistep Word Problems

1. A pair of jeans cost \$80 last week. Now they are 20% off. Find the new cost of the jeans in two ways.

   a) Find 20% of \$80. Then subtract this amount from \$80. ____________

   b) 100% − 20% = 80%. Find 80% of \$80. ____________

2. A daily planner cost \$12.50 last year. The price of this year's planner has increased 20%. What is the new price?

3. A game sells for \$25 plus 14% tax. Is \$28 enough to buy the game?

4. a) 115% = 46 (46 ÷ 115)

   What is 1%? 0.4

   What is 100%? 40

   b) 175% = 35

   What is 1%? ______

   What is 100%? ______

   c) 150% = 45

   What is 1%? ______

   What is 100%? ______

5. The cost of a T-shirt with 14% tax included is \$23.00. The total price is 114% of the original price. What was the original price?

6. A grocery store buys organic apples at 80 cents each and sells them for \$1 each. What percent does the store mark up the price of each apple?

7. There are 20 more students in the band this year than last year, which is a 10% increase.

   a) How many were in the band last year?

   b) How many are in the band this year?

8. The tax on a purchase of \$20 is \$2.80. How much tax will there be on a purchase of \$45.50?

9. Milly went to a city and bought something that was priced at \$6.95. The total bill was \$7.61. What is the sales tax rate in that city? (Round the answer to one decimal place.)

10. Calculate the percentage. Round to one decimal place, if necessary.

    a) 25% of 50%

    = 0.25×0.50

    = $0.125 = 12.5\%$

    b) 10% of 60%

    = ____________

    = ____________

    c) 80% of 30%

    = ____________

    = ____________

11. Bo gave 60% of his stamp collection to his brother. Bo sold 20% of the remaining amount. What percent of his stamp collection did Bo sell?

Answer all problems in your notebook.

12. An 8-slice pizza is shared among 3 people. Amy eats 2 pieces, David eats 3 pieces, and Karen eats 3 pieces. The pizza costs $12.99 plus a 14% tax. How much should each person pay?

13. Two hockey goalies, Jin and Mona, are comparing their records. Jin saved 53 out of 60 shots in 3 games. Mona saved 65 out of 70 shots in 2 games.

a) Find the percentage of shots each person saved (to one decimal place).

b) Find the average number of goals allowed per game by each player (to one decimal place).

c) Who do you think is the better goalie? Why?

14. Ed gave away 45% of his hockey cards.

a) What fraction of his cards did Ed keep?

b) Ed put his remaining cards in a scrapbook. Each page holds 18 cards and he filled $23\frac{5}{6}$ pages. How many cards did Ed put in the book?

c) How many cards did Ed have before he gave part of his collection away?

15. 24-karat gold is pure, so that means 12-karat gold is 50% pure and 18-karat gold is 75% pure.

a) How pure is 15-karat gold?

b) Tina has a gold bracelet weighing 50 g. It is 15-karat gold. If pure gold costs $23.64 per gram, what is a fair price for the bracelet?

16. Rick gave $\frac{2}{7}$ of his savings to charity and spent $\frac{3}{5}$ of the remainder on holiday gifts.

a) What fraction of Rick's money is left?

b) If Rick has $300 left, how much money did he have to start with?

17. A book costs $17.50. The salesperson tells you that the total price, including tax, is $21.43. How can you tell if the total price is reasonable without using a calculator? Hint: No state has tax higher than 12%.

Bonus ▶ Two years ago, a calculator cost $120. The price increased by 10% last year. This year, the price increased 12%. What is this year's price? What percent did the price increase over the two years?

Bonus ▶ A population increased by 10% one year and 15% the next year. Explain why there was not a 25% increase in the poplutaion over the two years.

EE7-13 Solving Equations—Guess and Check

Remember: Finding the value of a variable that makes an equation true is called solving for the variable. Sara uses a table to solve $2x + 1 = 7$.

x	$2x + 1$	Is the equation true?
1	3	✗
2	5	✗
3	7	✓

So $x = 3$ makes the equation true.

1. Complete the table, then solve for x.

a) $4x + 1 = 21$

x	$4x + 1$	True?
1	$4(1) + 1 = 5$	✗
2	$4(2) + 1 = 9$	✗
3		
4		
5		

So $x =$ ______

b) $3x + 4 = 16$

x	$3x + 4$	True?
1	$3(1) + 4 = 7$	✗
2		
3		
4		
5		

So $x =$ ______

c) $5x - 3 = 12$

x	$5x - 3$	True?
1		
2		
3		
4		
5		

So $x =$ ______

2. Replace n with 5 and say whether 5 is too high, too low, or just right to solve the equation. Then try a lower or higher number if you need to.

a) $4n - 1 = 23$

n	$4n - 1$	Answer
5	$4(5) - 1$	19

5 is *too low*.

b) $5n - 4 = 16$

n	$5n - 4$	Answer
5	$5(5) - 4$	

5 is ____________.

c) $2n - 5 = 7$

n	$2n - 5$	Answer
5		

5 is ____________.

d) $3n + 2 = 17$

n	$3n + 2$	Answer
5		

5 is ____________.

e) $4n + 3 = 19$

n	$4n + 3$	Answer
5		

5 is ____________.

f) $8n - 1 = 31$

n	$8n - 1$	Answer
5		

5 is ____________.

3. Solve for n by guessing small values for n, checking, and revising.

a) $4n + 2 = 22$ b) $5n - 2 = 33$ c) $4n - 1 = 27$

d) $6n - 5 = 19$ e) $8n - 2 = 22$ f) $9n + 2 = 65$

4. Complete the table. When n increases, does the expression increase or decrease?

a)

n	$n - 2$
1	
2	
3	
4	

As n increases, $n - 2$ ________________.

b)

n	$2 - n$
1	
2	
3	
4	

As n increases, $2 - n$ ________________.

c)

n	$-2n + 3$
1	
2	
3	
4	

As n increases, $-2n + 3$ ________________.

When the coefficient of n is negative, increasing n makes the expression smaller.

You can use this to solve $15 - 2n = 7$ by guessing and checking. Guess $n = 5$ and evaluate:

$15 - 2(5) = 15 - 10 = 5$

The answer is too *low*, so 5 is too *high*. Try $n = 4$ in the expression:

$15 - 2(4) = 15 - 8 = 7$

So $n = 4$ solves the equation.

5. Replace n with 5 and say whether 5 is too high or too low to solve the equation. Then try a lower or higher number.

a) $30 - 4n = 14$

n	$30 - 4n$	Answer
5		

5 is ________________.

b) $50 - 5n = 20$

n	$50 - 5n$	Answer
5		

5 is ________________.

c) $22 - 3n = 4$

n	$22 - 3n$	Answer
5		

5 is ________________.

6. Solve for n by guessing small values for n, checking, and revising.

a) $20 - 3n = 8$ b) $5n - 4 = 26$ c) $50 - 7n = 15$

d) $32 - 6n = -4$ e) $9n - 34 = 2$ f) $6n - 25 = 5$

7. Would you solve $\frac{7}{3} - \frac{1}{8}x = \frac{2}{5}$ by guessing, checking, and revising? Explain.

EE7-14 Preserving Equality to Solve Equations

1. Show the operation you need to do to get back to x.

a) $3x$ $\quad$ $3x \div 3$ ______

b) $x - 3$ ______

c) $x + 7$ ______

d) $8 + x$ ______

e) $\frac{x}{8}$ ______

f) $1.5x$ ______

g) $x - 9$ ______

h) $x + \frac{3}{4}$ ______

> To solve an equation, put the variable by itself on one side of the equation, with coefficient 1.
>
> Example: $x - 3 = 4$ $\quad$ Adding 3 gets $x - 3$ back to x, so add 3 to both sides of the equation.
>
> $x - 3 + 3 = 4 + 3$ $\quad$ Since both sides are equal before adding 3, they are equal after adding 3.
>
> $x = 7$ $\quad$ Now x is by itself, with coefficient 1, so you can read the answer: $x = 7$.

2. Get back to x on the left side. Do the same operation to the right side to solve the equation.

a) $x - 3 = 5$

$x - 3 + 3 = 5 + 3$

$x = 8$

b) $x + 8 = 11$

c) $3.2 + x = 4.6$

d) $x - \frac{2}{7} = 5$

e) $x - 2 = -7$

$x - 2 + 2 = -7 + 2$

$x = -5$

f) $x + 7 = 4$

g) $2.7 + x = -6.1$

h) $x + \frac{5}{8} = \frac{1}{2}$

3. Check your answers to Question 2 by replacing x with your answer. Is the equation true?

a) $8 - 3 = 5$ ✓ $\quad$ b) $\quad$ c) $\quad$ d)

e) $\quad$ f) $\quad$ g) $\quad$ h)

> REMINDER: $(+) \times (+) = +$ $\quad$ $(+) \times (-) = -$ $\quad$ $(-) \times (+) = -$ $\quad$ $(-) \times (-) = +$
>
> $(+) \div (+) = +$ $\quad$ $(+) \div (-) = -$ $\quad$ $(-) \div (+) = -$ $\quad$ $(-) \div (-) = +$

4. Multiply or divide.

a) $3 \times (-2) =$ ____

b) $8 \div (-4) =$ ____

c) $(-9) \times (-3) =$ ____

d) $(-9) \div (-3) =$ ____

e) $-9 \times 5 =$ ____

f) $-20 \div 5 =$ ____

Bonus ▶ $(-18) \div (-4.5) =$ ______

5. Get back to x on the left side. Do the same thing to the right side to solve the equation.

a) $3x = 12$ b) $\frac{x}{-4} = 20$ c) $0.8x = -4.8$ d) $\frac{x}{-5} = -6$

Sometimes you need two steps to solve an equation.

Step 1: Do the same thing to both sides to get the variable term by itself.

Step 2: Do the same thing to both sides to make the coefficient equal to 1.

Example: Solve $-2x + 3 = 11$.

Subtract 3 from both sides:

$-2x + 3 - 3 = 11 - 3$

$-2x = 8$

Divide both sides by -2:

$-2x \div (-2) = 8 \div (-2)$

$x = -4$

6. Do the same operation to both sides to get the variable term by itself. Do not solve.

a) $2x - 5 = 17$

$2x - 5 + 5 = 17 + 5$

$2x = 22$

b) $3x + 4 = 13$

c) $-3x + 14 = -10$

d) $7x - 13 = 22$ e) $-x - 3 = -10$ f) $2x + 5 = -3$

7. Solve the equation. Check your answer in your notebook by substituting your answer for x in the original equation.

a) $3x - 5 = 16$

$3x - 5 + 5 = 16 + 5$

$3x = 21$

$3x \div 3 = 21 \div 3$

$x = 7$

b) $2x - 9 = -5$

c) $-3x + 5 = -19$

d) $\frac{x}{5} + 4 = 3$ e) $\frac{x}{-3} + 8 = 3$ f) $-\frac{x}{2} - 3 = 7$

8. Abdul can rent skis for \$3 an hour. A ski ticket costs \$20 for the day.

a) How much does it cost to ski for 3 hours?

b) How many hours can Abdul ski if he has \$41?

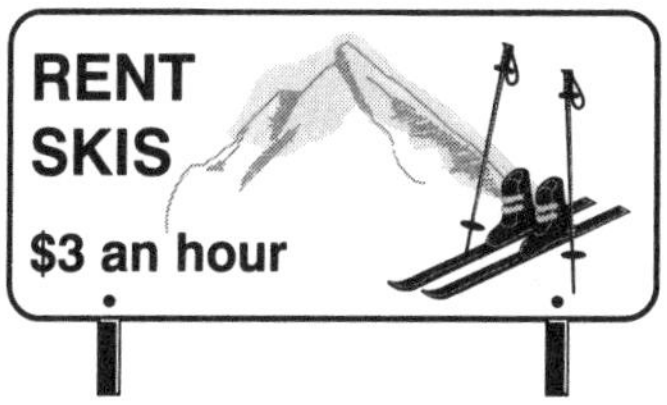

9. Use the distributive property to rewrite the equation without brackets.

a) $2(x + 3) = 16$

$2x + 6 = 16$

b) $3(5 - x) = 12$

c) $-3(x + 2) = 6$

d) $-2(x - 3) = 8$

e) $-4(3 - x) = 20$

f) $-2(-5x + 4) = 11$

10. Use cross multiplication to rewrite the equation without fractions.

a) $\frac{2x-3}{5} = 4$

b) $\frac{2(4x+1)}{3} = 14$

c) $\frac{x+8}{3} = \frac{2}{-5}$

d) $\frac{2x-5}{-3} = \frac{-4}{7}$

e) $\frac{5-3x}{3} = \frac{-1}{4}$

Bonus ▶ $\frac{2}{3}(5-3x) = 8$

11. Rewrite the equation if you need to. Then solve the equation.

a) $4(x - 7) = 12$

b) $\frac{x+4}{5} = 4$

c) $-3(x + 4) = 15$

d) $22 = 3x + 4$

e) $15 + 2x = 9$

f) $3(x - 5) = 12$

g) $-3(x + 2) = 6$

h) $\frac{x+11}{2} = 3$

i) $\frac{x}{2} + 7 = 4$

j) $\frac{x}{2} + 3 = 9$

k) $\frac{x-5}{4} = 1$

l) $-5x + 2 = -13$

12. Solve $3(x + 4) = 21$ two ways. Make sure you get the same answer both ways.

a) Start by expanding $3(x + 4)$.

b) Start by dividing both sides of the equation by 3.

EE7-15 Solving Two-Step Equations—A Shortcut

Here are two ways to solve $x + 3 = 7$.

Method 1: Use preserving equality.

$$x + 3 = 7$$
$$x + 3 - 3 = 7 - 3$$
So $x = 7 - 3$

Method 2: Use logic.

$x + 3 = 7$ means you have to add 3 to x to get 7.

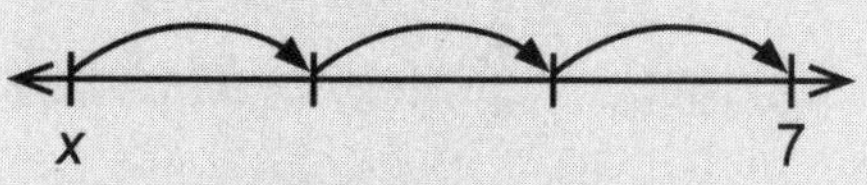

So you have to subtract 3 from 7 to get x.

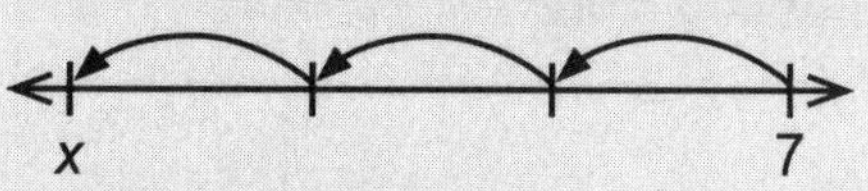

So $x = 7 - 3$.

In both methods, the 3 moved to the other side and was subtracted instead of added.

1. To get the variable term by itself, move the constant term to the right side. Remember to change addition to subtraction.

a) $x + 7 = 15$

$x = 15 - 7$

b) $3x + 4 = 19$

c) $-x + 9 = 12$

d) $2x + 10 = 4$

e) $7 + 4x = 15$

f) $7 + 2x = 3$

g) $5 - 3x = 8$

$-3x = 8 - 5$

h) $7 - 2x = 3$

i) $0.8 - 2.6x = -7$

You can solve $x - 3 = 7$ two ways.

Method 1: Use preserving equality.

$$x - 3 = 7$$
$$x - 3 + 3 = 7 + 3$$
So $x = 7 + 3$.

Method 2: Use logic.

$x - 3 = 7$ means you have to subtract 3 from x to get 7. So you have to add 3 to 7 to get x.

So $x = 7 + 3$.

In both ways, the 3 moved to the other side and was added instead of subtracted.

2. To get the variable term by itself, move the constant term to the right side. Remember to change subtraction to addition.

a) $2x - 5 = 11$

$2x = 11 + 5$

b) $x - 7 = 11$

c) $4x - 5 = 6$

d) $3x - 4 = -10$

e) $0.6x - 5 = 1$

f) $-4 + 3x = 8$

You can move any term to the other side of an equation. Just change addition to subtraction and subtraction to addition. Example:

You have to subtract 2 from A to get B. So you have to add 2 to B to get A.

$\underbrace{5x - 3x + 4x}_{A} - \mathbf{2} = \underbrace{7 + 3 - 8}_{B}$ $\underbrace{5x - 3x + 4x}_{A} = \underbrace{7 + 3 - 8}_{B} + \mathbf{2}$

3. Move all the variable terms to the left side and all the constant terms to the right side. Do not solve the equation.

a) $3x + 5 - x = 7$

$3x - x = 7 - 5$

b) $8x + 4 = 3x - 11$

$8x - 3x = -11 - 4$

c) $7 - 4x = x - 3$

d) $2x + 8 - 5x = 14$

e) $9x - 5 = 11x + 5$

f) $2x - 8 = 5x + 1$

An equation with all the variable terms on one side and all the constant terms on the other side is easy to solve.

Step 1: Simplify the side with the variable terms and evaluate the side with the constant terms.

Example: $3x - x - 4x = 7 - 9 + 8$

$-2x = 6$

Step 2: Divide both sides by the coefficient of the variable.

$-2x \div (-2) = 6 \div (-2)$

$x = -3$

4. Solve the equation.

a) $x + 6x - 4x = 10 - 1$

$3x = 9$

$x = 3$

b) $7x - 5x = 7 - 1$

c) $9x - 2x + x = 5 + 7 - 2 + 6$

d) $5x - 4x + x = -8 - (-2)$

e) $3x - 7x = 2 - (-10)$

f) $2x - 4x - x = 7 - 5 - 8$

g) $7x - 9x = 11 - 5$

h) $2x - 4x - x = 7 - 13$

i) $x - 5x = -1 - 2 - 8 + 4 - 1$

5. Rewrite the equation without brackets. Then move all the variable terms to the left side and all the constant terms to the right side. Do not solve the equation.

a) $3(x - 5) = 13 - x$

$3x - 15 = 13 - x$

$3x + x = 13 + 15$

b) $2(x + 3) = x - 5$

c) $2(7 - 2x) = 5(x - 8)$

d) $3(5 - x) - 2 = 7(x - 1)$

e) $4(9 - x) = 3x - 13$

f) $2(3x + 4) = 4(5 - 3x)$

To solve an equation:

Step 1: Rewrite the equation without brackets if you need to.

Example: $3(2x - 3) + 4 = -2(x + 4) - 5$

$6x - 9 + 4 = -2x - 8 - 5$

Step 2: Move all the variable terms to one side and all the constant terms to the other side.

$6x + 2x = 9 - 4 - 8 - 5$

Step 3: Simplify both sides of the equation.

$8x = -8$

Step 4: Divide by the coefficient of x.

$x = -1$

You just solved for x!

6. Solve the equation.

a) $-x - 3 = x - 9$

b) $3x - 17 = 5x - 9$

c) $3(x + 5) = x + 7$

d) $3(5 - x) = 2(4 - 5x)$

e) $6 + \frac{2}{3}x = 11 - x$

f) $\frac{3}{5} + 5x = \frac{7}{5} - 3x$

g) $3(x + 4) - 10 = 2(x - 2)$

h) $2(3x + 7) = 5(9 - 2x) + 1$

i) $3(2x - 5) = 2x + 9$

7. Check your answers to Question 6 by substituting your answer into the original equation.

EE7-16 Solving Problems Algebraically

When you use a variable to solve a word problem, you are solving it **algebraically**. Always start by letting the variable represent what you want to know.

1. What would you use x to represent?

a) Clara has 5 times as many apples as Matt. Clara has 35 apples. How many apples does Matt have?

Let x be *the number of apples that Matt has* ____.

b) Randi needs to save \$60. She makes \$12 an hour. How many hours does she need to work?

Let x be ____________________.

c) Tim works 15 hours and makes \$10 an hour. How much money does he make altogether?

Let x be ____________________.

d) Tess is three times as old as Sal. Sal is four years younger than Mona. Tess is 15 years old. How old is Mona?

Let x be ____________________.

e) Pedro bought 250 pencils for 15¢ each. He sells them for 25¢ each. How much profit does he make?

Let x be ____________________.

f) May buys pencils for 15¢ each. She sells them for 25¢ each. She wants her profit to be \$30. How many pencils should she buy?

Let x be ____________________.

2. Three children have 30 apples altogether. Nick has x apples. Complete the table and write the equation.

a)

	Expression
Lynn has 2 more apples than Nick.	$x + 2$
Josh has twice as many apples as Nick.	$2x$

Equation:

$x + x + 2 + 2x = 30$

(x: Nick's apples; $x + 2$: Lynn's apples; $2x$: Josh's apples)

b)

	Expression
Lynn has 4 times as many apples as Nick.	
Josh has 6 more apples than Nick.	

Equation:

3. Solve the equations in Question 2. How many apples does each child have?

4. a) Three children have 40 apples altogether. Jen has x apples. Complete the table.

i)

	Expression
Ross has twice as many apples as Jen.	$2x$
Sun has 5 more apples than Ross.	$2x + 5$

ii)

	Expression
Ross has 5 times as many apples as Jen.	
Sun has 4 fewer apples than Ross.	

iii)

	Expression
Ross has 2 more apples than Jen.	
Sun has 6 fewer apples than Ross.	

iv)

	Expression
Ross has 5 fewer apples than Jen.	
Sun has 5 times as many apples as Ross.	

b) Write an equation you could solve to find x.

i) $x + 2x + 2x + 5 = 40$

ii) ____________________

iii) ____________________

iv) ____________________

c) Solve your equations from part b). How many apples does each child have? Check your answer.

5. a) Raj has 30 apples. Zara has x apples. Complete the table.

i)

	Expression
Sam has 4 times as many apples as Zara.	$4x$
Raj has 2 more apples than Sam.	$4x + 2$

ii)

	Expression
Sam has 5 times as many apples as Zara.	
Raj has 5 fewer apples than Sam.	

iii)

	Expression
Sam has 2 more apples than Zara.	
Raj has 3 fewer apples than Sam.	

iv)

	Expression
Sam has 2 fewer apples than Zara.	
Raj has 5 times as many apples as Sam.	

b) Use an equation to find x. How many apples does each child have?

6. Nancy has twice as many apples as Jay. Jay has 3 more apples than Ava. Nancy has 22 apples. How many apples does Ava have?

7. Bo has 8 times as many apples as Amy. Bo has 7 more apples than Don. Don has 41 apples. How many apples does Amy have?

8. Kami buys pens for \$4 each and sells them for \$4.50 each. How many pens does she need to sell to make a profit of \$50?

EE7-17 Comparing Numerical and Algebraic Solutions

REMINDER: A rectangle with length ℓ and width w has:

area $A = \ell \times w$ perimeter $P = 2\ell + 2w$

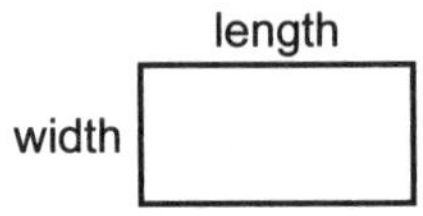

1. Solve the problem numerically (without variables) and algebraically (with variables).

a) A triangle has all sides equal. Its perimeter is 24 cm. How long is each side?

b) A square has perimeter 18 cm. How long is each side?

c) The area of a rectangle is 72 in^2. The length of the rectangle is 9 in. What is its width?

d) The perimeter of a rectangle is 60 in. The width of the rectangle is 3 in. How long is the rectangle?

2. Look at your answers to Question 1. Circle the parts of the algebraic solutions that use the same steps as the numerical solutions.

When two quantities are unknown, you can pick either of them to be the variable.

Example: Two numbers add to 42. One number is twice the other number. What are the numbers?

Solution: Let x be the smaller number. Then the other number is $2x$.

They add to 42, so $x + 2x = 42$, or $3x = 42$, so $x = 14$.

The two numbers are $x = 14$ and $2x = 28$.

3. Read the problem below:

Two numbers add to 20. One number is 4 more than the other number. What are the numbers?

a) Let x be the smaller number. Then the larger number is ________________.

The sum of the two numbers is ________________ = 20.

Solve the equation: x is ________.

The two numbers are ________ and ________.

b) Let x be the larger number. Then the smaller number is ________________.

The sum of the two numbers is ________________ = 20.

Solve the equation: x is ________.

The two numbers are ________ and ________.

c) Did you get the same answer both ways? If not, find your mistake.

4. Solve the problem algebraically. Be sure to say what the variable represents.

a) A rectangle is 5 times as long as it is wide. Its perimeter is 24 in. How long and how wide is the rectangle? Hint: Write an equation for half the perimeter.

b) The length of a rectangle is twice as long as its width. Its perimeter is 18 in. How long and how wide is the rectangle?

c) A triangle has all sides equal. A rectangle has width twice as long as the side of the triangle and length three times as long as the side of the triangle. The perimeter of the rectangle is 20 in. What is the perimeter of the triangle?

Bonus ▶ The perimeter of a rectangle is 3 times the length. How does the width compare to the length?

5. Read the problem below:

Jane is 3 times as old as John. Their ages add to 20 weeks. How old are they?

a) What is wrong with the following solution?

Let x be John's age. Then Jane's age is $3x$, so $x + 3x = 20$ or $4x = 20$, so $x = 5$. Therefore, John is 5 years old and Jane is 15 years old.

____

____

b) Why is it important to be precise when recording what the variable represents?

____

____

EE7-18 Unit Ratios, Equations, and Verbal Descriptions

1. In the recipe, what do you multiply the first column by to get the second column?

a)

Cups of milk	Cups of flour
1	4
2	8
3	12

Multiply by _____

b)

Cups of nuts	Cups of fruit
2	6
4	12
6	18

Multiply by _____

c)

Cups of apples	Cups of raisins
1	$\frac{1}{4}$
2	$\frac{1}{2}$
3	$\frac{3}{4}$

Multiply by _____

d)

Cups of rice	Cups of water
1	1.5
2	3
3	4.5

Multiply by _____

You can write an equation from any ratio table.

Examples:

Input	Output
1 (× 2 →)	2
2 (× 2 →)	4
3 (× 2 →)	6

The equation is output = 2 × input.

Input	Output
1 (× 5 →)	5
3 (× 5 →)	15
6 (× 5 →)	30

The equation is output = 5 × input.

The multiplier in the equation is the output given by input 1 in the table.

2. Write an equation for the ratio table.

a)

Input	Output
1	6
2	12
3	18

output = ____ × input

b)

Hours	Miles
1	11
2	22
3	33

miles = ____ × hours

c)

h	m
1	$\frac{2}{5}$
2	$\frac{4}{5}$
3	$\frac{6}{5}$

m = ____ × h

d)

a	b
1	0.3
2	0.6
3	0.9

b = ____ × a

3. Complete the ratio table for parts of red paint to parts of blue paint.

a)

Red	Blue
1	2
3	

× 2

b)

Red	Blue
1	2
7	

× 2

c)

Red	Blue
1	2
6	

× 2

d)

Red	Blue
1	2
r	

× 2

4. a) Complete the ratio table for parts of red (r) paint to parts of blue (b) paint.

i)

r	**b**
1	3
5	

× 3

ii)

r	**b**
1	3
0.8	

× 3

iii)

r	**b**
1	3
$\frac{2}{3}$	

× 3

iv)

r	**b**
1	3
r	

× 3

b) Write an equation for the ratio $r : b = 1 : 3$. $b =$ ________________

When you know the unit ratio, you can write an equation. Here are three ways of saying the same thing:

$r : b = 1 : 7$ $\quad$ b is 7 times as much as r. $\quad$ $b = 7r$

5. Write an equation from the ratio.

a) $s : t = 1 : 5$ b) $t : w = 1 : 12$ c) $m : p = 1 : 4.2$ d) $x : y = 1 : \frac{8}{5}$

________________ ________________ ________________ ________________

6. Write the ratio with 1 in the first position. Then write an equation.

a) $r : b = 5 : 1$, so *b : r = 1 : 5*.

Equation: *r = 5b*

b) $c : s = 7 : 1$, so ________________.

Equation: ________________

c) $b : r = 0.8 : 1$, so ________________.

Equation: ________________

d) $t : n = \frac{3}{2} : 1$, so ________________.

Equation: ________________

7. Write the ratio in a table with 1 in the first column. Then write an equation.

a) $b : r = 4 : 1$

r	**b**
1	*4*

b = 4r

b) $b : r = 1 : 3$

b	**r**
1	

____

c) $r : b = 8 : 1$

1	

____

d) $r : b = 1 : 0.6$

1	

____

e) $b : r = 1 : 45$

1	

____

f) $b : r = \frac{11}{5} : 1$

1	

____

g) $r : b = 4.5 : 1$

1	

____

h) $r : b = 1 : \frac{3}{2}$

1	

____

8. Use the description to write a ratio with 1 in the first position. Then write an equation.

a) For every 1 part blue, 3 parts red.

b	*r*
1	

$r =$ ________

b) 5 parts blue for every 1 part red.

1	

____

c) 2.5 parts blue for every part red.

d) For every part blue, $\frac{1}{2}$ part red.

9. Write two descriptions for the equation.

a) $b = 2r$

For every 1 part red, 2 parts blue.

2 parts blue for every 1 part red.

b) $r = 10b$

____

____

c) $r = 0.25b$

d) $b = \frac{2}{3}r$

10. Write variables in the brackets. Use the variables to write an equation.

a) 3 parts yellow (*y*) per part white (*w*) $y = 3w$

b) 2 cups of flour (______) per cup of milk (______) ________

c) 4 triangles (______) per square (______) ________

d) 1.5 lemons (______) per liter of water (______) ________

e) $\frac{3}{4}$ cup of cereal (______) per serving (______) ________

If you know the unit ratio $r : b$, you can find the unit ratio $b : r$.

r	*b*
1	4
$\frac{1}{4}$	1

(÷4 on both sides)

You can write the equation in two ways:

$r : b = 1 : 4$, so $b = 4r$

$b : r = 1 : \frac{1}{4}$, so $r = \frac{1}{4}b$

11. The unit ratio $r : b$ is given. Find the unit ratio $b : r$ and write two equations.

a)

r	*b*
1	5
	1

(÷5 on both sides)

$b =$ ________

$r =$ ________

b)

r	*b*
1	12

$b =$ ________

$r =$ ________

c)

r	*b*
1	$\frac{2}{5}$

$b =$ ________

$r =$ ________

d)

r	*b*
1	$\frac{7}{4}$

$b =$ ________

$r =$ ________

EE7-19 Equations, Ratio Problems, and the Constant of Proportionality

To solve a ratio problem:

Step 1: Decide what the variables represent. Use y for what you don't know.

Step 2: Set up a ratio table. It is convention to write x in the first column.

Step 3: Make $x = 1$ to write the equation.

Step 4: Plug in what you know for x to find y.

1. Decide what the variables represent. Remember to write the units.

a) Marta rides her bike 8 km per hour. How many km can she bike in 3 hours?

Let y be *the distance (in km)*.

Let x be *the time (in hours)*.

b) There are 3 cups of red paint for every cup of blue paint. How many cups of blue paint are there for 12 cups of red paint?

Let y be ______________________.

Let x be ______________________.

c) Use 2 tsp of sugar per cup of tea. How much sugar do you need for 2 cups of tea?

Let y be ______________________.

Let x be ______________________.

d) Pencils cost $0.20 each. How many pencils can you buy for a dollar?

2. Find the unit rate and write an equation.

a)

x pounds	y dollars
5	15
1	

$y =$ __________

b)

x hours	y miles
6	270
1	

$y =$ __________

c)

x hours	y dollars
12	78
1	

$y =$ __________

d)

x minutes	y gallons
5	1.5
1	

$y =$ __________

3. Use the equation to find y for the given x.

a) Equation: $y = 10x$

$x = 7$, so $y =$ *10(7) = 70*

b) Equation: $y = 1.5x$

$x = 5$, so $y =$ ______________

c) Equation: $y = \frac{2}{3}x$

$x = 9$, so $y =$ ______________

d) Equation: $y = \frac{3}{4}x$

$x = 6$, so $y =$ ______________

4. Solve the ratio problem. Include the units in your answer.

a) Every 5 books cost $10.
How much do 3 books cost?

Let y be ______________________

Let x be ______________________

x books	y dollars (cost)
5	10
1	2

(÷5 on both sides)

Equation: $y = 2x$

$x = $ 3, so $y = $ $2(3) = 6$

3 books cost ______________.

b) I walk 6 km every 2 hours.
How far do I walk in 5 hours?

Let y be ______________________

Let x be ______________________

x	y

Equation: ______________

$x = $ ______, so $y = $ ______________

I walk ______________ in 5 hours.

c) I earn $20 for every 4 hours.
How long does it take to earn $35?

Let y be ______________________

Let x be ______________________

x	y

Equation: ______________

$x = $ ______, so $y = $ ______________

It takes ______________ to earn $35.

d) My heart beats 420 times in 7 minutes.
How long do 240 beats take?

Let y be ______________________

Let x be ______________________

x	y

Equation: ______________

$x = $ ______, so $y = $ ______________

240 beats take ______________.

e) Mix 3 cups of blue paint for every 5 cups of red paint.
How much red paint for 2 cups of blue paint?

f) Mix 2 cups of blue paint for every 3 cups of yellow paint.
How much blue paint for 8 cups of yellow paint?

Bonus ▶ Use 3 tsp of sugar per cup of tea. How much tea do you need for 8 tsp of sugar?

The constant of proportionality is the number that multiplies the unit to get the other quantity.

The unit ratio 1 : 12 and the equation $y = 12x$ have a constant of proportionality of 12.

5. Complete the table.

a)

Unit ratio $x : y$	**Constant of proportionality**	**Equation**
1 : 3		
		$y = 4x$
	0.7	

b)

Unit ratio $x : y$	**Constant of proportionality**	**Equation**
	10	
$1 : \frac{4}{7}$		
		$y = 1.2x$

6. Complete the table.

Ratio $x : y$	5 : 4	3 : 18	$6 : \frac{2}{3}$	$\frac{1}{4} : 5$	$\frac{1}{2} : \frac{1}{3}$
Unit ratio	$1 : \frac{4}{5}$	1 :	1 :		
Constant of proportionality	$\frac{4}{5}$				
Equation	$y = \frac{4}{5}x$	$y =$	$y =$		

7. Andy babysat one night for 4 hours and was paid \$30. Another night, he babysat for 6.5 hours and was paid \$48.75.

a) Make a table relating the hours he worked to his pay.

***x* hours**	***y* dollars (pay)**

b) Is this relationship proportional? __________

Hint: Do you multiply the first column by the same number to get the second column?

c) What is the constant of proportionality? __________

d) How much would Andy be paid if he babysat for 2 hours? Write an equation to solve the problem.

EE7-20 Graphing Ratios on Coordinate Planes

An ordered pair is a pair of numbers in brackets.
It determines the location of a point on a coordinate grid.
The point (0, 0) is called the origin.

A (4, 1) — *x*-coordinate, *y*-coordinate

B (1, 4) — *x*-coordinate, *y*-coordinate

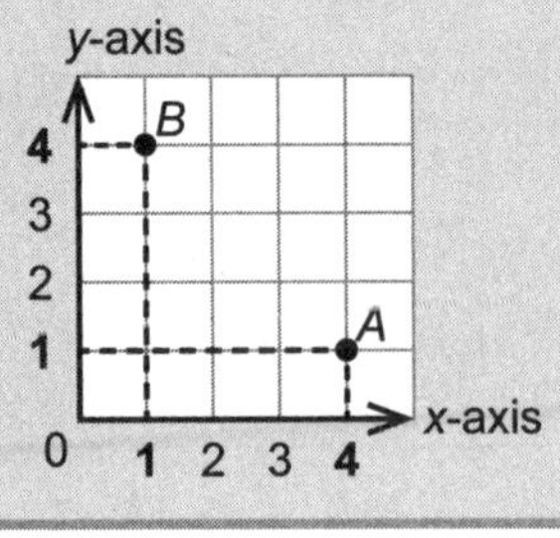

1. Write the coordinates of each point.

A (2 , 3) *B* (,) *C* (,)

D (,) *E* (,) *F* (,)

G (,) *H* (,) *I* (,)

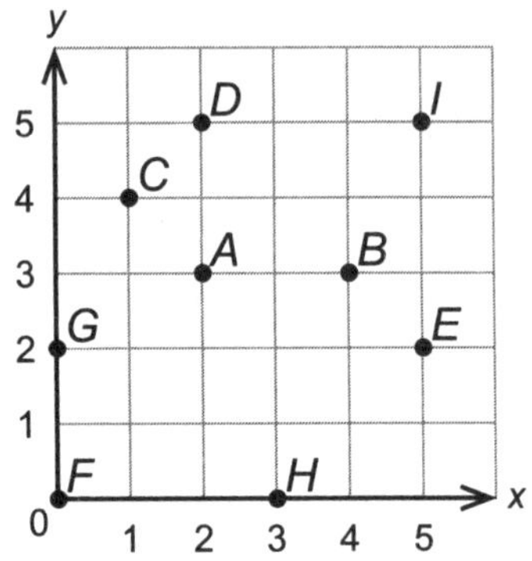

2. Plot and label the points on the coordinate grid.
Cross out the points as you go.

~~*A* (3, 4)~~ *B* (2, 1) *C* (4, 2)

D (0, 0) *E* (1, 2) *F* (1, 0)

G (0, 3) *H* (4, 5) *I* (5, 0)

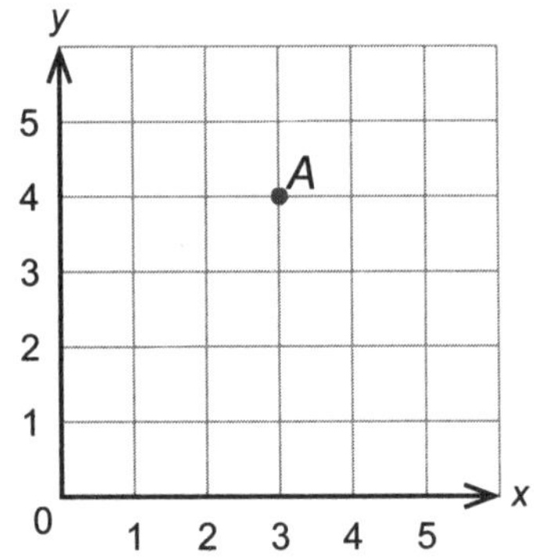

3. Mark the approximate location of the points on the number line.

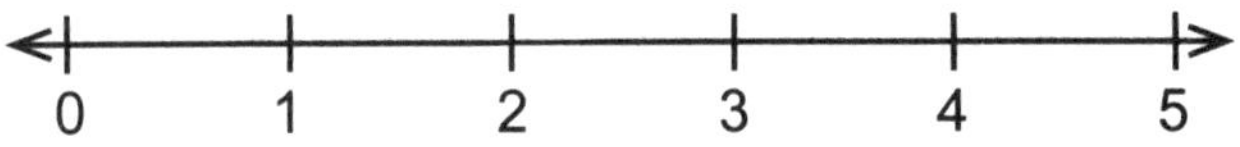

T. 3.5 ***M.*** 0.5 ***H.*** $4\frac{3}{4}$ ***A.*** $2\frac{1}{2}$

4. Plot and label the points on the coordinate grid.
Cross out the points as you go.

~~*A* (2.5, 3)~~ *B* (0.5, 4) *C* (4.75, 5)

D ($3\frac{1}{2}$, 0) *E* ($4\frac{3}{4}$, 2) *F* ($2\frac{1}{2}$, 2)

G (0, 2.5) **Bonus ▶** *H* (0.75, $1\frac{1}{4}$)

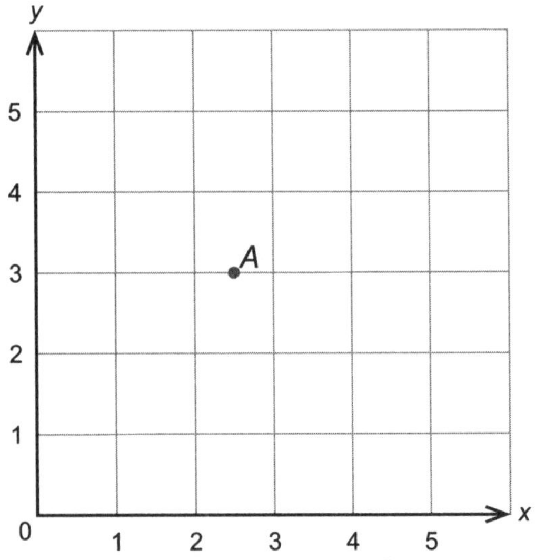

To graph a ratio:

Step 1: Make a ratio table.

Step 2: Write an ordered pair for each row of the table.

Step 3: Plot the ordered pairs.

5. a) Make a ratio table for the ratio. Write an ordered pair for each row of the table.

i) 1 : 2

1	*2*	*(1, 2)*
2	*4*	*(2, 4)*
3	*6*	*(3, 6)*
4	*8*	*(4, 8)*

ii) 1 : 1

1		
2		
3		
4		

iii) 2 : 3

2		
4		
6		
8		

b) Plot the ordered pairs on the grid and connect the points.

i)

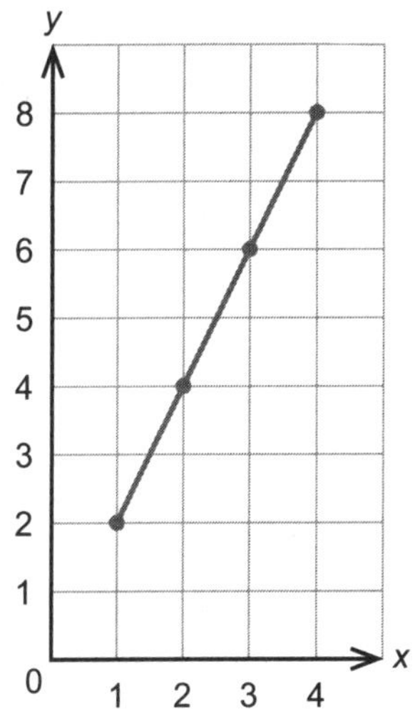

ii)

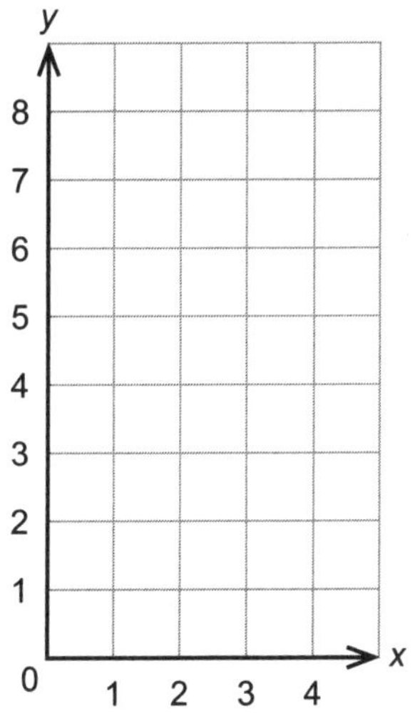

iii)

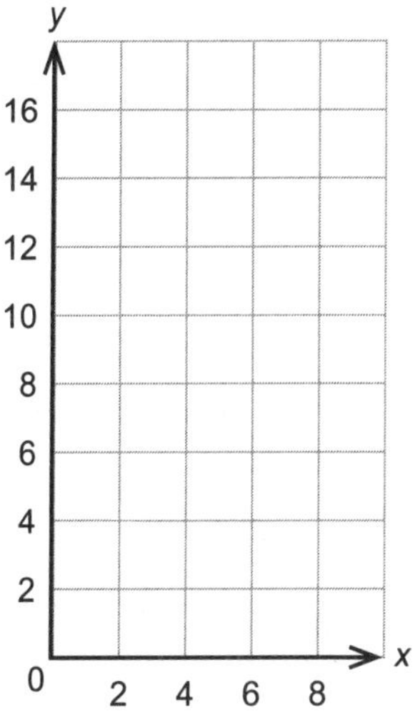

c) Do the points lie on a straight line?

i) __________ ii) __________ iii) __________

d) Extend each line to intersect the *x*-axis. Where does the line meet the *x*-axis?

i) (______, 0) ii) (______, 0) iii) (______, 0)

The graph of a ratio is a straight line that passes through the origin (0, 0).

6. Graph the ratio. Is the graph a straight line that passes through the origin? If not, find your mistake.

a) 3 : 2 b) 1 : 4 c) 4 : 1

If a relationship is proportional, it can be put in a ratio table and its graph will be a straight line that passes through the origin.

If a relationship is not proportional, it can be put in a T-table and graphed.

Examples:

x tickets	*y* dollars paid
0	0
1	2
2	4
3	5

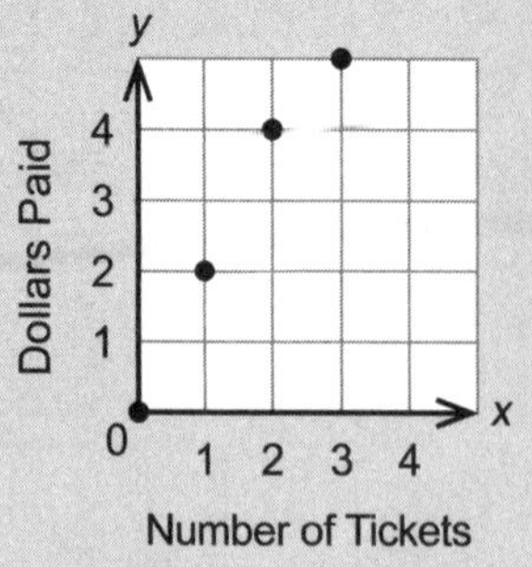

This graph is not a straight line.
The relationship is not proportional.

x miles	*y* dollars (taxi fare)
0	2
1	2.50
2	3
3	3.50

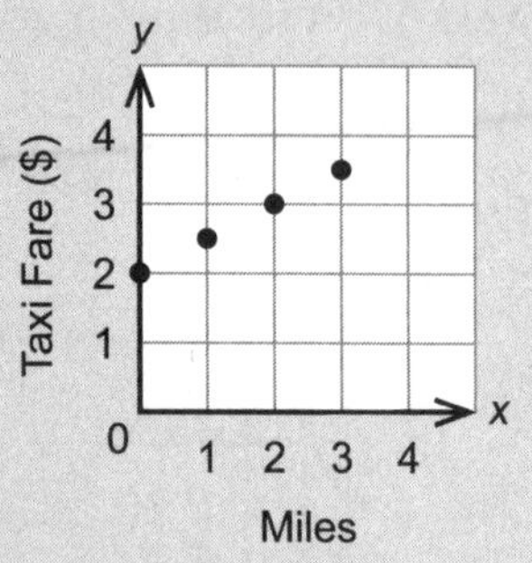

This graph does not pass through (0, 0).
The relationship is not proportional.

7. a) Graph the relationship.

i)

x hours worked	*y* dollars earned
2	16
3	24
4	32

ii)

x hours rented	*y* dollars paid
1	6
2	10
3	14

iii)

x sheets of paper	*y* dollars paid
100	3
200	6
300	7

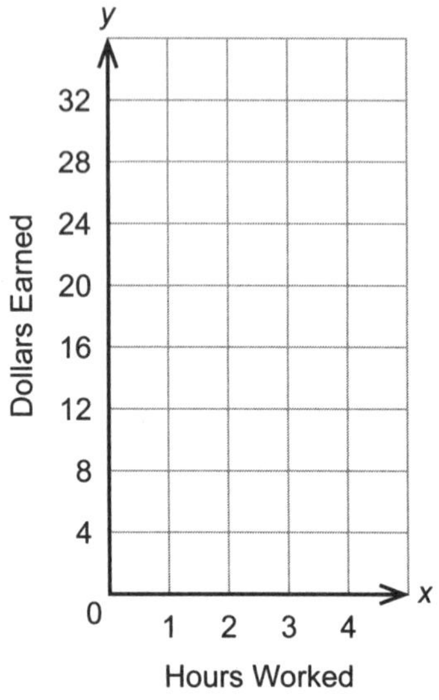

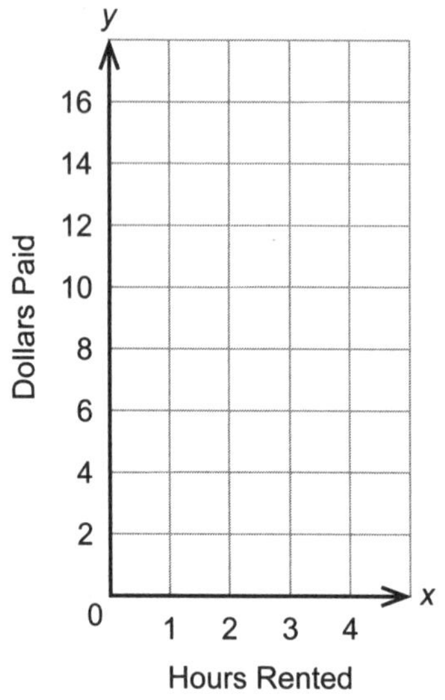

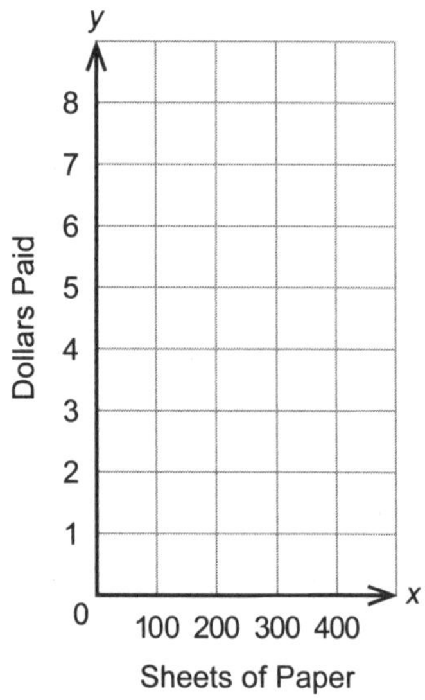

b) Is the relationship proportional? Use the graph to explain how you know.

i) ______________________________

ii) ______________________________

iii) ______________________________

Ratios, Equations, and Coordinate Systems

1. This graph shows the price of concert tickets.

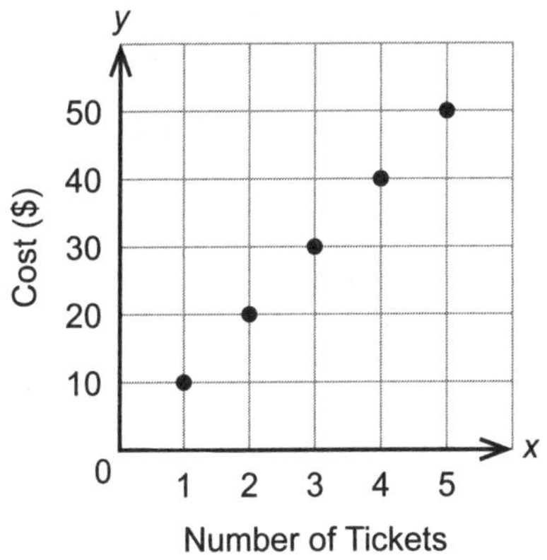

a) The point (1, 10) tells us that *one ticket costs $10* ________.

b) The point (2, 20) tells us that ________________________.

c) The point (0, 0) tells us that ________________________.

d) Does the point (3.5, 35) tell us anything? ________

Explain. ______________________________

2. This graph shows the distance a plane traveled over time.

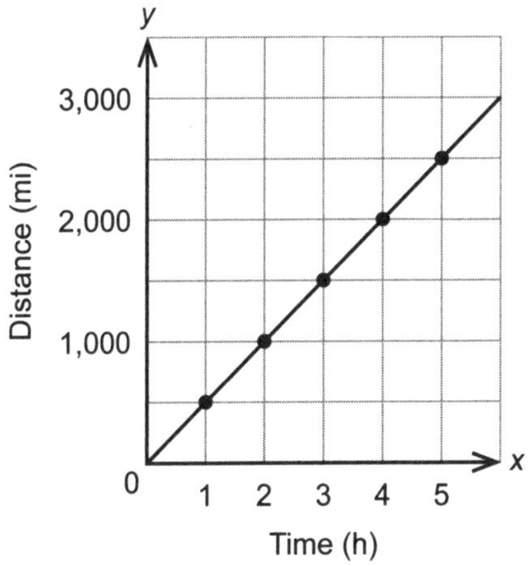

a) What point tells us how far the plane traveled in 4 hours?

(*4* , *2,000*)

b) What point tells us how many hours it took the plane to travel 2,500 miles?

(,)

c) What point tells us how far the plane traveled in 3 hours?

(,)

d) What point tells us how far the plane traveled in 1 hour?

(,)

> If you want to find the constant of proportionality c on a graph, look at the y-value when $x = 1$.
>
> The equation of the graph is $y = cx$.

3. a) Identify the constant of proportionality c on the graph by finding the value of y when $x = 1$.

i)

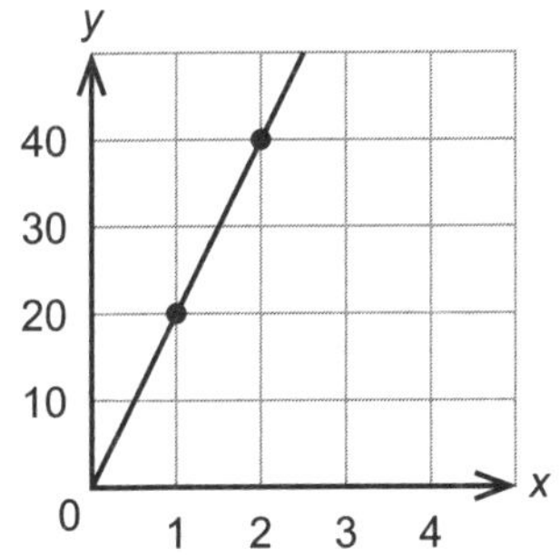

$c =$ ________

ii)

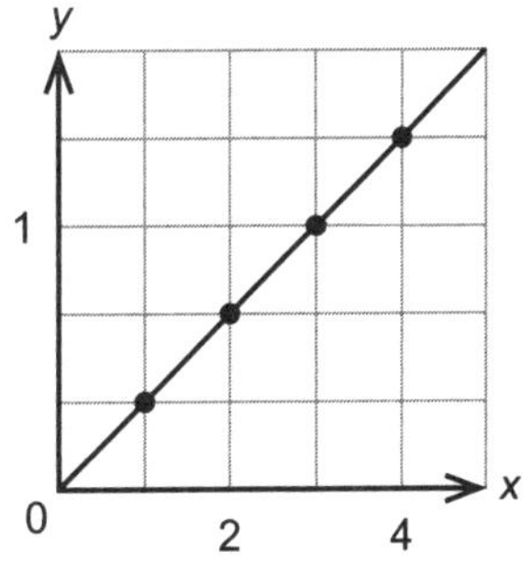

$c =$ ________

iii)

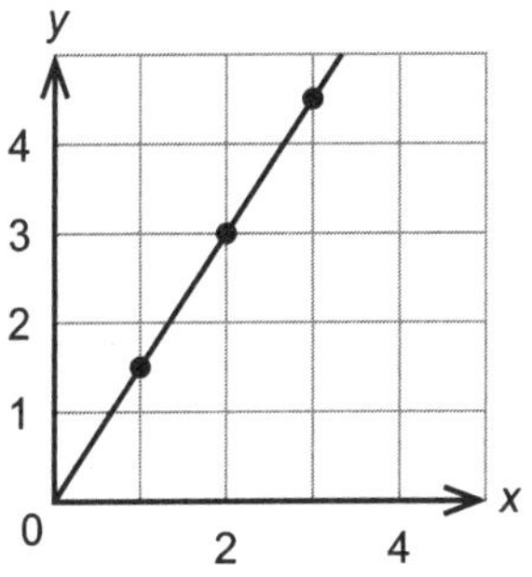

$c =$ ________

b) Write an equation for the graph.

i) $y =$ ________ ii) $y =$ ________ iii) $y =$ ________

4. Make a ratio table for the equation $y = 0.2x$. Draw a graph from the ratio table.

x	y
1	
2	
3	
4	

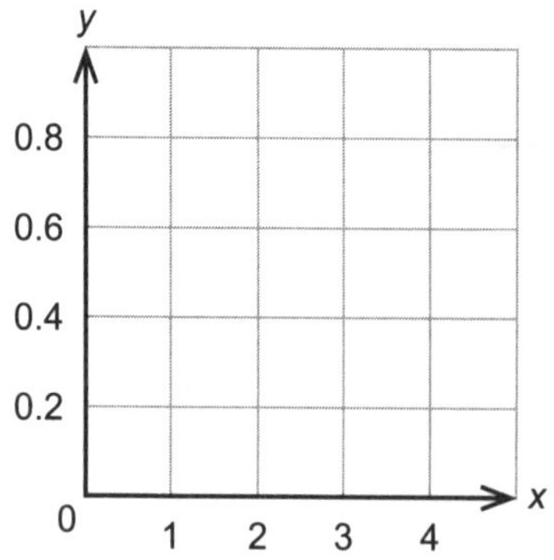

5. a) Every 4 pens cost $3.

i) Complete the table. Write an equation and plot the two points.

x pens	y dollars (cost)
4	3
1	

$y =$ __________

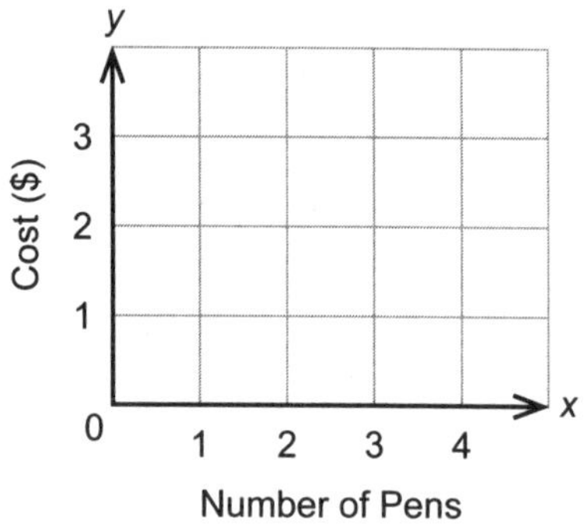

ii) Use the equation to find how much 2 pens cost.

$x =$ __________, so $y =$ __________

iii) Show this point on the graph.

b) Every 2 hours, Kevin walks 3 miles.

i) Complete the table. Write an equation and plot the two points.

x hours	y miles
2	
1	

$y =$ __________

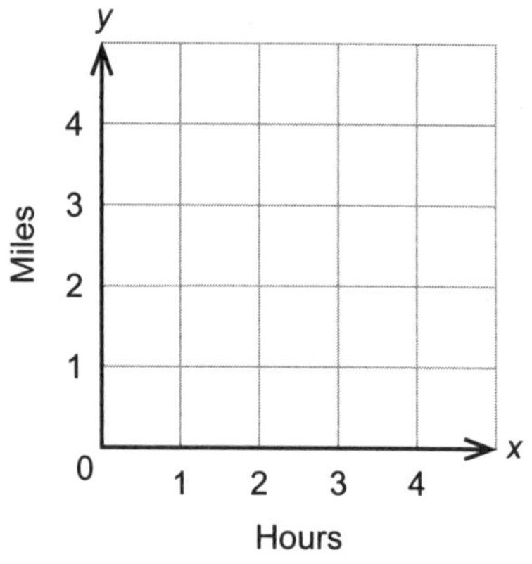

ii) Use the equation to find how far he can walk in 3 hours.

$x =$ __________, so $y =$ __________

iii) Show this point on the graph.

6. For each graph in Question 5, what does the point represent when $x = 1$?

7. a) Every 5 classes, Karen writes 3 pages. Draw a graph on grid paper using x for the number of classes and y for the number of pages.

b) What does the point represent when $x = 1$?

EE7-22 Constant of Proportionality (Advanced)

The value of y when $x = 1$ tells you the constant of proportionality. You can get this from a ratio table or a graph.

x	y
1	3 ← When $x = 1$, $y = 3$
2	6
3	9
4	12

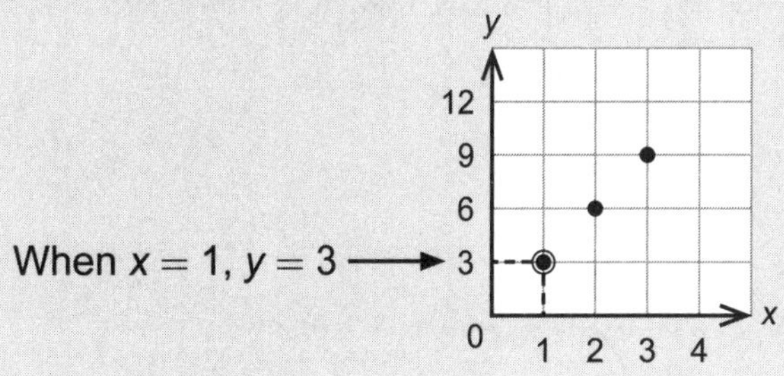

The table and the graph both show that the constant of proportionality is 3.

1. Write the constant of proportionality c. Then find the increase in y for each increase of 1 in x.

a)

x	y
1	5
2	10
3	15
4	20

(+1) (+1) (+1)

$c =$ ________

y increases by ________

b)

x	y
1	0.2
2	0.4
3	0.6
4	0.8

(+1) (+1) (+1)

$c =$ ________

y increases by ________

c)

x	y
1	1.5
2	3
3	4.5
4	6

(+1) (+1) (+1)

$c =$ ________

y increases by ________

d)

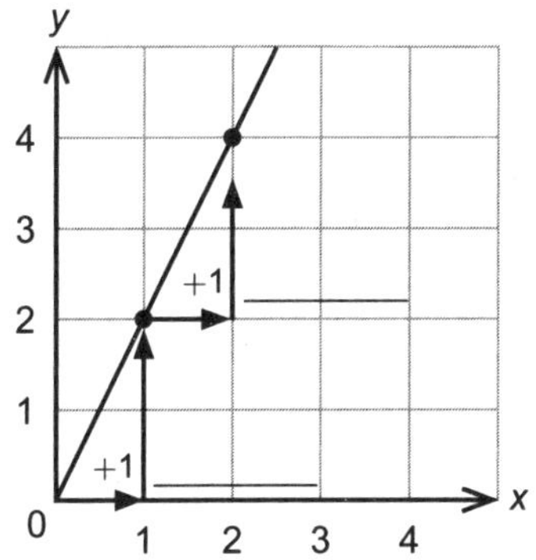

$c =$ ________

y increases by ________

e)

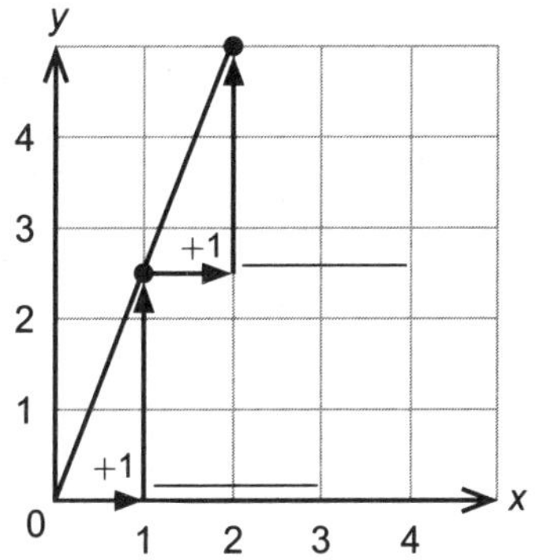

$c =$ ________

y increases by ________

f)

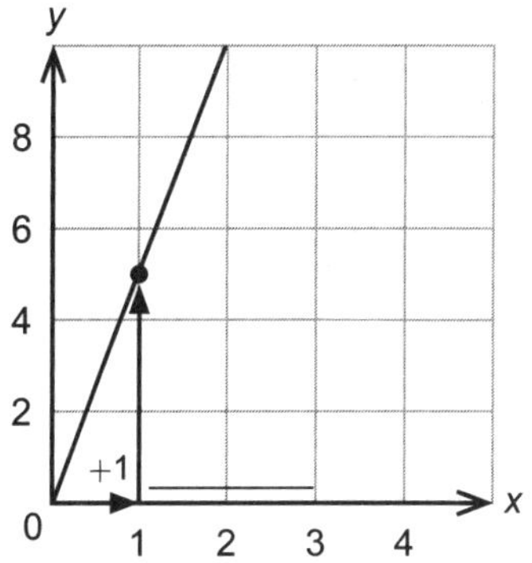

$c =$ ________

y increases by ________

2. Look at your answers to Question 1. What is the relationship between the constant of proportionality and the amount that y increases for each increase of 1 in x?

____

____

The constant of proportionality is the amount that y increases by when x increases by 1.

3. a) Draw triangles to show how many units you go up when you move one unit to the right.

i)

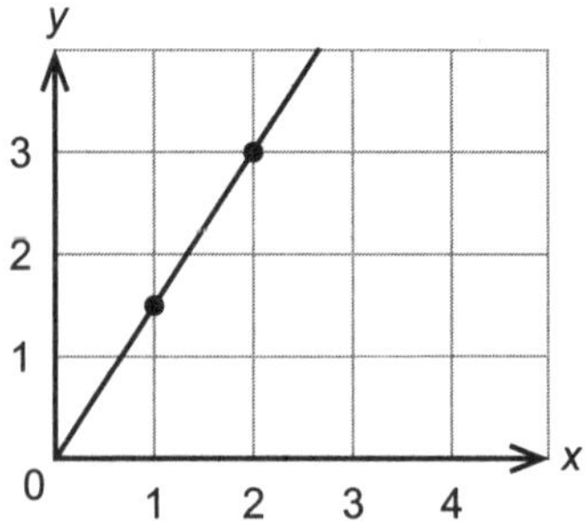

ii)

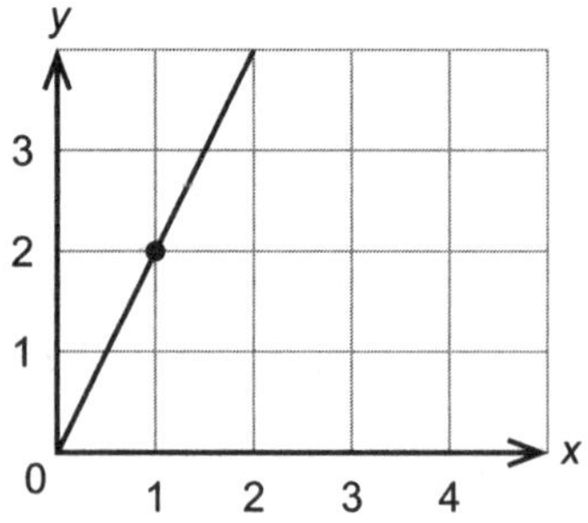

b) For the graphs in part a), identify the constant of proportionality c and write an equation.

i) $c =$ ________

$y =$ ________

ii) $c =$ ________

$y =$ ________

4. a) Fill in the missing values in the diagram and the ratio table.

i)

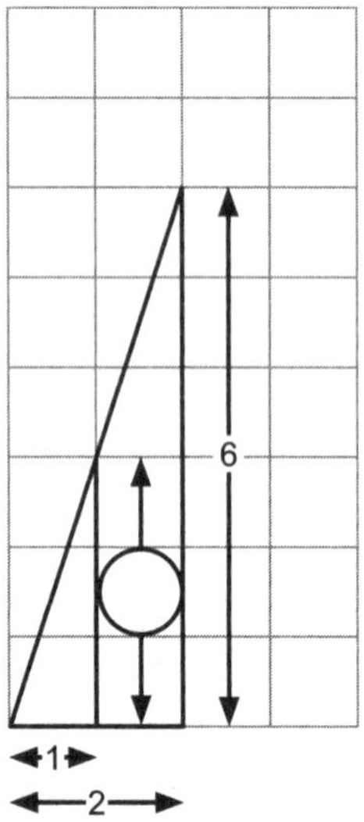

2	6
1	

ii)

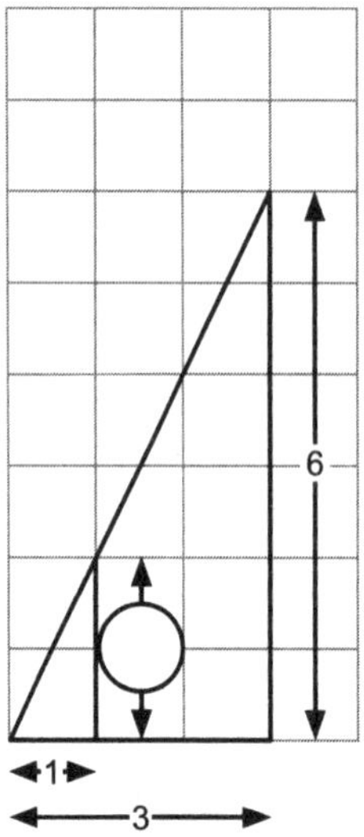

3	6
1	

iii)

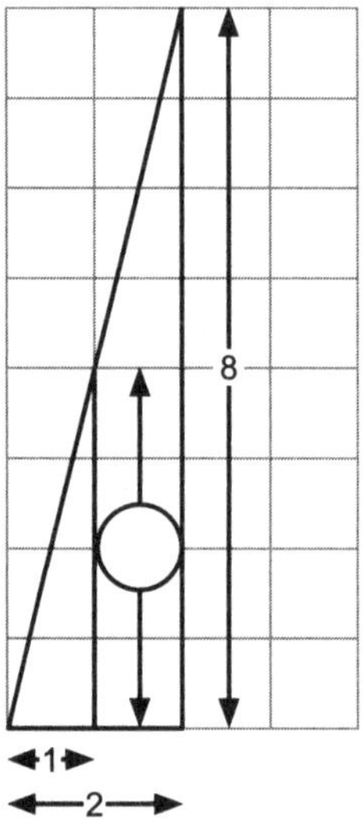

2	8
1	

iv)

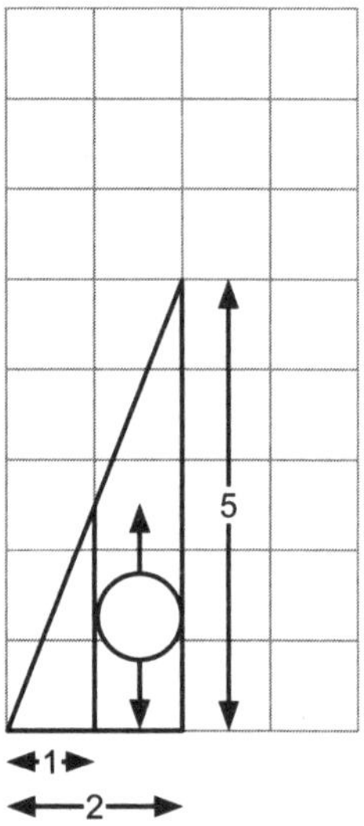

2	5
1	

b) What is the constant of proportionality for the relationships shown in part a)?

i) ________ ii) ________ iii) ________ iv) ________

EE7-23 Introduction to Inequalities

$=$	$<$	$>$	$\leq$	$\geq$
equals	less than	greater than	less than or equal to	greater than or equal to

1. Write the symbol for the description.

a) w is less than or equal to 7. $\underline{\quad w \leq 7 \quad}$

b) w is equal to -5. ____________

c) w is greater than or equal to -0.5. ____________

d) w is less than $-5\frac{1}{2}$. ____________

2. Write the meaning of the symbol in words.

a) $w > 8$ ____________

b) $8 \geq x$ ____________

c) $z \leq 0$ ____________

d) $r < -5$ ____________

You can write every inequality in two ways. For example, you can write the inequality "*w* is greater than 80" as "80 is less than *w*."

3. Write the inequality another way.

a) x is greater than 4. ____________

b) x is less than or equal to -2.6. ____________

c) x is less than 0. ____________

d) x is greater than or equal to $\frac{5}{3}$. ____________

4. Use a symbol to write the inequality another way.

a) $x > 5$ $\underline{\quad 5 < x \quad}$

b) $-3 \leq x$ ____________

c) $x \geq -0.4$ ____________

d) $x \leq 3.2$ ____________

e) $x < -4$ ____________

f) $-5 < x$ ____________

g) $x \leq \frac{8}{11}$ ____________

h) $-7 \geq x$ ____________

You can use different phrases to mean the same thing.

Greater than or equal to 5:	Less than or equal to 5:
• At least 5	• At most 5
• 5 or more	• 5 or less
• Not less than 5	• Not more than 5

5. Write symbols for the words. Use x for the unknown number.

a) A number is at most 8.

x ≤ 8

b) A number is 7 or more.

c) A number is not more than 4.

d) A number is less than or equal to 9.

e) A number is -7 or less.

f) A number is not less than $-\frac{7}{4}$.

Han lifts 80 pounds and Alexa lifts more than 80 pounds. If w is the weight Han lifts, then the inequality $w > 80$ represents what we know about the weight Alexa lifts.

6. Represent the situation with an inequality. Use x for the variable.

a) A heavyweight boxer weighs more than 200 pounds. ___________

b) A box of bananas weighs 35 pounds or more. ___________

c) The temperature in the fridge is colder than 40°F. ___________

d) The temperature in the freezer is warmer than or equal to 0°F. ___________

e) David has at least $35. ___________

f) Eva has at most $60. ___________

The number 3 is a **solution** to the inequality $x < 5$ because substituting $x = 3$ makes the statement true: $3 < 5$

7. Is 3 a solution to the inequality?

a) $x > -2$ ___________

b) $x \leq 3$ ___________

c) $x \geq 4$ ___________

d) $x \leq -3$ ___________

The statement $x > -2$ represents all numbers on the number line that are greater than -2.

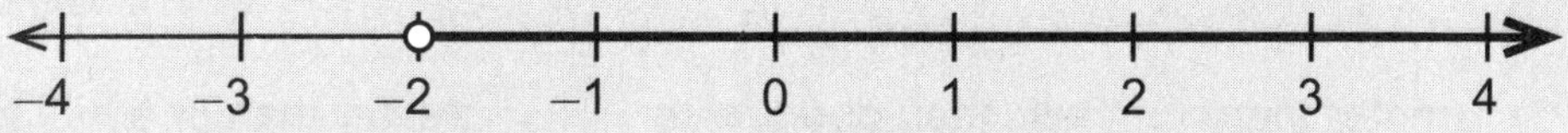

The circle is not filled in because -2 does not satisfy the statement.

The statement $x \geq -2$ represents all numbers on the number line that are greater than or equal to -2.

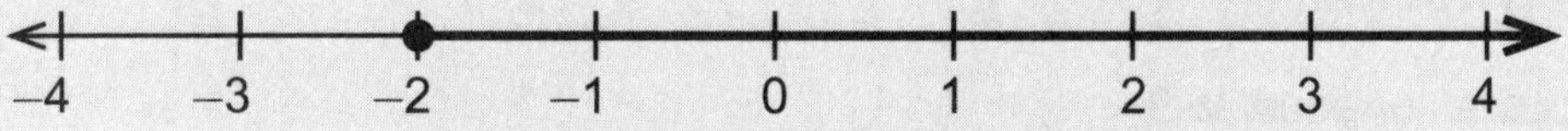

The circle is filled in because -2 does satisfy the statement.

8. Write an inequality for the picture.

a) 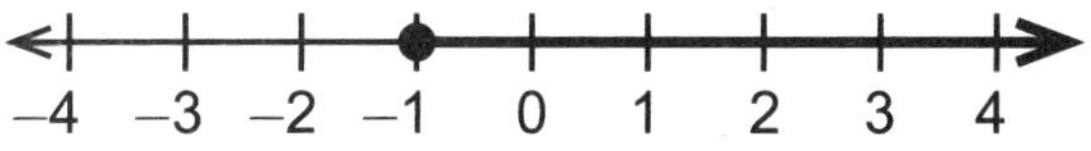

____

b) 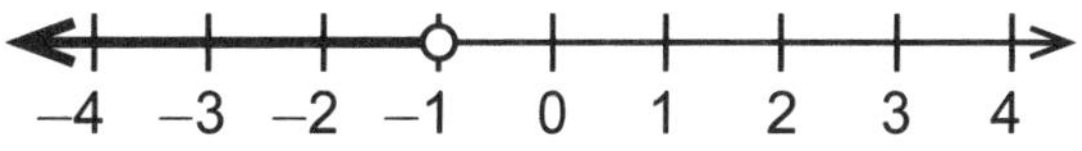

____

c) 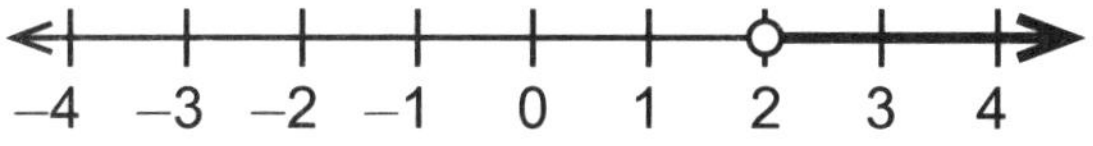

____

d) 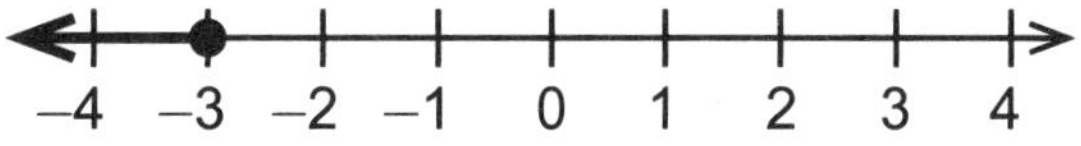

____

e) 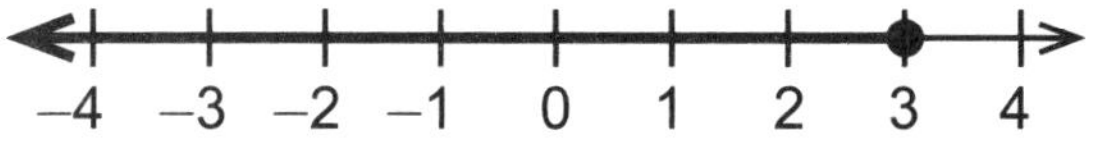

____

f) 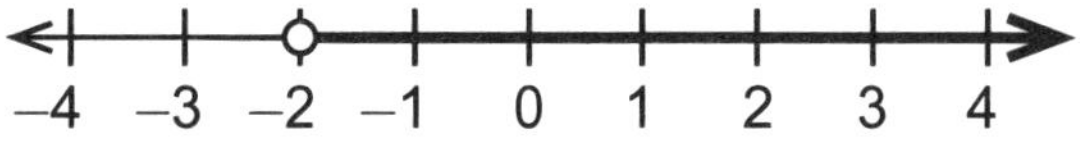

____

9. Draw a ray to show the solution of the inequality on the number line.

a) $x < -2$

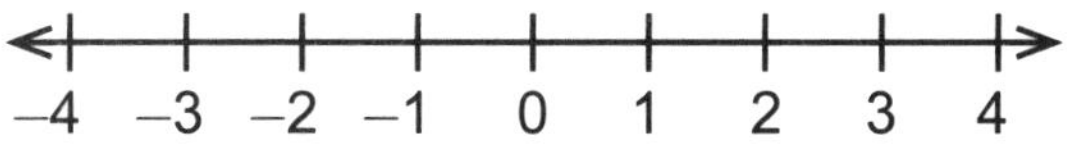

b) $x \leq 0$

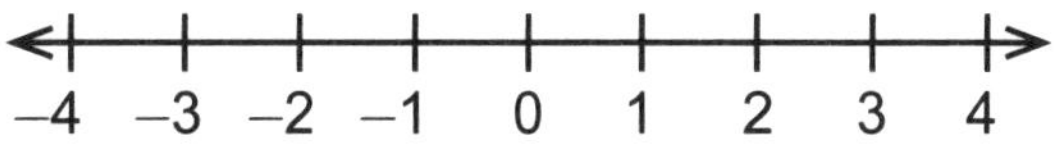

c) $x \geq -3$

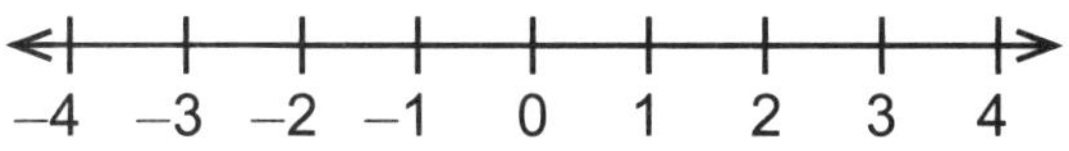

d) $x > 1$

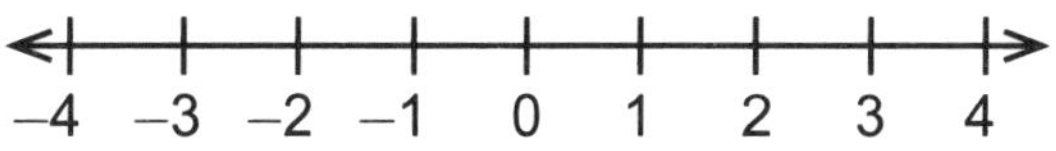

e) $x \leq 1$

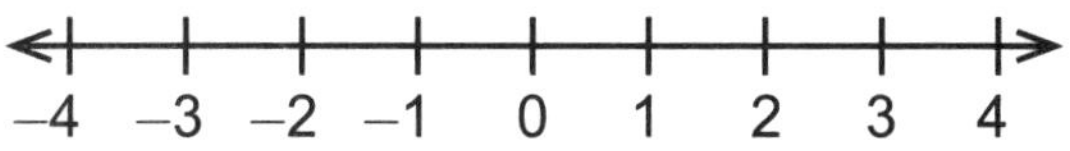

f) $x \geq -1$

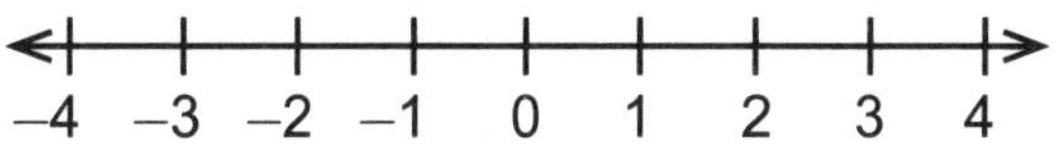

EE7-24 More Inequalities

REMINDER:	$<$	$>$	$\leq$	$\geq$
	less than	greater than	less than or equal to	greater than or equal to

1. Write an inequality for the description.

a) 5 more than a number is less than 8. *$x + 5 < 8$*

b) Twice a number is less than or equal to 9. ______________

c) 7 more than a number is greater than or equal to -3. ______________

d) Three times a number is greater than $\frac{8}{11}$. ______________

e) Three times 5 less than a number is less than or equal to 7. ______________

f) Six less than twice a number is greater than or equal to 1.5. ______________

2. Write the meaning of the inequality in words.

a) $w + 4 \geq 8$ *4 more than a number is greater than or equal to 8.*

b) $x - 5 \leq 9$ ______________

c) $2x - 1 > 7$ ______________

d) $0 \geq 3z$ ______________

REMINDER: You can write $x + 4 > 7$ as $7 < x + 4$.

3. Write the inequality another way.

a) $x - 5 \leq 8$ ______________

b) $3 < 2x - 8$ ______________

c) $-4 \leq x + 1$ ______________

d) $3x - 4 > 5$ ______________

4. Is 2 a solution to the inequality?

a) $x + 5 \leq 7$

$2 + 5 = 7$

Is $7 \leq 7$? ✓

b) $5 - x < 3$

$5 - 2 = 3$

Is $3 < 3$? ✗

c) $2x + 3 \geq 8$

d) $7 - 3x \leq 1$

e) $8 - 3x \leq 0$

f) $5x > 9$

g) $10 - 3x > 4$

h) $\frac{1}{3}x \leq 1$

5. Write symbols for the words. Use x for the unknown number.

a) $\underbrace{\text{Three more than a number}}_{x+3}\ \underbrace{\text{is at most 9.}}_{\leq 9}$

b) $\underbrace{\text{Four times a number}}\ \underbrace{\text{is 12 or more.}}$

c) 0.2 less than a number is not less than 0.3.

d) One fifth of a number is less than −3.

e) Five more than twice a number is more than 18.

f) Twice as much as five more than a number is 9 or less.

6. Can 5.4 be the number?

a) Three more than a number is at most 9.

b) Four less than a number is not less than 2.

7. Complete the table.

a)

x	$2x$	$2x + 1$	Is $2x + 1 < 4$?
−2	*−4*	*−3*	*yes*
−1			
0			
1			
2			

b)

x	$3x$	$5 - 3x$	Is $5 - 3x < 8$?
−2	*−6*	*5 − (−6) = 11*	*no*
−1			
0			
1			
2			

8. Look at your answers to Question 7. Predict the answer to each question.

a) Is −3 a solution to $2x + 1 < 4$? ________

Is +3 a solution to $2x + 1 < 4$? ________

b) Is −3 a solution to $5 - 3x < 8$? ________

Is +3 a solution to $5 - 3x < 8$? ________

EE7-25 Solving Inequalities with Balances and Logic

The pictures below show balances, so the side with more weight is down. Each circle weighs 1 kg.

1. Write an inequality for the weight in one bag.

a) 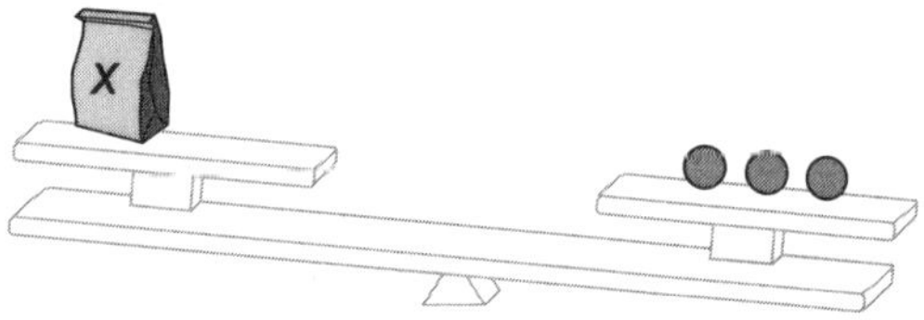

x < 3

b) 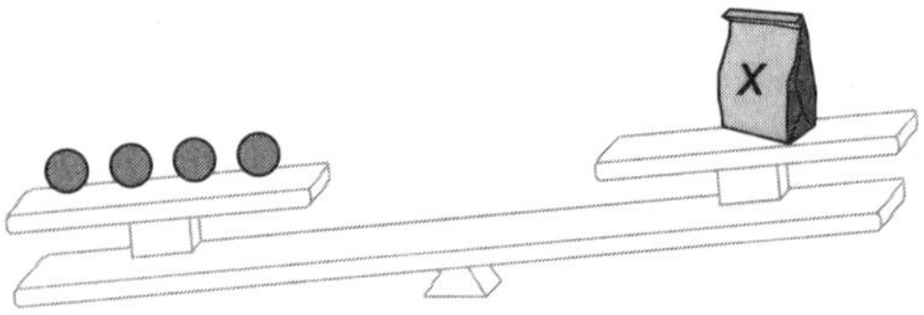

____

c) 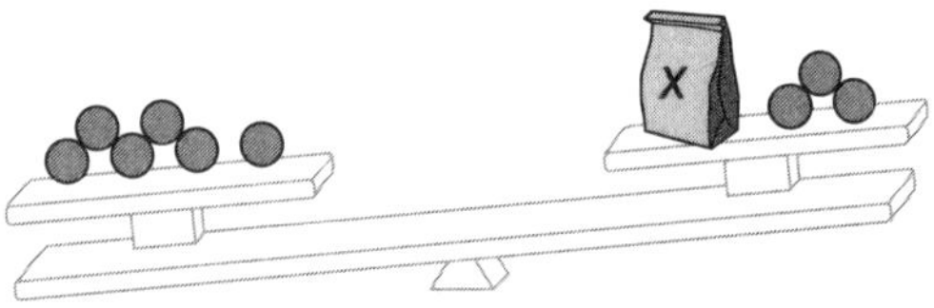

____

d) 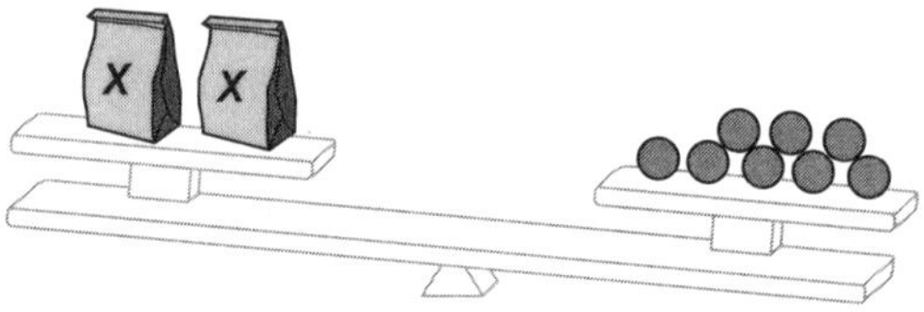

____

e) 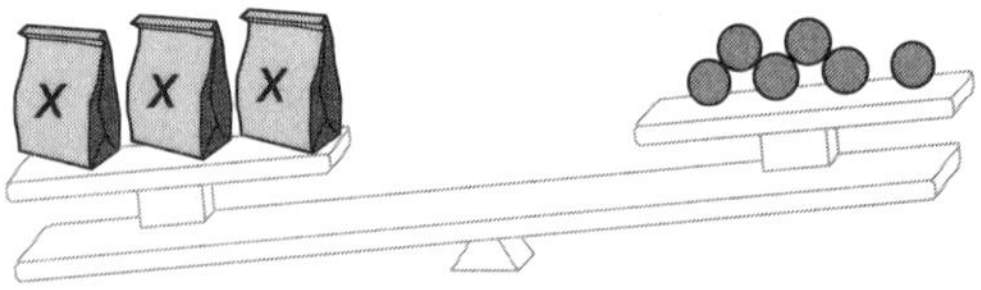

____

f) 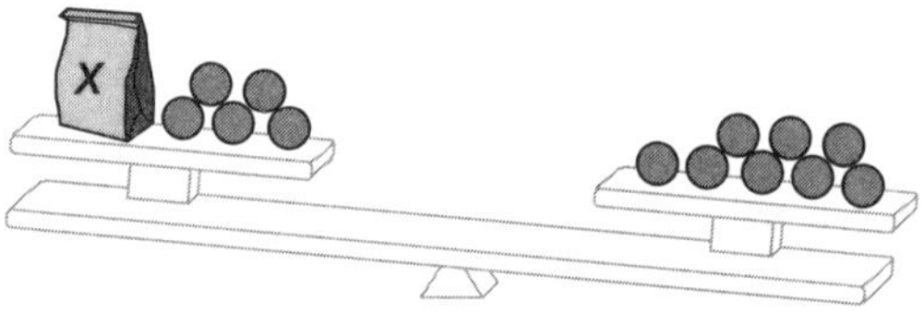

____

g) 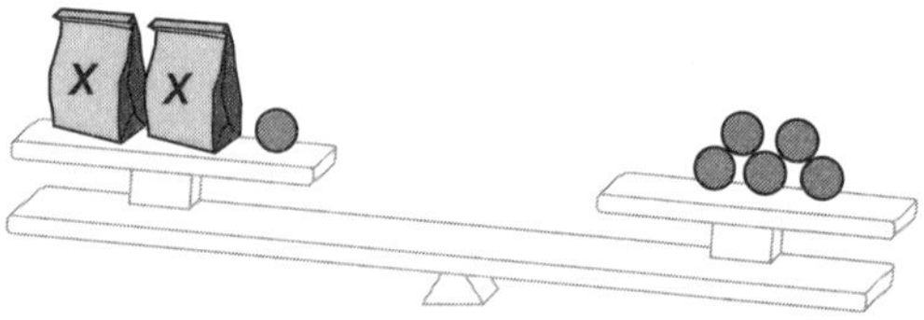

____

h) 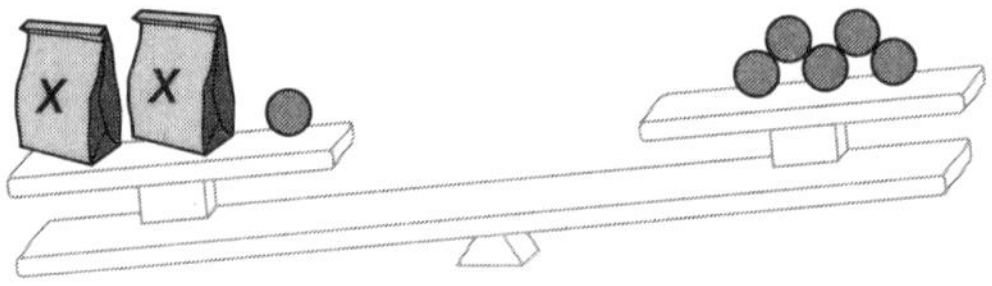

____

i) 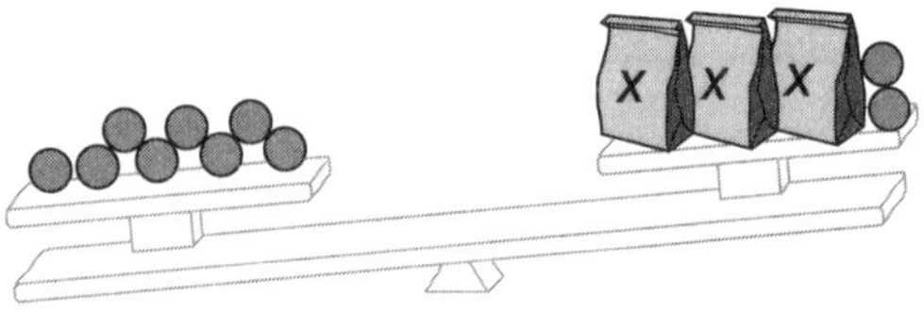

____

j) 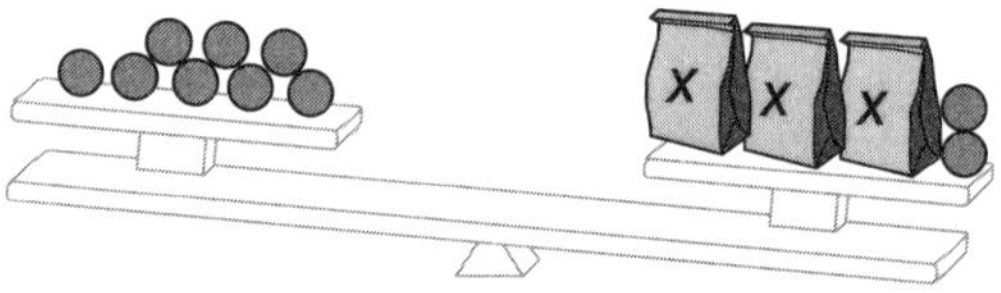

____

2. Write the inequality, then remove 3 circles from each side. Write the new inequality.

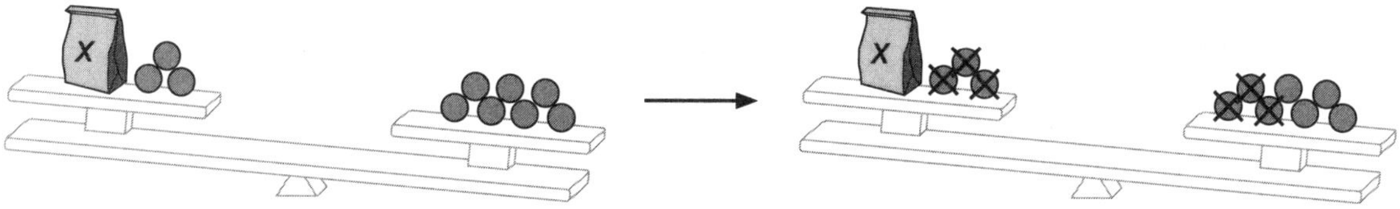

$x + 3 < 7$ ______   ______

3. Can you use the balance model to solve $x - 4 < 9$? Explain.

4. The inequality represents two weights in kg. Remove the same weight from both sides. Then write a new inequality.

a) $x + 7 > 12$ So $x >$ 5

b) $x + 9 < 15$ So $x <$ ______

c) $x + 4 \leq 9$ So $x \leq$ ______

d) $x + 5 \geq 8$ So $x \geq$ ______

You can use logic to solve $3x < 15$. Divide the 15 circles into 3 equal bags.

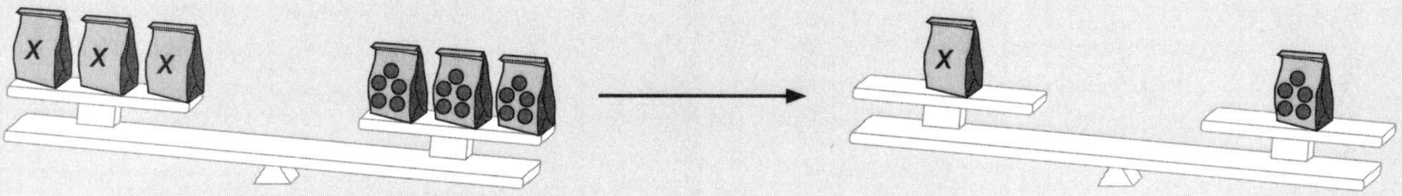

3 bags weighing x kg each weigh less than 3 bags weighing 5 kg each.

So 1 bag weighing x kg weighs less than 1 bag weighing 5 kg. So $x < 5$.

5. The inequality represents two weights in kg. Divide both weights by the same number. Then write a new inequality.

a) $5x > 30$ So $x >$ ______

b) $4x \leq 20$ So $x \leq$ ______

c) $2x \geq 18$ So $x \geq$ ______

d) $3x < 12$ So $x <$ ______

6. a) Blanca's parrot weighs 180 g. That's less than the weight of five identical toy parrots together. What can you say about the weight of each toy parrot?

b) Billy sold 180 raffle tickets last year for a school fundraiser. This year, he wants to sell more than that. He has five months to sell. How many should he try to sell each month?

c) How are parts a) and b) the same? How are they different?

7. In three years, everyone in Carl's family will be old enough to ride the roller coaster shown in the picture. What can you say about the age of everyone in Carl's family?

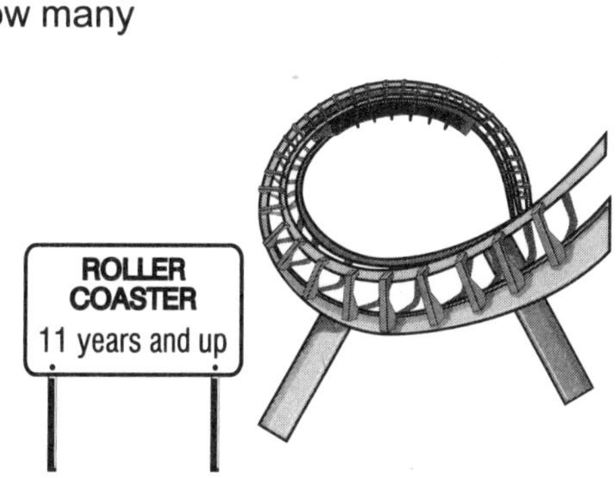

EE7-26 Using Equations to Solve Inequalities

To solve an inequality, you can:

- Move terms to the other side and change addition to subtraction or subtraction to addition.
- Multiply or divide the same positive number on both sides.

1. Solve the equation and the inequalities.

a) $3x + 5 = 20$ $\quad$ $3x + 5 < 20$ $\quad$ $3x + 5 > 20$

$3x = 20 - 5$ $\quad$ $3x < 20 - 5$ $\quad$ $3x > 20 - 5$

$3x = 15$ $\quad$ $3x < 15$ $\quad$ $3x > 15$

$x = 5$ $\quad$ $x < 5$ $\quad$ $x > 5$

b) $4x - 3 = 5$ $\quad$ $4x - 3 < 5$ $\quad$ $4x - 3 > 5$

c) $5 + 2x = 11$ $\quad$ $5 + 2x < 11$ $\quad$ $5 + 2x > 11$

d) $5x + 4 = 34$ $\quad$ $5x + 4 < 34$ $\quad$ $5x + 4 > 34$

2. If $x = 73$ is the solution to the equation $9x + 83 = 740$, what is the solution to the inequality?

a) $9x + 83 > 740$ ______ $\quad$ b) $9x + 83 \geq 740$ ______ $\quad$ c) $9x + 83 < 740$ ______ $\quad$ d) $9x + 83 \leq 740$ ______

To solve $2x - 9 \leq 11$, use the same steps you would use to solve $2x - 9 = 11$.

$$2x - 9 \leq 11$$
$$2x \leq 11 + 9$$
$$2x \leq 20$$
$$x \leq 10$$

Notice that the inequality stays in the same direction:

variable term	$\leq$	constant term		variable term	$\leq$	constant term
$2x - 9$	$\leq$	11	so	x	$\leq$	10

This makes sense because, as x increases, so does $2x - 9$.

3. Solve the inequality.

a) $2x + 3 \leq 7$

b) $3x - 5 < 10$

c) $4x - 3 \geq 5$

d) $2x + 8 \leq 11$

e) $4x + 7 > 18$

f) $4x - 5 \geq 2$

g) $2x + 7 \leq 3$

h) $3x + 10 \geq 4$

i) $2x + 11 > 8$

j) $5x + 8 < -2$

k) $3x - 5 \leq -11$

l) $8x - 3 > -1$

To solve $8 - 3x \geq 2$:

Step 1: Move the variable term to the other side so that subtraction becomes addition. $8 \geq 3x + 2$

Step 2: Solve $8 \geq 3x + 2$ or $3x + 2 \leq 8$.

$$3x + 2 \leq 8$$
$$3x \leq 8 - 2$$
$$3x \leq 6$$
$$x \leq 6 \div 3$$
$$x \leq 2$$

Notice that the inequality reverses direction:

variable term $\geq$ constant term		variable term $\leq$ constant term
$8 - 3x \quad \geq \quad 2$	so	$x \quad \leq \quad 2$

This makes sense because, as x increases, $8 - 3x$ decreases.

4. Solve the inequality.

a) $18 - 5x \geq 3$

b) $13 - 2x \leq 7$

c) $17 - 4x < 2$

d) $-4x + 7 > -5$

e) $-5x + 9 \geq -6$

f) $-5x + 10 \leq -7$

g) $7 \geq -3 - 2x$

h) $11 \leq -4x - 5$

i) $-3 - 5x < 8$

EE7-27 More Solving Inequalities (Advanced)

1. Multiply or divide both sides of the inequality by the same number. Change $<$ to $>$ if you need to.

		$3 < 4$	$90 < 100$	$0 < 5$
a)	Multiply by $+3$.	$9 < 12$		
b)	Multiply by -1.	$-3 > -4$		
c)	Multiply by $\frac{1}{2}$.			
d)	Multiply by -2.			
e)	Multiply by $-\frac{1}{10}$.			
f)	Divide by 4.			
g)	Divide by -4.			

2. In Question 1, when did you have to change $<$ to $>$?

When I multiplied by ______, ______, or ______ and when I divided by ______.

> You can multiply or divide both sides of an inequality by any number.
>
> If the number you multiply or divide by is positive, keep the direction of the inequality the same.
> Example: If $x < 4$, then $3x < 12$
>
> If the number you multiply or divide by is negative, reverse the direction of the inequality.
> Example: If $x < 4$, then $-3x > -12$

3. Multiply the expression by -1.

a) x ______ b) $-x$ ______ c) $5 - x$ ______ d) $-3 - x$ ______

e) $2x$ ______ f) $-2x$ ______ g) $7 - 3x$ ______ h) $-8 - 5x$ ______

4. Multiply both sides of the inequality by -1 to make the coefficient positive.

a) $8 - x < 2$
$-8 + x > -2$

b) $-x + 4 \geq 3$ ______

c) $-x - 2 \leq -5$ ______

d) $-x - 5 > 7$ ______

e) $-2x + 3 \leq 4$ ______

f) $5 - 3x > 4$ ______

g) $7 - 5x \leq -2$ ______

h) $-3x + 4 < -8$ ______

> To solve the inequality $3 - 2x < 11$:
>
> **Step 1:** Make the coefficient positive by multiplying both sides of the inequality by -1. $\quad -3 + 2x > -11$
>
> **Step 2:** Solve the new inequality.
>
> $2x > -11 + 3$
>
> $2x > -8$
>
> $x > -4$

5. Solve the inequality.

a) $14 - 5x \leq 4$ b) $8 - 3x \geq -1$ c) $-3x + 4 < -5$

6. Write an integer solution for the last inequality. Check that it is a solution for the first inequality.

a)

$10 - 3x < 4$

$-10 + 3x > -4$

$3x > -4 + 10$

$3x > 6$

$x > 2$

$x =$ __3__ satisfies $x > 2$

Check: *10 – 3(3) = 10 – 9*

= 1

Is 1 < 4? ✓

b)

$-8x + 5 < -4$

$8x - 5 > 4$

$8x > 4 + 5$

$8x > 9$

$x > \frac{9}{8}$

$x =$ ______ satisfies $x > \frac{9}{8}$

Check:

c)

$10 - 3x \geq 1$

$-10 + 3x \leq -1$

$3x \leq -1 + 10$

$3x \leq 9$

$x \leq 3$

$x =$ ______ satisfies $x \leq 3$

Check:

7. Check your answers to Question 5 by making sure that a solution for the last inequality is a solution of the first one.

a) b) c)

8. Solve the inequality. Check your answer.

a) $2x + 5 > 13$

b) $2x - 5 < 13$

c) $7 - 2x \leq 15$

d) $-2x - 5 \leq 3$

e) $-4x + 7 \geq 23$

f) $9 - 5x \geq 7$

To solve the inequality $5 - 2x < 11$, you can make the coefficient positive in two ways.

Method 1: Move the variable to the other side and change subtraction to addition.

$5 < 2x + 11$

Method 2: Multiply both sides of the inequality by -1 and change $<$ to $>$.

$-5 + 2x > -11$

9. Solve $5 < 2x + 11$, then $-5 + 2x > -11$.

$5 < 2x + 11$

$-5 + 2x > -11$

Did you get the same answer? __________

10. Solve the inequality two ways. Make sure you get the same answer both ways.

a) $10 - 4x < -2$

b) $6 - 11x \geq 28$

c) $18 - 4x < 30$

d) $-2 - 5x \leq 3$

EE7-28 Inequalities and Word Problems

1. Lily has $20 to spend this week. She has to spend $14 on school supplies. If smartphone apps cost $2 each, how many apps could Lily buy?

   a) What do you want to find? Let x be ______________________________.

   b) Write an expression, in terms of x, for the amount Lily spends this week. ____________

   c) Write an inequality and solve it.

   d) How many apps could Lily buy? ______, ______, ______, or ______.

2. Greg can spend at most $200. He has to spend $80 on clothes. If DVDs cost $15 each, how many DVDs could Greg buy?

   a) What do you not know? Let x be ______________________________.

   b) Write an expression, in terms of x, for the total amount Greg spends. ____________

   c) How does the expression from part b) compare to $200? Write an inequality.

   ____

   d) Solve the inequality from part c) to answer the question.

   e) Why might Greg choose to buy less than the maximum number of DVDs?

   ____

3. Surfboards cost $30 an hour to rent, plus a $10 flat fee. Rob has $100. How many hours can he surf for?

   a) Let x be ______________________________.

   b) Write an inequality in terms of x. ____________

   c) Solve your inequality to answer the question.

4. Mindy is paid $70 each week plus $2 for each sale she makes. This week she wants her pay to be at least $200. Write an inequality for the number of sales Mindy needs to make and solve it.

5. Massimo's backyard is very long, but only 11 feet wide. He wants to enclose part of his backyard as a rectangular pen for chickens. Fencing costs \$20 per foot.

a) Massimo can spend at most \$1,000 on fencing. How long can his enclosure be?

b) If each chicken needs at least 4 square feet of space to run, how many chickens can he raise?

6. Sharon has \$300. Each time she goes out for lunch, she spends \$10. She needs to keep \$100 for school supplies before the school year starts.

a) What is the maximum number of times she can go out for lunch?

b) Why might Sharon choose to go out for lunch less than the maximum number of times?

c) Write an inequality that shows all the possibilities for the number of times Sharon can go out for lunch.

7. If a store sells each shirt for $\$p$, the store will sell $100 - 5p$ shirts each day.

a) How many people will buy a shirt if each shirt costs …

i) \$20 ii) \$10 iii) \$0 (free)

b) The store sold 30 shirts yesterday. What was the price of each shirt?

c) The store wants to sell at least 70 shirts. What range of prices will ensure this?

d) In part c), did the store need to make the price at least a certain amount or at most that amount? Why does that make sense?

8. a) In which part of Question 7 did you solve an equation? ____________________

b) In which part of Question 7 did you solve an inequality? ____________________

G7-11 Complementary Angles and Supplementary Angles

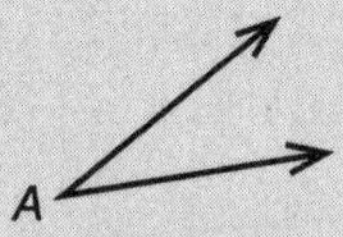

A is the vertex.
∠*A* is the angle.

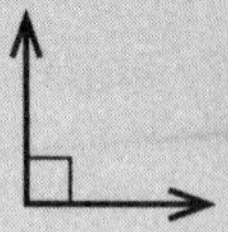

Right angles (90°) are marked with a square.

Straight angles measure 180°.

1. Use a corner of a sheet of paper to look for right angles. Mark the right angles with a square.

a) 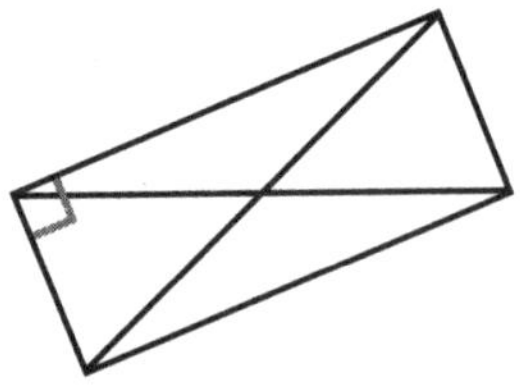

b) 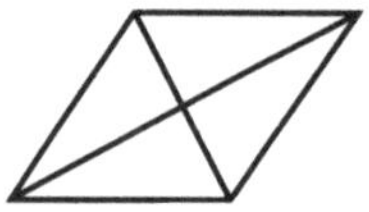

c) 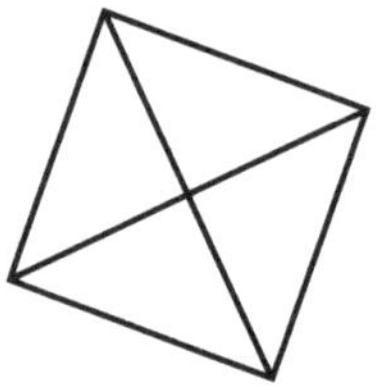

Two angles are **complementary** if their measures add to 90°. Two angles are **supplementary** if their measures add to 180°.

2. Fill in the blanks.

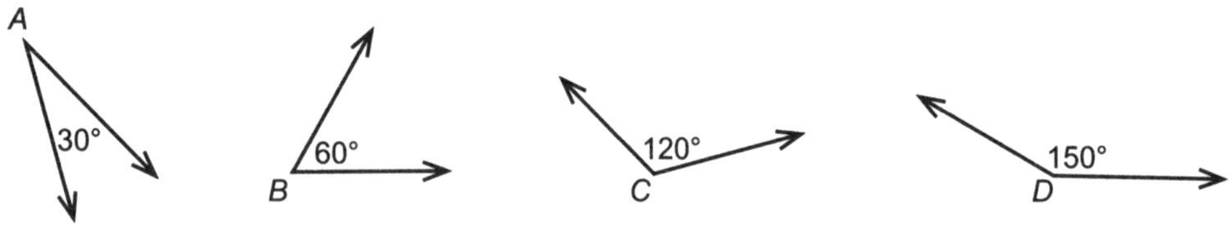

a) ∠*A* and ∠______ are complementary.

b) ∠*A* and ∠______ are supplementary.

c) ∠*B* and ∠______ are complementary.

d) ∠*B* and ∠______ are supplementary.

When two angles share a vertex, you can write the label for each angle inside the angle.

3. Write "complementary" or "supplementary."

a) 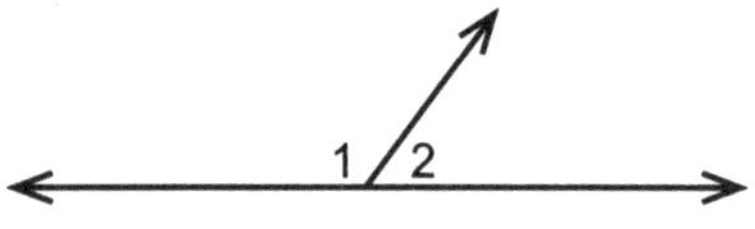

∠1 and ∠2 are ____________________.

b) 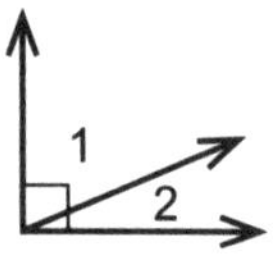

∠1 and ∠2 are ____________________.

c) 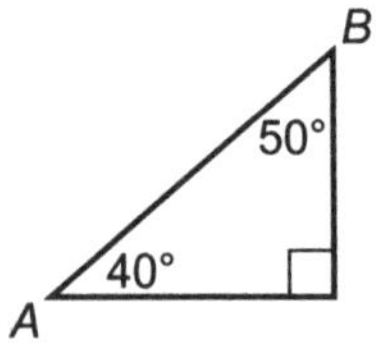

∠*A* and ∠*B* are ____________________.

d) 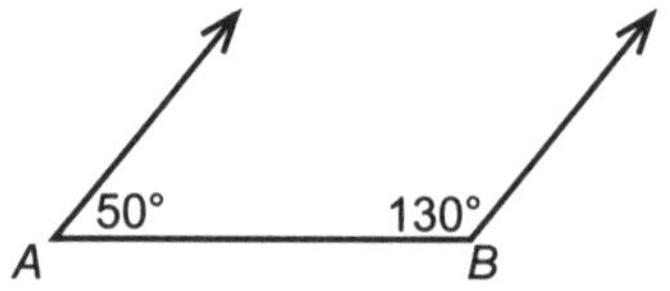

∠*A* and ∠*B* are ____________________.

Solve for x. You do not need to write the degree symbol (°) in equations when you do your rough work, but you do need to write it in the answer.

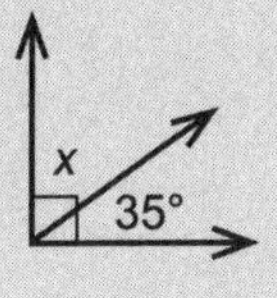

Rough work:

$x + 35 = 90$

$x = 90 - 35$

$x = 55$ So $x = 55°$

4. Use an equation to find x.

a) 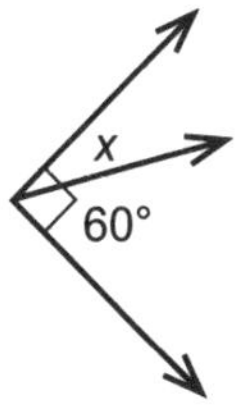

b) 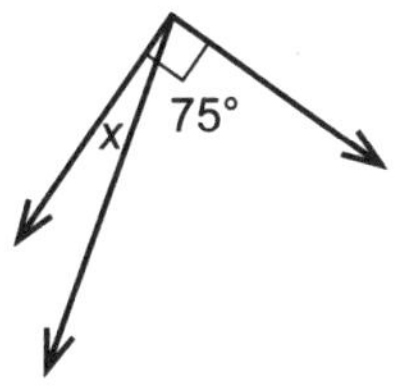

c) 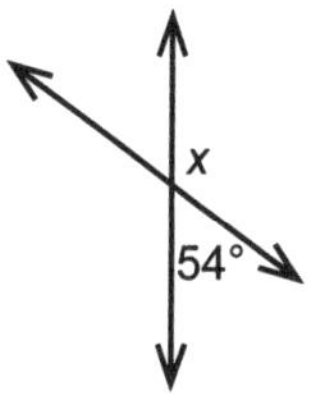

You may need to simplify the equation before solving it.

d) 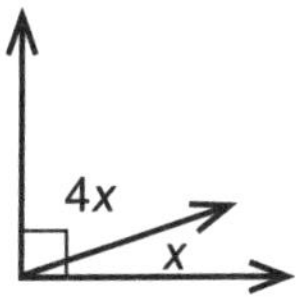

$4x + x = 90$

$5x = 90$

$x = 90 \div 5$

$x = 18$

So $x = 18°$

e) 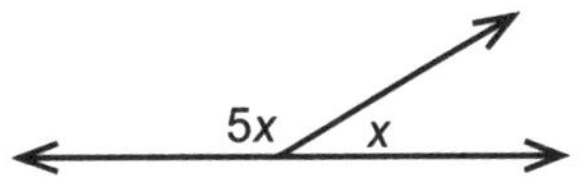

f) 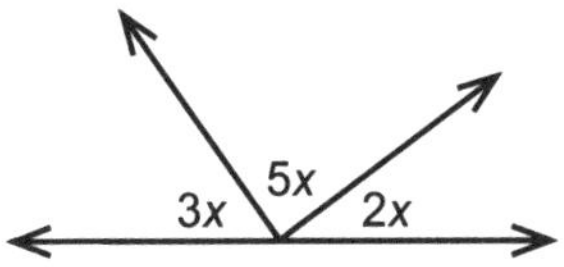

g) 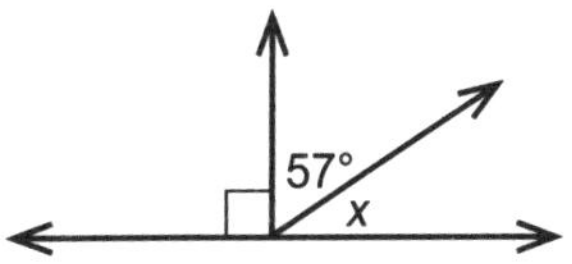

h) 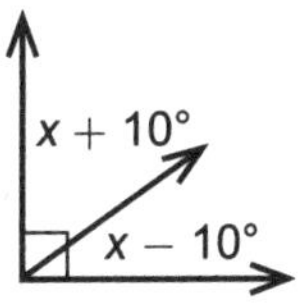

i) 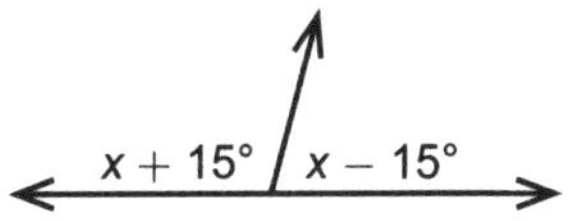

5. Use a protractor to measure the angles in parts a) and b). Were you correct? ____________________

Some equations require two steps to solve.

Example: Find x.

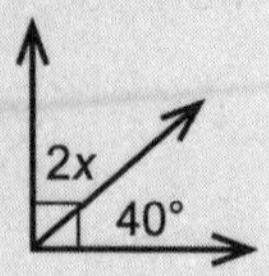

Rough work:

$2x + 40 = 90$

$2x = 90 - 40$

$2x = 50$

$x = 50 \div 2$

$x = 25$ So $x = 25°$

6. Use an equation to find x.

a)

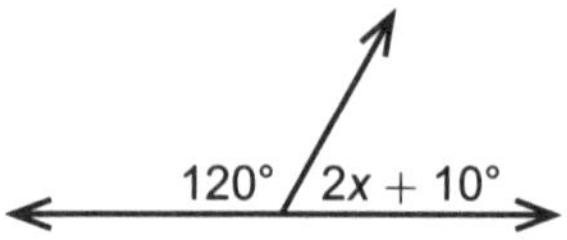

b)

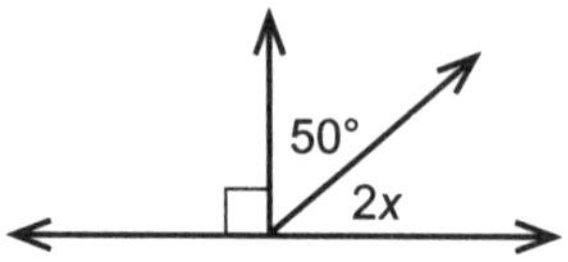

c)

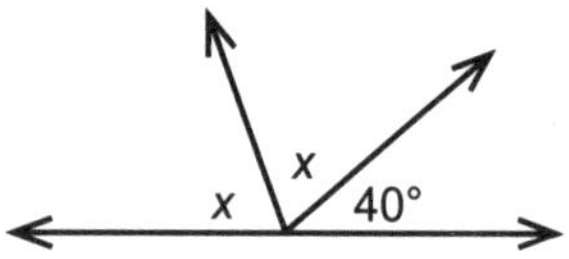

d)

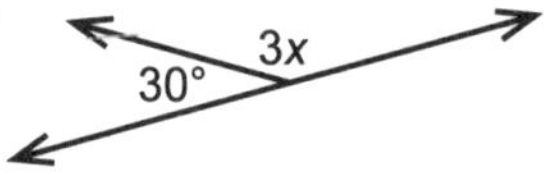

e)

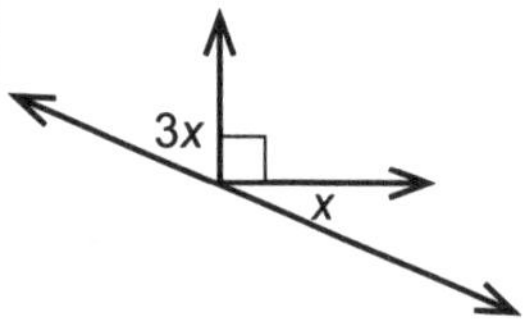

f)

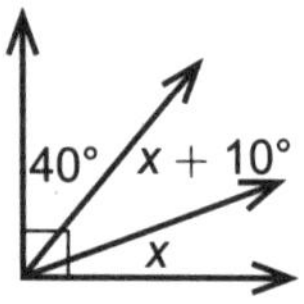

To solve the problems below, ignore the information you do not need.

g)

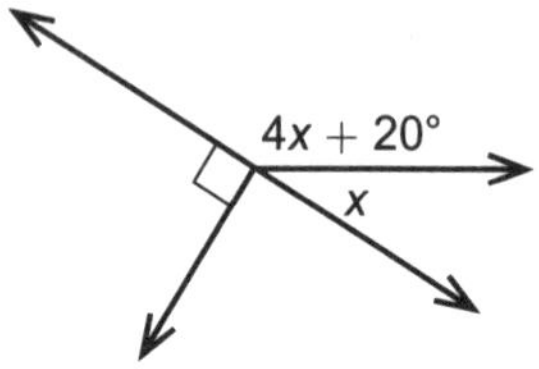

h)

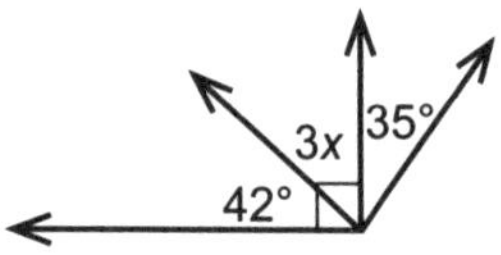

i)

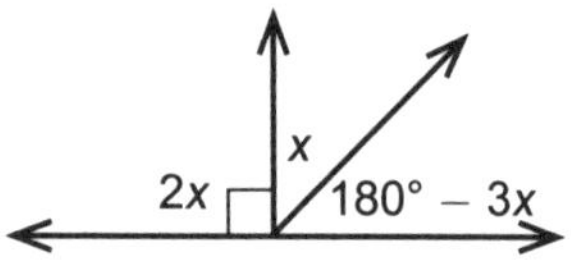

7. $\angle A$ measures 100°.

a) $\angle B$ is supplementary to $\angle A$. What is the measure of $\angle B$? ________

b) $\angle C$ is supplementary to $\angle B$. What is the measure of $\angle C$? ________

c) $\angle D$ is complementary to $\angle B$. What is the measure of $\angle D$? ________

d) Can you draw $\angle E$ so that $\angle E$ is complementary to $\angle A$? Explain.

G7-12 Adjacent Angles and Vertical Angles

Adjacent angles share a vertex and an arm.

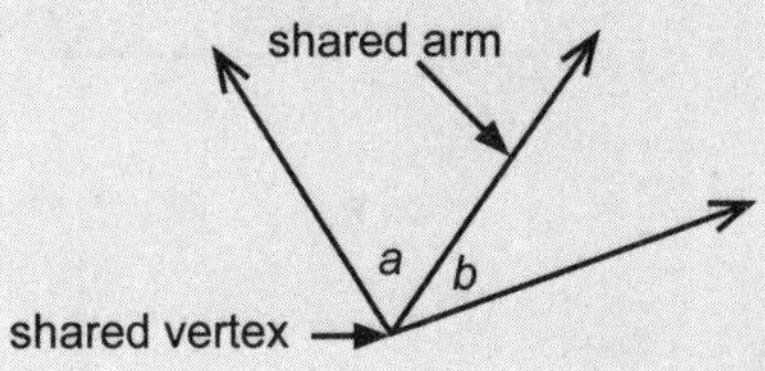

Vertical angles are the non-adjacent angles formed by two intersecting lines.

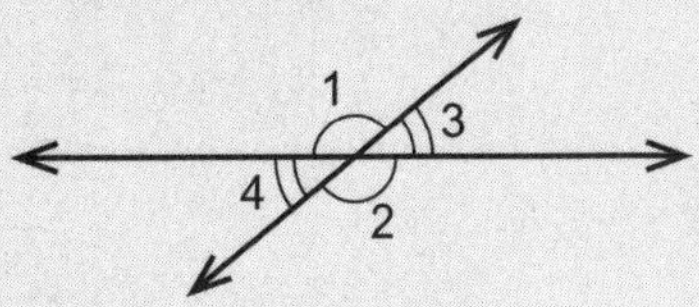

∠1 and ∠2 are vertical angles.

∠3 and ∠4 are also vertical angles.

1. Write "adjacent" or "vertical."

a) ∠1 and ∠2 are ______________________.

b) ∠1 and ∠4 are ______________________.

c) ∠3 and ∠2 are ______________________.

d) ∠3 and ∠6 are ______________________.

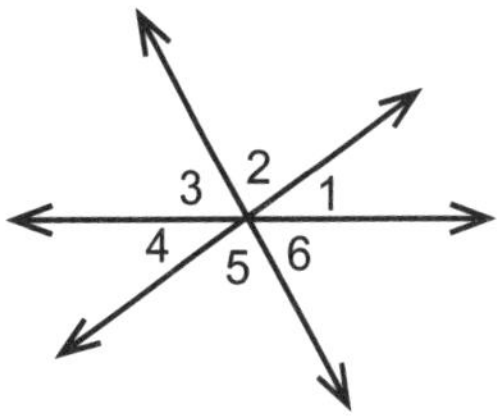

2. The measures of two vertical angles are *x* and *y*. Find *x* and *y*. Include the units.

a)

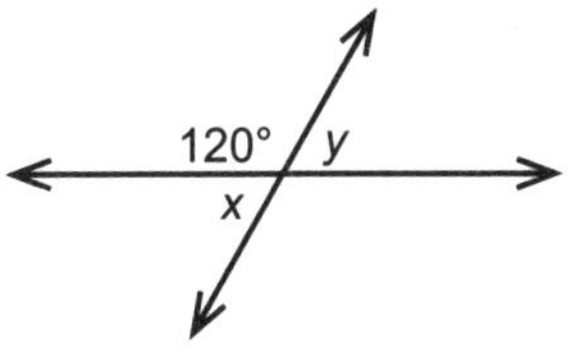

$x =$ ______, $y =$ ______

b)

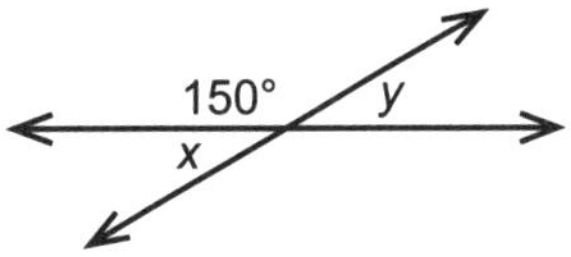

$x =$ ______, $y =$ ______

c)

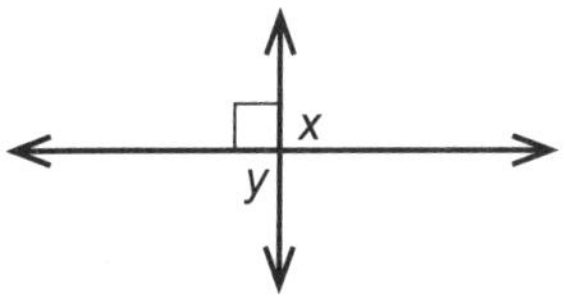

$x =$ ______, $y =$ ______

3. Look at your answers to Question 2. What do you notice about the measures of vertical angles?

____

The measures of two vertical angles are always equal.

4. Find *x* and *y*. Include the units.

a)

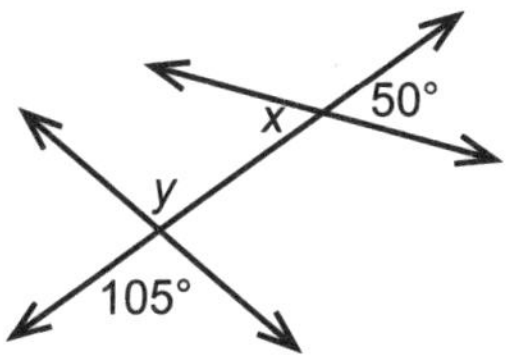

$x =$ ______, $y =$ ______

b)

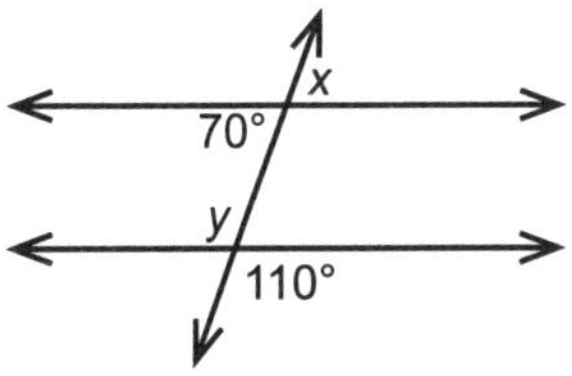

$x =$ ______, $y =$ ______

c)

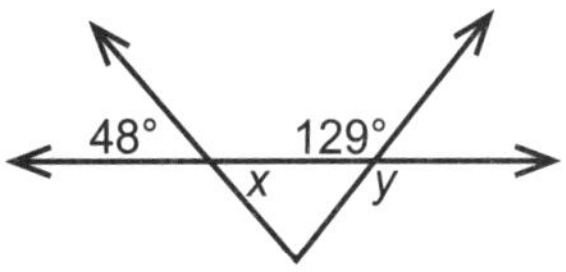

$x =$ ______, $y =$ ______

5. Write an equation, then solve it for x.

a)

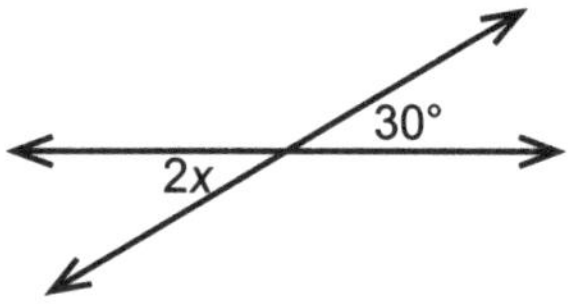

b)

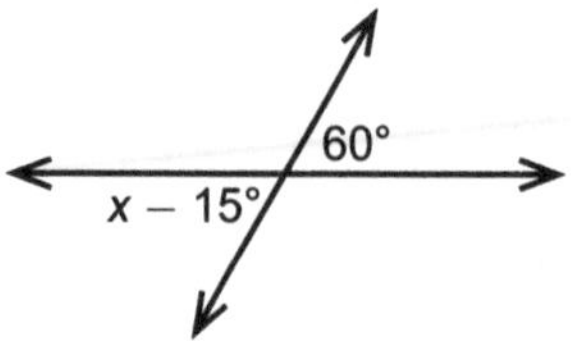

c)

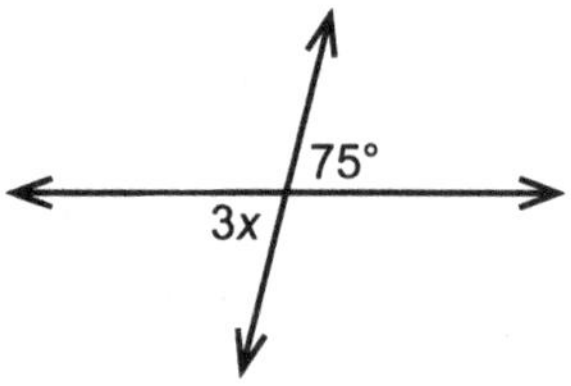

d)

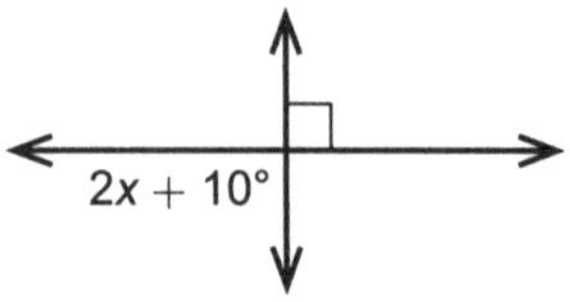

e)

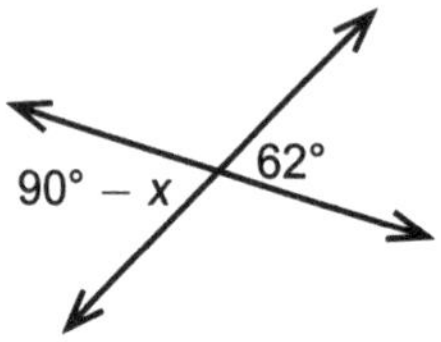

f)

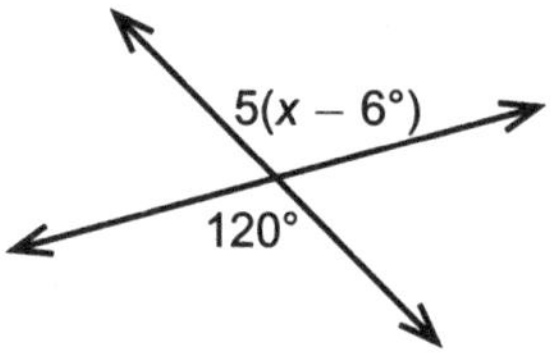

6. Draw an arc to mark the angle that is vertical to the angle shown.

a)

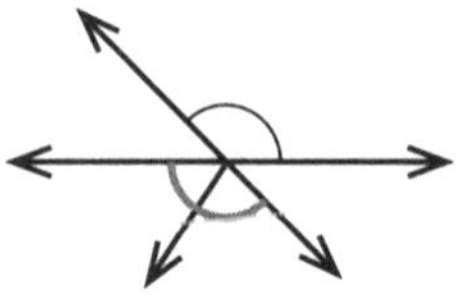

b)

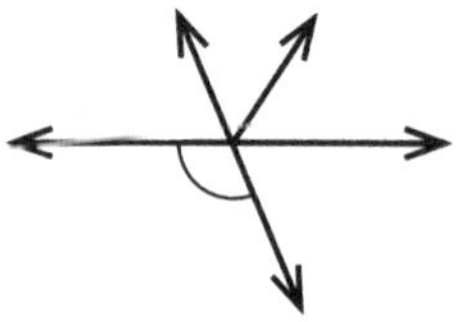

c)

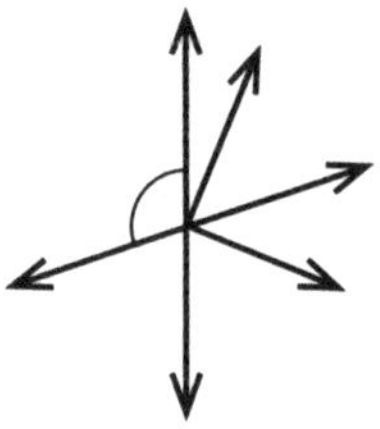

7. Use vertical angles to write an equation. Then solve the equation for x.

a)

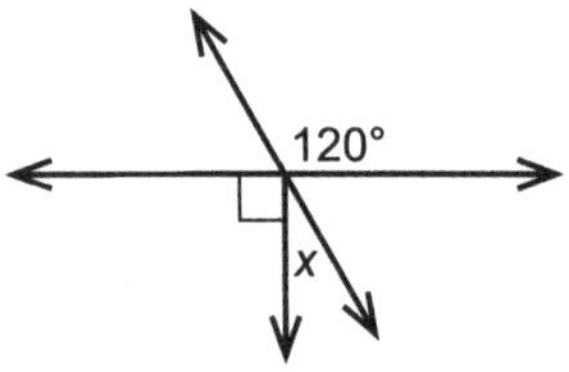

b)

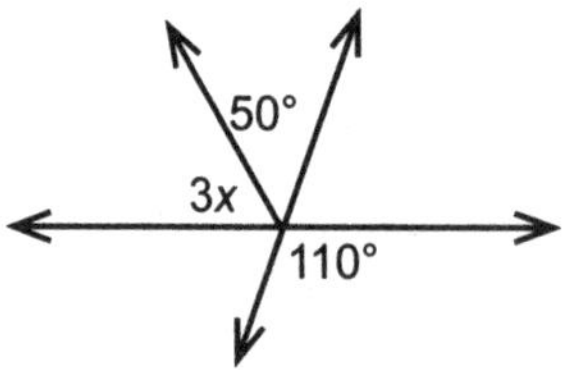

c)

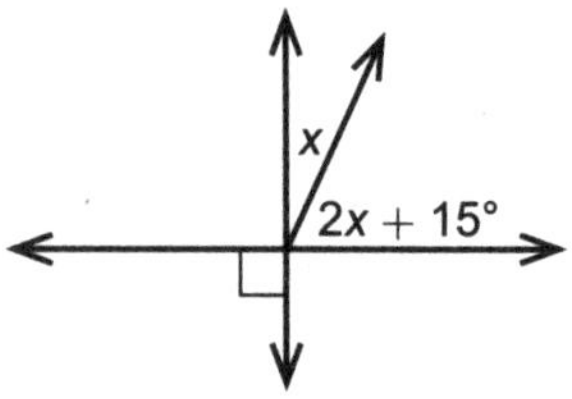

G7-13 Solving Problems Using Angle Properties

1. Write "vertical," "complementary," or "supplementary."

a) ∠1 and ∠2 are ______________________.

b) ∠3 and ∠4 are ______________________.

c) ∠3 and ∠5 are ______________________.

d) ∠5 and ∠6 are ______________________.

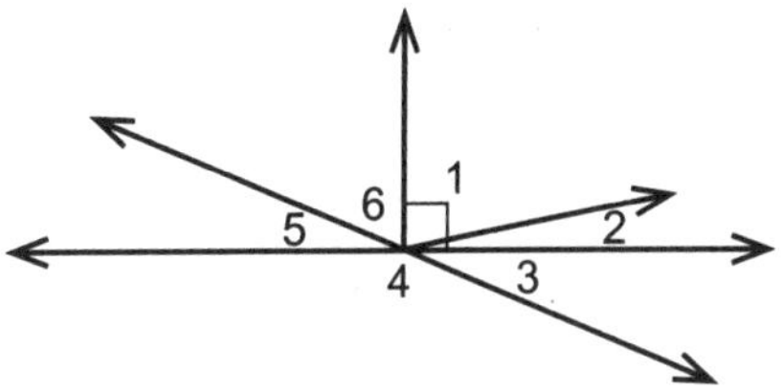

2. Find *x*, *y*, and *z*. Include the units.

a)

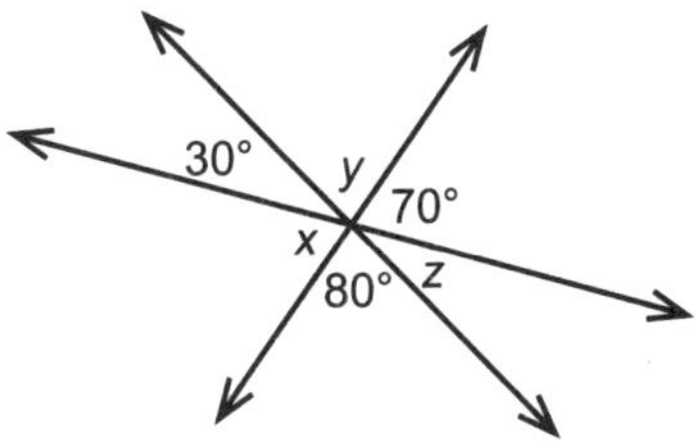

$x =$ ______

$y =$ ______

$z =$ ______

b)

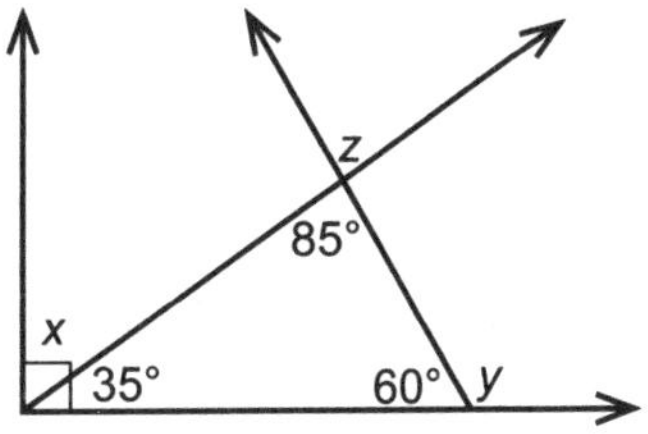

$x =$ ______

$y =$ ______

$z =$ ______

c)

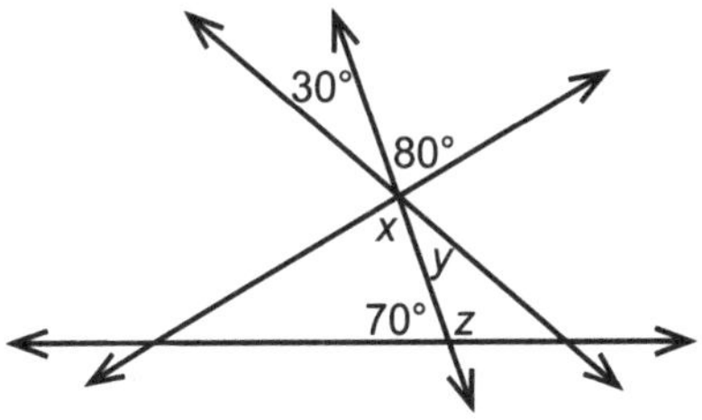

$x =$ ______

$y =$ ______

$z =$ ______

REMINDER: The angle in a full rotation is 360°. 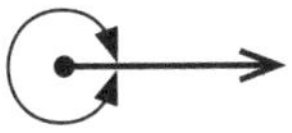

3. Write an equation, then solve it to find x.

a)

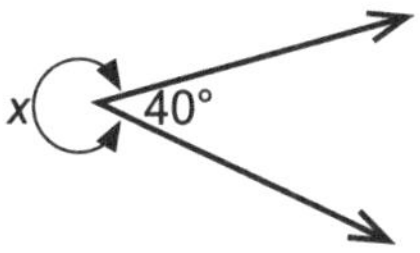

b)

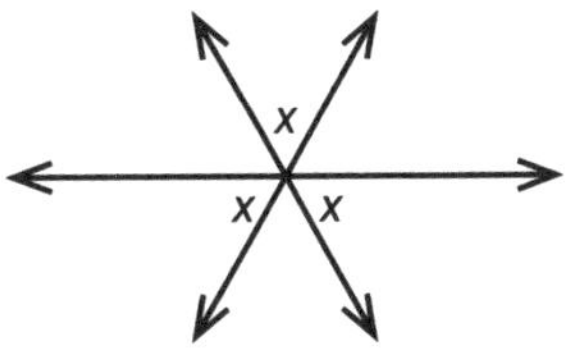

c)

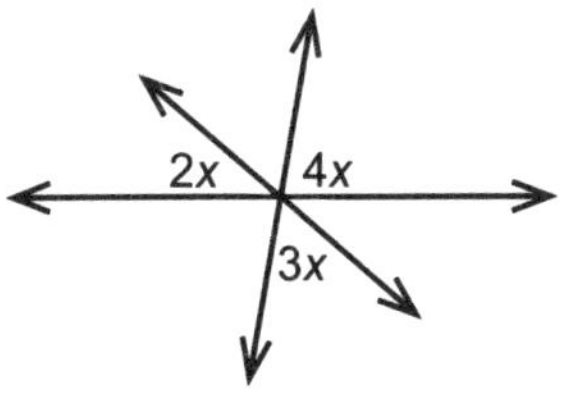

REMINDER: The angles in a triangle add to 180°.

4. Write an equation for x and solve it.

a) 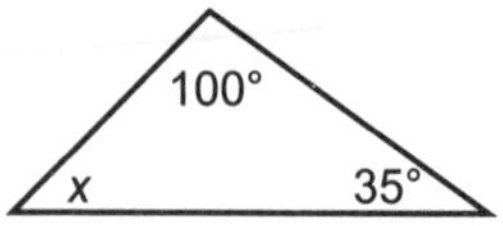

b) 

5. Evaluate the variables. Include the units.

a) 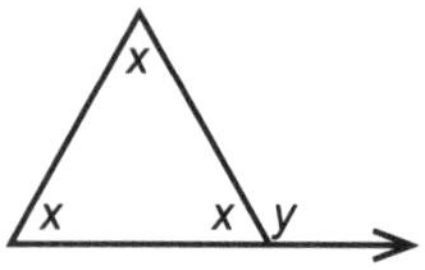

$x =$ ______, $y =$ ______

b) 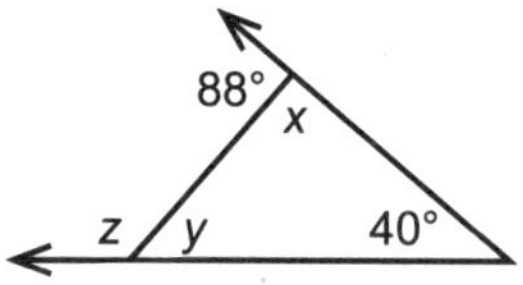

$x =$ ______, $y =$ ______, $z =$ ______

c) 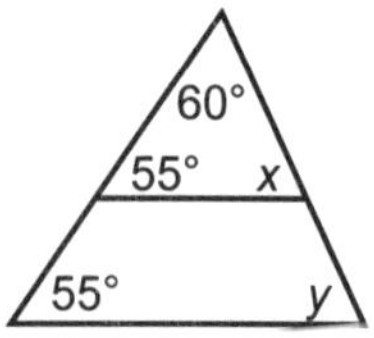

$x =$ ______, $y =$ ______

d) 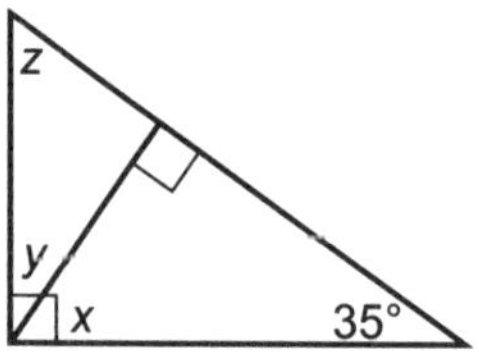

$x =$ ______, $y =$ ______, $z =$ ______

e) 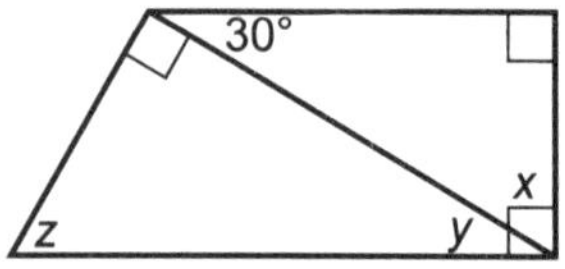

$x =$ ______, $y =$ ______, $z =$ ______

f) 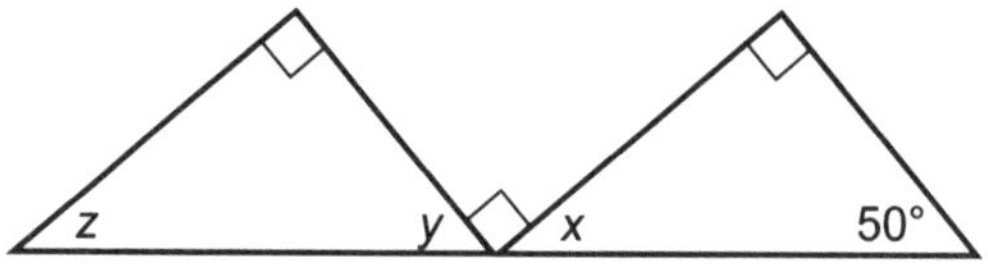

$x =$ ______, $y =$ ______, $z =$ ______

g) 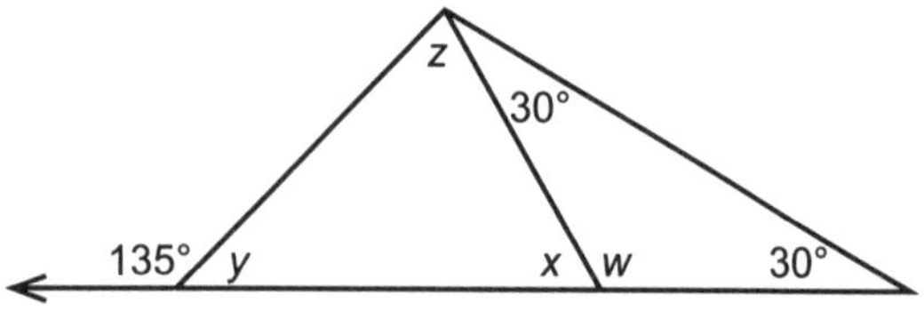

$w =$ ______, $x =$ ______,

$y =$ ______, $z =$ ______

h) 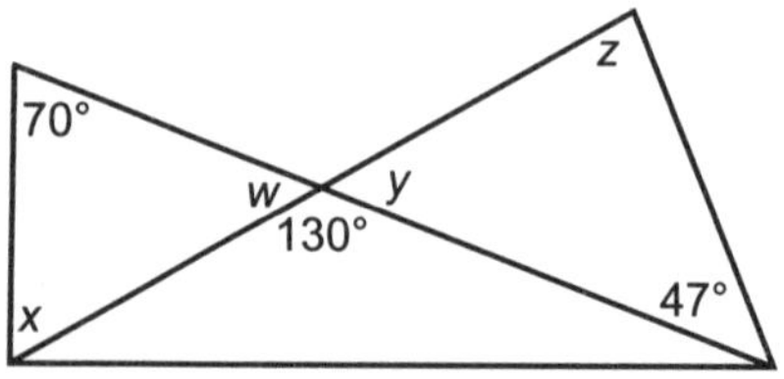

$w =$ ______, $x =$ ______,

$y =$ ______, $z =$ ______

You can name angles using points on the arms. Always write the vertex in the middle.

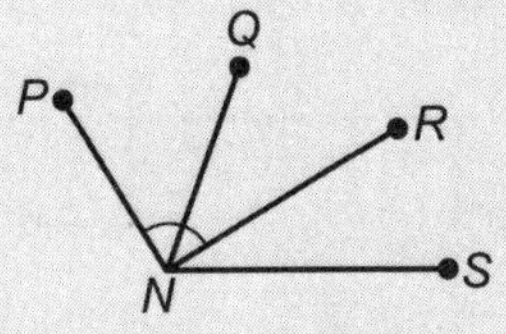

∠PNR or ∠RNP

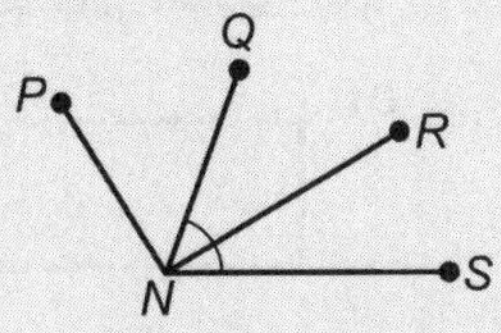

∠QNS or ∠SNQ

6. Name the angle two ways.

a)

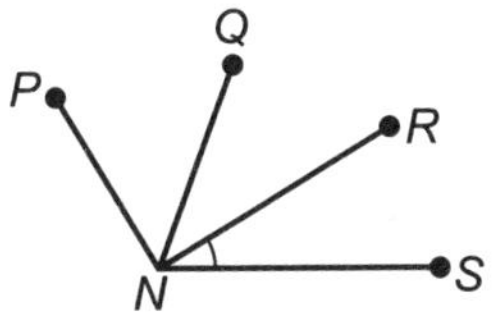

∠________ or ∠________

b)

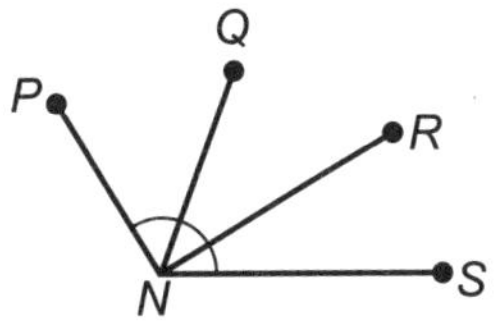

∠________ or ∠________

c)

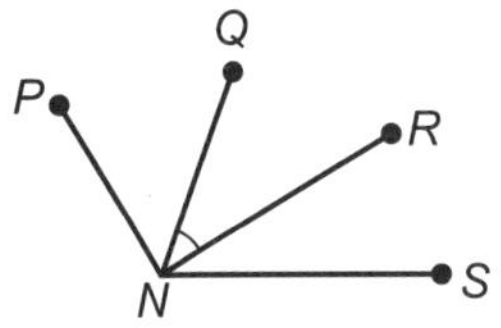

∠________ or ∠________

7. Circle all the possible names for the angle shown.

∠ACT   ∠ATB   ∠BTC   ∠CBT

∠CTA   ∠BTA   ∠ACB   ∠BCA

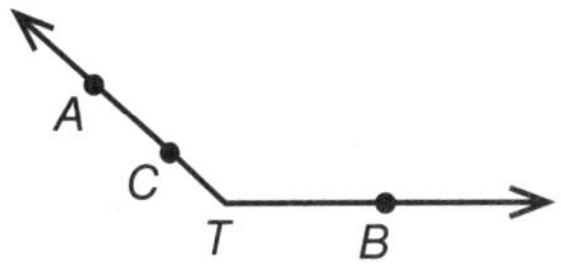

8. a) Show the measures of the angles on the diagram.

∠ADB = 60°   ∠ABD = 70°

∠BAC = 50°   ∠BDC = 120°

∠DBC = 40°

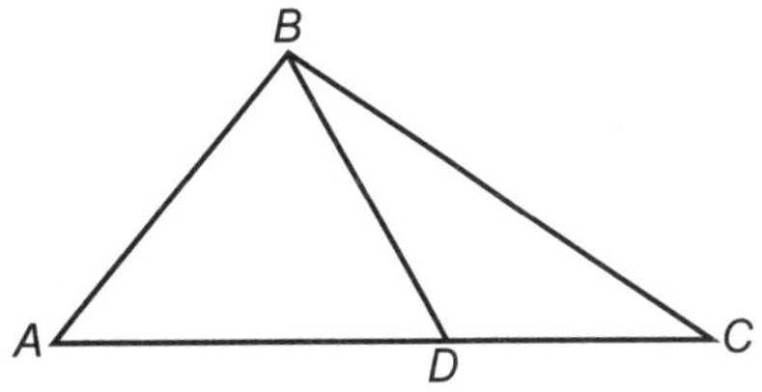

b) What is ∠ABC? ________

c) Which two angles are supplementary? ________ and ________

How could you have predicted this from the picture? ________________________________

____

9. Find the measure of ∠XYZ.

a)

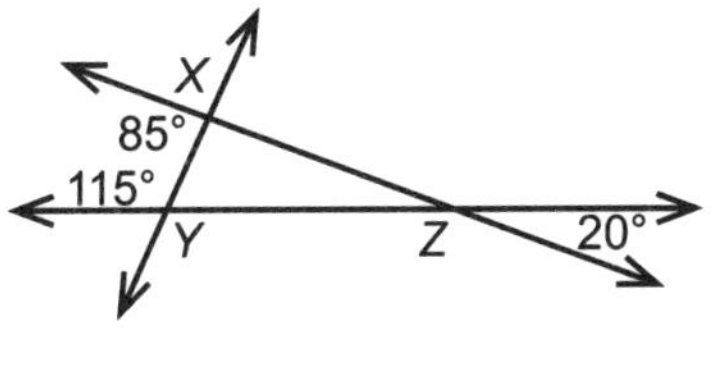

________°

b)

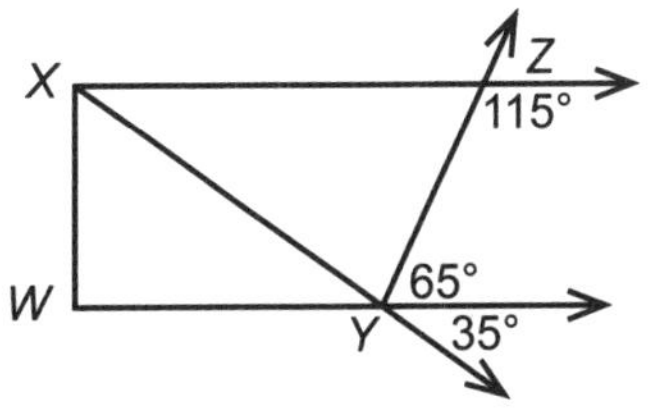

________°

c)

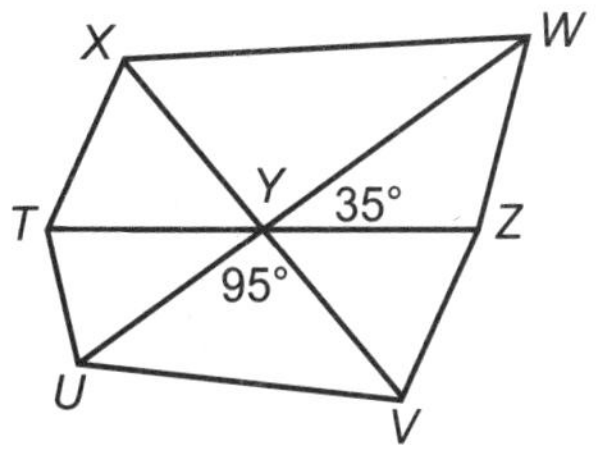

________°

G7-14 Area of Rectangles and Triangles

1. Use the length (ℓ) and width (w) of the rectangle to find the area, $A = \ell \times w$.

a)

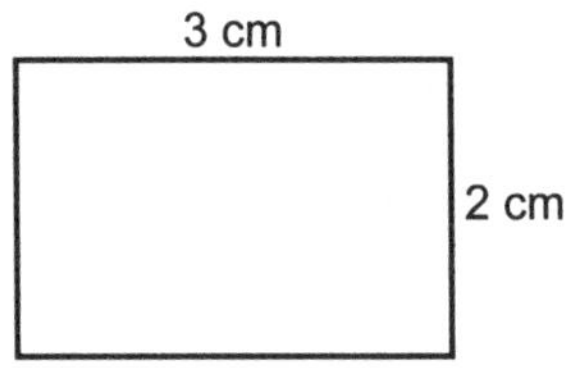

Area = ______ cm²

b)

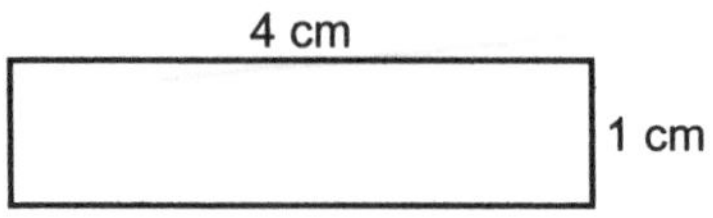

Area = ______ cm²

c)

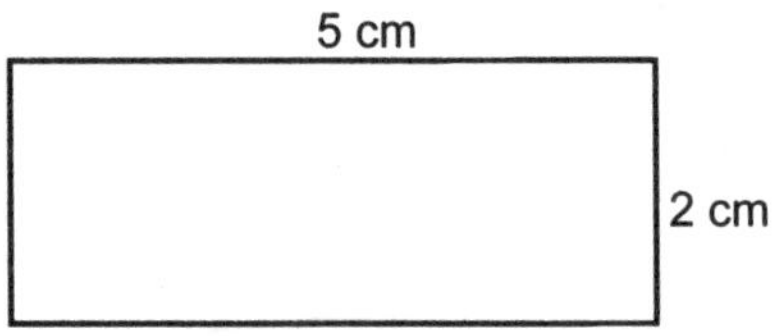

Area = ______ cm²

2. Find the area of the shaded triangle in square centimeters.

a)

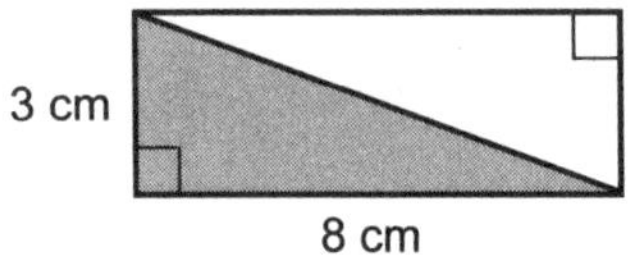

Area of rectangle = ______ cm²

Area of triangle = ______ cm²

b)

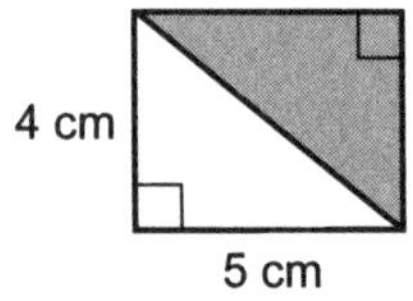

Area of rectangle = ______ cm²

Area of triangle = ______ cm²

3. Use the area of the first two triangles to find the area of the third triangle.

a)

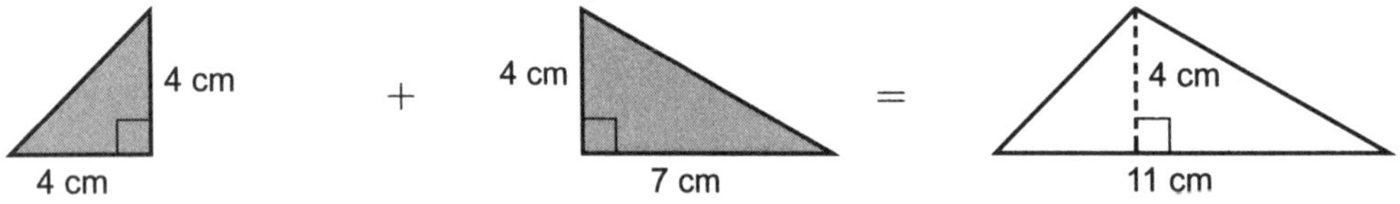

(4 × ______) ÷ 2 + (4 × ______) ÷ 2 = (4 × ______) ÷ 2 = ______ ÷ 2 = ______

So the area of the third triangle is ________.

b)

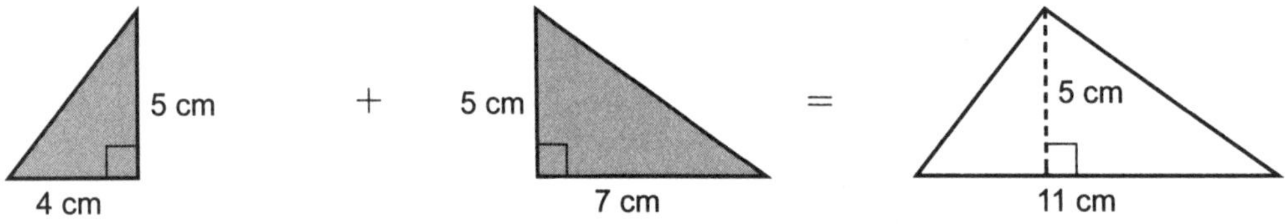

(5 × ______) ÷ 2 + (5 × ______) ÷ 2 = (5 × ______) ÷ 2 = ______ ÷ 2 = ______

So the area of the third triangle is ________.

c)

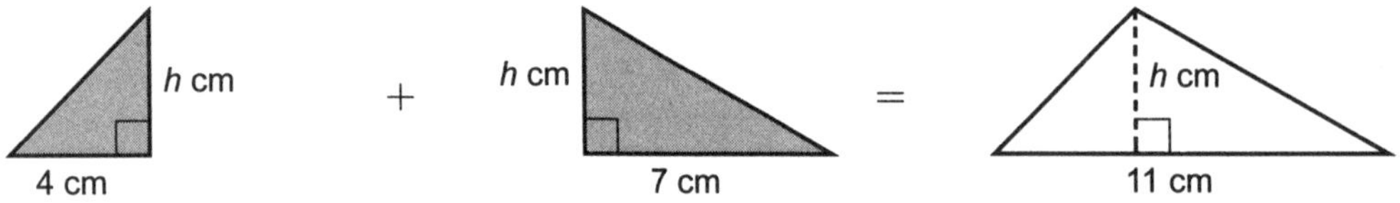

(h × ______) ÷ 2 + (h × ______) ÷ 2 = (h × ______) ÷ 2

So the area of the third triangle is ________________.

4. Use the area of the first two triangles to find the area of the third triangle.

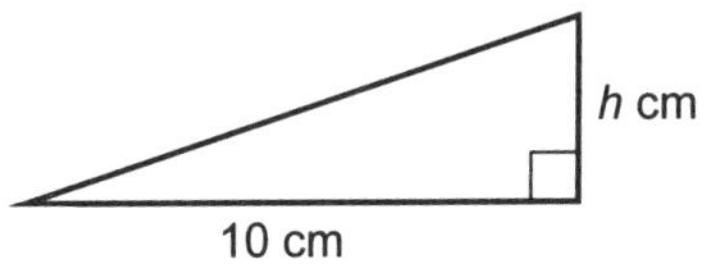

−

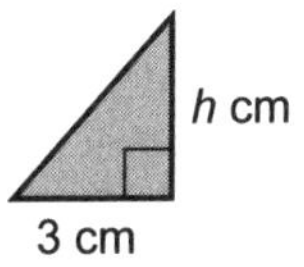

=

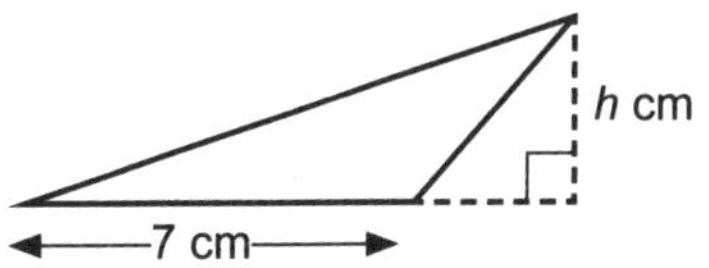

$(h \times \_\_\_\_\_) \div 2$ − $(h \times \_\_\_\_\_) \div 2$ = $(h \times \_\_\_\_\_) \div 2$

So the area of the third triangle is ________________.

To find the area of a triangle:

Step 1: Measure the length of any side. Both the side and its length are called the **base** of the triangle.

Step 2: Measure the distance from the base to the vertex opposite the base. The distance should be measured **perpendicular** (at a right angle) to the base. This distance is called the **height**.

Examples: In the triangles below, the thick side is the base. The arrow shows the height.

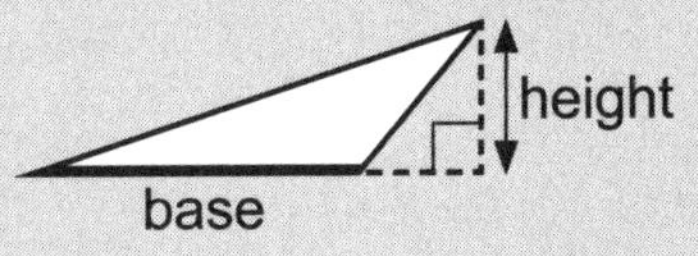

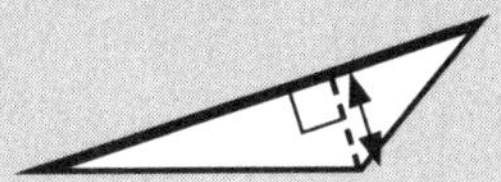

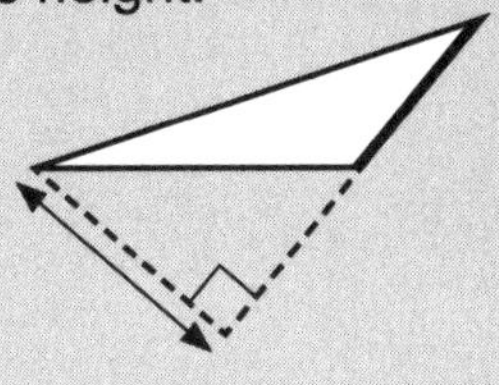

5. The thick side is the base. Circle the vertex that is opposite the base.

a) 

b) 

c) 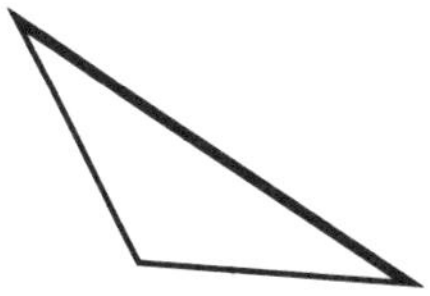

6. The thick side is the base. Draw the height. Hint: You may need to extend the base.

a) 

b) 

c) 

Step 3: Calculate the area of the triangle using:

Area = base × height ÷ 2 or $A = b \times h \div 2$

7. Find the area of the triangle.

a) 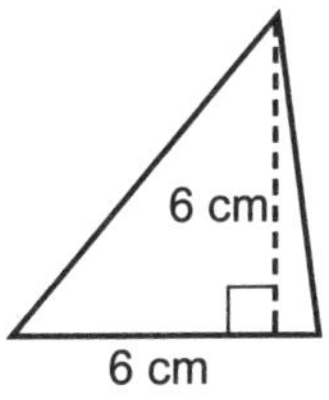

b) 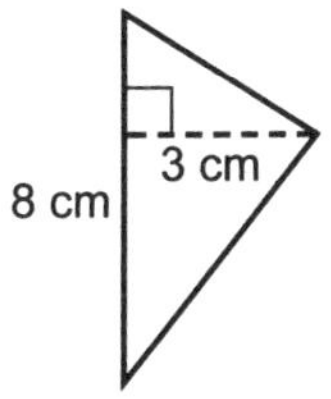

c) 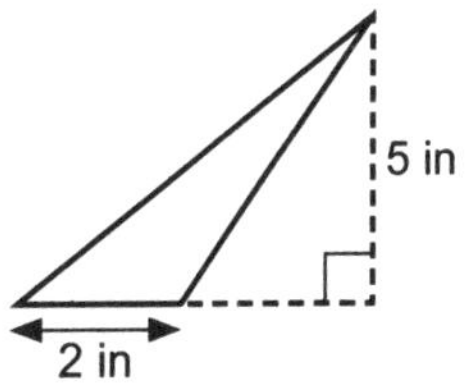

d) 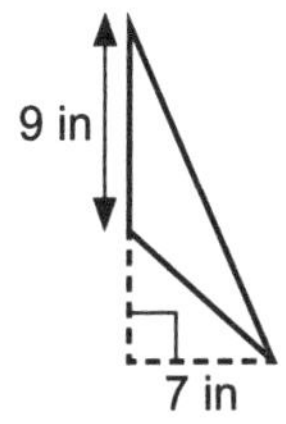

__________ __________ __________ __________

8. a) Find the area of the triangle in two ways, using different sides as the base.

i)

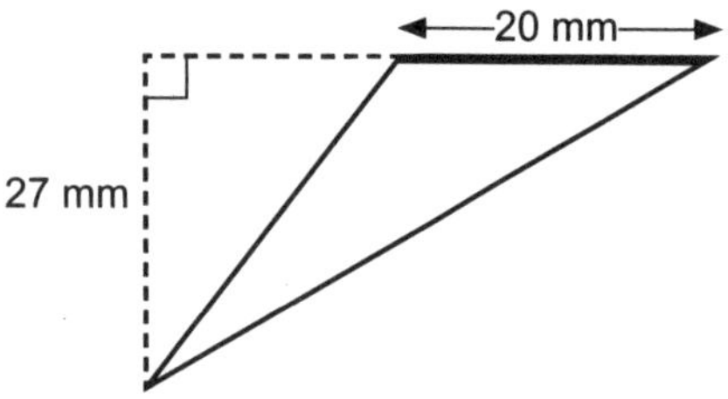

ii)

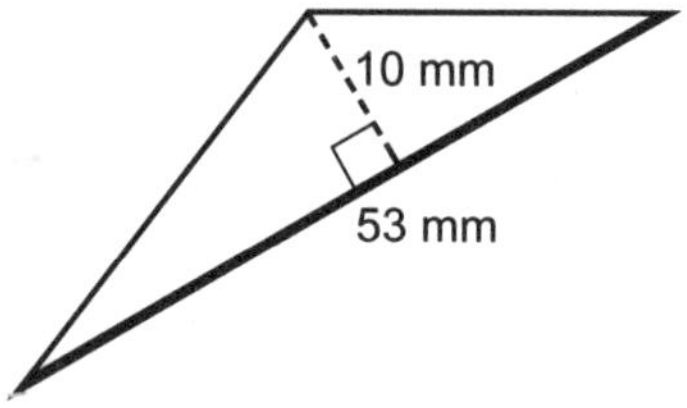

b) Did you get exactly the same answer both ways? __________

c) How far apart are the areas you found in part a)? __________

Show the difference in area measurements on the centimeter square.

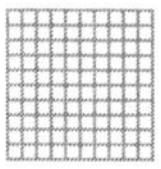

Is it a large difference or a small difference in measurement? ____________________

9. Find the area in two ways to make an equation. Then solve for *x* to the nearest millimeter.

a)

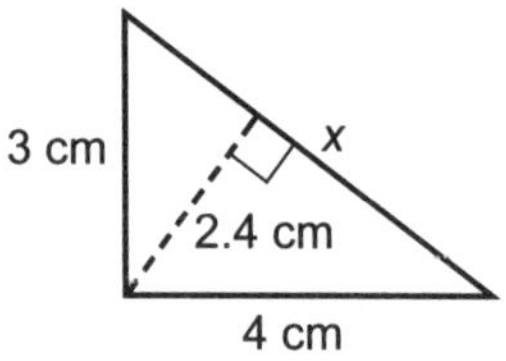

b)

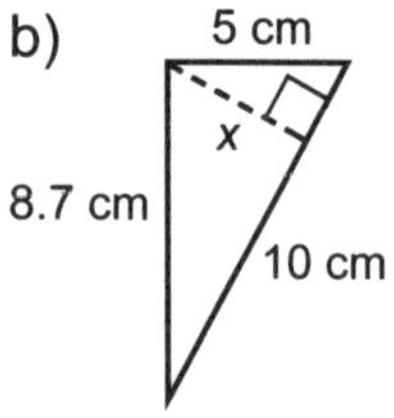

c)

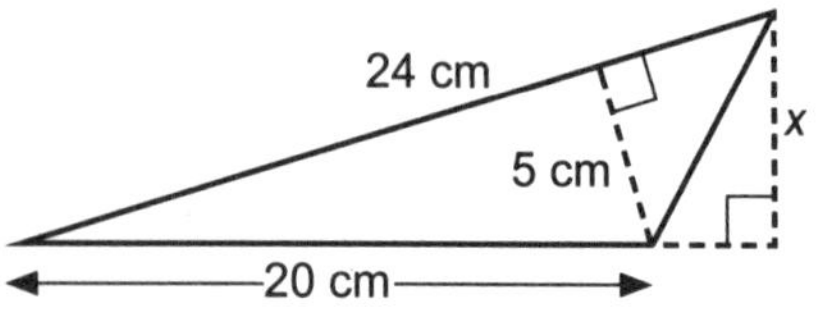

d)

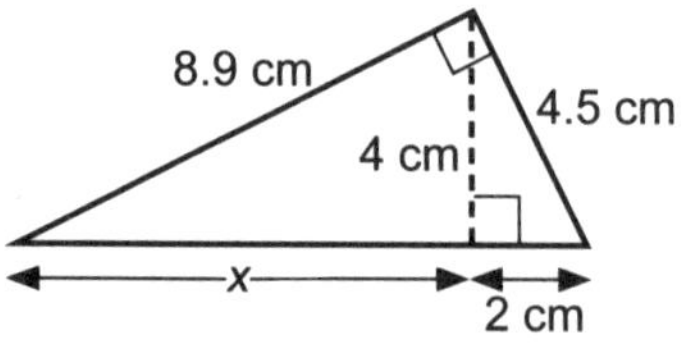

10. The area is 18 ft^2. Find *x*.

a)

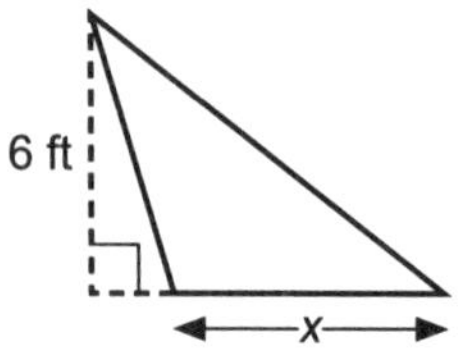

b)

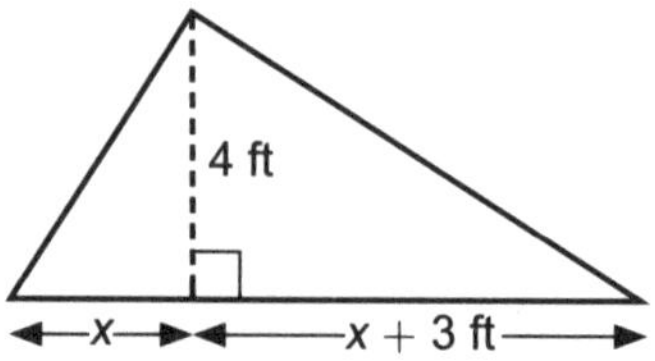

G7-15 Area of Parallelograms

Parallel lines are like the long, straight rails on a railroad track. Parallel lines:

- are straight
- are always the same distance apart
- point in the same two directions

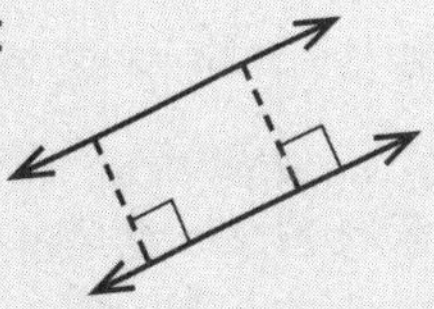

1. Measure the distance (in millimeters) between the lines from two different points. Make sure you measure the distances perpendicular to one of the lines. Are the lines parallel?

a) 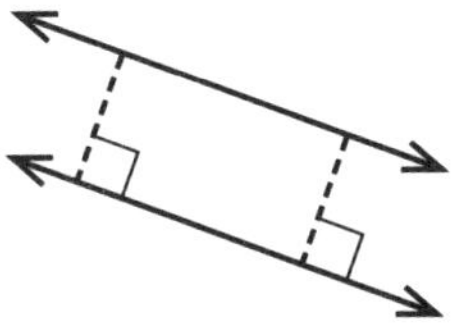 ________

b) 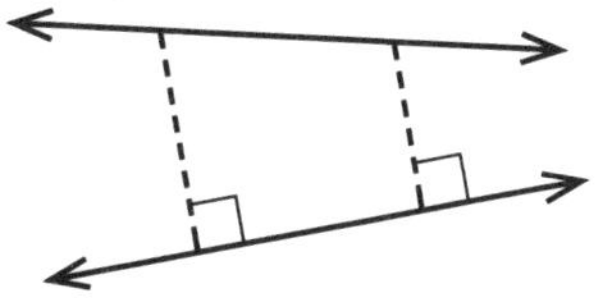 ________

c) 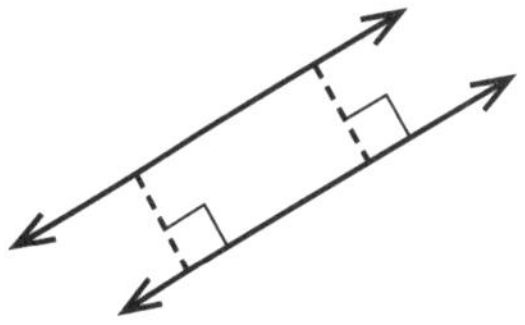 ________

A **parallelogram** is a quadrilateral with 2 pairs of parallel sides. The opposite sides of a parallelogram are equal.

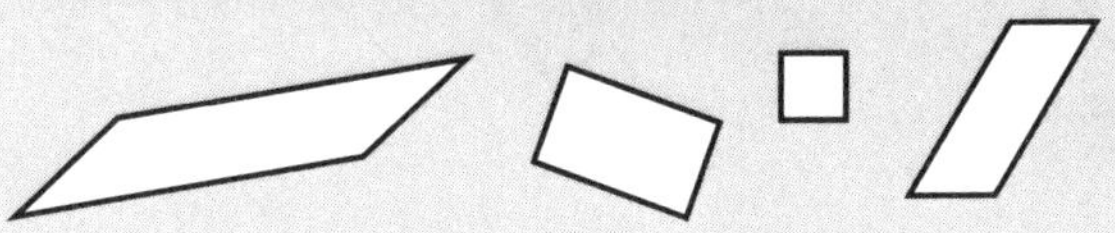

A **trapezoid** is a quadrilateral with only one pair of parallel sides.

2. Write "P" for parallelogram and "T" for trapezoid.

a) 

b) 

c) 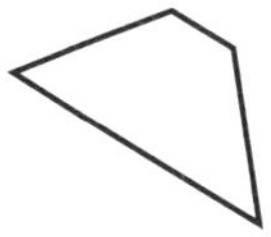

3. Find the area of the parallelogram. Include the units.

a) 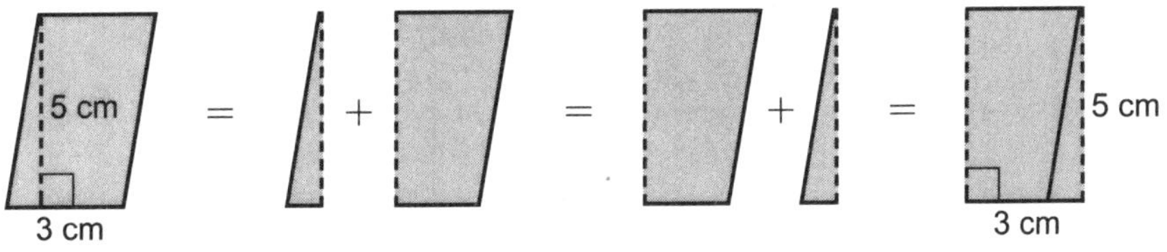

So the area of the parallelogram is ________.

b) 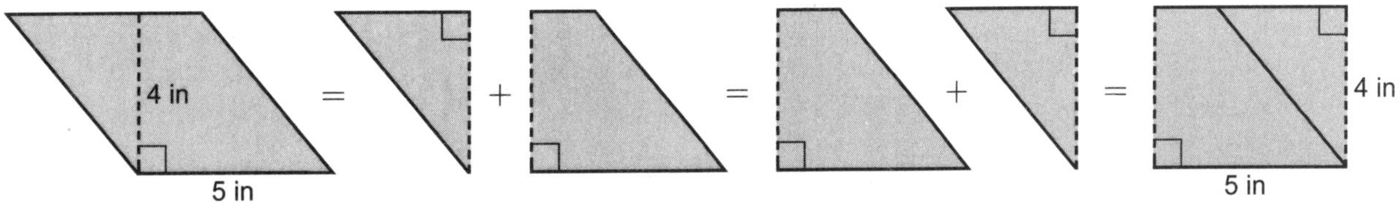

So the area of the parallelogram is ________.

The area (A) of a parallelogram is equal to

A = base (b) × height (h).

Any side of a parallelogram can be used as a base. The height is measured perpendicular to the base, from the opposite side.

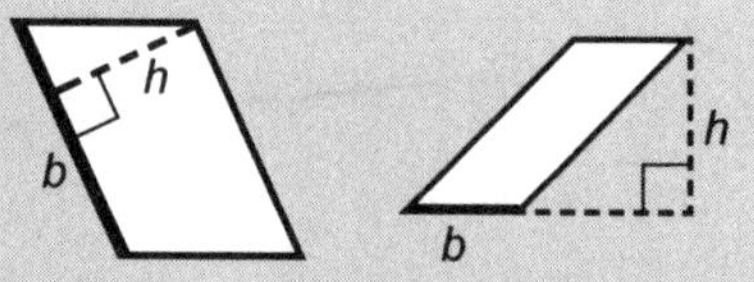

4. Find the area (A) of the parallelogram. Include the units.

a)

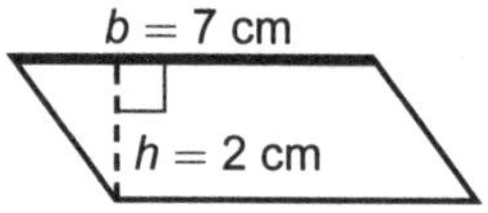

A = ________

b)

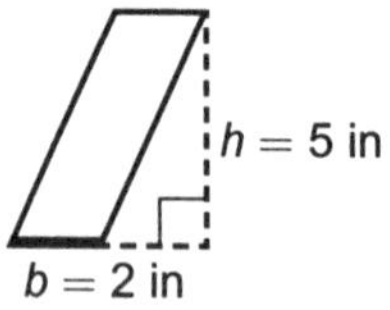

A = ________

c)

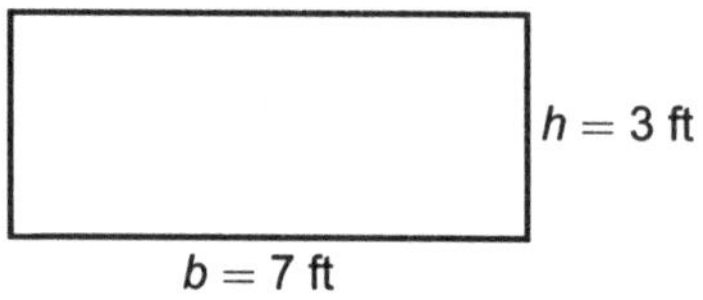

A = ________

5. Use different sides as the base to find the area in two ways.

a)

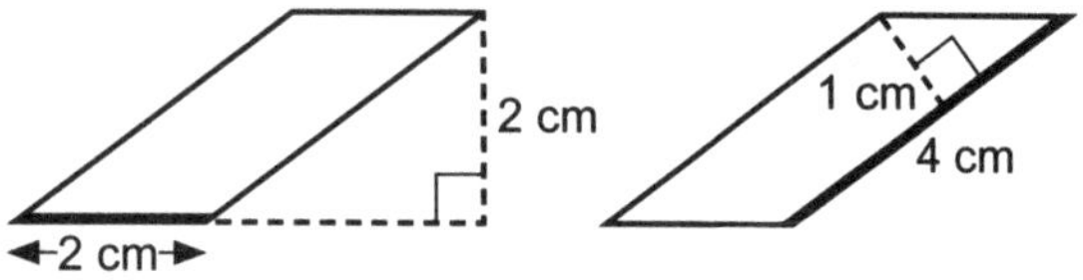

Area = ________________

Area = ________________

b)

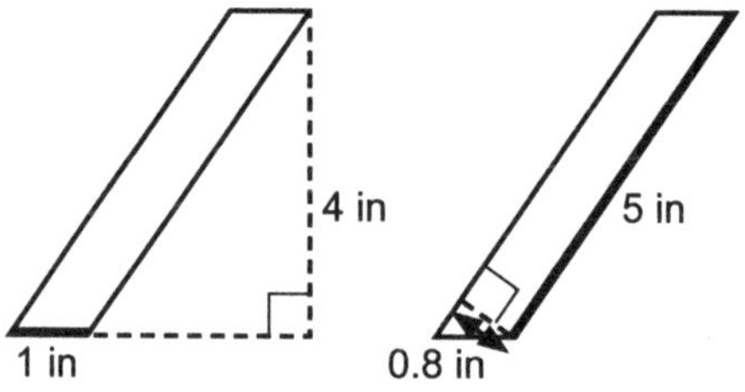

Area = ________________

Area = ________________

6. Find the area two ways to make an equation. Then solve for x. All measurements are in inches.

a)

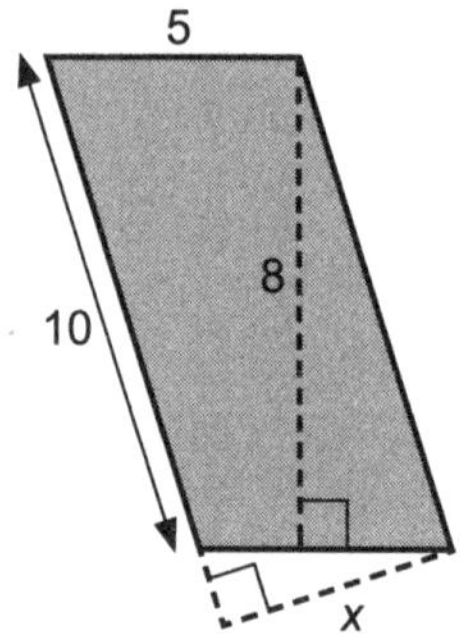

5(8) = 10x

10x = 40

x = 40 ÷ 10

x = 4 in

b)

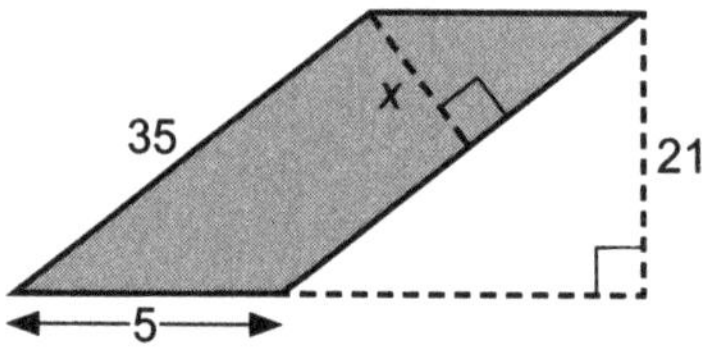

c)

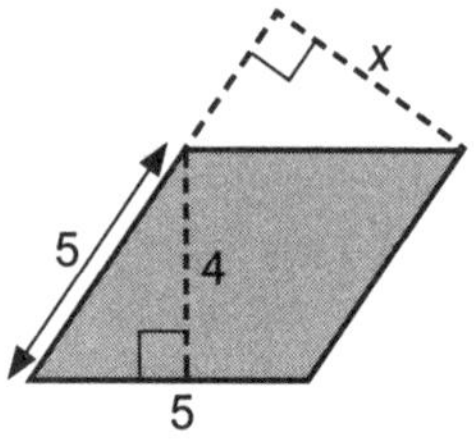

d)

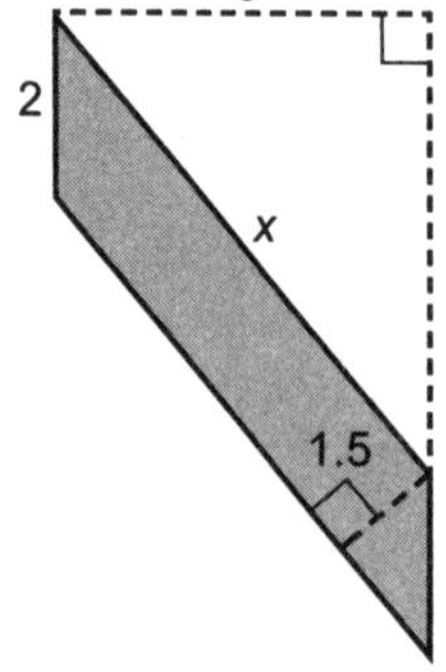

Area of Trapezoids

1. Draw an upside down copy of the trapezoid, as shown in part a), to create a parallelogram. Then fill in the blanks.

a)

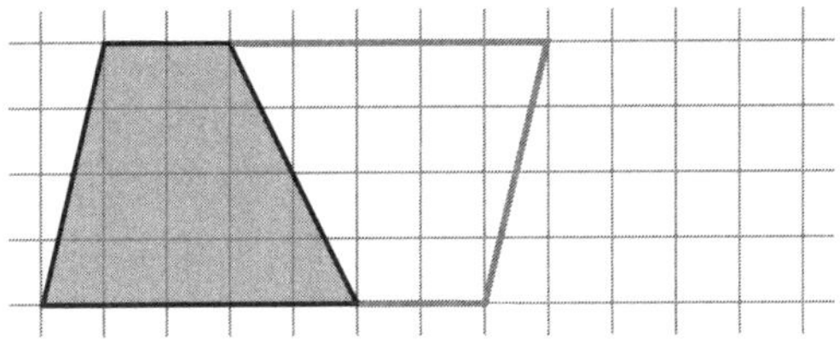

Base of parallelogram = 7 ← 5 + 2

Height of parallelogram = ______

Area of parallelogram = ______

Area of trapezoid = ______

b)

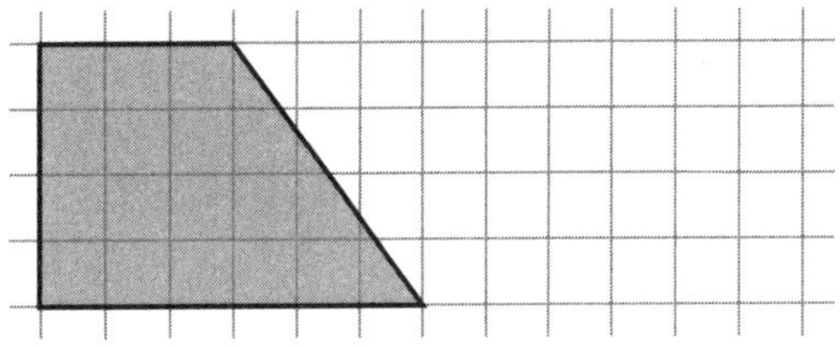

Base of rectangle = ______

Height of rectangle = ______

Area of rectangle = ______

Area of trapezoid = ______

In a trapezoid, the two parallel sides are the bases.
The height (h) is the perpendicular distance between them.

Area of trapezoid = $(b_1 + b_2) \times h \div 2$

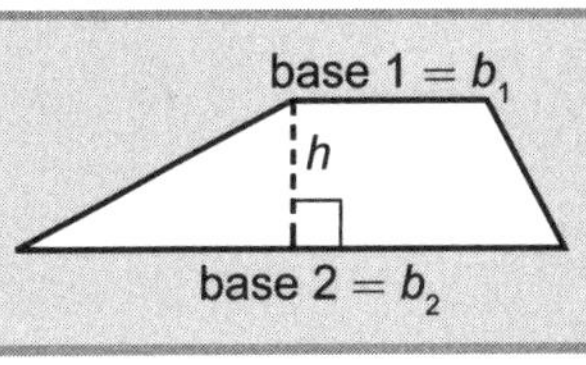

2. Use the formula to find the area of the trapezoid. All lengths are in inches.

a)

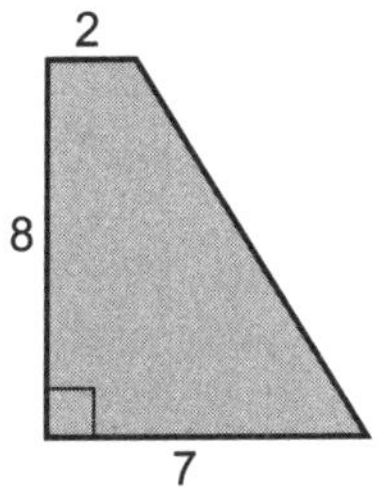

(2 + 7) × 8 ÷ 2

= 9 × 8 ÷ 2

= 72 ÷ 2

= 36

So area = 36 in²

b)

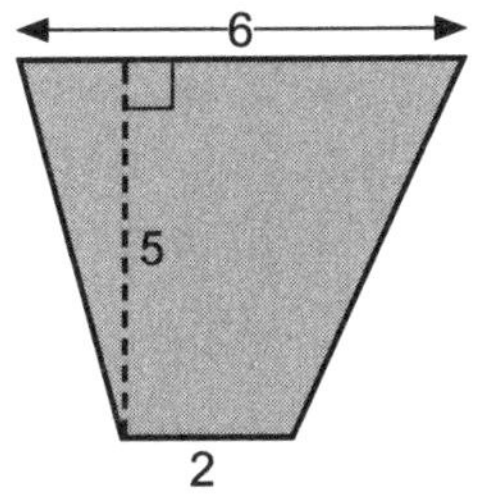

c)

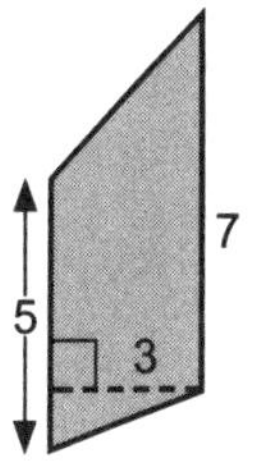

3. To find the area, circle the information in the diagram that you need and ignore the rest. All measurements are in centimeters

a)

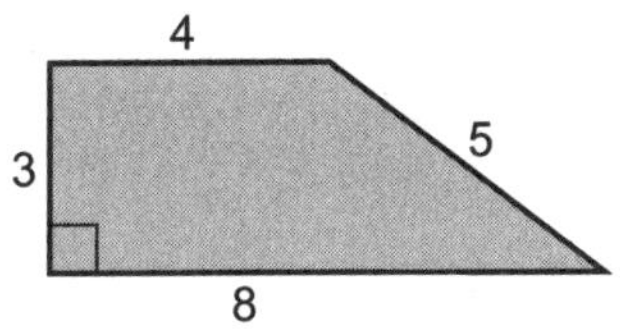

b)

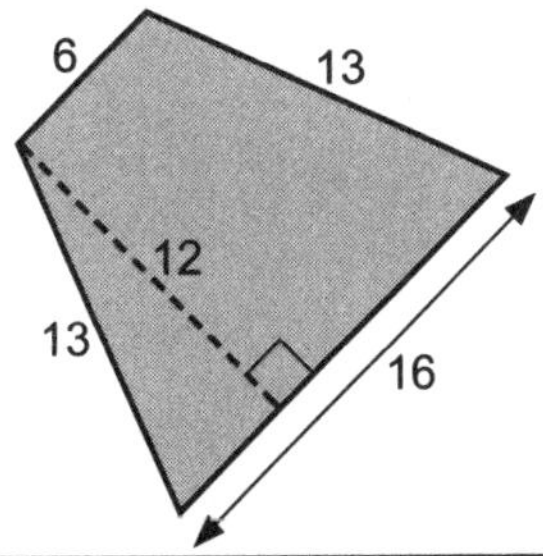

c)

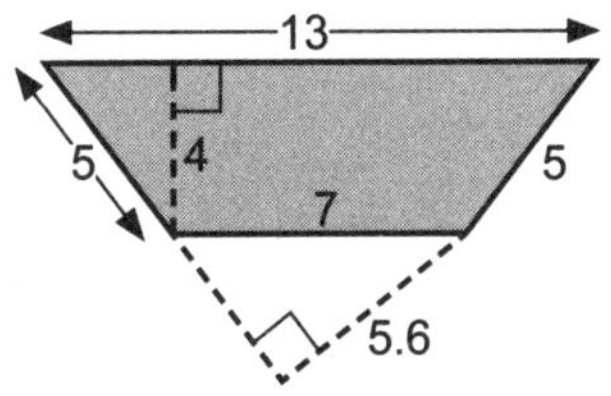

4. Find the area of the same trapezoid by …

a) adding two areas.

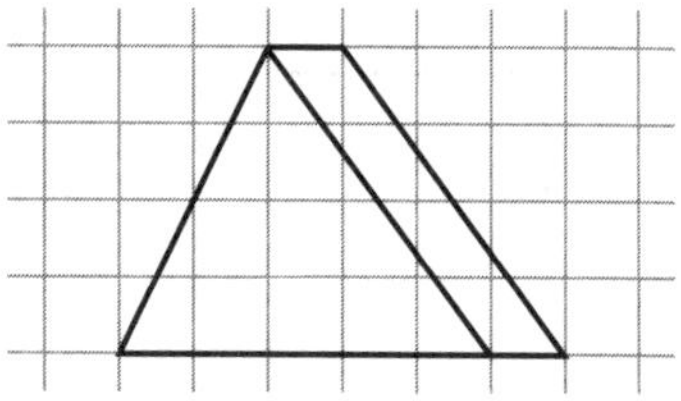

_____ + _____ = _____

b) adding three areas.

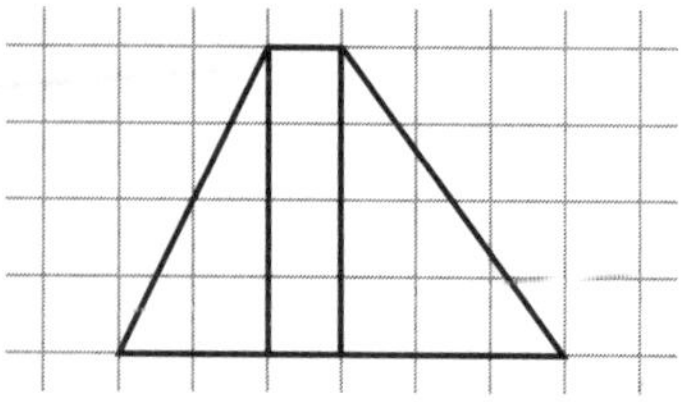

_____ + _____ + _____ = _____

c) using the formula for the area of a trapezoid.

5. Use the formula to find the area of the two trapezoids. Then find the area of the triangle.

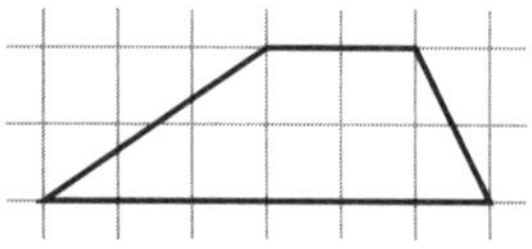

(____ + ____) × ____ ÷ 2

=

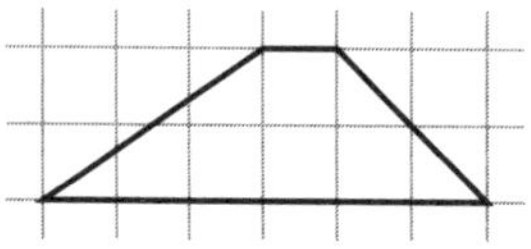

(____ + ____) × ____ ÷ 2

=

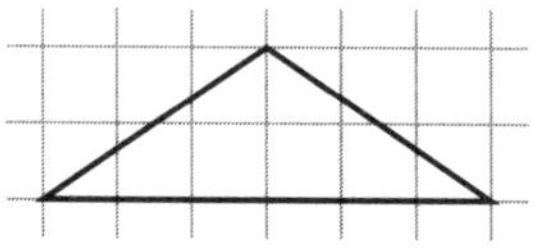

____ × ____ ÷ 2

=

Bonus ▶ Put $b_1 = 0$ into the formula for the area of a trapezoid. What formula do you get?

6. The area of the trapezoid is 30 in². Write an equation and solve for x. The first one is started for you.

a)

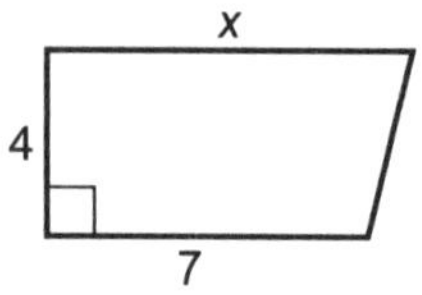

$4(7 + x) \div 2 = 30$

$4(7 + x) =$ _____

$7 + x =$ _____

$x =$ _____

b)

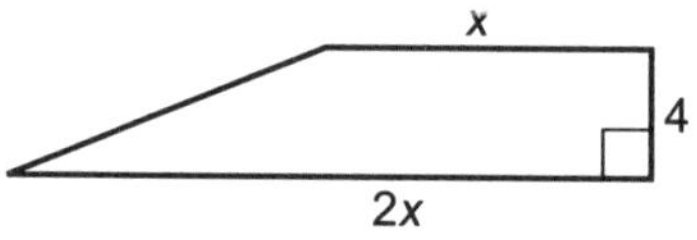

c)

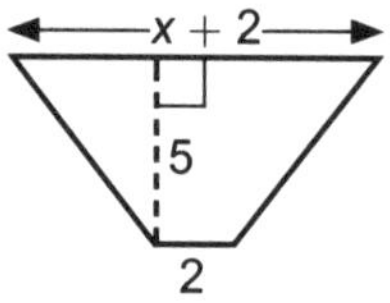

7. The area of the trapezoid must be at least 150 ft². What is the measure of x?

a)

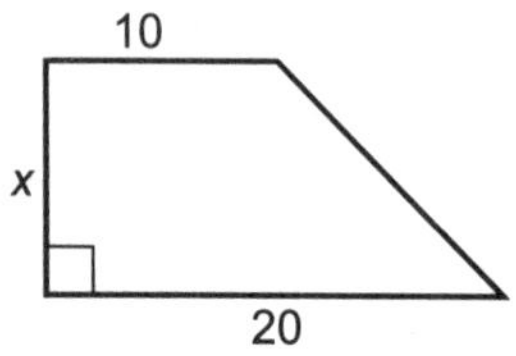

b)

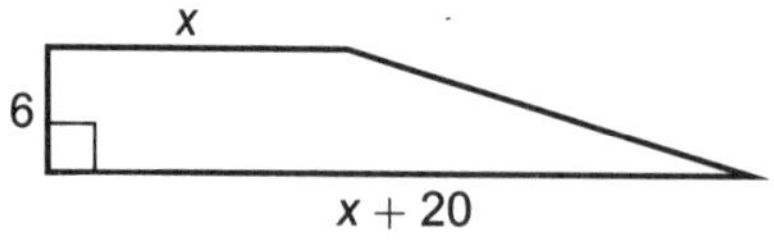

c)

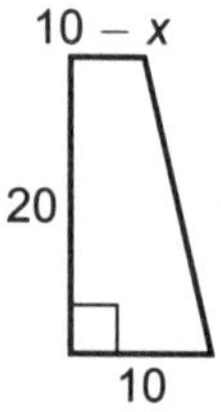

8. A train has 80 windows that are parallelograms with height 1 m and base 1.4 m. Glass costs $26 for each 1 m². How much will it cost to replace the glass in all 80 windows?

G7-17 Area of Composite Shapes

1. Find the missing side lengths. All measurements are in inches.

a) 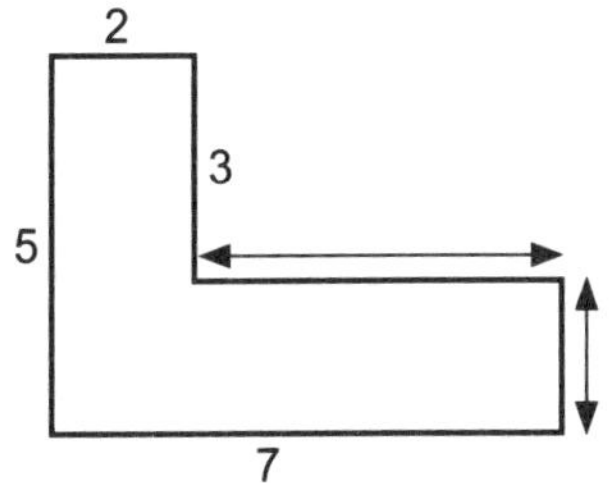

b) 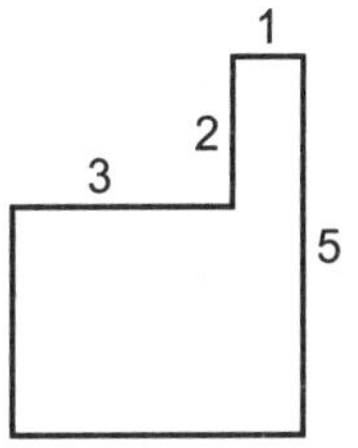

c) 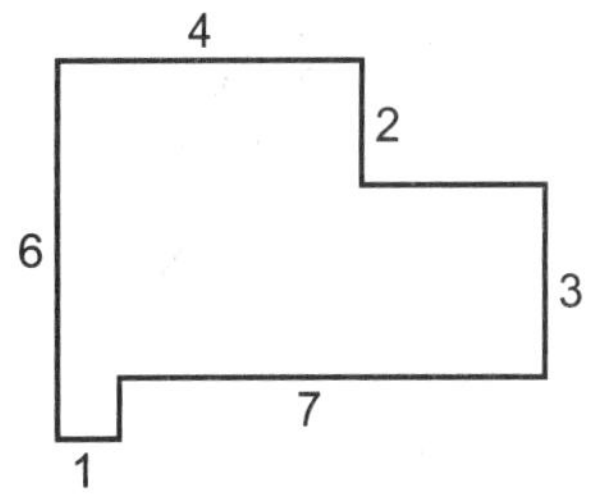

2. Break the shape into rectangles to find its area. All measurements are in feet.

a) 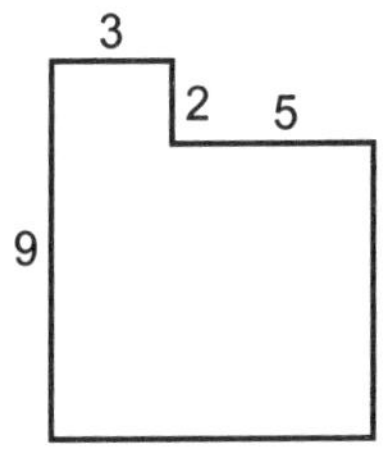

b) 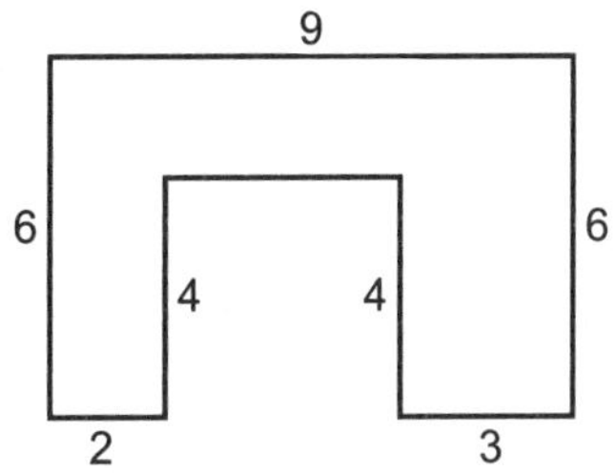

c) 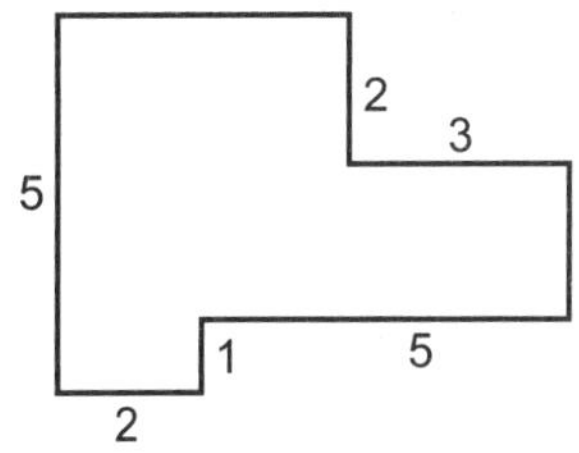

3. Find the area of the shape in Question 2.a) by subtracting the areas of one rectangle from another. Make sure you get the same answer.

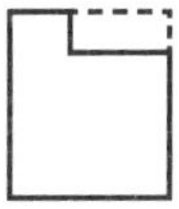

4. 1 cm = ______ mm, so 1 cm^2 = ______ mm^2.

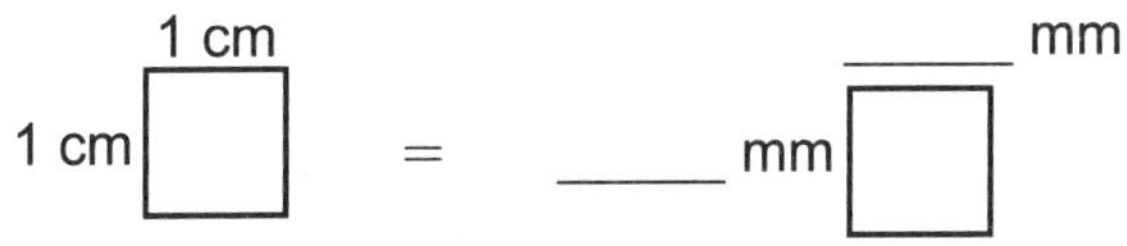

5. a) Find the area in two ways by …

i) changing all the measurements to centimeters.

ii) changing all the measurements to millimeters.

b) Did you get the same answer both ways? Explain how you know.

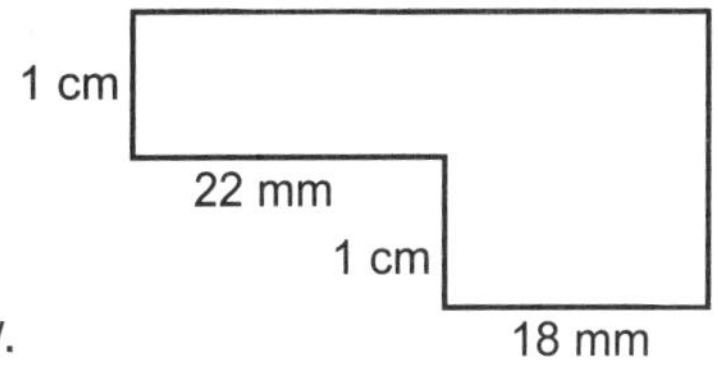

6. Find the area of the composite shapes. All measurements are in meters.

a) 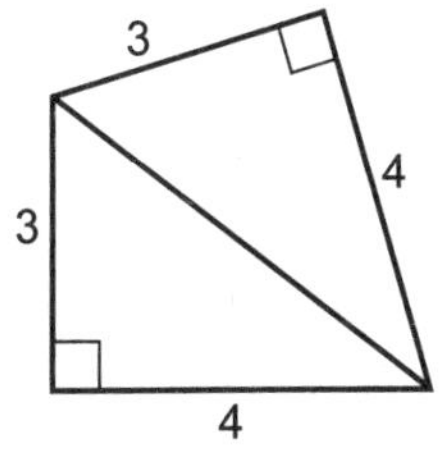

b) 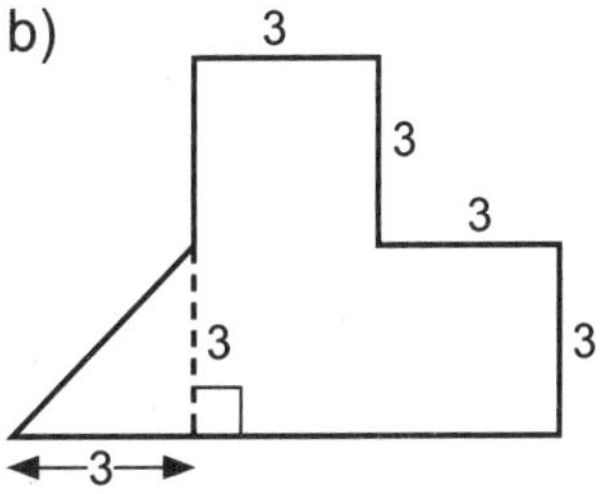

c) 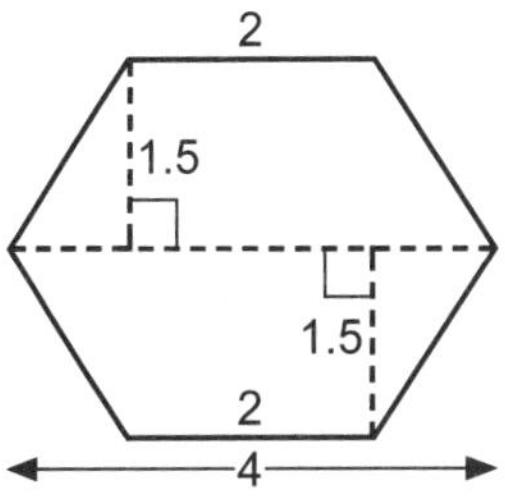

7. a) Find the total area of the figure in two ways by …

i) splitting the shape into two trapezoids.

ii) splitting the shape into a triangle and a rectangle.

b) Did you get the same answer both ways? If not, find your mistake.

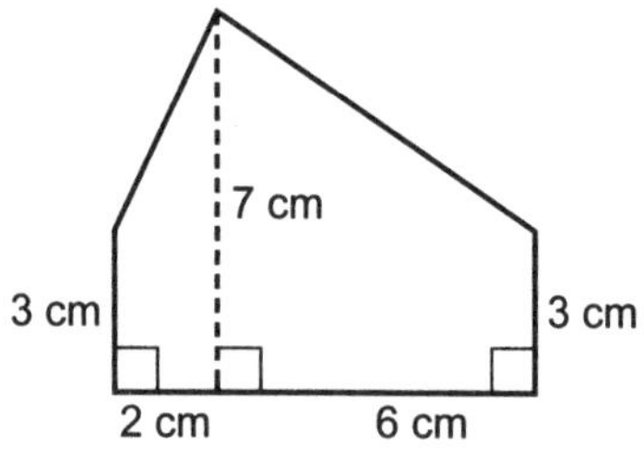

8. John is painting a mural of red crayons. He has a can of red paint that covers 350 square feet of wall. How many red crayons can he paint?

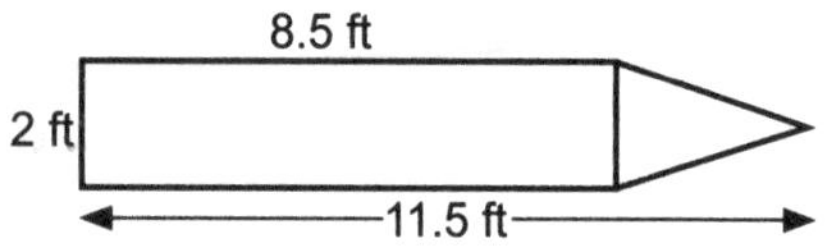

9. All measurements shown are in meters. The area of the shaded figure is 45 m^2. Evaluate x.

a)

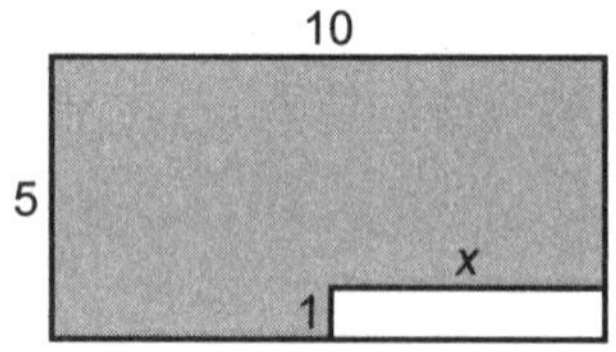

b)

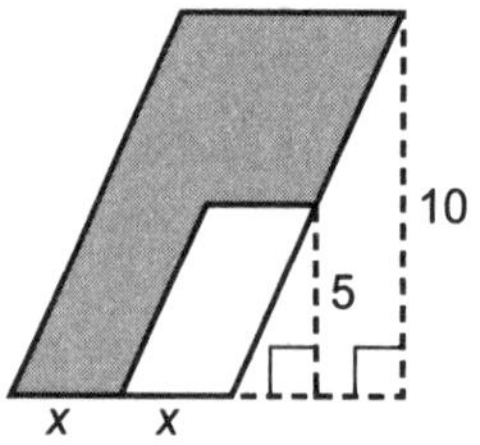

c)

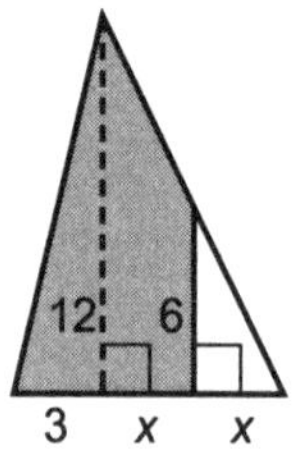

To find the total area of two overlapping shapes:

Step 1: Add the area of the two shapes.

Step 2: Subtract the area of the overlapping shape because you counted it twice.

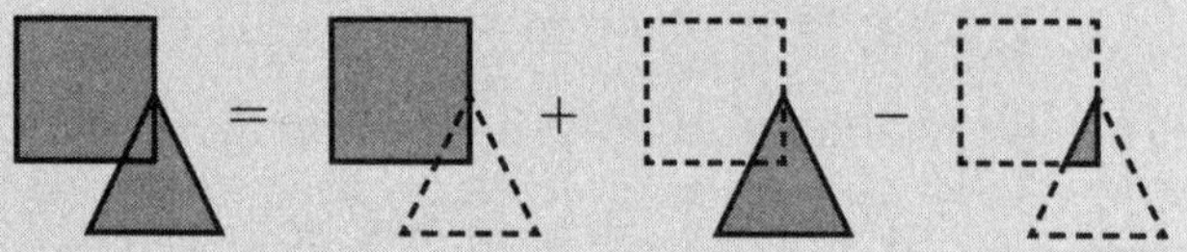

10. Find the total area. All measurements are in feet.

a)

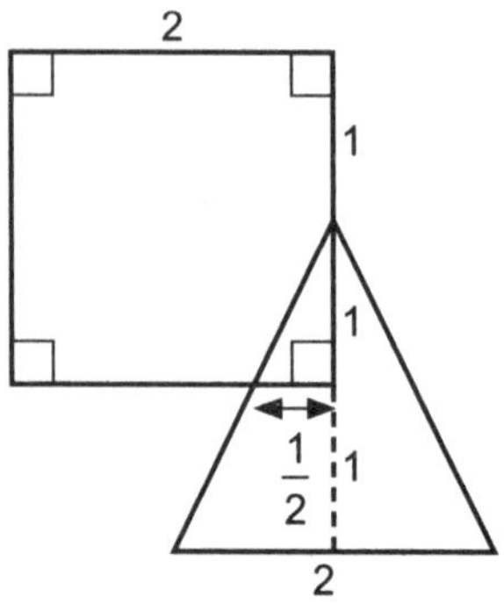

b)

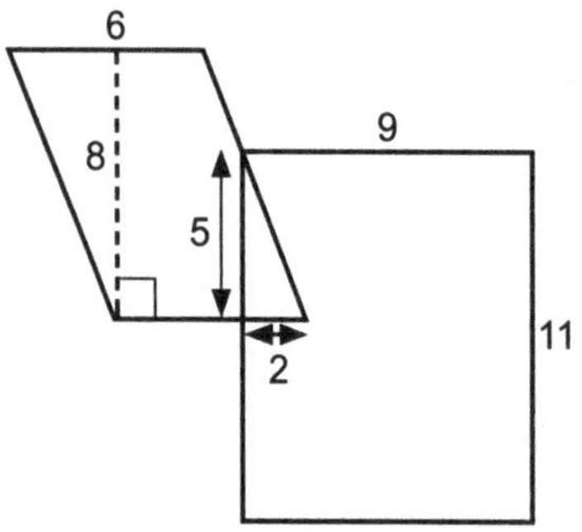

c)

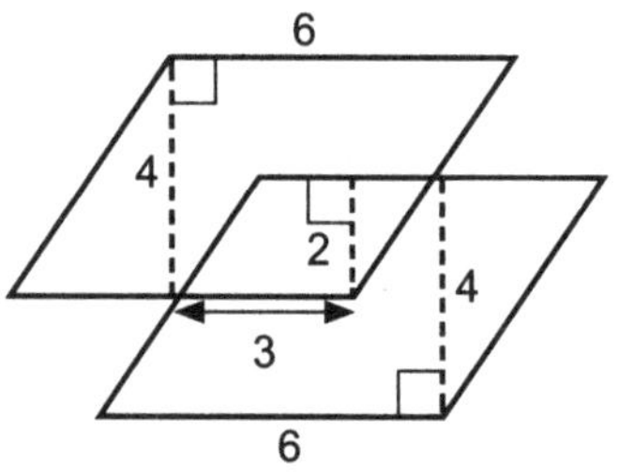

G7-18 Area of Scale Drawings

1. Make a scale drawing with the scale (original) : (new) = 1 : 2. Then find the area of both shapes.

a) 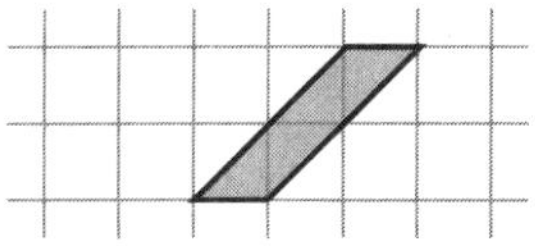

Area = ______

Scale drawing:

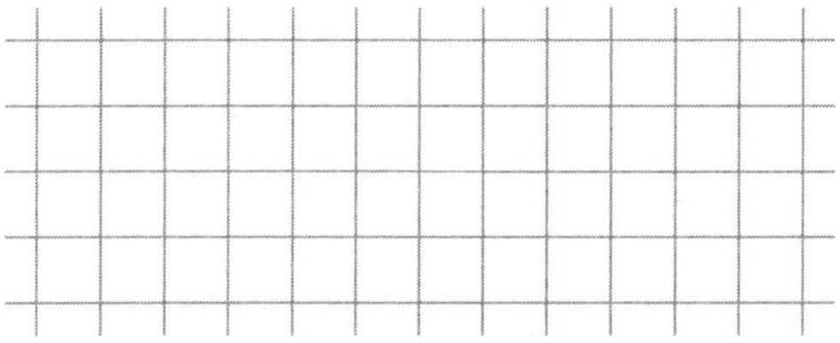

Area = ______

b) 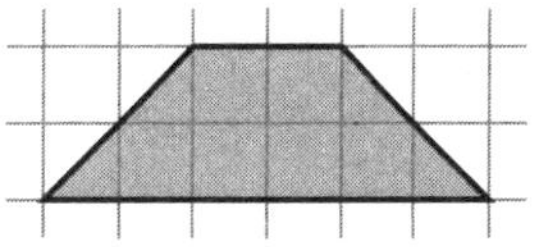

Area = ______

Scale drawing:

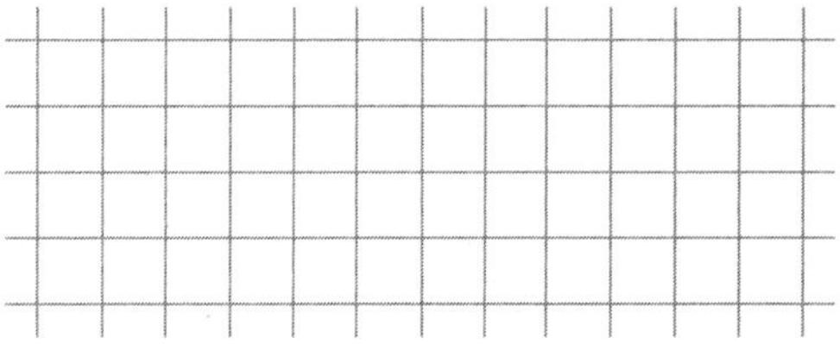

Area = ______

c) 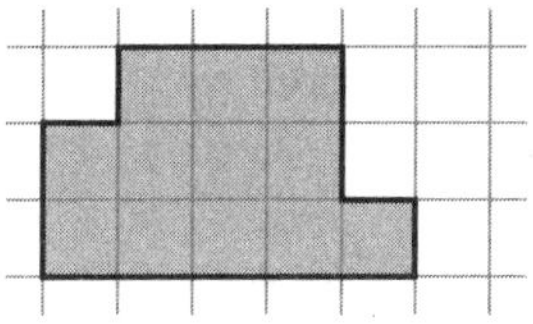

Area = ______

Scale drawing:

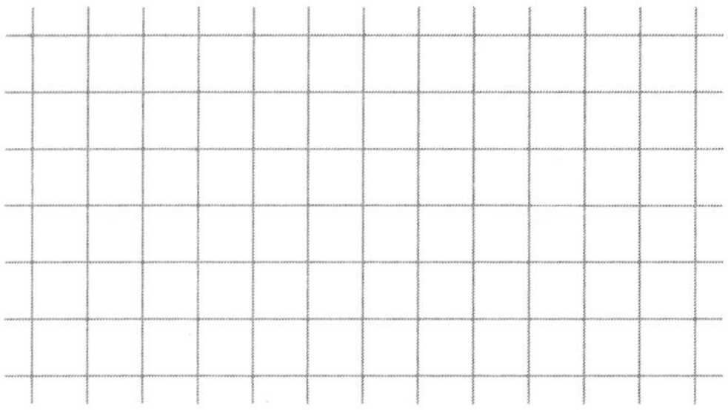

Area = ______

d) 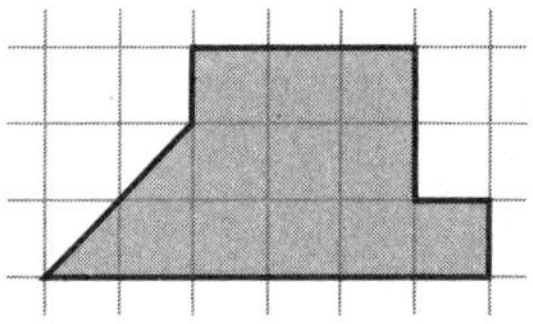

Area = ______

Scale drawing:

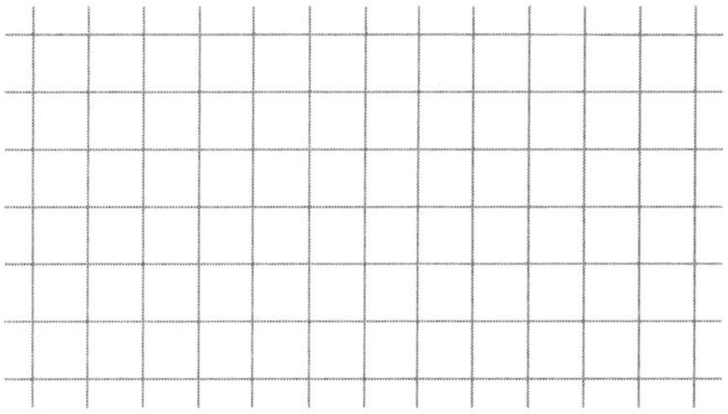

Area = ______

Bonus ▶ 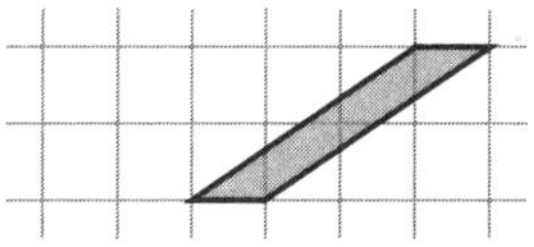

2. In Question 1, (area of scale drawing) = ______ × (area of original drawing).

3. a) Find the base and height of the scale drawings. Then calculate the areas.

Original triangle	(original) : (new) = 1 : 2	(original) : (new) = 1 : 3	(original) : (new) = 1 : 4
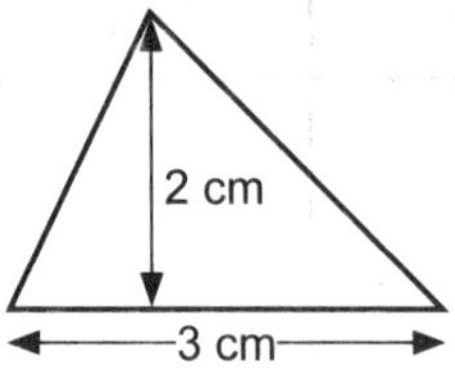 2 cm; 3 cm	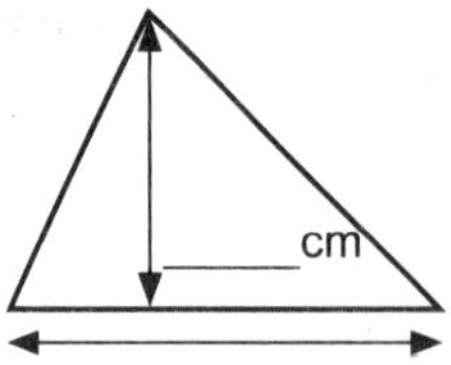 ______ cm; ______ cm	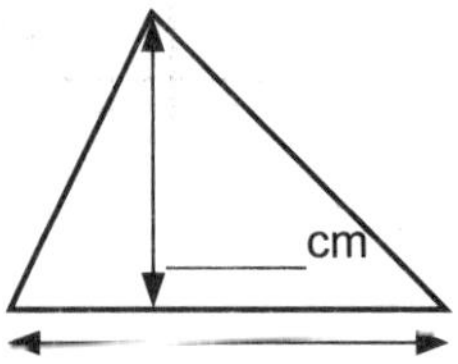 ______ cm; ______ cm	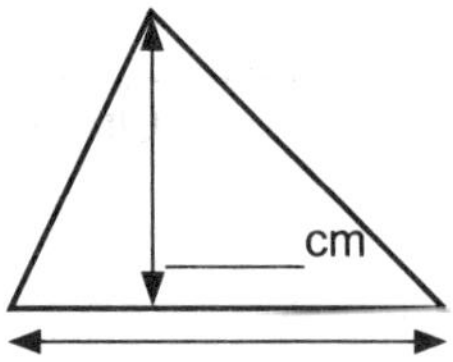 ______ cm; ______ cm
Area = 3 cm²	Area = ______ cm² = 3 cm² × ______	Area = ______ cm² = 3 cm² × ______	Area = ______ cm² = 3 cm² × ______

b) How can you get the area of a scale drawing if you know the scale and the area of the original drawing?

____

____

4. The area of a star is 8 cm². A scale drawing is drawn with the scale (original) : (new) = 1 : 3.

What is the area of the scale drawing? __________

5. a) 1 yard is 3 feet, so 1 yd² is ______ ft².

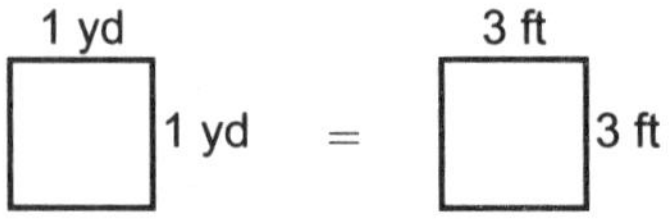

b) Use the floor plans to find the area of each room. Which room is bigger?

A.

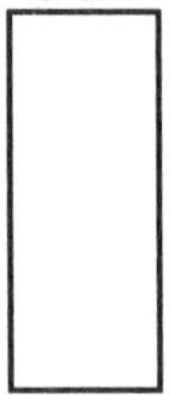

Scale: 1 cm = 2 ft

B.

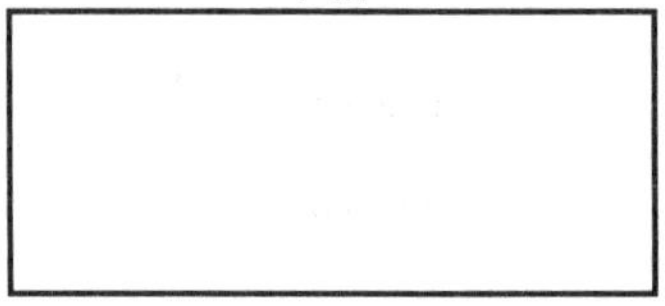

Scale: 1 in = 1 yd

6. The picture is a scale drawing of the state of Colorado with the scale 1 cm = 20 mi. Find the area of Colorado in two ways.

a) Find the area of the scale drawing, then use it to find the area of the actual state.

b) Find the actual length and width of the state, then use them to find its actual area. Did you get the same answer both ways? If not, find your mistake.

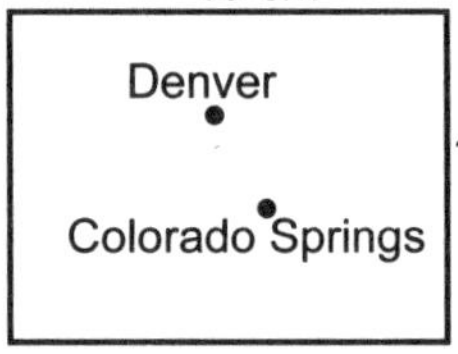

7. The original rectangle is shown. Find the length, width, and area of a rectangle drawn to the given scale.

		Length (cm)	Width (cm)	Area (cm^2)
a)	Original rectangle 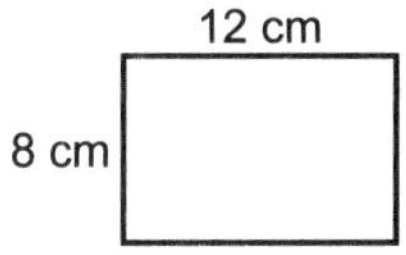	*12*	*8*	*96*
b)	(original) : (new) = 1 : 3			
c)	(original) : (new) = $1 : \frac{1}{2}$			
d)	(original) : (new) = $1 : \frac{1}{4}$			
e)	(original) : (new) = $1 : \frac{3}{4}$			

The area of a scale drawing with (original) : (new) = 1 : s is

A = (original area) × s^2 or A = (original area) × s × s

8. Use the formula to find the areas in Questions 7, parts b) to e). Make sure you get the same answers as in Question 7.

b) $96 \times 3 \times 3 =$

c) $96 \times \frac{1}{2} \times \frac{1}{2} =$

d) $96 \times \frac{1}{4} \times \frac{1}{4} =$

e) $96 \times \frac{3}{4} \times \frac{3}{4} =$

9. The area of a pentagon is 80 m^2. A scale drawing is drawn with the scale (original) : (new) = $1 : \frac{3}{4}$. What is the area of the drawing?

10. The area of a trapezoid is 60 cm^2. A scale drawing is drawn with the scale (original) : (new) = 5 : 2. What is the area of the drawing?

11. The area of a professional soccer field is 8,514 yd^2. A school soccer field is one third as long and one third as wide. What is the area of the school soccer field?

12. The area of an Olympic swimming pool is 1,250 m^2. A park has a swimming pool that is one fifth as long and one fifth as wide. What is the area of the park swimming pool?

G7-19 Circles

All points on a circle are the same distance from the **center** of the circle.

To construct a circle with center *O* and passing through point *P*, use a compass:

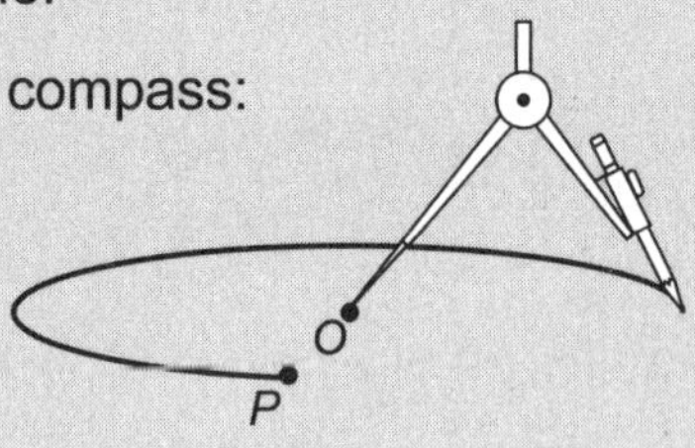

Step 1: Put the point of the compass at the center of the circle.

Step 2: Put the pencil of the compass at point *P*.

Step 3: Keeping the point at the center, and without changing the width of the compass, draw the circle.

1. Draw a circle with center *O* that passes through point *P*.

a)

b)

c)

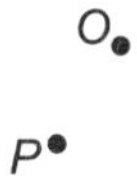

The **radius** of a circle is the distance of any point on the circle from the center.

To construct a circle with center *O* and radius 3 cm, use a compass:

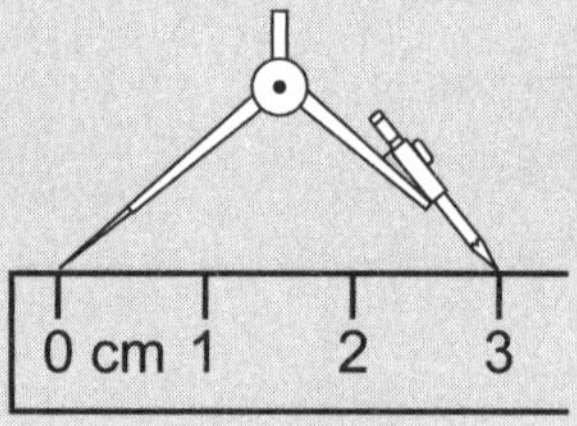

Step 1: Set the width of the compass to be 3 cm.

Step 2: Put the point of the compass on the center of the circle. Keep the width the same!

Step 3: Draw the circle.

2. Draw a circle with center *O* and given radius *r*.

a) $r = 2$ cm

b) $r = 15$ mm

c) $r = 25$ mm

The **diameter** of a circle is a line segment that passes through the center of the circle and joins two points on the circle. The length of the diameter is also called the diameter (d). The diameter is:

- the largest width across the circle.
- always double the radius (r), so $d = 2 \times r$.

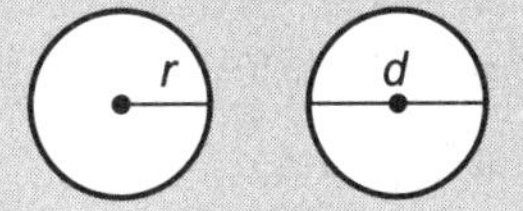

3. Which is given, the radius or the diameter? Find the measure that is not given.

a)
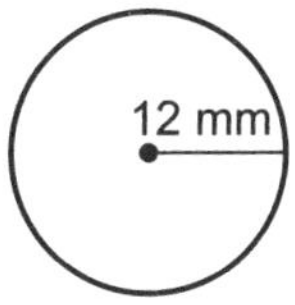

$r =$ ______ mm

$d =$ ______ mm

b)
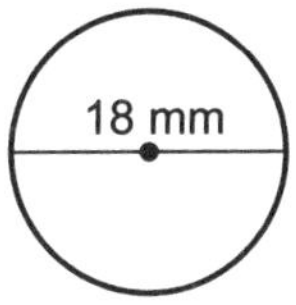

$r =$ ______ mm

$d =$ ______ mm

c)

$r =$ ______ mm

$d =$ ______ mm

4. Draw a line through the center of the circle. Measure the radius and the diameter.

a)
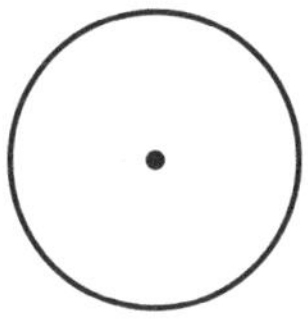

$r =$ ______ mm

$d =$ ______ mm

b)

$r =$ ______ mm

$d =$ ______ mm

c)

$r =$ ______ mm

$d =$ ______ mm

5. Use a ruler to find the point on the circle farthest from the given point. Then draw the diameter through those two points and find its length.

a)
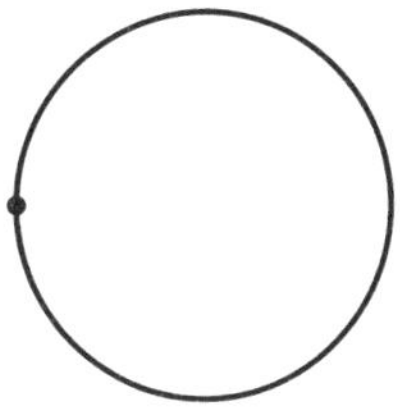

Diameter = ______ mm

b)
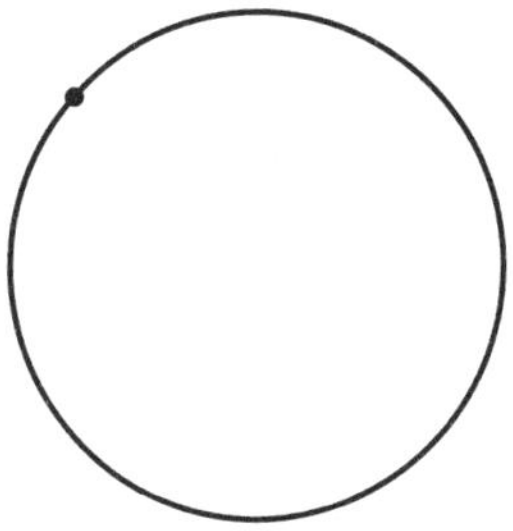

Diameter = ______ mm

c)
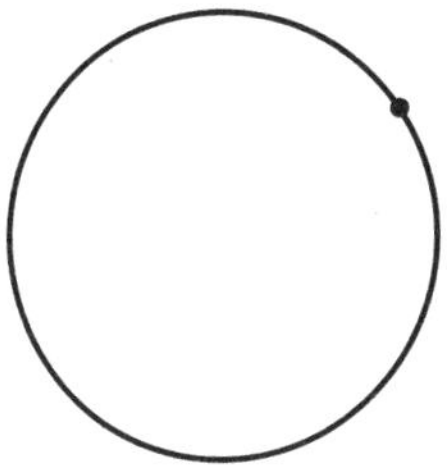

Diameter = ______ mm

6. a) For each circle in Question 5, draw another diameter. Measure the length of the new diameter. If you do not get the same length both times, find your mistake.

b) How can you tell where the center of the circle is?

7. Construct a circle with diameter 7 cm.

To draw a triangle with given side lengths 2 cm, 3 cm, and 4 cm:

Step 1: Draw the longest side horizontally. Label the endpoints.

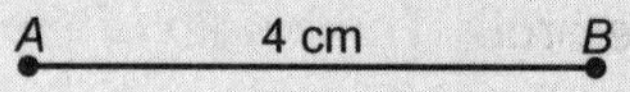

Step 2: Use a compass to draw a circle with radius 2 cm and center *A*.

Step 3: Use a compass to draw a circle with radius 3 cm and center *B*.

Any point of intersection of the two circles can be the third vertex of the triangle. Label it *C*.

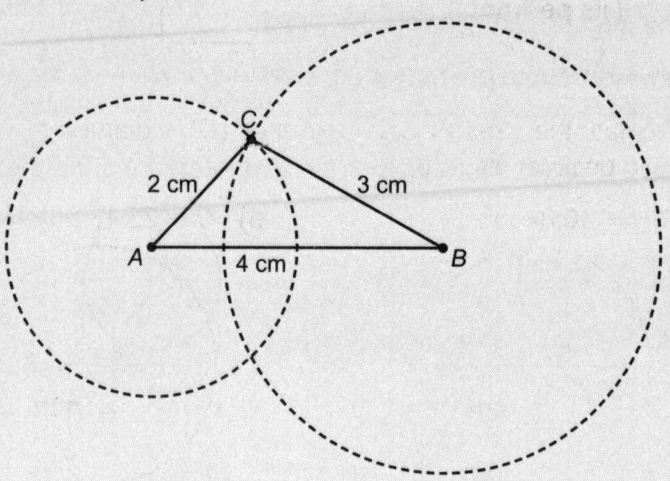

8. Draw a triangle with the given side lengths. The longest side is drawn for you.

a) 2 cm, 2 cm, 3 cm

3 cm

b) 3 cm, 3 cm, 4 cm

4 cm

c) 3 cm, 4 cm, 5 cm

Hint: You do not need to draw the whole circle.

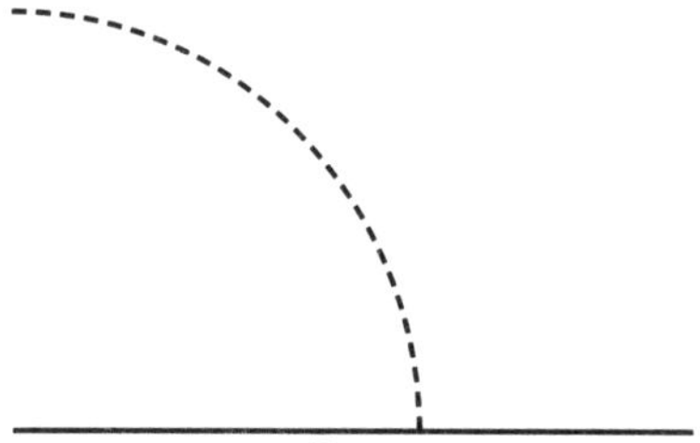

5 cm

d) 2 cm, 4 cm, 5 cm

5 cm

9. Try to use a compass to draw a triangle with sides 3 cm, 4 cm, and 7 cm. What happens?

G7-20 Circumference

The distance around a polygon is called its **perimeter**.

The distance around a circle is called its **circumference**.

1. Calculate the quotient circumference (C) $\div$ diameter (d). Round your answer to two decimal places.

a) $C = 16.34$ cm

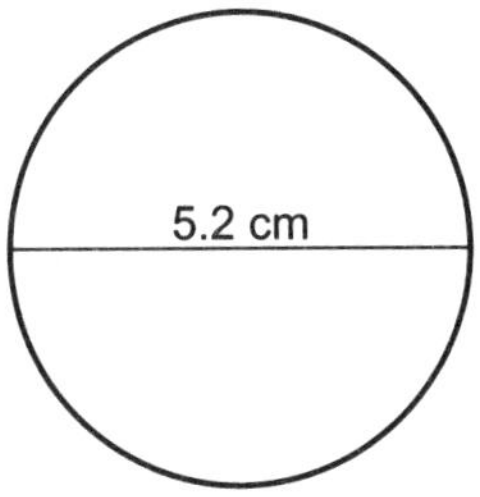

$C \div d =$ __________

b) $C = 25.13$ mi

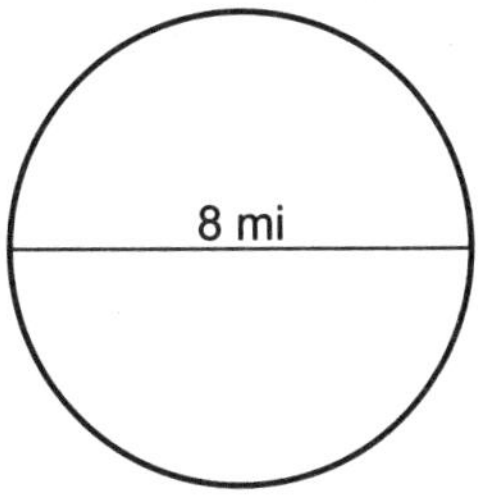

$C \div d =$ __________

c) $C = 56.55$ ft

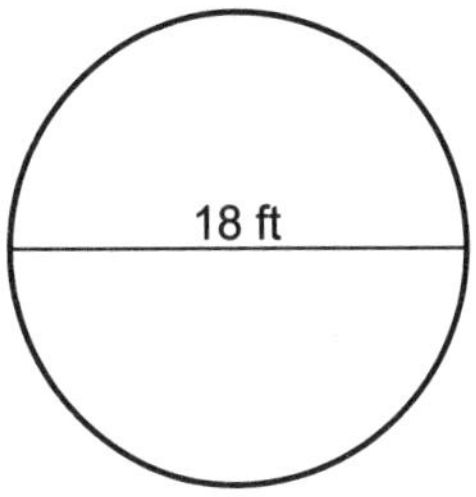

$C \div d =$ __________

d) $C = 8$ cm

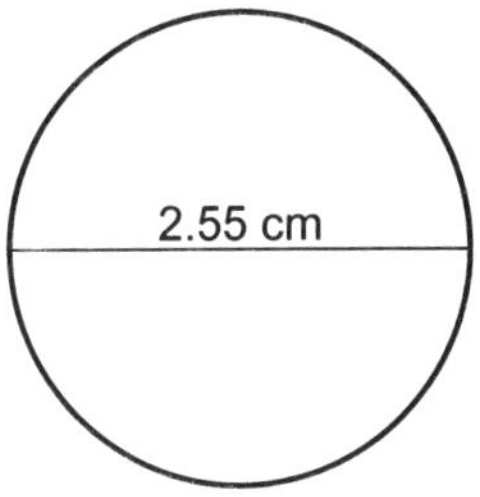

$C \div d =$ __________

e) $C = 13$ yd

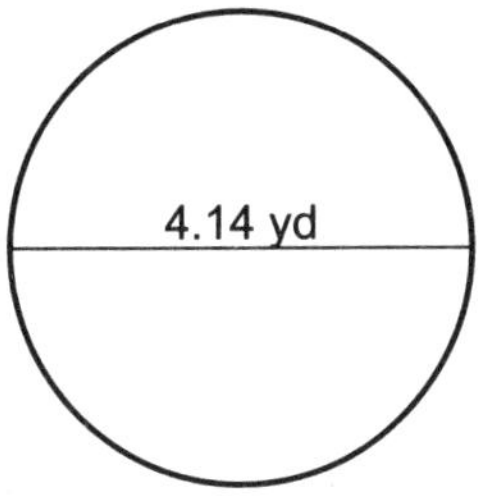

$C \div d =$ __________

Bonus ▶ $C = 94.25$ in

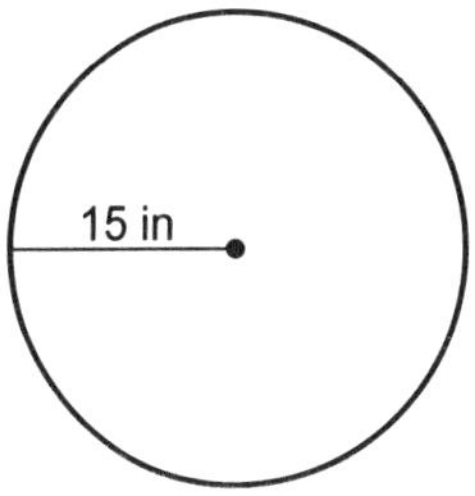

$C \div d =$ __________

2. What do you notice about your answers to Question 1? ______________________________

____

The quotient $C \div d$ is the same for all circles. Mathematicians give the quotient a special name:

$$\pi = C \div d$$

The symbol π is pronounced "pie." The number π has an infinite number of digits after the decimal point. To six decimal places,

$$\pi \approx 3.141593$$

3. Round π to the given decimal place.

a) $\pi \approx$ __________ (tenths)

b) $\pi \approx$ __________ (hundredths)

c) $\pi \approx$ __________ (thousandths)

d) $\pi \approx$ __________ (ten thousandths)

If you know the diameter (d) of a circle, you can find the circumference (C).

$$C = \pi \times d \text{ (or } C = \pi d\text{)}$$

You can use 3.14 for π to get a good approximation.

Example: If $d = 4$ inches, then use $C = \pi \times 4 \approx 12.57$.

So, $C \approx 12.57$ inches

4. Find the circumference of the circle with the given diameter. Include the units in your answer.

a)

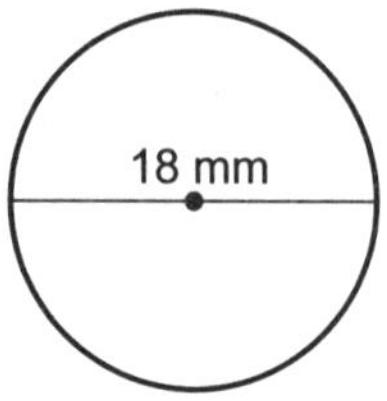

$C \approx$ *3.14 × 18*

$C \approx$ *56.52 mm*

b)

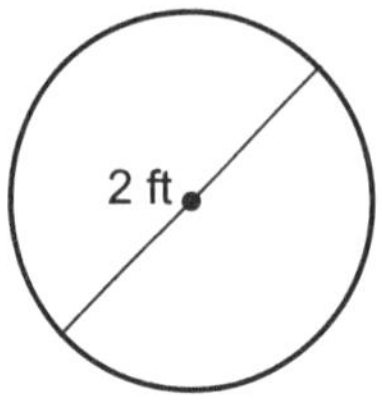

$C \approx$ ____________

$C \approx$ ____________

c)

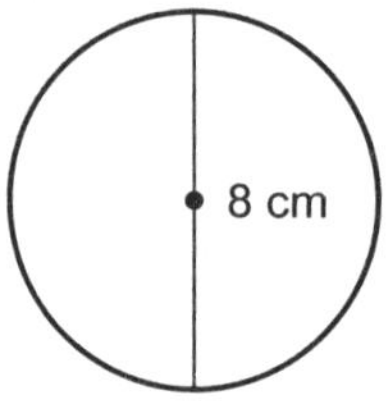

$C \approx$ ____________

$C \approx$ ____________

d)

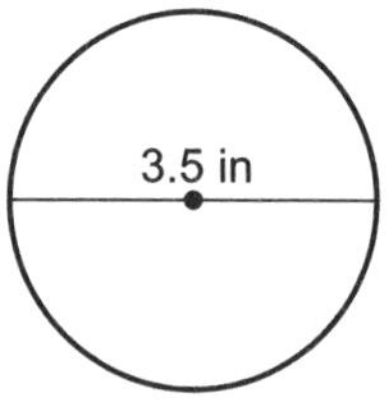

$C \approx$ ____________

$C \approx$ ____________

If you know the radius of a circle, you can find the circumference:

$$\begin{aligned} C &= \pi \times d \\ &= \pi \times 2 \times r \\ &= 2\pi r \end{aligned}$$

5. Find the circumference of the circle with the given radius. Include the units. Use 3.14 for π.

a)

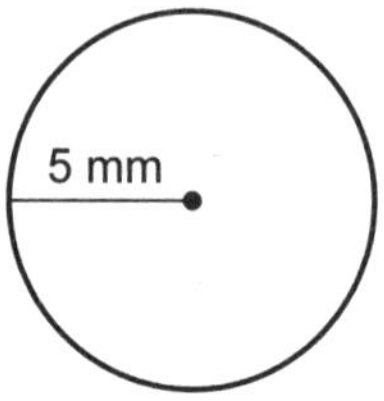

$C \approx$ ____________

$C \approx$ ____________

b)

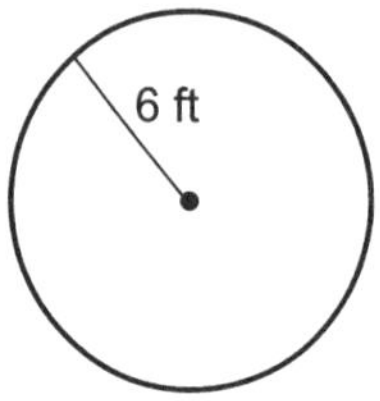

$C \approx$ ____________

$C \approx$ ____________

c)

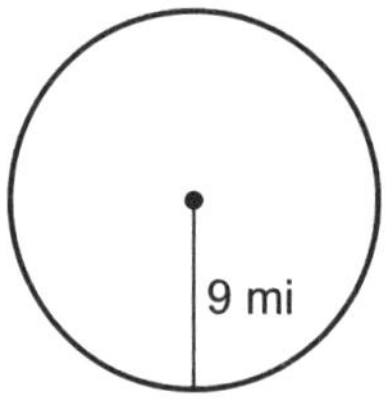

$C \approx$ ____________

$C \approx$ ____________

d)

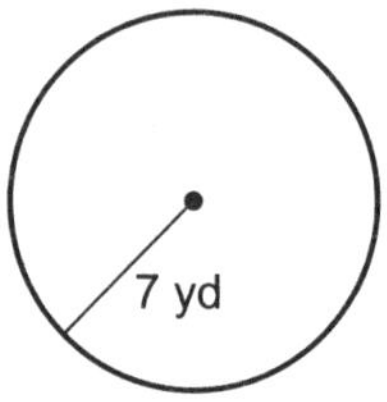

$C \approx$ ____________

$C \approx$ ____________

6. Write the formula you would use ($2\pi r$ or πd) to find the circumference of the circle.

a)

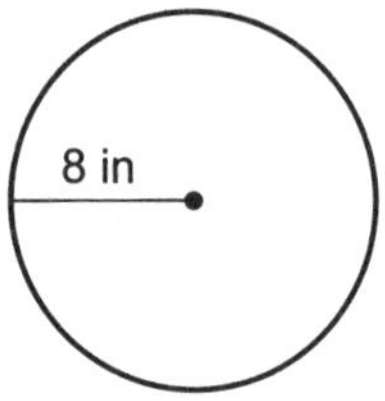

____

b)

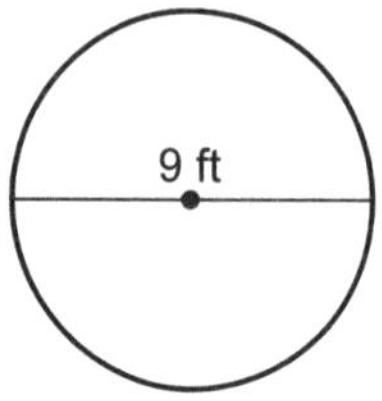

____

c)

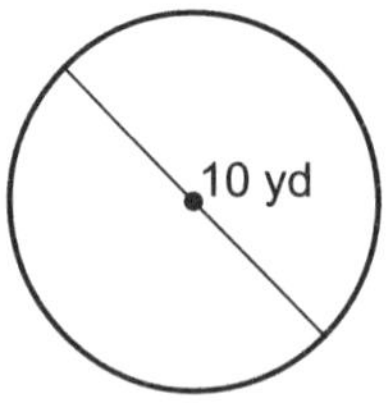

____

d)

____

7. Find the circumference. Include the units.

a) 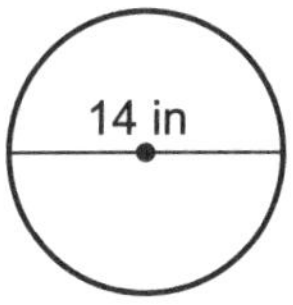

$C \approx$ ______________

b) 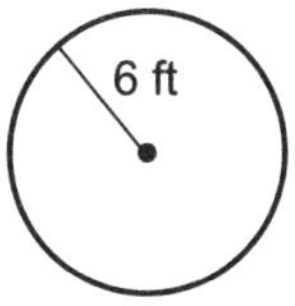

$C \approx$ ______________

c) 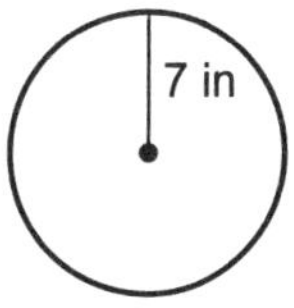

$C \approx$ ______________

d) 

$C \approx$ ______________

8. Which two parts of Question 7 have the same answer? Why is this the case?

If you can find the distance the whole way around the circle, then you can find the distance partway around the circle.

A full turn is 360°. So you can find what fraction of a turn has been made by deciding what fraction of 360° the turn has covered.

9. What fraction of the circumference is thick? Write your answer in lowest terms.

a) 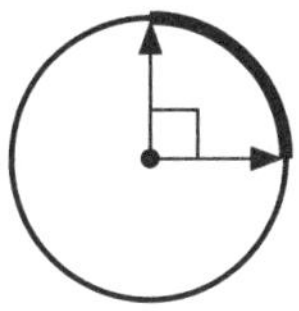

$\frac{90^\circ}{360^\circ} = \frac{1}{4}$

b) 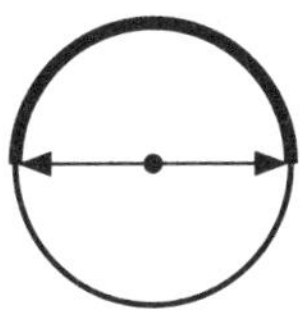

c) 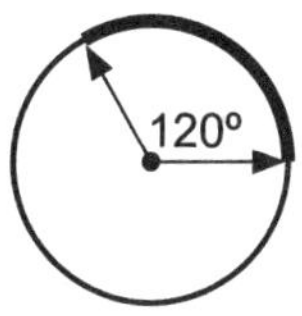

d) 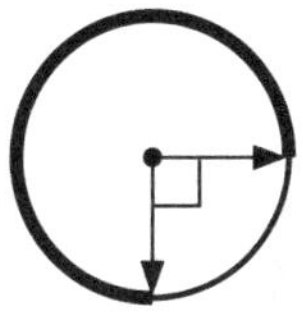

10. Each circle in Question 9 has diameter 2 inches.

a) Find the circumference of each circle in Question 9.

b) Use the fraction of the circumference covered to find the length of the thick part of the circle.

11. Find the distance (D) around the shape.

a) 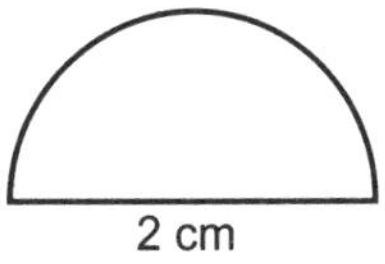

$2 + \frac{1}{2}\pi d = 2 + \frac{1}{2}\pi(2)$

$= 2 + \pi$, so $D \approx 5.14$ cm.

b) 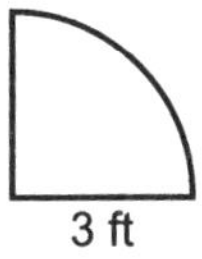

c) 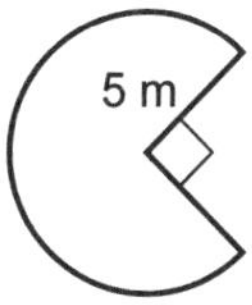

d) 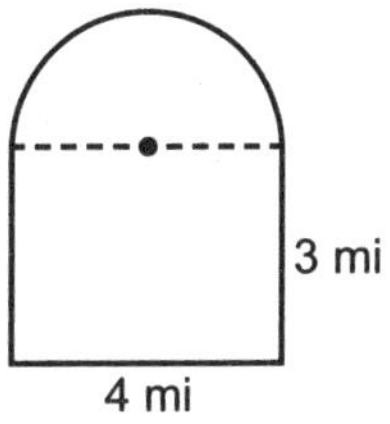

G7-21 Area of Circles

The area A of a circle with radius r is $A = \pi r^2$. Use 3.14 for π.

1. Find the area of the circle with the given radius.

a) 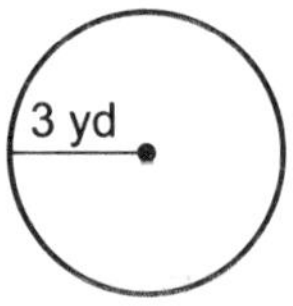

$A \approx$ ____________

$A \approx$ ____________

b) 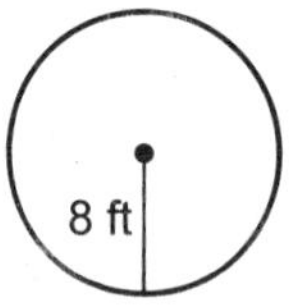

$A \approx$ ____________

$A \approx$ ____________

c) 

$A \approx$ ____________

$A \approx$ ____________

d) 

$A \approx$ ____________

$A \approx$ ____________

2. Find the radius of the circle. Then find the area.

a) 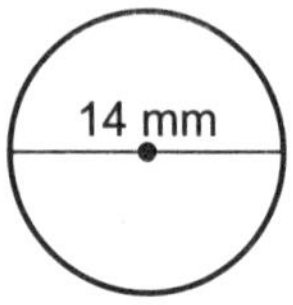

$r =$ *7 mm*

$A \approx$ $(3.14)(7)^2$

$A \approx$ *153.86 mm²*

b) 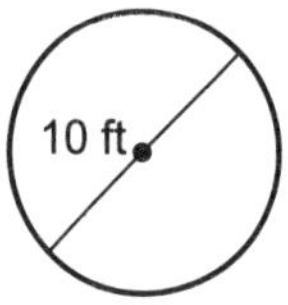

$r =$ ____________

$A \approx$ ____________

$A \approx$ ____________

c) 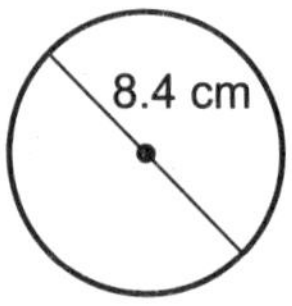

$r =$ ____________

$A \approx$ ____________

$A \approx$ ____________

d) 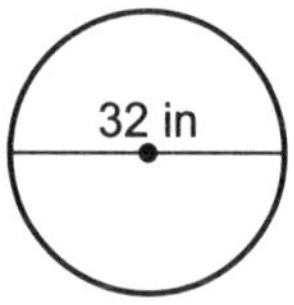

$r =$ ____________

$A \approx$ ____________

$A \approx$ ____________

3. A circle has area 36 cm². Find the area of the shaded part.

a) 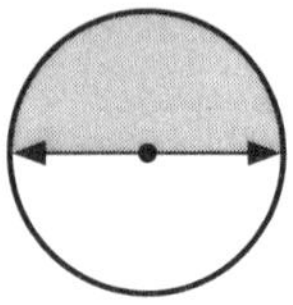

$A = \frac{1}{2} \times 36$

$A =$ *18 cm²*

b) 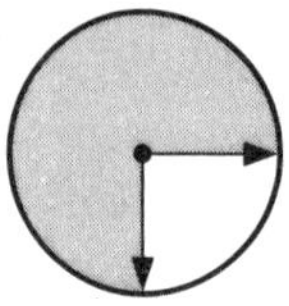

$A =$

$A =$ ____________

c) 

$A =$

$A =$ ____________

d) 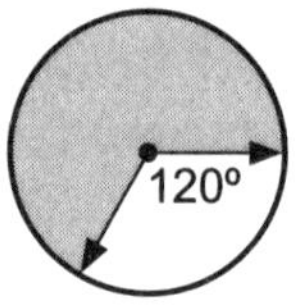

$A =$

$A =$ ____________

4. Find the area of the shape made from circle parts and/or rectangles. Use 3.14 for π.

a) 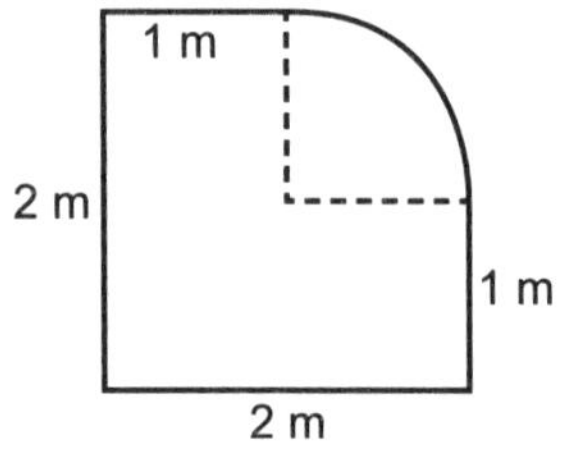

b) 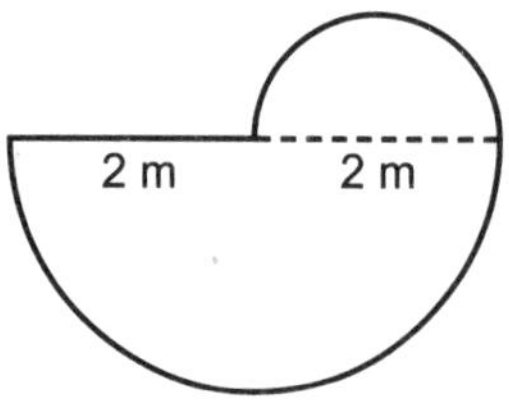

c) 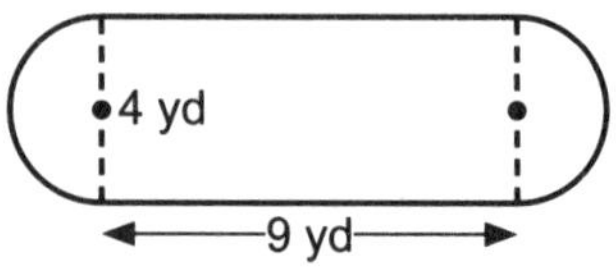

5. Use the exercises below to show why the formula $A = \pi r^2$ makes sense.

a) Draw a large circle with a compass. Use radius 10 cm or more.

b) Cut out the circle and fold it in half three times.

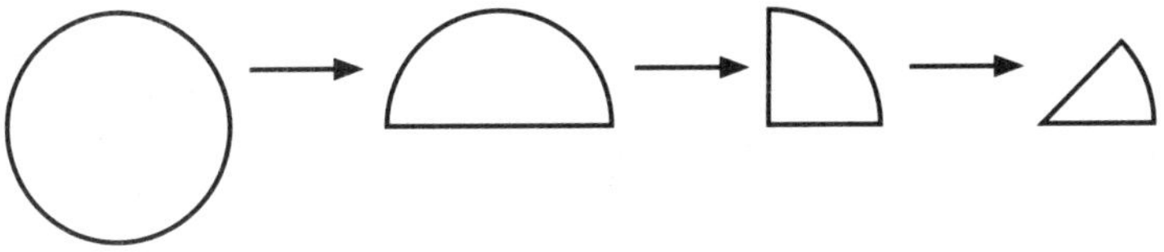

c) Unfold your circle. It should have fold marks as shown. Now color one half of the circle.

d) Cut out the eight pieces:

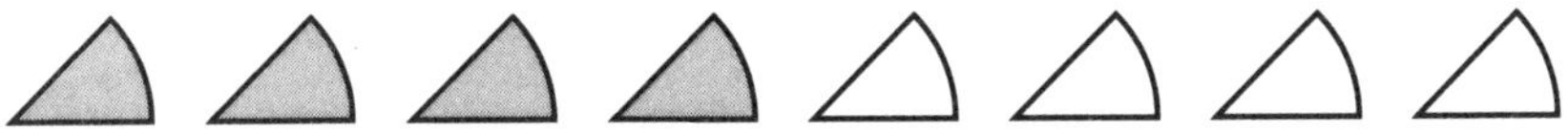

e) Arrange the pieces as shown. Then cut one of the pieces in half and move one of the halves to the other side.

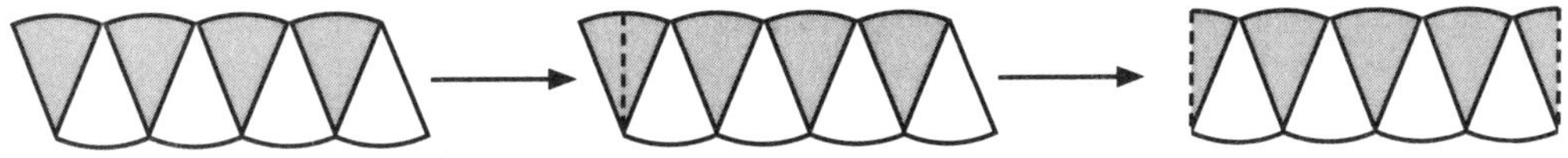

f) What distance does the arrow show? Write "radius" or "circumference."

i) 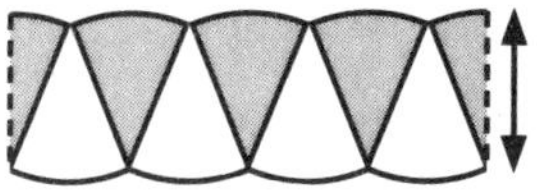

____

ii) 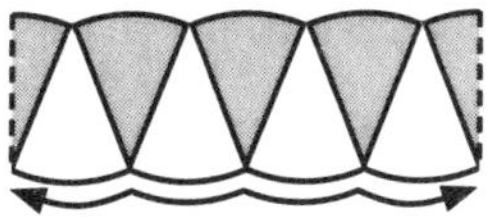

$\frac{1}{2}$ of ______________________

g) Draw or imagine a rectangle around the pieces. Write "width" (smaller side) or "length" (longer side).

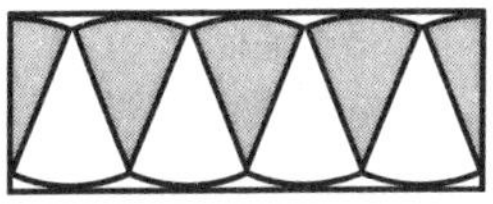

The ______________________ of the rectangle is equal to the radius of the circle.

The ______________________ of the rectangle is close to half of the circumference.

h) Explain why half of the circumference is $\pi \times r$. ____

____

i) The area of the circle is about equal to the area of the rectangle.

The area of the rectangle is (length) $\times$ (width) $\approx$ __________ $\times$ __________.

Does your answer equal πr^2? If not, find your mistake.

G7-22 Using a Sketch to Solve Problems

1. Circle the sketch (or sketches) that shows the given information correctly.

a) A parallelogram has a base that is 5 cm long. The height is 2 cm shorter than the base.

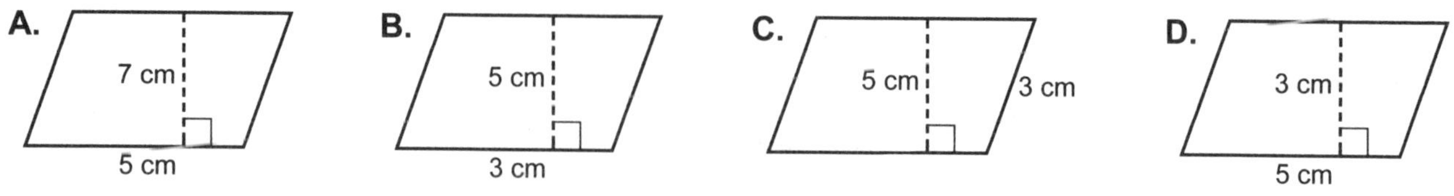

b) The base of a triangle is twice as long as its height. The base is 5 cm long.

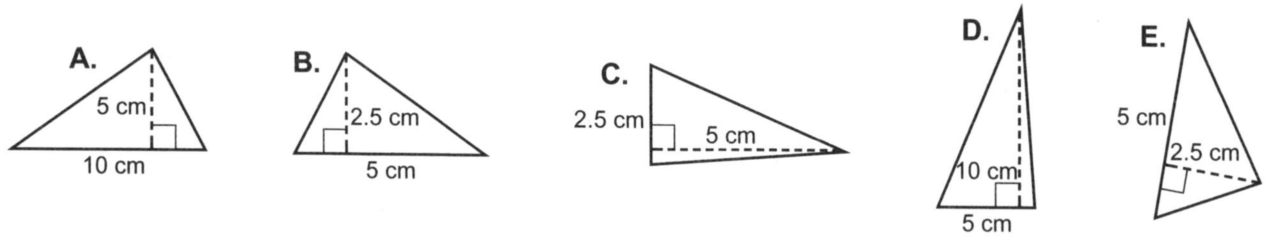

2. Draw a sketch to show the information. Then find the area.

a) The base of a parallelogram is three times as long as the height. The height is 2 cm.

b) A right-angled trapezoid is made from a square and a right triangle. The base and height of the right triangle, and the side length of the square, are all 3 in long.

c) One base of a trapezoid is twice as long as the other base. The height is half the length of the shortest base. The longest base is 8 in long.

3. Match the sketch with the description.

A.

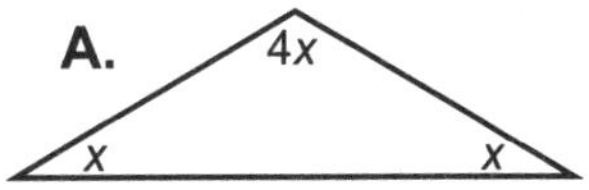

B.

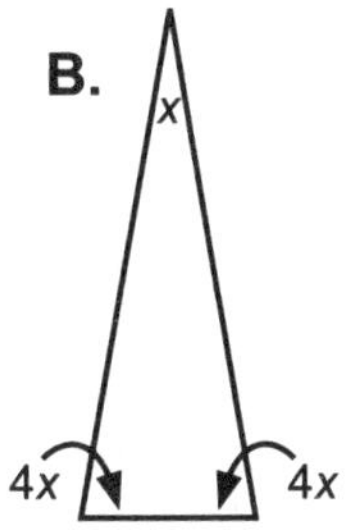

C.

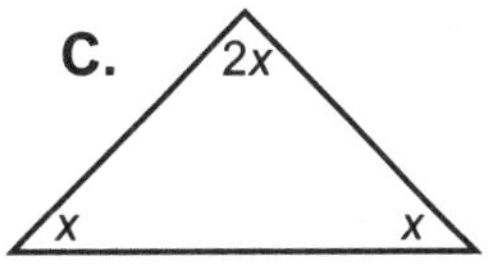

D.

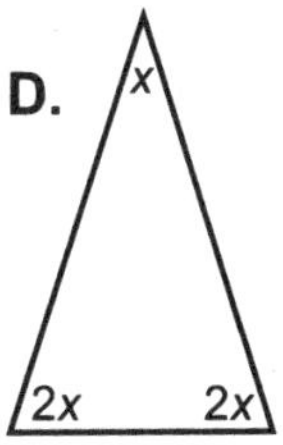

a) The two smallest angles are equal.

   i) The largest angle is 4 times as large as the smallest. ______

   ii) The largest angle is twice as large as the smallest. ______

b) The two largest angles are equal.

   i) The largest angle is 4 times as large as the smallest. ______

   ii) The largest angle is twice as large as the smallest. ______

REMINDER: The sum of the angles in a triangle is 180°.

4. a) For each triangle in Question 3, write an equation for x and solve it.

A. *$6x = 180°$ so $x = 30°$* ____________ **B.** ______________________________

C. ______________________________ **D.** ______________________________

b) Which triangles have an obtuse angle ($> 90°$)? __________

c) Which triangles have all angles acute ($< 90°$)? __________

d) Which triangles are right-angled? __________

5. Sketch the triangle and use an equation to find both of the acute angles.

a) In a right triangle, one acute angle is 4 times as large as the other acute angle.

b) In a right triangle, one acute angle is 20° more than the other acute angle.

6. A triangle has two equal angles.

a) One of the angles measures 100°. What are the other angles?

b) One of the angles measures 20°. What are the other angles?
Hint: There are two solutions.

c) How are parts a) and b) different? Why do they have a different number of solutions?

G7-23 Using a Formula

REMINDER: A formula tells you how to get one quantity using other quantities.

Example: The formula for the area of a rectangle is:

Area = length × width or $A = \ell \times w$

1. What is each formula for?

a) $C = \pi d$ (or $C = 2\pi r$) ______________________

b) $A = b \times h \div 2$ ______________________

c) $A = (b_1 + b_2) \times h \div 2$ ______________________

d) $A = \pi r^2$ ______________________

e) $A = b \times h$ ______________________

2. Write the formula you need to find the area. Label on the picture what each variable in the formula represents.

a) 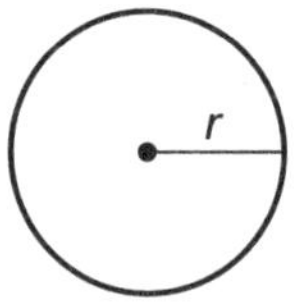

$A = \pi r^2$

b) 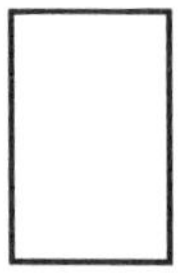

____

c) 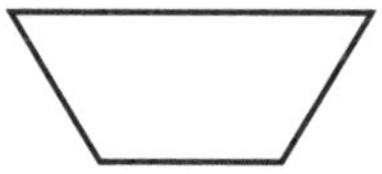

____

d) 

____

3. Decide what you are given, what you need to find, and the formula you would use.

a) Find the area of a triangle with height 2 cm and base 6 cm.

Given: *height = 2 cm* | Find: *area of triangle*

base = 6 cm | Formula: *Area = base × height ÷ 2*

b) A triangle with base 5 cm has area 10 cm². What is its height?

Given: ______________ Find: ______________

______________ Formula: ______________

c) A circle has radius 5 cm. What is its area?

Given: ______________ Find: ______________

Formula: ______________

d) A trapezoid has bases 3 cm and 5 cm, and area 32 cm². What is its height?

12 in = 1 ft   10 mm = 1 cm   3 ft = 1 yd

4. Convert the measurement if needed. Replace the parts of the formula with the given information. Then solve the equation for the unknown. Include the units in your final answer.

a) $b = 45$ mm = __*4.5*__ cm

A = 18 cm^2

Find: height (h) of parallelogram

Formula: $A = b \times h$

$18 = 4.5h$

$h = 18 \div 4.5$

$h = 4$ cm

b) $b = 8$ ft = __$\frac{8}{3}$__ yd

A = 2 yd^2

Find: height (h) of triangle

Formula: $A = b \times h \div 2$

c) Base 1 = 45 mm = __*4.5*__ cm

Base 2 = 35 mm = ______ cm

Area = 16 cm^2

Find: height (h) of trapezoid

Formula: $A = (b_1 + b_2) \times h \div 2$

d) Base 1 = 30 in = ______ ft

Height = 20 in = ______ ft

Area = 5 ft^2

Find: base 2 (b_2) of trapezoid

Formula: $A = (b_1 + b_2) \times h \div 2$

e) Circumference = 6.28 cm

Find: radius of circle (use $\pi = 3.14$)

Formula: $C = 2\pi r$

f) Diameter = 14 in

Find: area of circle (use $\pi = 3.14$)

Formula: $A = \pi r^2$

5. a) Two circles are drawn on 1 cm grid paper. Find the areas. Use $\pi = 3.14$.

b) How many times greater is the radius of B than the radius of A?

c) How many times greater is the area of B than the area of A?

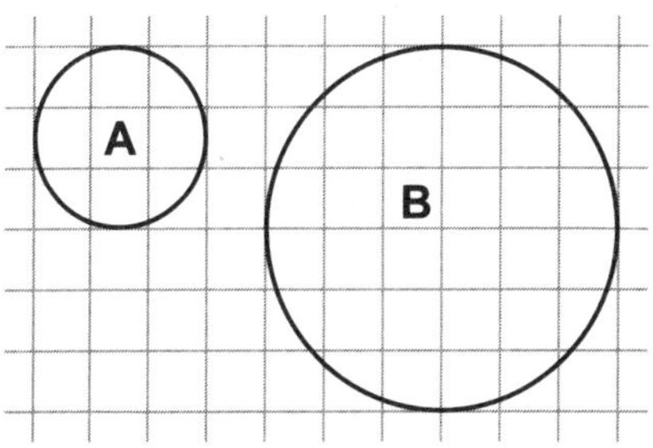

In the questions below, round your answers to two decimal places. Use $\pi = 3.14$.

6. a) Find the area of each shaded part and unshaded part. Use 3.14 for π.

i)

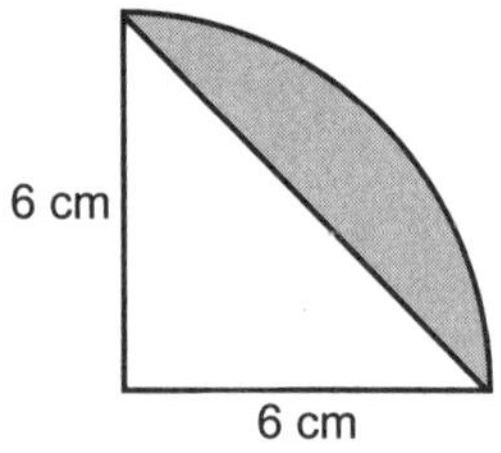

ii)

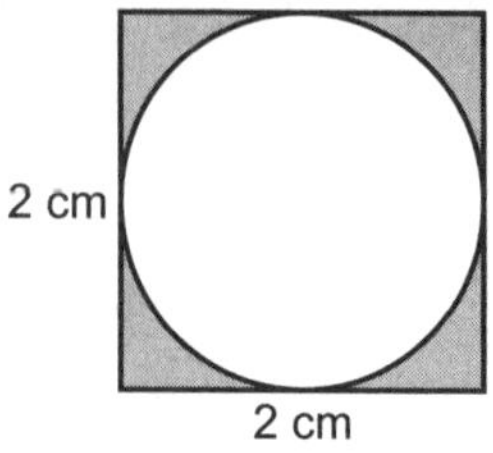

iii)

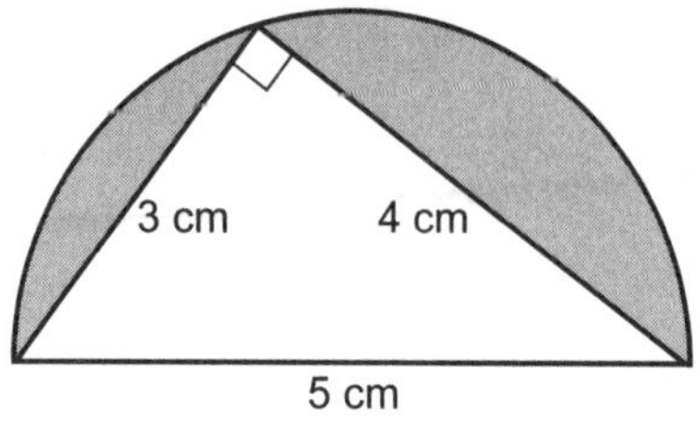

b) Look at the pictures in part a). Is the area of the shaded part more or less than the area of the unshaded part? Do your answers for part a) make sense with the pictures?

7. A window has the shape of a rectangle with a semicircle on top. The width of the rectangle and the diameter of the circle are both 90 cm. The height of the rectangle is 1.4 m. If glass costs \$25 per 1 m^2, what is the cost of the glass needed to build the window?

8. A garden has a path that is an outer layer of a quarter circle, as shown. The shaded areas are flowerbeds.

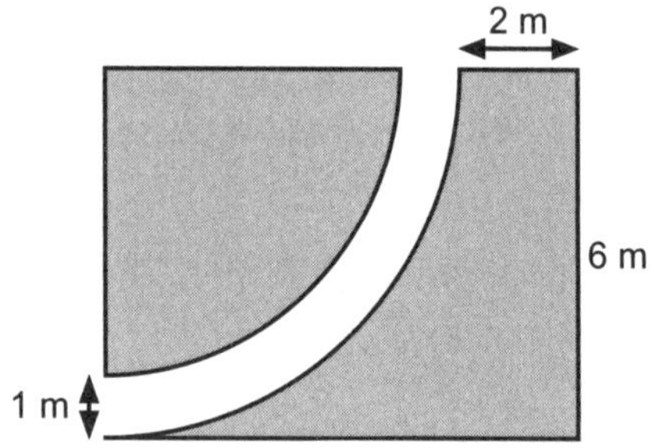

a) What is the area of the path?

b) What is the total area of the flowerbeds?

c) The path is covered in tiles. It cost \$3 per square meter to lay the tiles. It cost \$5 per square meter to plant the flowerbeds. How much did it cost to create the garden?

9. The London Eye is a giant Ferris wheel in downtown London, England.

a) The diameter of the wheel is about 135 m. What is the circumference of the wheel?

b) The wheel turns about 0.3 m every second. About how long does it take for the wheel to rotate once?

c) The London Eye has 32 evenly spaced capsules that can each hold 25 people.

i) How many people can ride the Ferris wheel at the same time?

ii) How far apart are the capsules?

d) The High Roller is a Ferris wheel in Las Vegas. Its 28 cabins each hold 40 people and are 17.8 m apart.

i) How many people can use the High Roller at one time?

ii) Which is taller, the High Roller or the London Eye? How do you know?

NS7-46 2-Digit Division

To divide 176 ÷ 38:

Step 1: Round the divisor to the nearest ten. → (40)

Step 2: Estimate the quotient. Use 176 ÷ 40 or 17 ÷ 4. → 4

$$\begin{array}{r} 4 \\ 38\overline{)176} \\ -\underline{152} \\ 24 \end{array}$$

Step 3: Multiply the divisor by the estimated quotient: 38 × 4 = 152.

Step 4: Subtract to find the remainder.

So, 176 ÷ 38 = 4 R 24.

1. Round the divisor to the nearest ten. Then estimate the quotient.

a) (*50*) $48\overline{)163}$ quotient: *3* b) ( ) $33\overline{)204}$ c) ( ) $59\overline{)342}$ d) ( ) $71\overline{)695}$

2. Multiply the divisor by the estimated quotient. Write the answer below the dividend.

a) $38\overline{)128}$ quotient: 3; *114*

	3 (carry *2*)	*8*
×		*3*
1	*1*	*4*

b) $23\overline{)118}$ quotient: 5

×		

c) $57\overline{)184}$ quotient: 3

×		

d) $46\overline{)350}$ quotient: 7

×		

3. Subtract to find the remainder.

a) 62)

			4
62)	2	7	3
−	2	4	8
		2	*5*

b) 51)

			7
51)	3	7	9
−	3	5	7

c) 28)

			9
28)	2	7	8
−	2	5	2

d) 63)

			7
63)	4	7	0
−	4	4	1

4. Write the quotient and the remainder for each division in Question 3.

a) 273 ÷ 62 = *4 R 25* b) 379 ÷ 51 = ________ c) 278 ÷ 28 = ________ d) 470 ÷ 63 = ________

5. Complete the long division.

a) (60)

			4
58)	2	5	3
−	2	3	2
		2	1

	5	8
×		4
2	3	2

So, 253 ÷ 58 = *4 R 21*

b) ( )

43)	2	7	3
−			

×		

So, 273 ÷ 43 = ________

c) 68)639 d) 19)103 e) 52)445 f) 39)187

6. Circle the first part of the dividend that is at least as big as the divisor.

a) 18)(37)2

Is 3 at least 18? No.
Is 37 at least 18? Yes.

b) 24)137 c) 64)821 d) 31)124

e) 63)574 f) 19)504 g) 52)529 h) 79)629

7. Estimate how many times the divisor goes into the circled number. Write your estimate above the ones digit of the circled number.

a) 34)(139) — *4*

b) 56)(64)1 c) 65)(518) d) 23)(71)3

8. Divide. Hint: Circle the first part of the dividend that is at least as big as the divisor.

a) 47)322 b) 25)623 c) 21)655 d) 56)435

322 ÷ 47 = ________

623 ÷ 25 = ________

655 ÷ 21 = ________

435 ÷ 56 = ________

Bonus ▶ 4,104 ÷ 216

9. Divide as though the dividend is a whole number. Then put the decimal point in the correct place.

a) $69.3 \div 33 =$ ________ b) $8.82 \div 21 =$ ________ c) $874.2 \div 93 =$ ________

10. Determine the sign of the quotient. Then use the absolute values to divide.

a) $8.82 \div (-42) =$ ________ b) $-2{,}628 \div 73 =$ ________ c) $-35.19 \div (-69) =$ ________

d) $387 \div (-43)$ e) $79.2 \div 33$ f) $-99.6 \div 83$

11. Jake shares 276 amusement park tickets equally among 12 friends. How many tickets does each friend get?

12. On Mercury, the temperature can change by −90°F per hour. At this rate, how many hours have passed if the temperature changed by −1,080°F?

13. a) Kate is dividing 253 by 34. Will the quotient have 1 digit or 2 digits? ______

b) Carlos is dividing 651 by 34. Will the quotient have 1 digit or 2 digits? ______

c) Explain how you can predict the number of digits in the quotient.

14. Twenty-one neighbors equally share the profits from a community garage sale. If the profit is $1,094.94, how much money does each neighbor get?

NS7-47 2-Digit Division—Guess and Check

When estimating the quotient in a division problem, your estimate might be too high or too low.

Examples:

$$\begin{array}{r} 7 \\ 23\overline{)156} \\ -\underline{161} \end{array}$$

negative number
7 is too high.

$$\begin{array}{r} 6 \\ 16\overline{)123} \\ -\underline{\ \ 96} \end{array}$$

27 but 27 > 16
6 is too low.

1. Find the remainder. Is the estimate too high or too low?

a) $\begin{array}{r} 7 \\ 32\overline{)218} \\ -\underline{224} \end{array}$

7 is too ________.

b) $\begin{array}{r} 4 \\ 29\overline{)147} \\ -\underline{116} \end{array}$

4 is too ________.

c) $\begin{array}{r} 6 \\ 36\overline{)266} \\ -\underline{216} \end{array}$

6 is too ________.

d) $\begin{array}{r} 8 \\ 41\overline{)322} \\ -\underline{328} \end{array}$

8 is too ________.

2. Use the first estimate to make a better estimate. Then divide.

a) $\begin{array}{r} 8 \\ 47\overline{)438} \\ -\underline{376} \end{array}$

62 but 62 > 47

8 is *too low*.

			9
47)	4	3	8
–	*4*	*2*	*3*
		1	*5*

b) $\begin{array}{r} 7 \\ 32\overline{)215} \\ -\underline{224} \end{array}$

negative number

7 is *too high*.

32)	2	1	5
–			

c) $\begin{array}{r} 9 \\ 24\overline{)195} \\ -\underline{216} \end{array}$

9 is ________.

24)	1	9	5
–			

d) $\begin{array}{r} 5 \\ 25\overline{)171} \\ -\underline{125} \end{array}$

5 is ________.

25)	1	7	1
–			

e) $\begin{array}{r} 4 \\ 68\overline{)348} \\ -\underline{272} \end{array}$

4 is ________.

68)	3	4	8
–			

f) $\begin{array}{r} 6 \\ 51\overline{)304} \\ -\underline{306} \end{array}$

6 is ________.

51)	3	0	4
–			

3. Divide.

a) $468 \div 76$ b) $168 \div 43$ c) $212 \div 31$ d) $612 \div 65$

4. Round the divisor to the nearest ten to estimate how many times it goes into the circled number. Multiply to check your estimate. Is the estimate good, too high, or too low?

a) $24\overline{)\,9{,}851}$ (9,8 circled); quotient 4; $-\,96$; remainder 2

Estimate is *good*.

b) $24\overline{)\,1{,}295}$ (1,29 circled)

Estimate is ____________.

c) $37\overline{)\,925}$ (92 circled)

Estimate is ____________.

d) $37\overline{)\,1{,}517}$ (1,51 circled)

Estimate is ____________.

e) $33\overline{)\,617}$ (61 circled)

Estimate is ____________.

f) $49\overline{)\,1{,}492}$ (1,49 circled)

Estimate is ____________.

5. a) For which parts of Question 4 did you round the divisor up? _____, _____, _____

b) For which parts of Question 4 was your estimate too high? _____, _____

c) When rounding the divisor up, can your estimate be too high? Explain how you know.

____

____

____

6. Divide. Hint: Circle the first part of the dividend that is at least as big as the divisor.

a) $43\overline{)\,9\;3\;7}$

$937 \div 43$

= ____________

b) $84\overline{)\,3\;2\;6\;8}$

$3{,}268 \div 84$

= ____________

c) $37\overline{)\,2\;3\;7\;8}$

$2{,}378 \div 37$

= ____________

REMINDER: To divide by a decimal, make the divisor a whole number. Multiply both the dividend and the divisor by the same power of 10.

Examples:

$1.5\overline{)7.5}$	$0.15\overline{)7.5}$	$0.015\overline{)7.5}$
↓	↓	↓
$15\overline{)75.}$	$15\overline{)750.}$	$15\overline{)7500.}$

Then divide by the whole number using long division

7. Divide. Hint: Make the divisor a whole number.

a) 0.78 ÷ 2.6 b) 6.48 ÷ 0.54 c) 43 ÷ 0.025

8. Determine the sign of the quotient. Then use the absolute values to divide.

a) −13.5 ÷ (−0.18) b) 1,976 ÷ (−52) c) −16.56 ÷ 4.6

d) 0.2405 ÷ 3.7 e) −0.0408 ÷ (−0.12) f) 0.8316 ÷ (−0.036)

9. Twenty-eight students equally share the cost of a field trip. If the cost is $210.00, how much does each student pay?

10. Apples cost $0.45 each. Mandy spent $15.75. How many apples did she buy?

11. A sheet of paper is 0.012 cm thick. How many sheets are in a stack that is 5.4 cm thick?

12. The perimeter of a melting glacier changes at an average rate of −180 m each year. At this rate, how many years would it take for the perimeter to change by −15,480 m?

13. Fill in the blanks. Write the average change as an integer. Include the units.

a) A seagull descended from 84.5 ft to −35.5 ft in 1.5 minutes.

The seagull's elevation changed *−35.5 − 84.5 = −120 ft* in 1.5 minutes.

The average change in elevation was *−120 ÷ 1.5 = −80 ft per minute*.

b) A hot air balloon rose from −71.35 ft to 1,974.65 ft in 2.2 hours.

The balloon's elevation changed ____________________ in 2.2 hours.

The average change in elevation was ____________________.

c) The temperature fell from −17.6°F to −28.76°F in 3.6 hours.

The temperature changed ____________________ in 3.6 hours.

The average change in temperature was ____________________.

NS7-48 Writing Fractions as Decimals

Don wants to write $\frac{13}{20}$ as a decimal.
He writes 13 as 13.0 and divides 13.0 by 20.

He keeps adding 0s until the remainder is 0.

		0	. 6	5
20)	1	3	. 0	0
−	1	2	0	↓
		1	0	0
−		1	0	0
				0

So, $\frac{13}{20} = 0.65$.

1. Use long division to write the fraction as a decimal. Keep dividing until the remainder is 0.

a) $\frac{2}{5}$ = ________ b) $\frac{17}{25}$ = ________ c) $\frac{3}{8}$ = ________

		•
5)	2	• 0
−		

2. a) Calculate 2 ÷ 3 by writing 2 as 2.0, 2.00, and 2.000.

2.0 ÷ 3

	0	• *6*
3)	2	• 0
−	*1*	*8*
		2

2.00 ÷ 3

		•	
3)	2	• 0	0
−			
−			

2.000 ÷ 3

		•		
3)	2	• 0	0	0
−				
−				
−				

b) What patterns do you see in part a)?

c) Predict 2.0000 ÷ 3. Use long division to check your answer. Do you need to start the long division from the beginning again?

3. a) Use long division to find the first 3 numbers after the decimal point.

i) $\frac{5}{9} \approx$ ________ ii) $\frac{1}{3} \approx$ ________ iii) $\frac{4}{9} \approx$ ________

		•		
9)	5	• 0	0	0
−				
−				
−				

b) If you continued the divisions in part a), what remainders would you get?

i) _____ ii) _____ iii) _____

Anne wants to write $\frac{2}{3}$ as a decimal.

She writes 2 as 2.0 and divides 2.0 by 3.

She keeps adding 0s until she sees a pattern in the remainder.

She writes $\frac{2}{3} = 0.666\ldots$ to show the 6s continue forever.

	0	• 6	6	6
3)	2	• 0	0	0
−	1	8	↓	
		2	0	
−		1	8	↓
			2	0

Remainder repeats

4. Use long division to write the fraction as a decimal. Stop adding zeros to the dividend when the remainder is 0 or when you see a pattern.

a) $\frac{1}{9}$ = *0.111...* b) $\frac{12}{16}$ = *0.75* c) $\frac{56}{63}$ = ________

	0	• 1	1
9)	1	• 0	0
−		9	↓
		1	0
−			9
			1

		0	• 7	5
16)	1	2	• 0	0
−	1	1	2	↓
			8	0
−			8	0
				0

)				
−				
−				

d) $\frac{26}{40}$ e) $\frac{21}{-27}$ f) $\frac{-28}{32}$ g) $\frac{53}{-80}$ h) $\frac{-30}{-135}$ i) $-\frac{6}{9}$

NS7-49 Repeating Decimals and Terminating Decimals

A **repeating decimal** is a decimal with a digit or group of digits that repeats forever. You can use a bar to show the digit or group of digits that repeats.

Examples: $0.55555.... = 0.\overline{5}$ $4.12121212... = 4.\overline{12}$ $7.0161616... = 7.0\overline{16}$

A **terminating decimal** is a decimal that does not go on forever. Examples: 5.68, 0.444, 2.75

Some decimals do not terminate or repeat. Examples: $\pi = 3.14159...$, 0.1223334444...

1. Circle the repeating decimals.

0.12345 0.22222... 0.77 0.512512512... 0.112123... 0.0252525...

2. Write the decimal to eight decimal places.

a) $0.\overline{3} \approx 0.$ 3 ___ ___ ___ ___ ___ ___ ___

b) $0.0\overline{3} \approx 0.$ 0 3 3 3 ___ ___ ___ ___

c) $0.00\overline{3} \approx 0.$ ___ ___ ___ ___ ___ ___ ___ ___

d) $0.\overline{52} \approx 0.$ ___ ___ ___ ___ ___ ___ ___ ___

e) $0.\overline{817} \approx 0.$ ___ ___ ___ ___ ___ ___ ___ ___

f) $0.8\overline{17} \approx 0.$ ___ ___ ___ ___ ___ ___ ___ ___

g) $0.9\overline{26} \approx 0.$ ___ ___ ___ ___ ___ ___ ___ ___

h) $0.25\overline{37} \approx 0.$ ___ ___ ___ ___ ___ ___ ___ ___

i) $7.2\overline{3} \approx 7.$ ___ ___ ___ ___ ___ ___ ___ ___

j) $8.2\overline{539} \approx 8.$ ___ ___ ___ ___ ___ ___ ___ ___

3. Use bar notation to write the repeating decimal.

a) 0.888888... = ______________

b) 0.343434... = ______________

c) 5.237237... = ______________

d) 57.11111... = ______________

e) 8.1626262... = ______________

f) 0.915091509150... = ______________

g) −5.0454545... = ______________

h) −17.777777... = ______________

4. Use long division to write the fraction as a decimal. Use bar notation.

a) $\frac{5}{9}$ b) $\frac{5}{6}$ c) $\frac{2}{15}$ d) $\frac{3}{11}$

e) $\frac{-32}{99}$ f) $\frac{5}{-18}$ g) $\frac{8}{11}$ h) $\frac{-13}{-22}$

5. a) Use long division to write $\frac{1}{11}, \frac{2}{11}, \frac{3}{11}$, and $\frac{4}{11}$ as decimals.

b) Extend the pattern to find $\frac{5}{11}, \frac{6}{11}, \frac{7}{11}, \frac{8}{11}, \frac{9}{11}$, and $\frac{10}{11}$.

NS7-50 Repeating Decimals and Terminating Decimals on Number Lines

REMINDER: 0.8 = 0.80 and 0.74 = 0.740

1. a) Write the hundredths marked with an X.

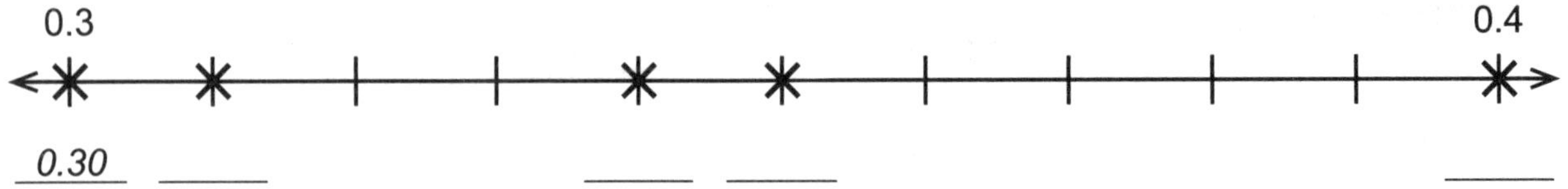

b) Write the thousandths marked with an X.

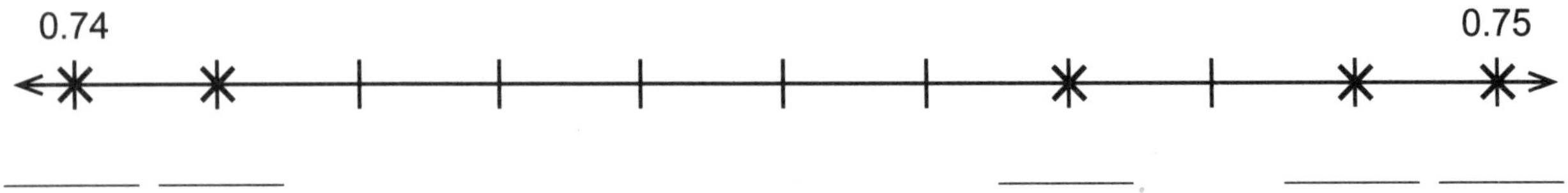

2. Circle the position of the terminating decimal on the number lines.

a) 0.269

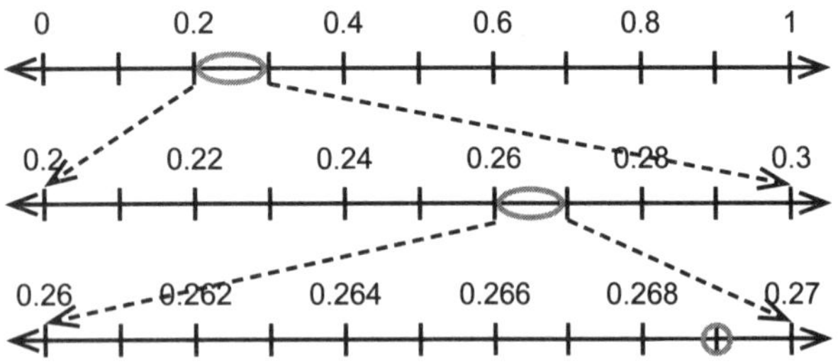

b) 0.583

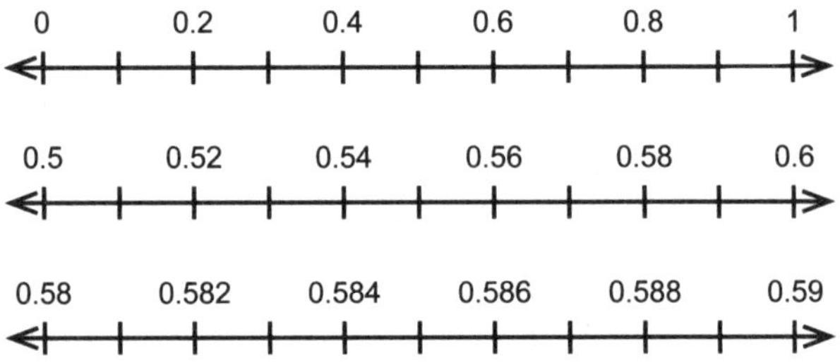

3. Do the terminating decimals in Question 2 each have an exact position on the third number line?

a) ______ b) ______

You can show the position of a terminating decimal on the number line by zooming in on the line until you find the number's exact position.

4. What two numbers is the given number between if you count by ones, tenths, and hundredths?

		Ones	Tenths	Hundredths
a)	0.487	*0 and 1*	*0.4 and 0.5*	*0.48 and 0.49*
b)	0.719			
c)	7.235			

Bonus ▶

d)	0.019			

5. Write the decimal to 4 decimal places. Circle the position of the repeating decimal on the number lines.

a) $0.\overline{7} \approx 0.$_________

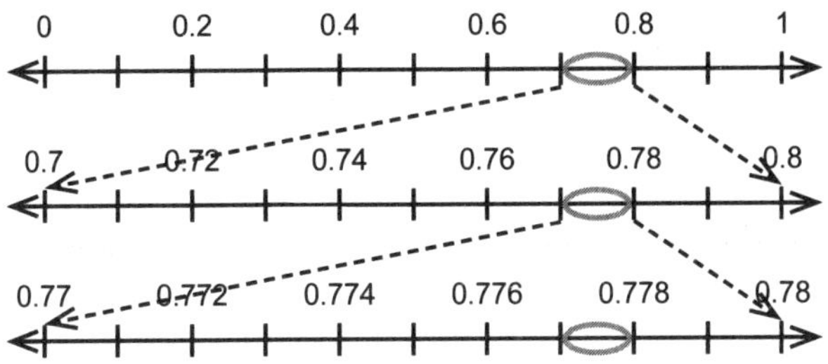

b) $0.\overline{3} \approx 0.$_________

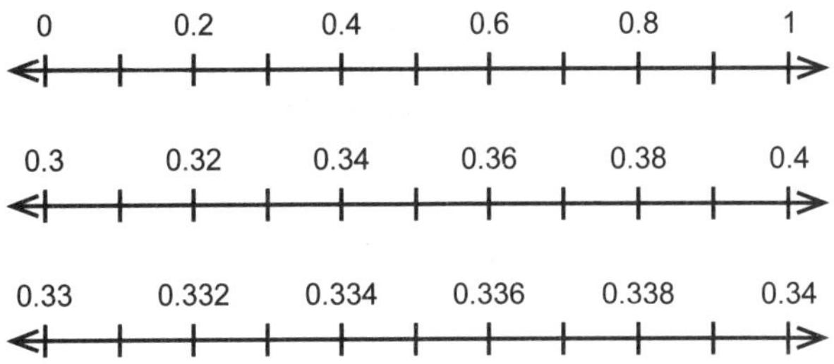

c) $0.1\overline{6} \approx 0.$_________

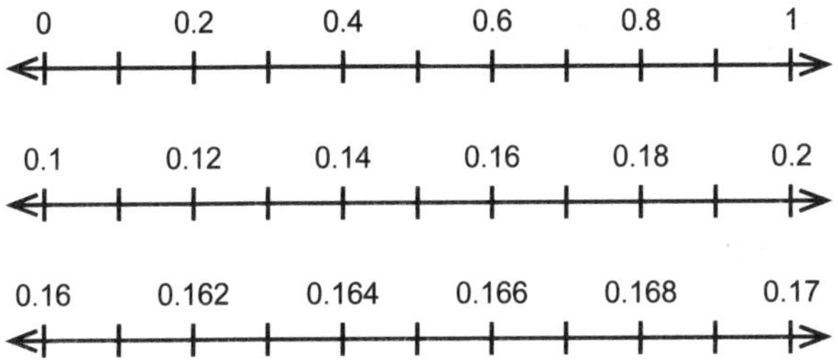

Bonus ▶ $0.\overline{45} \approx 0.$_________

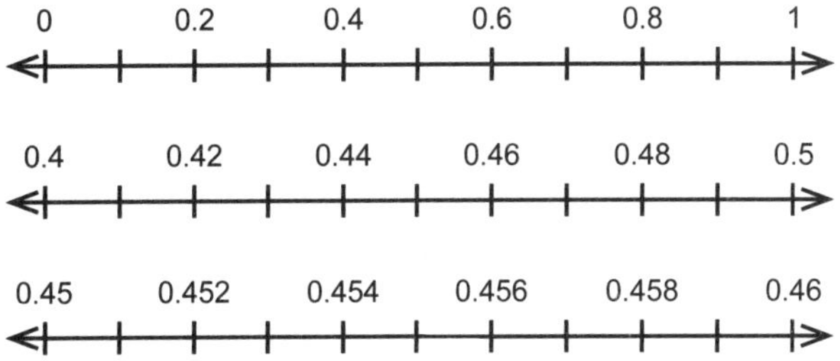

6. Do the repeating decimals in Question 5 each have an exact position on the third number line?

a) _______ b) _______ c) _______ **Bonus ▶** _______

> You can't determine the exact position of a repeating decimal on a number line divided into tenths, hundredths, thousands, etc. You can only estimate its position on these number lines.

7. What two numbers is the given number between if you count by tenths, hundredths, and thousandths?

		Tenths	**Hundredths**	**Thousandths**
a)	$0.\overline{5} = 0.5555...$	*0.5 and 0.6*	*0.55 and 0.56*	*0.555 and 0.556*
b)	$0.\overline{2}$			
c)	$0.8\overline{3}$			
d)	$0.\overline{26}$			

Bonus ▶

e)	$0.\overline{24}$			

8. Circle the numbers that have an exact position on a number line divided into hundredths.

0.34 $0.\overline{72}$ 0.845 $0.\overline{6}$ 0.09 0.2 $7.0\overline{5}$ −32.16

NS7-51 Is the Fraction a Repeating Decimal or a Terminating Decimal?

REMINDER: In a decimal fraction, the denominator is a power of ten.

Example: $\frac{3}{100}$ is a decimal fraction. $\frac{3}{100} = 0.03$

1. a) Write the decimal fraction as a decimal.

i) $\frac{3}{10} =$ ________ ii) $\frac{87}{100} =$ ________ iii) $\frac{429}{1,000} =$ ________

b) Which decimals in part a) are terminating decimals? ______________

If a fraction is equivalent to a decimal fraction, the fraction can be written as a terminating decimal.

2. a) Use long division to write the fraction as a decimal.

i) $\frac{5}{8}$ ii) $\frac{7}{12}$ iii) $\frac{11}{18}$ iv) $\frac{13}{25}$ v) $\frac{13}{2,000}$ vi) $\frac{4}{15}$

b) Which fractions in part a) can be written as terminating decimals? _____, _____, and _____

c) Write the fractions from part b) as decimal fractions.

___________ ___________ ___________

You can write powers of 10 as products of 2s and 5s.

$10 = 2 \times 5$

$100 = 10 \times 10$
$= 2 \times 5 \times 2 \times 5$

$1,000 = 10 \times 10 \times 10$
$= 2 \times 5 \times 2 \times 5 \times 2 \times 5$

3. Write the number as a product of only 2s and/or 5s.

a) $25 =$ ___________ b) $8 =$ ___________ c) $500 =$ ___________

4. a) Use long division to write the fraction as a decimal.

i) $\frac{4}{5}$ ii) $\frac{6}{11}$ iii) $\frac{7}{15}$ iv) $\frac{27}{50}$ v) $\frac{21}{22}$ vi) $\frac{11}{20}$

b) Which fractions in part a) can be written as terminating decimals? _____, _____, and _____

c) Which fractions in part a) have denominators that are products of only 2s and/or 5s?

_____, _____, and _____

To decide if a fraction can be written as a terminating decimal or a repeating decimal:

Step 1: Write the fraction in lowest terms.

Step 2: Look at the denominator. If it can be written as a product of only 2s and/or 5s, the decimal terminates. If it cannot be written as a product of only 2s and/or 5s, the decimal repeats.

5. a) Write the fraction in lowest terms.

i) $\frac{12}{40} =$ ii) $\frac{35}{60} =$ iii) $\frac{44}{80} =$

b) Can each denominator in part a) be written as a product of only 2s and/or 5s?

i) ________ ii) ________ iii) ________

c) Can each fraction in part a) be written as a terminating decimal?

i) ________ ii) ________ iii) ________

6. Predict whether the decimal will terminate. Check with long division. Hint: Write the fraction in lowest terms first.

a) $\frac{7}{8}$ b) $\frac{3}{4}$ c) $\frac{56}{80}$ d) $\frac{63}{77}$ e) $\frac{25}{55}$ f) $\frac{115}{400}$

7. a) Calculate the first few powers of 3. ($3, 3^2, 3^3, \ldots$)

b) Are the decimal equivalents for $\frac{1}{3}$, $\frac{1}{9}$, and $\frac{1}{27}$ repeating decimals? How can you tell without calculating the decimal?

8. a) Write the sixths from $\frac{1}{6}$ to $\frac{5}{6}$ in lowest terms.

b) Predict which of the sixths will terminate. Explain.

c) Use long division to calculate the decimal equivalents for each of the sixths.

d) Which of the sixths terminate? Was your prediction in part b) correct?

9. The denominators of $\frac{3}{6}$, $\frac{3}{12}$, $\frac{6}{12}$, $\frac{6}{15}$, $\frac{9}{15}$, and $\frac{12}{15}$ all have 3 as a factor, but they are all terminating decimals. Why?

Bonus ▶ Write a number to make a fraction that can be written as a terminating decimal.

a) $\frac{15}{30}$ b) $\frac{\_\_\_}{60}$ c) $\frac{\_\_\_}{45}$ d) $\frac{16}{\_\_\_}$ e) $\frac{3}{\_\_\_}$ f) $\frac{\_\_\_}{175}$

NS7-52 Operations with Repeating Decimals (Advanced)

1. Write the repeating decimal to 4 decimal places. Round the decimal to the nearest tenth, hundredth, and thousandth.

	Fraction	Decimal Equivalent (to 4 digits)	Nearest Tenth	Nearest Hundredth	Nearest Thousandth
a)	$\frac{5}{9}$	$0.\overline{5} \approx 0.5555$	≈ 0.6	≈ 0.56	
b)	$\frac{5}{11}$	$0.\overline{45}$			
c)	$\frac{5}{12}$	$0.41\overline{6}$			
d)	$\frac{5}{13}$	$0.\overline{3846150}$			

To compare decimals:

Step 1: Write the first few digits of each decimal.
(Add zeros at the end of the terminating decimals.)

Step 2: Circle the first digits where the decimals differ.

Step 3: The decimal with the greater circled digit is greater.

0.678 [?] $0.\overline{67}$

0.	6	7	(8)	0	0	0
0.	6	7	(6)	7	6	7

0.678 [>] $0.\overline{67}$

2. Compare the decimals.

a) 0.349 ☐ $0.3\overline{49}$

b) 0.278 ☐ $0.\overline{27}$

c) $0.\overline{613}$ ☐ $0.61\overline{3}$

3. a) Compare the fractions by writing them with common denominators.

i) $\frac{2}{7}$ and $\frac{5}{14}$

ii) $\frac{37}{99}$ and $\frac{4}{11}$

iii) $\frac{1}{6}$ and $\frac{2}{13}$

b) Compare the fractions in part a) by writing them as decimals.

c) Which do you prefer: the method you used in part a), or the method you used in part b)? Explain.

4. a) Use long division to write $\frac{4}{3}$ as a decimal.

b) $\frac{1}{3} = 0.\overline{3}$. What is $1\frac{1}{3}$ as a decimal?

c) Are your answers to parts a) and b) the same or different? Explain why.

5. Add or subtract the decimals by lining up the decimal places.

a) $0.\overline{25} + 0.33 =$ <u>$0.58\overline{25}$</u>

	0	• 2	5	2	5	2	5	2	5	…
+	0	• 3	3	0	0	0	0	0	0	
	0	• 5	8	2	5	2	5	2	5	…

b) $0.125 + 0.\overline{2} =$ ______________

		•							
+		•							
		•							

c) $0.\overline{34} + 0.\overline{61} =$ ______________

		•							
+		•							
		•							

d) $0.\overline{34} + 0.2\overline{5} =$ ______________

		•							
+		•							
		•							

e) $0.\overline{52} - 0.\overline{2} =$ ______________

		•							
−		•							
		•							

f) $0.\overline{345} - 0.\overline{123} =$ ______________

		•							
−		•							
		•							

Bonus ▶ Add $0.\overline{1} + 0.\overline{12} + 0.\overline{123}$. Hint: Write each decimal to 13 decimal places.

6. a) Add by lining up the decimal places.

i) $0.3 + 0.7$ ii) $0.33 + 0.77$ iii) $0.333 + 0.777$ iv) $0.3333 + 0.7777$

b) Use the pattern in part a) to predict $0.\overline{3} + 0.\overline{7}$. Why is it not possible to add $0.\overline{3} + 0.\overline{7}$ by lining up the decimal places?

c) $0.\overline{3} = \frac{1}{3}$ and $0.\overline{7} = \frac{7}{9}$. Add the fractions. Write your answer as a decimal. Was your prediction in part b) correct?

7. Calculate the first three products. Predict the fourth product.

a) $\begin{array}{r} 0.2 \\ \times \ 3 \\ \hline \end{array}$ $\begin{array}{r} 0.22 \\ \times \ 3 \\ \hline \end{array}$ $\begin{array}{r} 0.222 \\ \times \ 3 \\ \hline \end{array}$ $\begin{array}{r} 0.\overline{2} \\ \times \ 3 \\ \hline \end{array}$

b) $\begin{array}{r} 0.09 \\ \times \ 5 \\ \hline \end{array}$ $\begin{array}{r} 0.0909 \\ \times \ 5 \\ \hline \end{array}$ $\begin{array}{r} 0.090909 \\ \times \ 5 \\ \hline \end{array}$ $\begin{array}{r} 0.\overline{09} \\ \times \ 5 \\ \hline \end{array}$

8. Multiply.

a) $\begin{array}{r} 0.\overline{3} \\ \times \ 3 \\ \hline \end{array}$ b) $\begin{array}{r} 0.\overline{05} \\ \times \ 7 \\ \hline \end{array}$ c) $\begin{array}{r} 0.\overline{203} \\ \times \ 3 \\ \hline \end{array}$ d) $\begin{array}{r} 0.0\overline{2} \\ \times \ 12 \\ \hline \end{array}$

G7-24 Volume of Rectangular Prisms

Volume is the amount of space taken up by a three-dimensional (3-D) object.

We measure volume in unit cubes or cubic units. Examples: cubic inches (in^3) and cubic centimeters (cm^3)

1. Find the volume of the object made from unit cubes. Include units in your answer.

a) 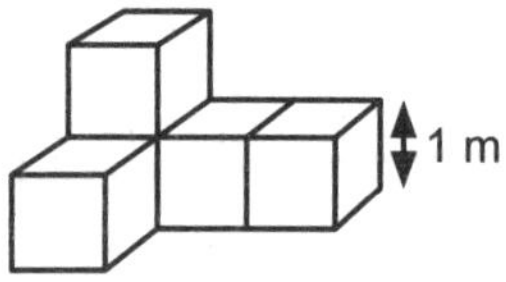

Volume = *5 m^3*

b) 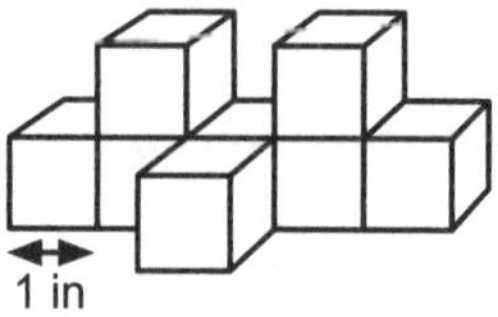

Volume = ____________

c) 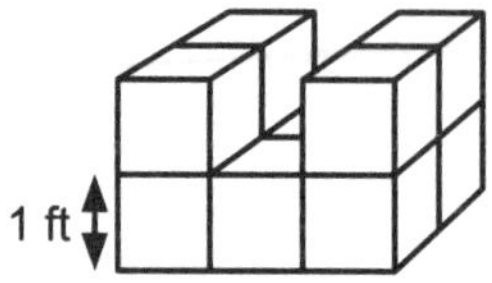

Volume = ____________

2. Blocks are stacked to make boxes.

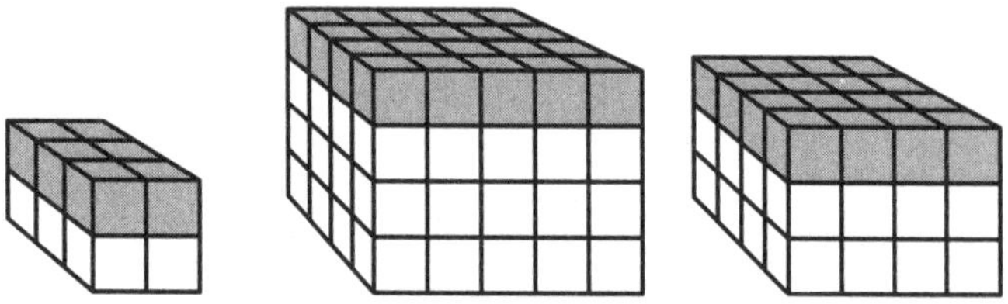

a) How many blocks are in the shaded layer?	*3 × 2 = 6*	____________	____________
b) How many blocks are in each layer?	*6*	____________	____________
c) How many horizontal layers are there?	*2*	____________	____________
d) How many bocks are in the whole box?	*6 × 2 = 12*	____________	____________

3. A box is ℓ blocks long, w blocks wide, and h blocks high.

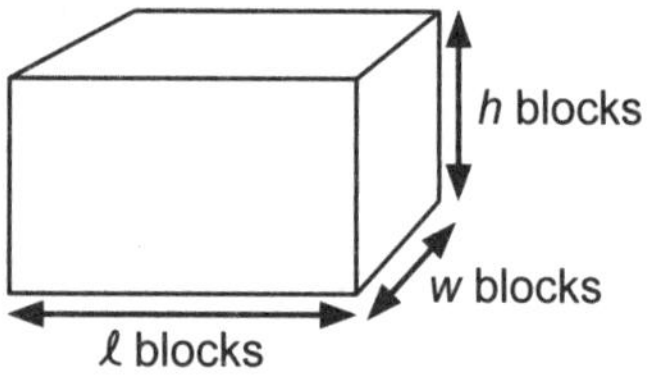

a) How many blocks are in each horizontal layer? ____________

b) How many layers are there? ________

c) How many blocks are in the whole box? ________________

Mathematicians call rectangular boxes **rectangular prisms**. For a rectangular prism:

Volume = length × width × height OR $V = \ell \times w \times h$

4. Label the length, width, and height on the diagram. Then find the volume.

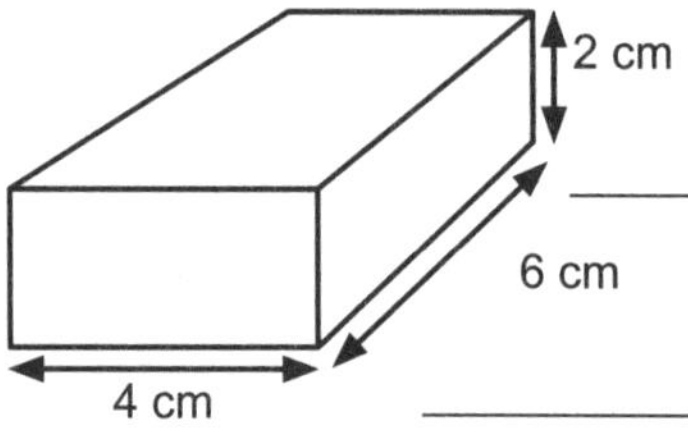

length

ℓ = *4 cm* w = ____________ h = ____________

V = *4 cm* × ____________ × ____________

= ____________ *cm^3*

5. Find the volume of the rectangular prism.

a) 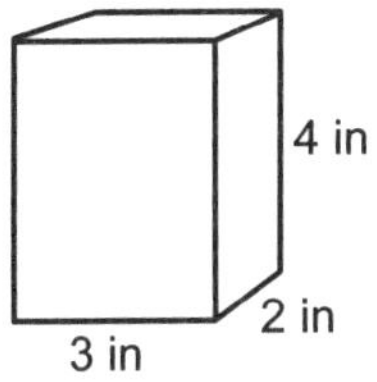

$V =$ ____________________

$=$ ______________

b) 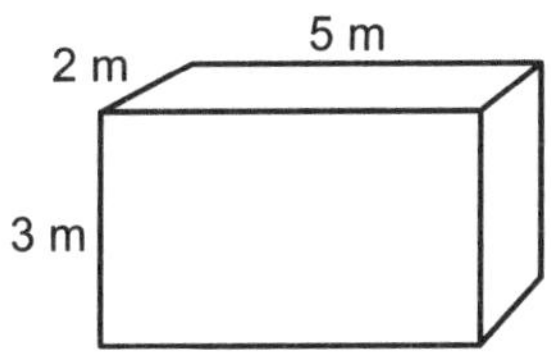

$V =$ ____________________

$=$ ______________

c) 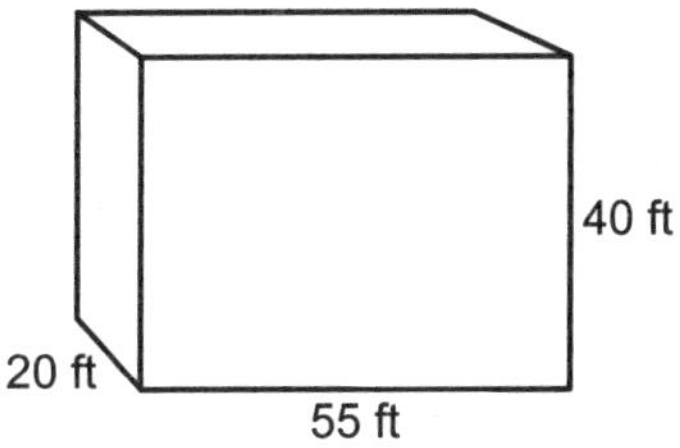

$V =$ ____________________

$=$ ______________

6. a) A bird feeder in the shape of a rectangular prism has length 4 inches, width 5 inches, and height 10 inches. How many cubic inches of bird seed does the bird feeder hold?

____

b) A 10-pound bag of bird seed has a volume of about 1,200 in^3. About how many times would one bag fill the bird feeder?

____

7. a) What is the volume of a rectangular prism with the given dimensions?

i) length 5 cm, width 4 cm, height 3 cm $V =$ ____________________

ii) length 4 cm, width 3 cm, height 5 cm $V =$ ____________________

b) Compare your answers from part a). What do you notice?

REMINDER: To multiply mixed numbers, convert them to improper fractions.

Example: $2\frac{1}{2} \times 4\frac{3}{4} = \frac{5}{2} \times \frac{19}{4} = \frac{5 \times 19}{2 \times 4} = \frac{95}{8} = 11\frac{7}{8}$

8. Find the volume of the rectangular prism.

a) 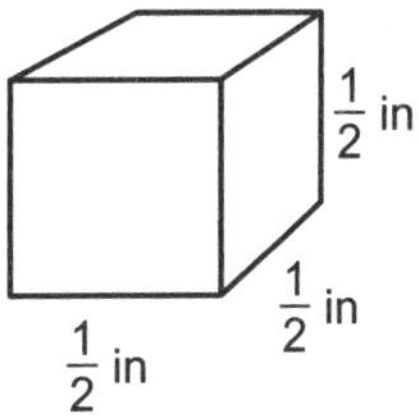

b) 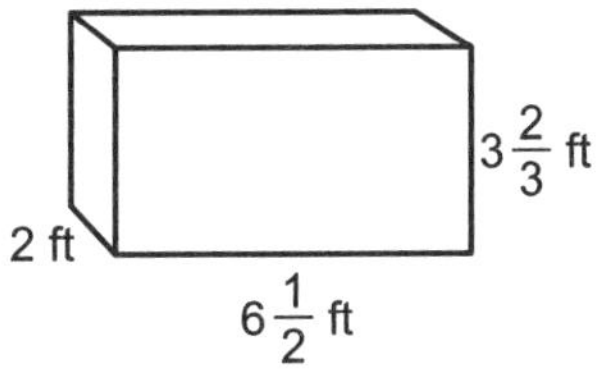

c) 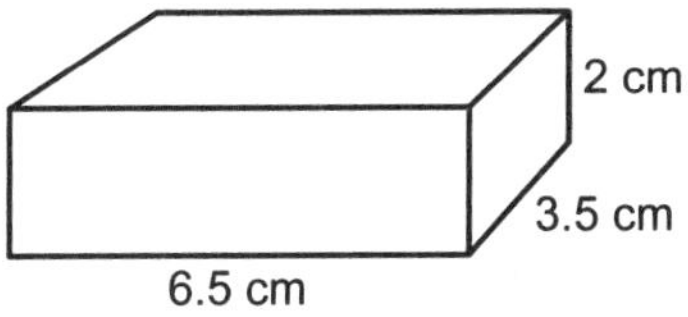

9. The dimensions of a cereal box are $7\frac{7}{8}$ inches by $3\frac{1}{3}$ inches by $11\frac{4}{5}$ inches. What is the volume of the cereal box in cubic inches?

10. A raised garden bed measures 4 ft by 8 ft by $\frac{3}{4}$ ft. If garden soil costs \$6 per cubic foot, how much would it cost to fill the garden bed with soil?

11. Find the missing edge length.

a)

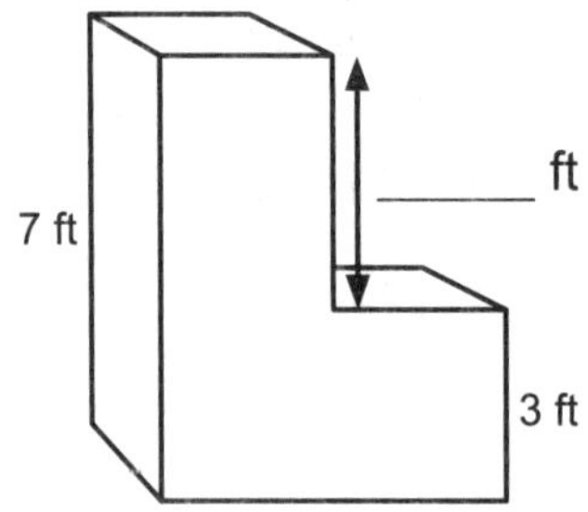

b)

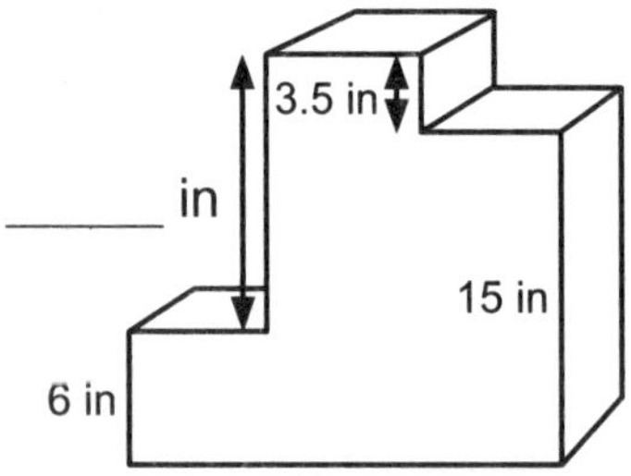

12. a) Find the volume of each prism. Then find the total volume of the whole shape.

i)

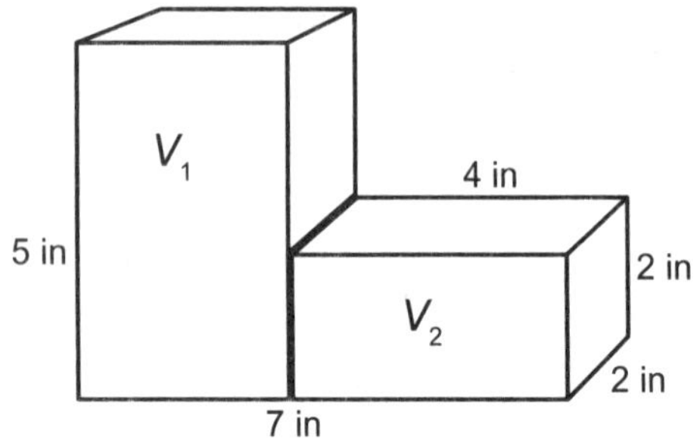

ii)

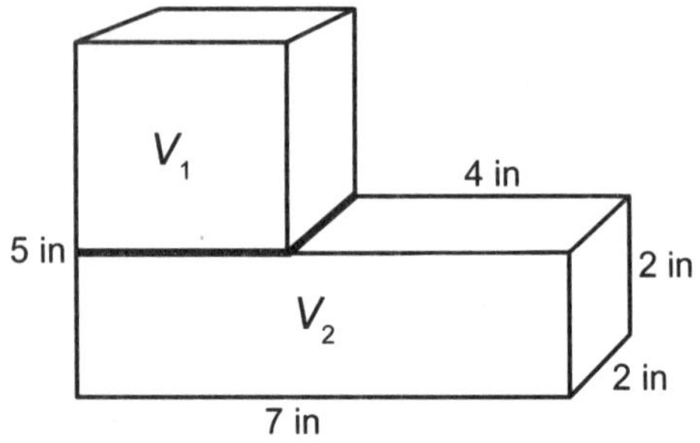

V_1 = *3 in × 2 in × 5 in = 30 in³*

V_2 = ______________________

Total volume = ______________

V_1 = ______________________

V_2 = ______________________

Total volume = ______________

b) Are the total volumes from part a) equal? Explain why.

13. Show how to divide the shape into rectangular prisms. Find the volume of each prism. Then find the total volume of the shape. All measurements are in inches.

a)

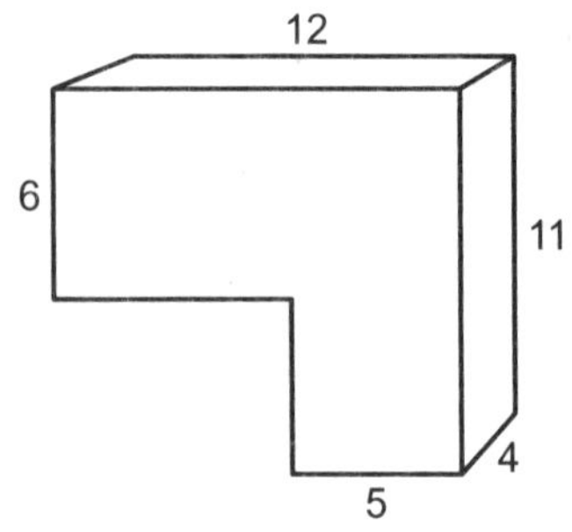

b)

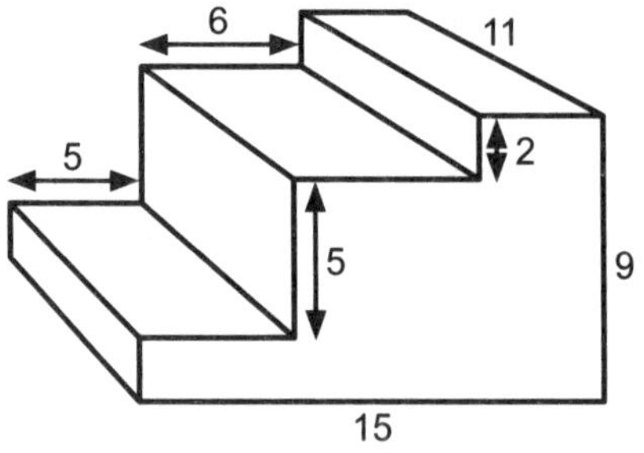

V_1 = ______________________

V_2 = ______________________

Total volume = ______________

V_1 = ______________________

V_2 = ______________________

V_3 = ______________________

Total volume = ______________

14. Check your answers to Question 13 by finding the volume in a different way.

15. Cam needs a box with a volume of at least 12 in^3. Circle the possible dimensions of the box.

1 in by 1 in by 6 in | 2 in by 2 in by 2 in | 2 in by 3 in by 4 in

3 in by 4 in by 1 in | $\frac{5}{2}$ in by 4 in by $\frac{1}{2}$ in | 2 in by 5 in by 1.2 in

Jennifer needs a box to have a volume of at least 48 in^3. The length is 6 inches and the width is 4 inches. What is the minimum height of the box?

$V \geq 48$

$\ell \times w \times h \geq 48$

$6(4)(x) \geq 48$

$24x \geq 48$

$x \geq 48 \div 24$

$x \geq 2$ in

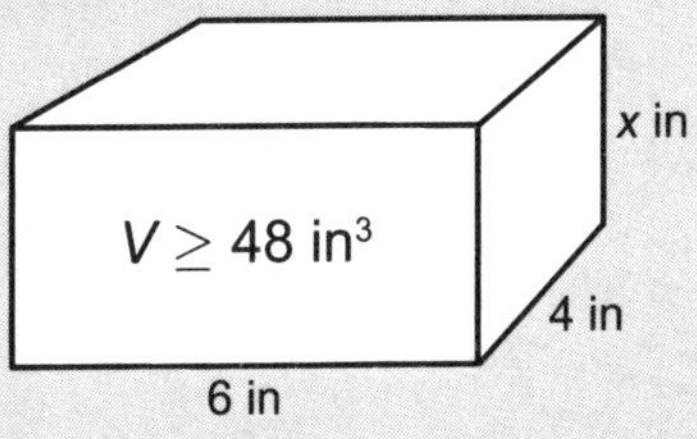

The height must be at least 2 inches to have a volume of at least 48 in^3.

16. Find the unknown dimension so that the volume is at most 48 ft^3. Write the answer as an inequality.

a)

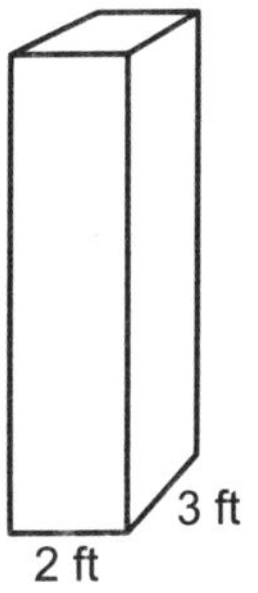

Find: *height of prism*

b)

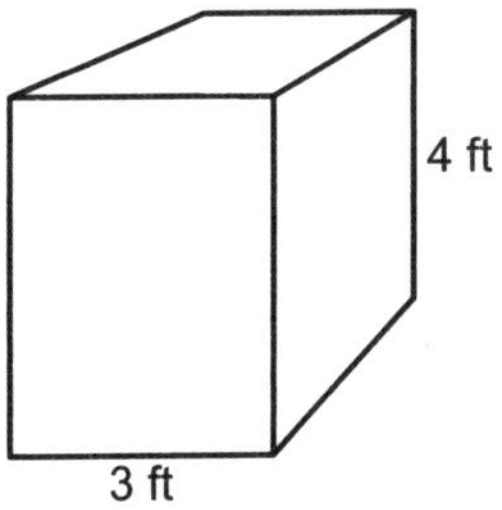

Find: ____________

c)

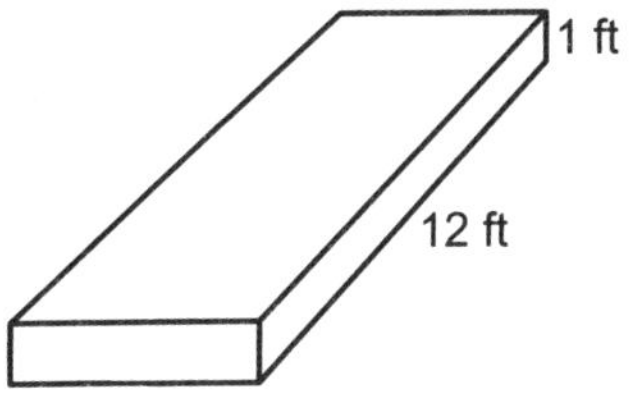

Find: ____________

17. Find the maximum width of a box with length 15 inches, height 12 inches, and volume no more than 1,440 in^3.

Bonus ▶ Billy needs a box that is 1 ft wide and $\frac{1}{2}$ ft high, and that has a volume of $\frac{3}{4}$ ft^3 or more. What is the minimum length of the box?

G7-25 Volume of Polygonal Prisms

Polygonal prisms are three-dimensional shapes that have two identical opposite faces called bases. The bases of a prism are congruent polygons. The prism is named for the shape of its base.

Examples:

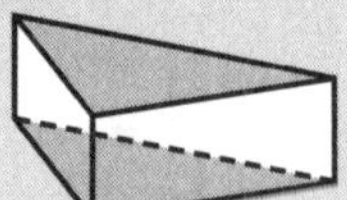
triangular prism

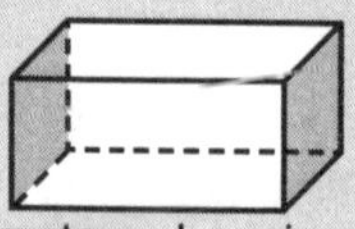
rectangular prism

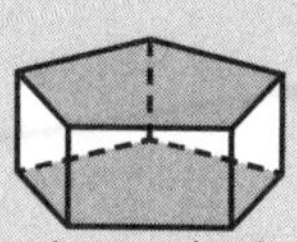
pentagonal prism

The bases have been shaded. Hidden edges are shown with dashed lines.

1. Shade the two bases of the prism. Identify the polygon that makes the base.

a) 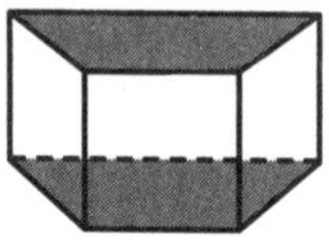
trapezoid

b) 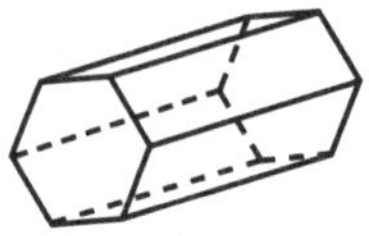
____

c) 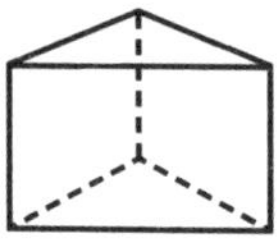
____

d) 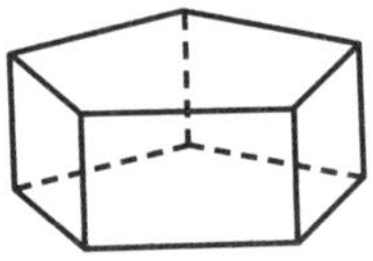
____

e) 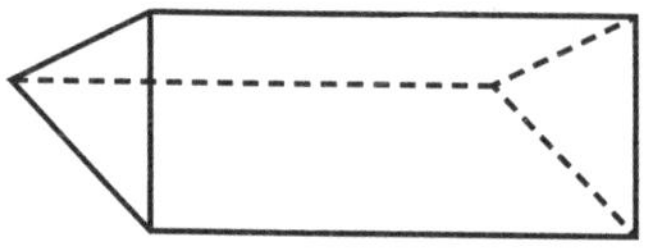
____

f) 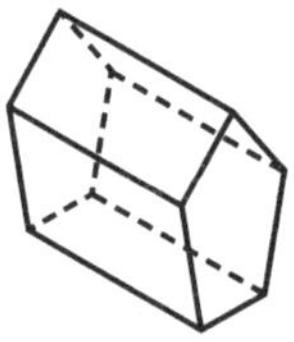
____

2. a) Count the cubes to determine the volume of the prism.

i) 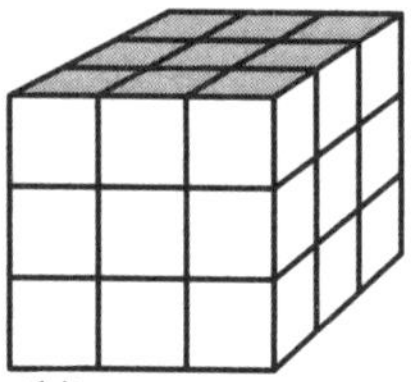

$V =$ *27 in³*

ii) 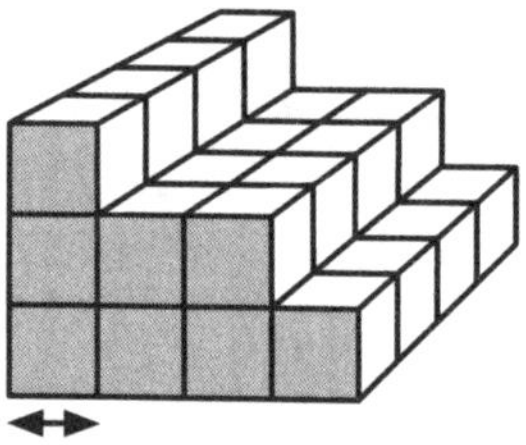

$V =$ __________

iii) 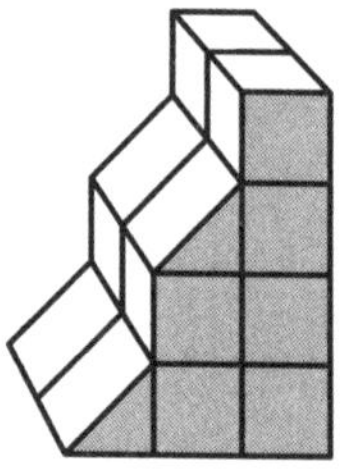

$V =$ __________

b) Complete the chart for each prism in part a).

	Area of Shaded Base (in^2)	Height (in)	Area of Shaded Base × Height (in^3)
i)	*9 in²*	*3 in*	*27 in³*
ii)			
iii)			

c) What do you notice about the volume of each prism in part a), and the product (area of base) × (height) in part b)? Write a formula for volume.

____

The height of a prism is the distance between its two bases.

3. Circle the measurement that gives the height of the prism. Hint: Shade the two bases.

a) 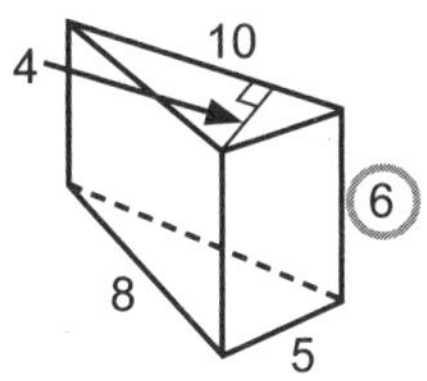

b) 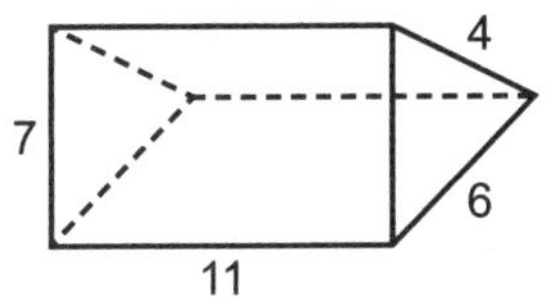

c) 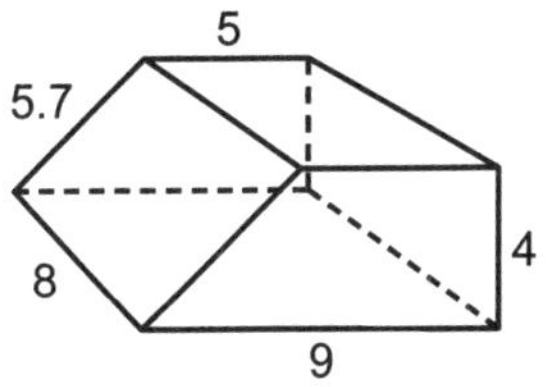

d) 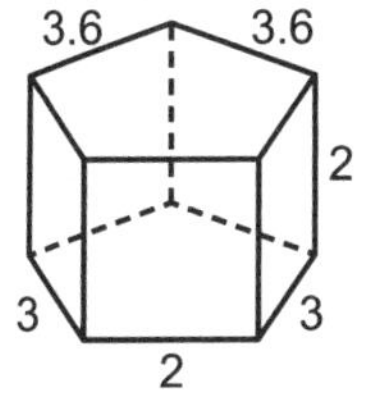

Volume of a prism = area of base × height OR $V = B \times h$

4. Calculate the volume of the prism.

a) 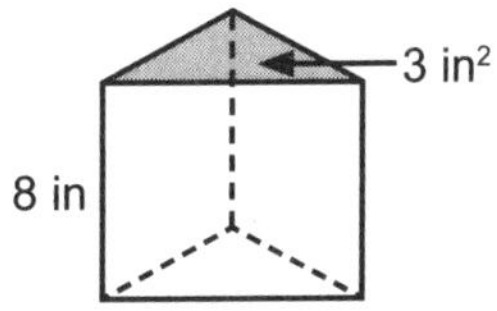

$B =$ ______________________

$h =$ ______________________

$V =$ ______________________

b) 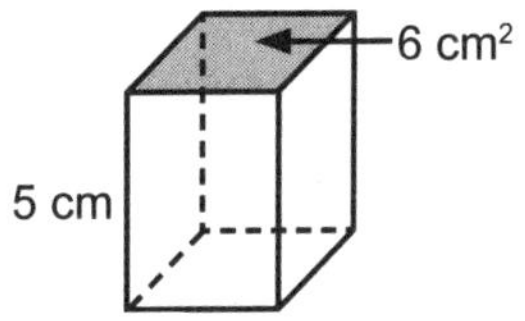

$B =$ ______________________

$h =$ ______________________

$V =$ ______________________

REMINDER:

Area of rectangle
= length × width

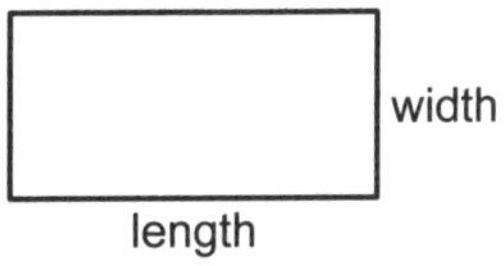

Area of triangle
= base × height ÷ 2

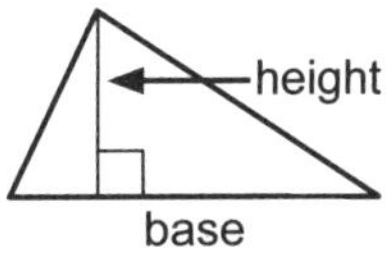

Area of parallelogram
= base × height

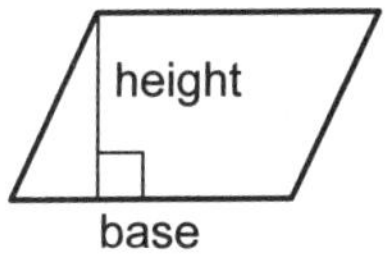

Area of trapezoid
= (base_1 + base_2) × height ÷ 2

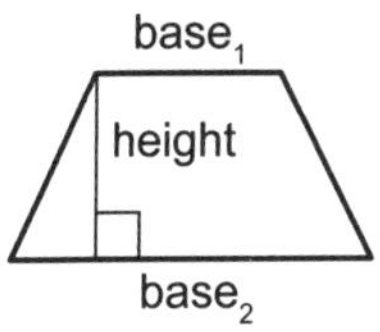

5. The diagram shows the base of a prism. Calculate the area of the base. Then use the given height to calculate the volume of the prism.

a) 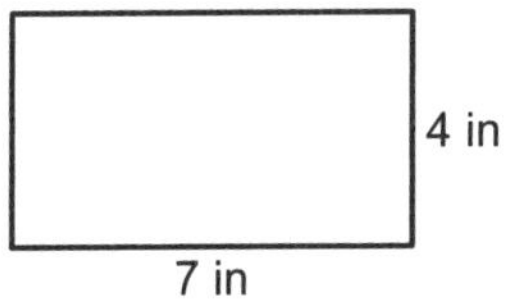

$B =$ ______________________

$h = 10$ in

$V =$ ______________________

b) 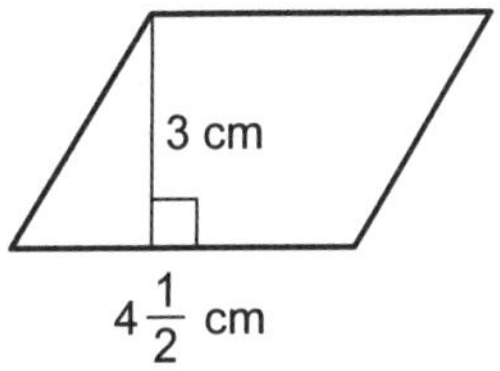

$B =$ ______________________

$h = 11\frac{2}{3}$ cm

$V =$ ______________________

6. Calculate the volume of the prism.

a)

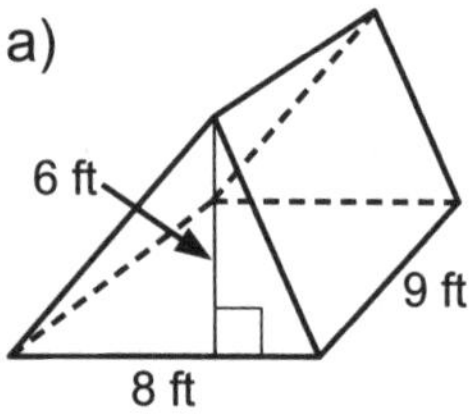

$B = $ <u>$8 \times 6 \div 2 = 24$ ft²</u>

$h = $ ____________

$V = $ ____________

b)

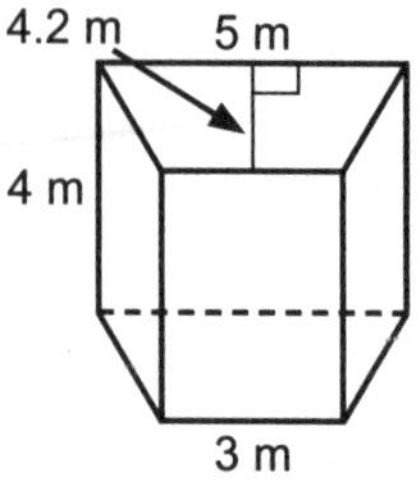

$B = $ ____________

$h = $ ____________

$V = $ ____________

7. a) Decompose the base into two polygons. Find the area of each polygon to find the total area of the base.

i)

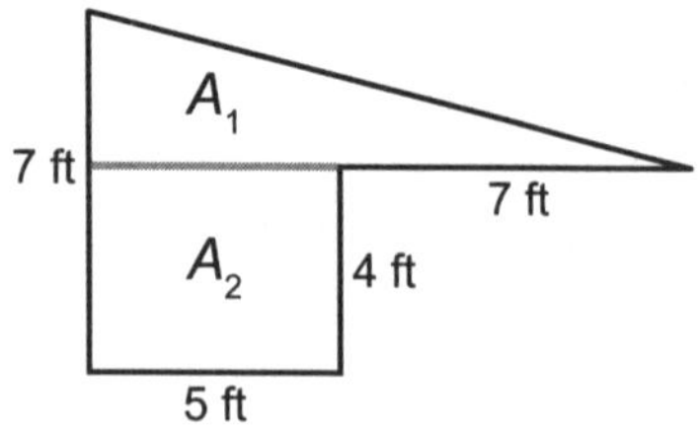

ii)

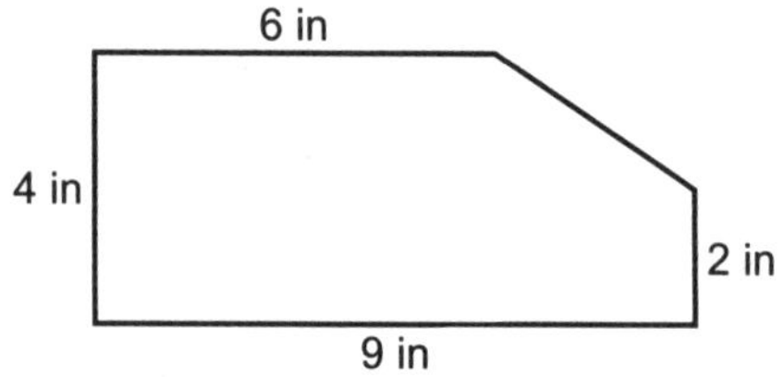

i) $A_1 = $ <u>12 ft $\times 3$ ft $\div 2 = 18$ ft²</u>

$A_2 = $ ____________

$B = $ ____________

ii) $A_1 = $ ____________

$A_2 = $ ____________

$B = $ ____________

b) Calculate the volume of a prism with the base shown in part a) and the given height.

i) $h = 7$ ft

$V = $ ____________

ii) $h = 5$ in

$V = $ ____________

Marla needs the triangular prism to have a volume of at least 60 in³. The height of the triangle is 4 inches, and the height of the prism is 5 inches. What is the minimum base of the triangle?

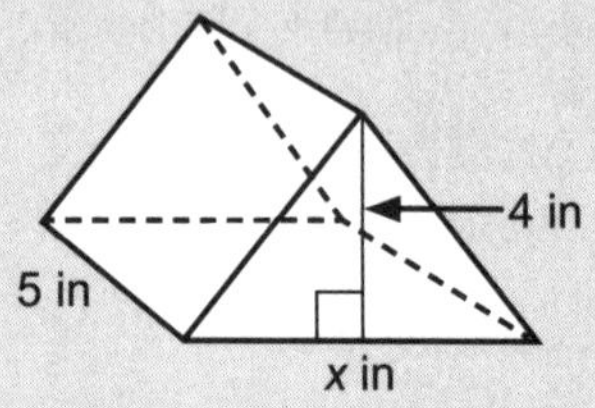

$V \geq 60$

$B \times h \geq 60$

$(2x)(5) \geq 60$

$10x \geq 60$

Area of base: $B = x \times 4 \div 2 = 2x$

$x \geq 60 \div 10$

Height of prism: $h = 5$

$x \geq 6$ in

The base of the triangle must be at least 6 in.

8. The volume of the prism is given. Find the unknown dimension. Write the answer as an inequality.

a) Volume is at least 45 in³

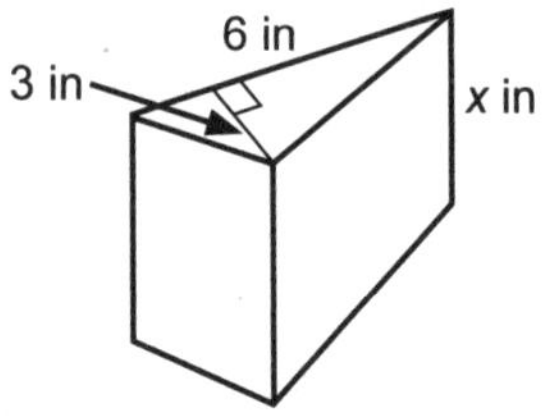

b) Volume is at most 56 ft³

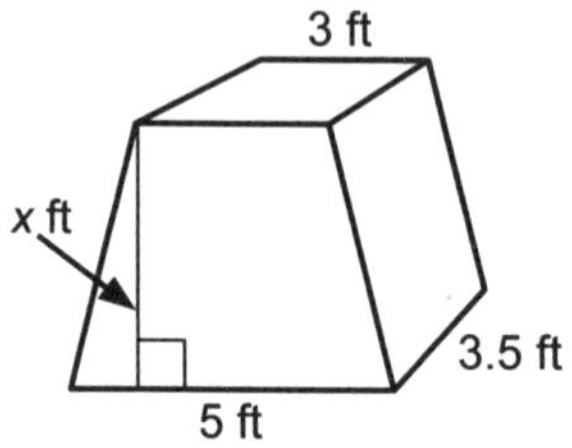

G7-26 Nets and Surface Area of Prisms

A **net** of a 3-D shape is a pattern that can be folded to make the shape.

Examples: rectangular prism

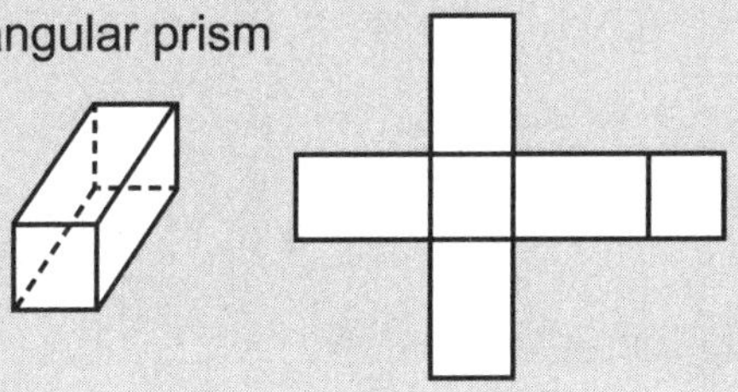

triangular prism

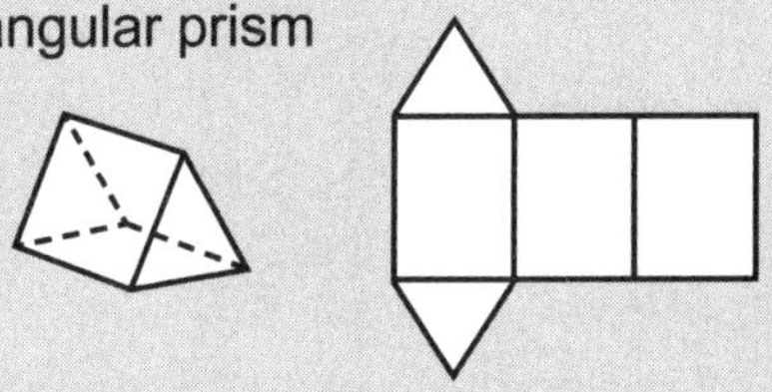

1. A net for the rectangular prism is shown on the grid. On the net, label each face of the prism. Each square on the grid represents 1 cm.

a)

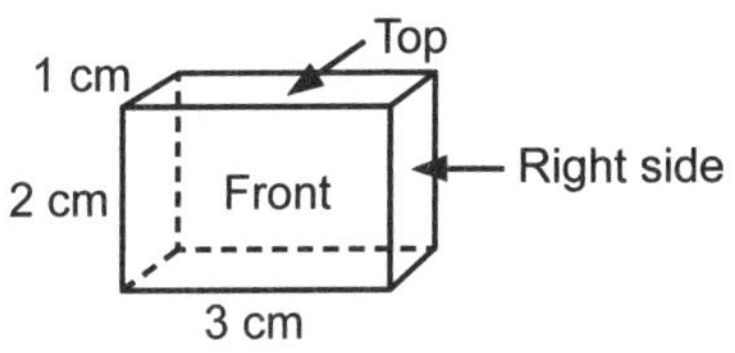

b)

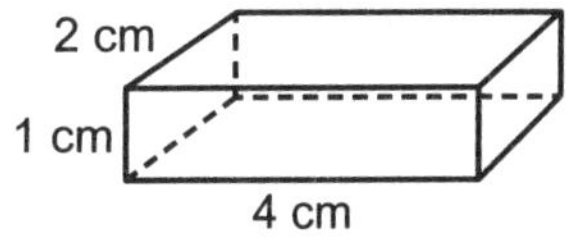

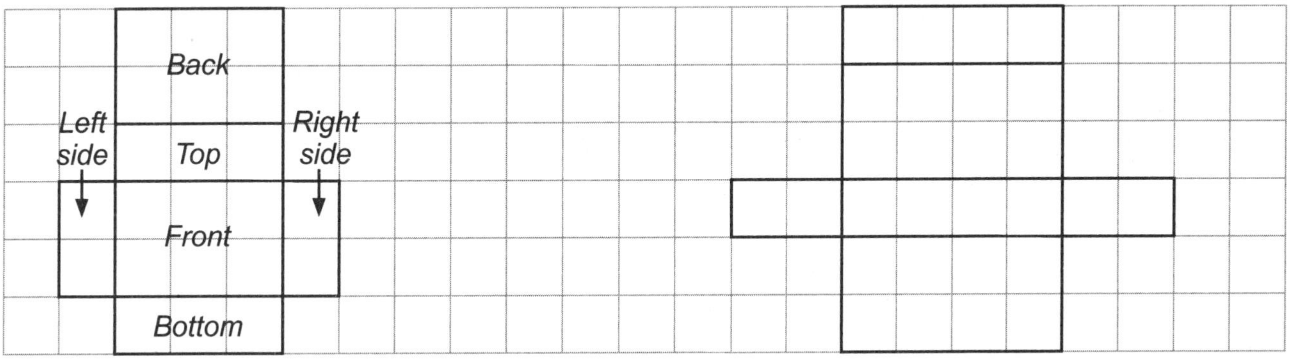

Surface area is the total area of all faces of a three-dimensional object.

We measure surface area in unit squares or square units. Example: square inches (in^2)

2. Write a multiplication equation for the area of each face for the rectangular prisms in Question 1. Then find the surface area of each prism.

a) Front *$2 \times 3 = 6$ cm^2*

Back ______________________

Right side ______________________

Left side ______________________

Top ______________________

Bottom ______________________

Surface area of prism ______________

b) Front ______________________

Back ______________________

Right side ______________________

Left side ______________________

Top ______________________

Bottom ______________________

Surface area of prism ______________

3. A net for the triangular prism is shown on the grid. On the net, label each face of the prism and write the length of each edge. Each square on the grid represents 1 cm^2.

a)

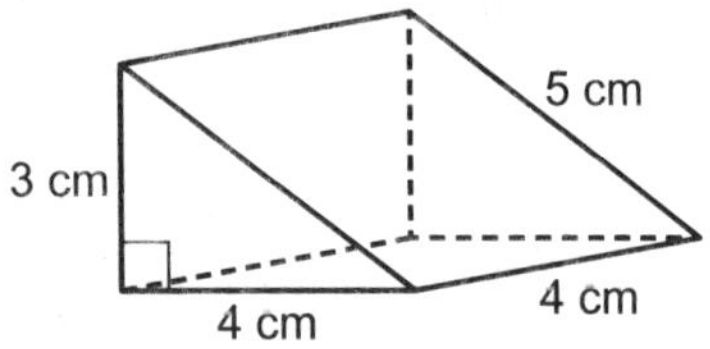

b)

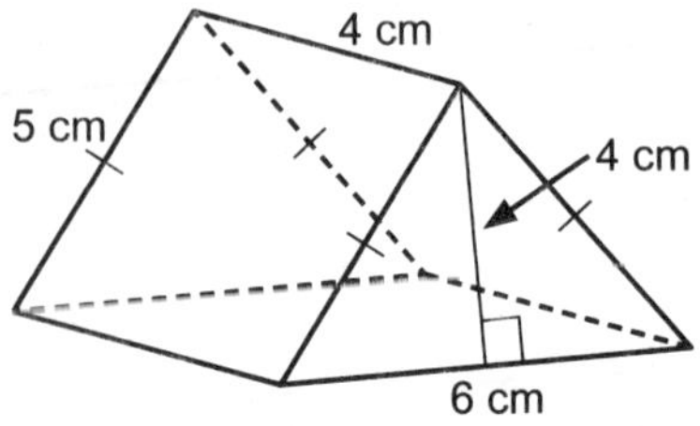

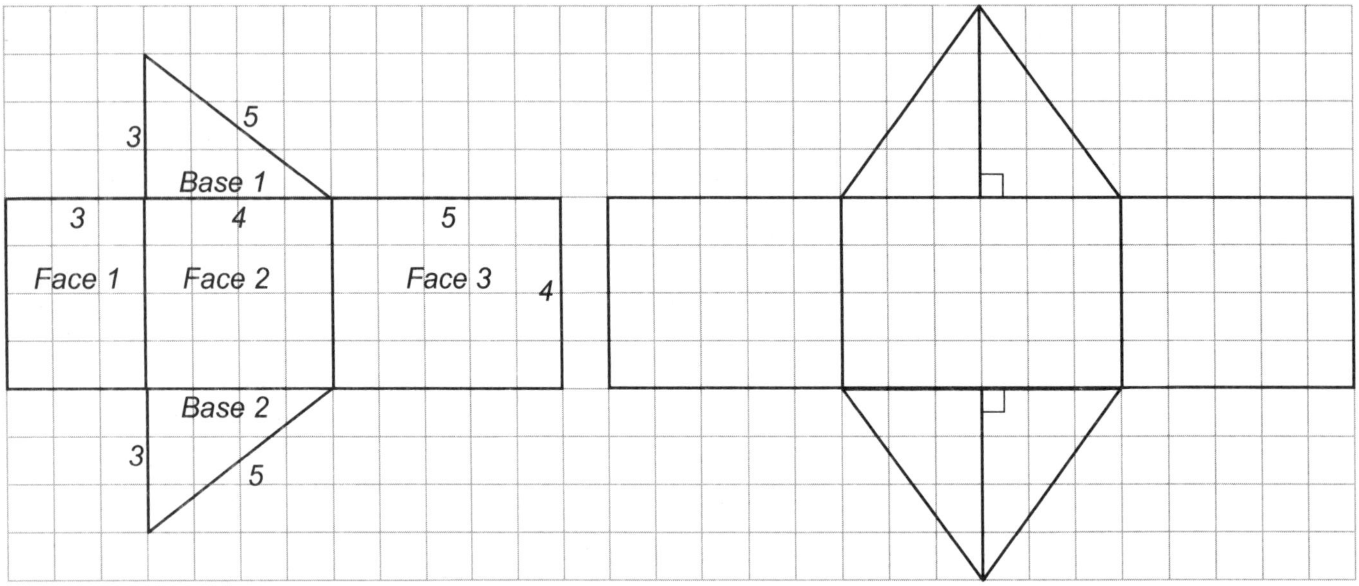

4. Write an equation for the area of each face for the triangular prisms in Question 3. Then find the surface area of each prism.

a) Base 1 $4 \times 3 \div 2 = 6\ cm^2$

Base 2 ______________

Face 1 ______________

Face 2 ______________

Face 3 ______________

Surface area of prism ______________

b) Base 1 ______________

Base 2 ______________

Face 1 ______________

Face 2 ______________

Face 3 ______________

Surface area of prism ______________

5. Explain how the net of a prism helps you find the surface area of the prism.

6. Find the surface area of the prism. Hint: Draw a net.

a)

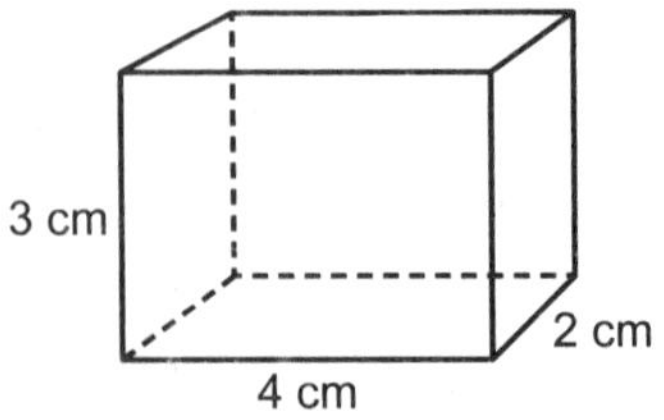

b)

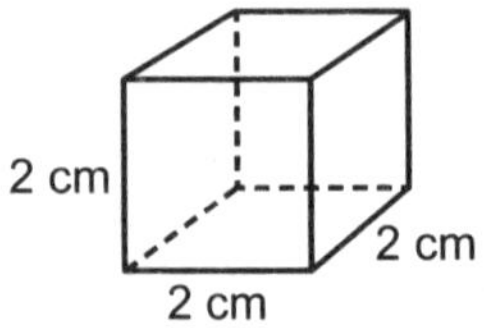

Surface Area of Rectangular Prisms

1. Shade the face that has the same area as the already shaded face.

a) 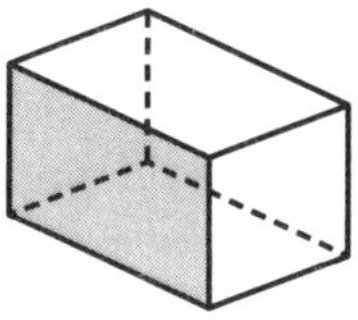

b) 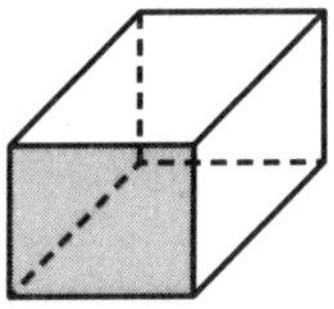

c) 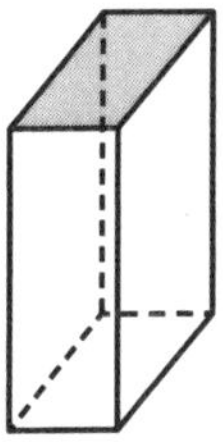

2. The area of each visible face is given. What is the area of each hidden face?

a) 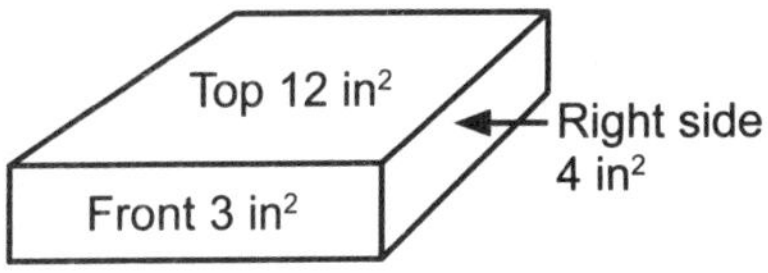

Back ____________

Bottom ____________

Left side ____________

b) 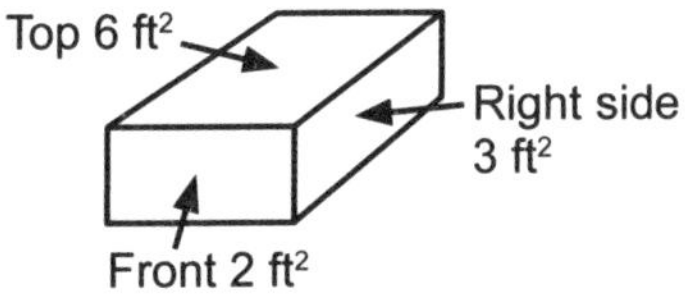

Back ____________

Bottom ____________

Left side ____________

c) 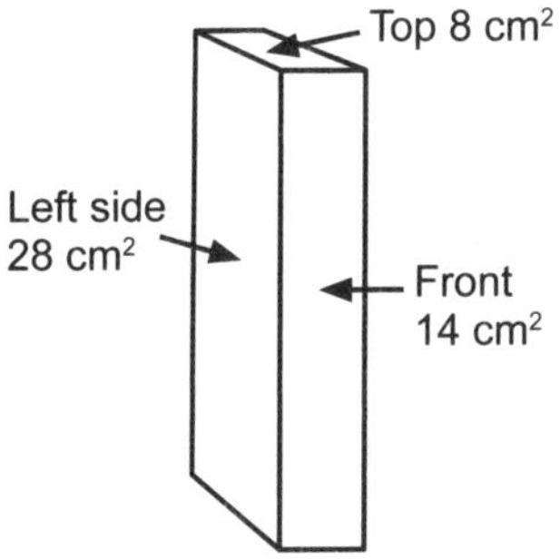

Back ____________

Bottom ____________

Right side ____________

3. Write the area of each visible face directly on the face. Double the area of the face to find the total area of each pair of opposite faces. Then find the surface area of the prism.

a) 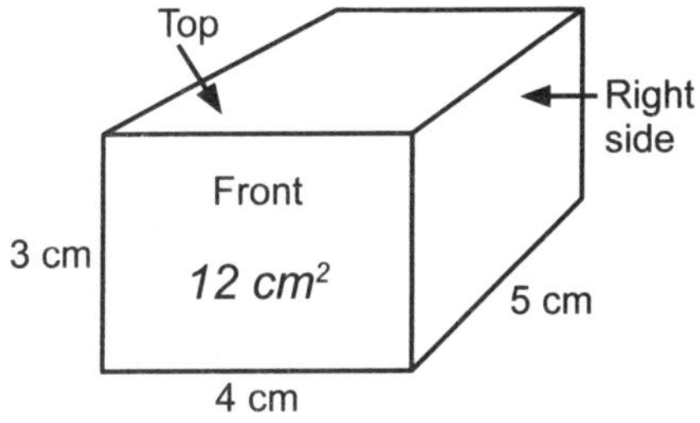

Front + back = *12 cm^2 × 2* = *24 cm^2*

Top + bottom = ____________ = ____________

Right + left sides = ____________ = ____________

Surface area = ________ + ________ + ________

= ____________

b) 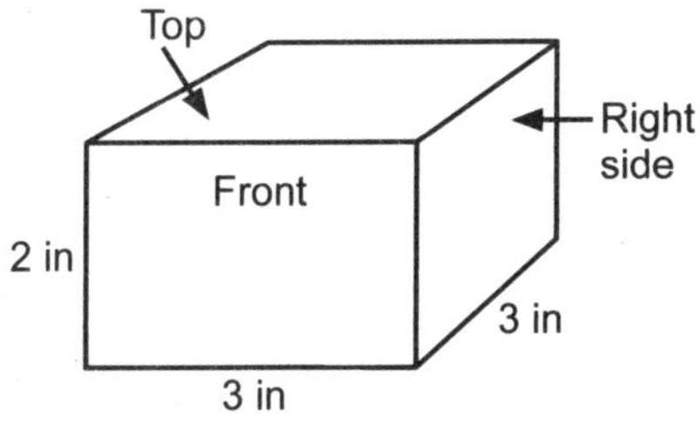

________ + ________ = ____________ = ________

________ + ________ = ____________ = ________

________ + ________ = ____________ = ________

Surface area = ________ + ________ + ________

= ____________

4. Find the surface area of the prism with length ℓ, width w, and height h.

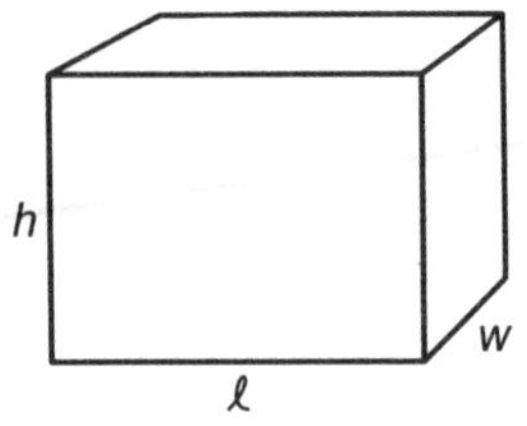

Front + back = $\underline{\ \ell \times h \times 2\ }$ = $\underline{\ 2\ell h\ }$

Top + bottom = ____________ = ________

Right + left sides = ____________ = ________

Surface area = ____________________

> The surface area of a rectangular prism = 2 × (area of front) + 2 × (area of top) + 2 × (area of right side)
>
> $SA = 2\ell h + 2\ell w + 2wh$ OR $2(\ell h + \ell w + wh)$

5. Find the surface area of the rectangular prism. Include units in your final answer.

a)

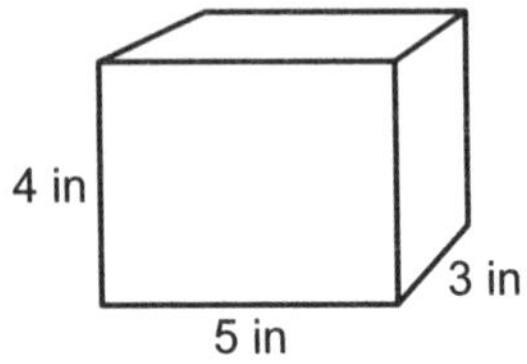

$SA = 2(\underline{\ 5\ })(\underline{\ 4\ }) + 2(\_\_\_)(\_\_\_) + 2(\_\_\_)(\_\_\_)$

= $\underline{\ 40\ }$ + ______ + ______

= __________

b)

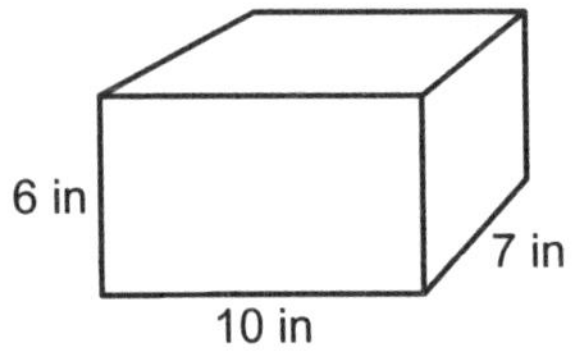

SA = __________ + __________ + __________

= ______ + ______ + ______

= __________

6. Jayden knows that the surface areas of the front, top, and right faces of a prism add to 28 in^2. How can he find the total surface area of the prism?

____

7. a) Helen says that she only needs to find the area of two faces of this prism to calculate the surface area. Is she correct? Explain.

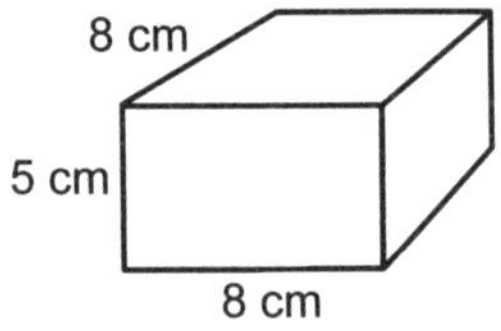

____

b) What is the surface area of the prism?

____

____

8. It costs about $0.10 per square foot to paint a room. About how much would it cost to paint only the walls of the room in the picture? You don't need to paint the door that measures 6.5 ft by 3 ft or the window that measures 4 ft by 5 ft.

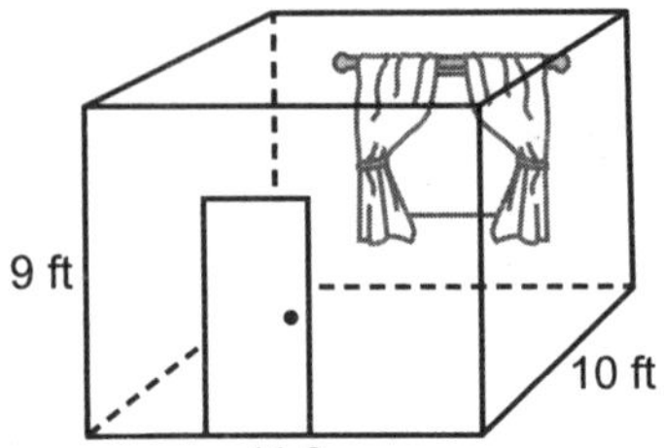

G7-28 Surface Area of Polygonal Prisms and Pyramids

To find the surface area of a polygonal prism, add the areas of each of its faces.

1. a) Find the area of the shaded face of the triangular prism.

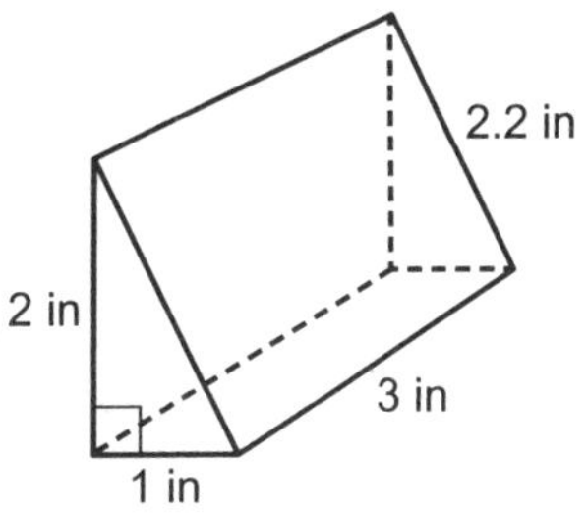

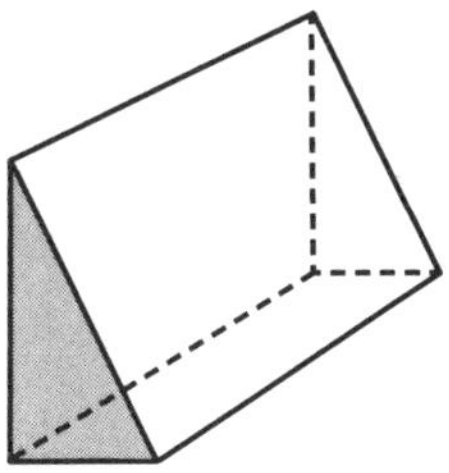

Area 1 = ___________

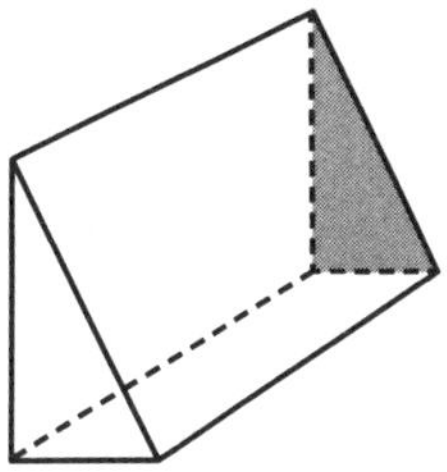

Area 2 = ___________

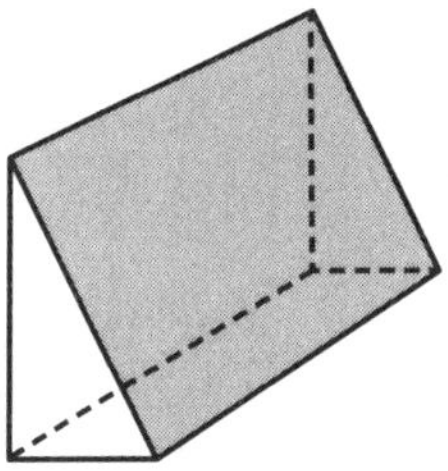

Area 3 = ___________

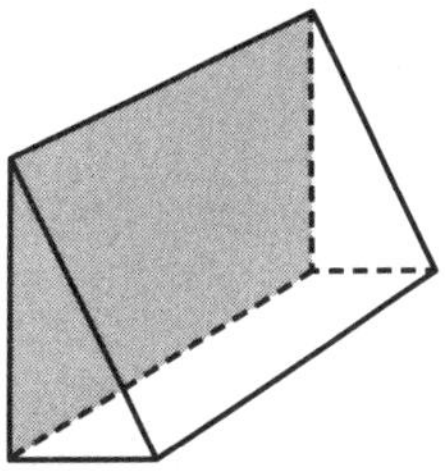

Area 4 = ___________

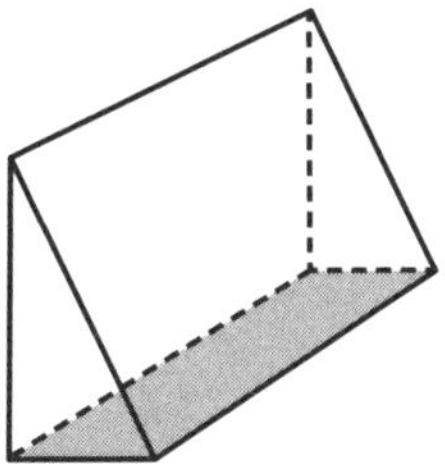

Area 5 = ___________

b) What is the surface area of the triangular prism in part a)? ___________________________

2. a) Shade one face of the trapezoidal prism at a time. Find the area of the shaded face.

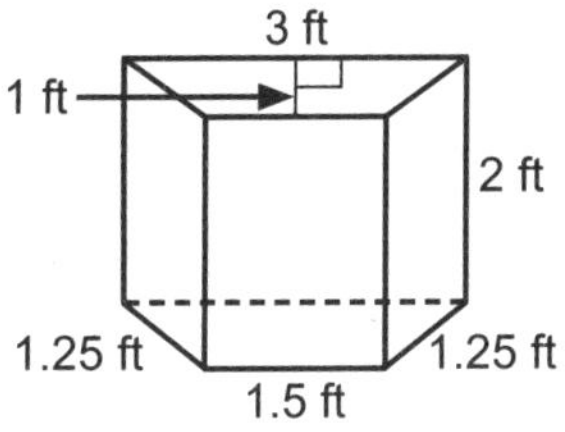

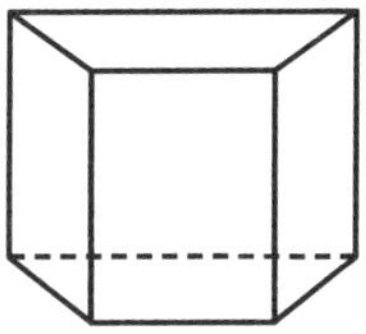

Area 1 = ___________

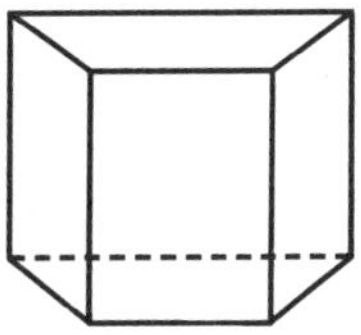

Area 2 = ___________

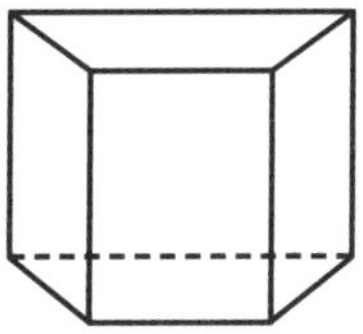

Area 3 = ___________

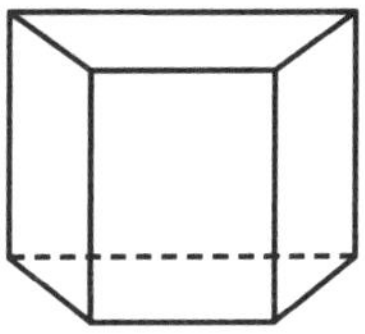

Area 4 = ___________

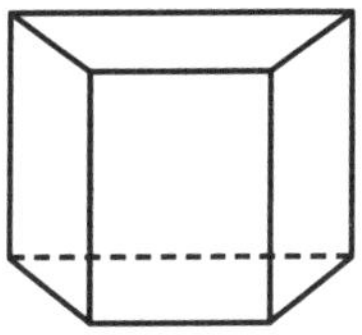

Area 5 = ___________

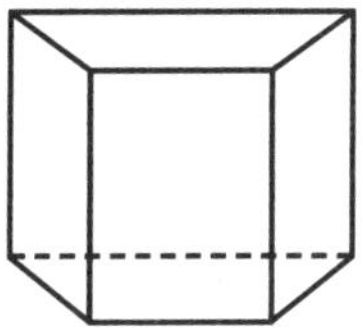

Area 6 = ___________

b) What is the surface area of the trapezoidal prism in part a)? ___________________________

c) Explain a simpler method to find the surface area of the prism in part a). Do you need to find the areas of all 6 faces? Hint: Which faces are congruent?

____

____

Pyramids have one base that is a polygon, and faces that are triangles. The faces meet at a vertex opposite to the base.

The bases of triangular pyramids are triangles.

The bases of rectangular pyramids are rectangles.

3. Find the area of each face to find the surface area of the pyramid. All measurements are in centimeters.

a)

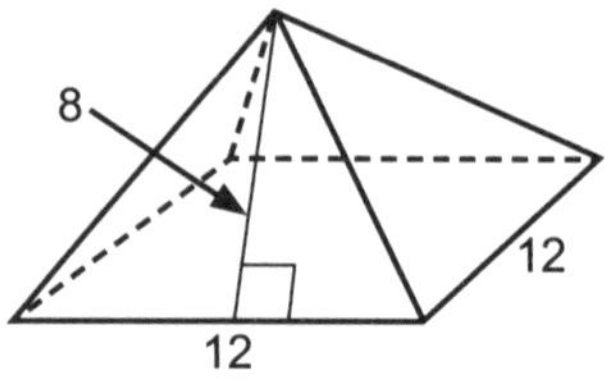

b)

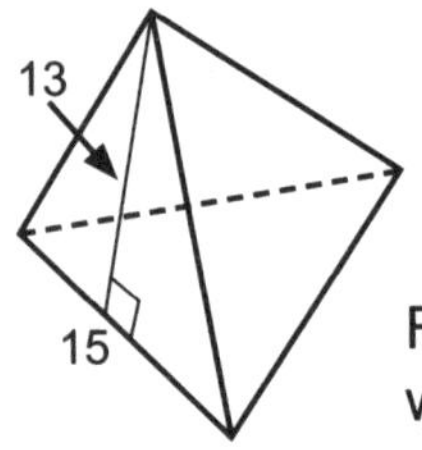

Faces are equilateral triangles with sides 15 cm.

4. Find the surface area of the prism. Hint: 1 inch = $\frac{1}{12}$ foot.

a)

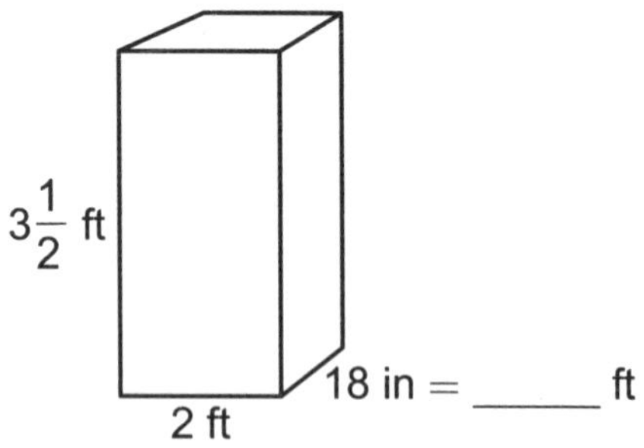

b)

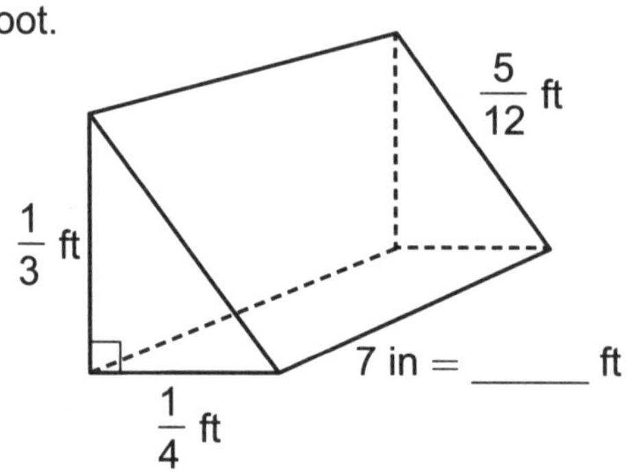

5. Two gifts boxes each have a volume of 120 in^3. Which box requires less material to make? All measurements are in inches.

Box A.

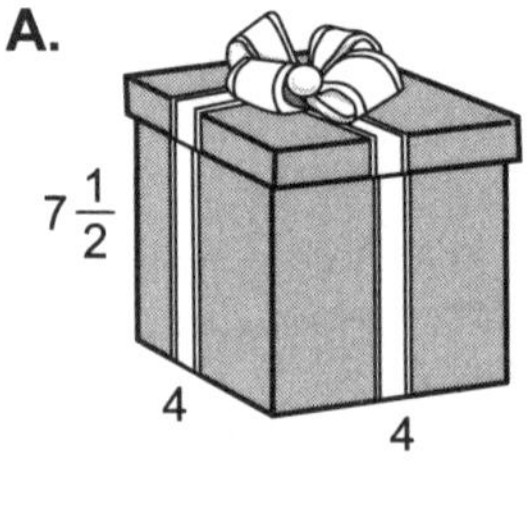

Box B.

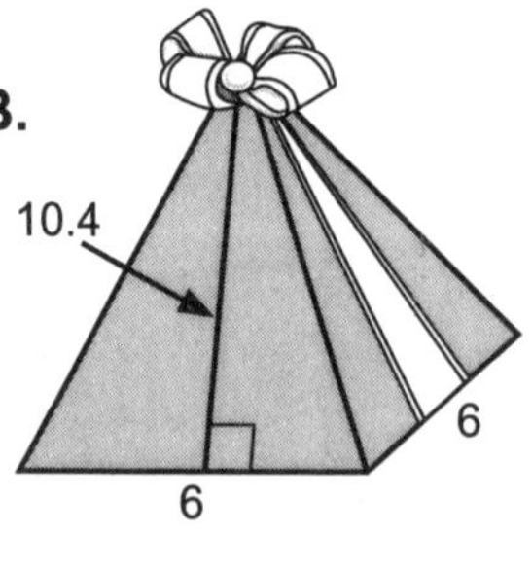

6. Glen is making an aquarium in the shape of a triangular prism. It will have glass sides, a glass bottom, and a plastic cover. If glass costs \$3 per ft^2, and Glen spends \$25 on other materials, how much will it cost to make the aquarium?

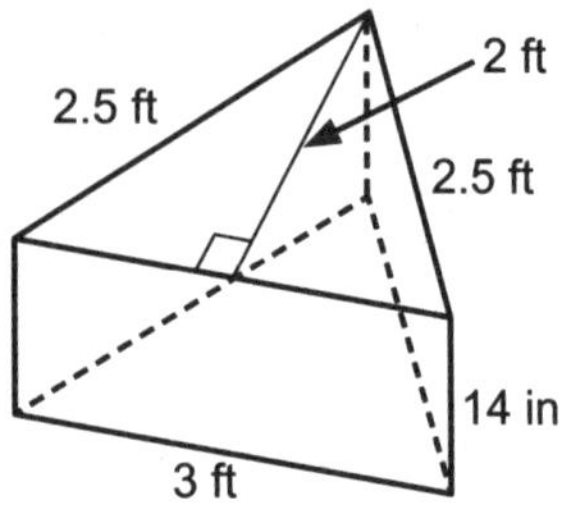

Alice wants to find the total surface area of this shape.

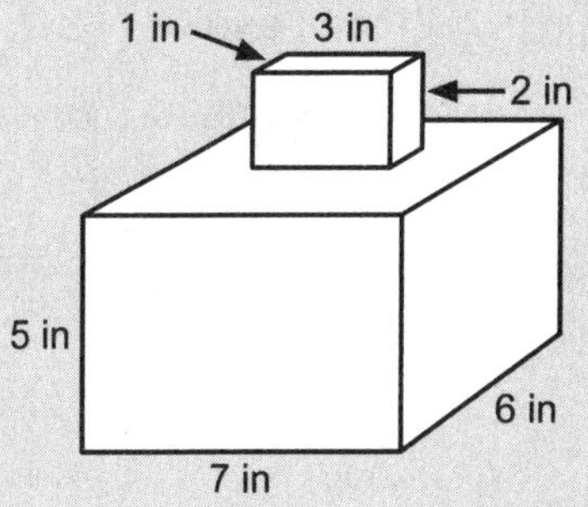

First, she finds the surface area of the bottom prism.	$2(7)(5) + 2(7)(6) + 2(6)(5)$ $= 70 + 84 + 60 = 214 \text{ in}^2$
Then, she finds the surface area of the top prism.	$2(3)(2) + 2(3)(1) + 2(1)(2)$ $= 12 + 6 + 4 = 22 \text{ in}^2$
Next, she finds the overlapping area.	$3(1) = 3 \text{ in}^2$
She adds the surface areas of the two prisms, and subtracts the overlapping area twice to find the total surface area.	$SA = 214 + 22 - 3 - 3$ $= 230 \text{ in}^2$

7. Find the surface area of the 3-D shape.

a)

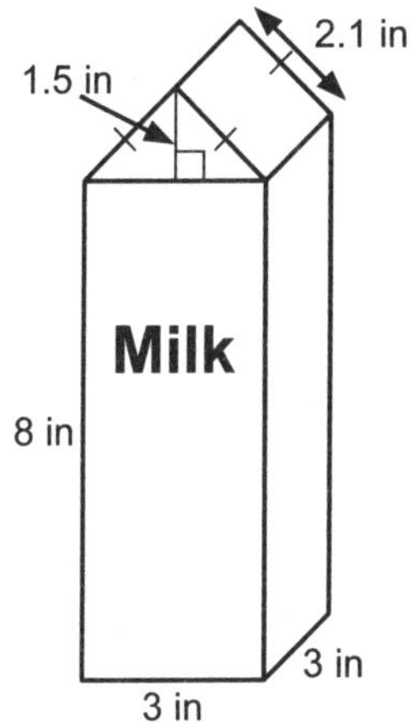

b)

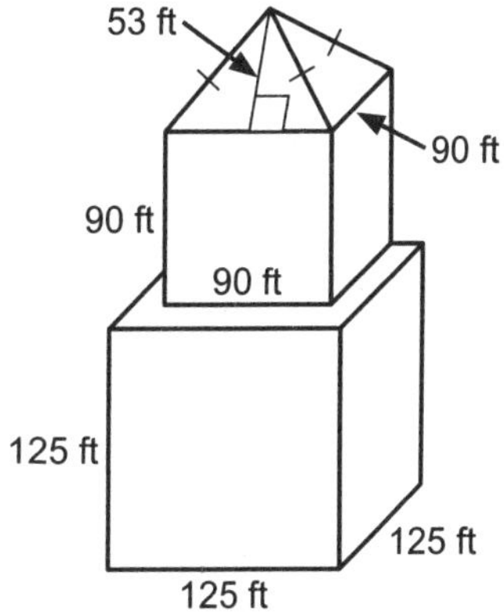

c)

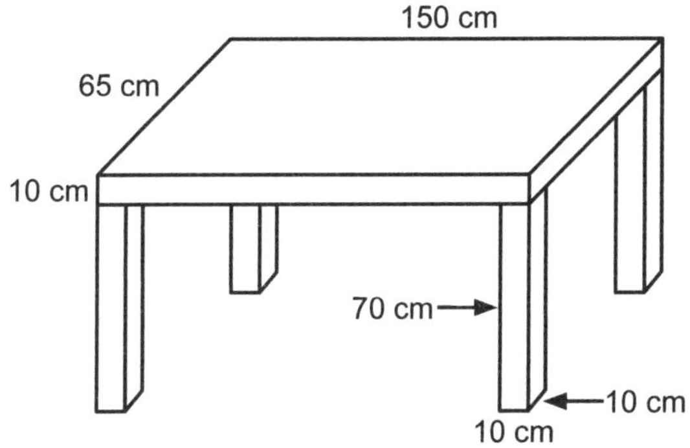

Bonus ▶ Hint: A rectangular prism is cut from the middle of this sculpture.

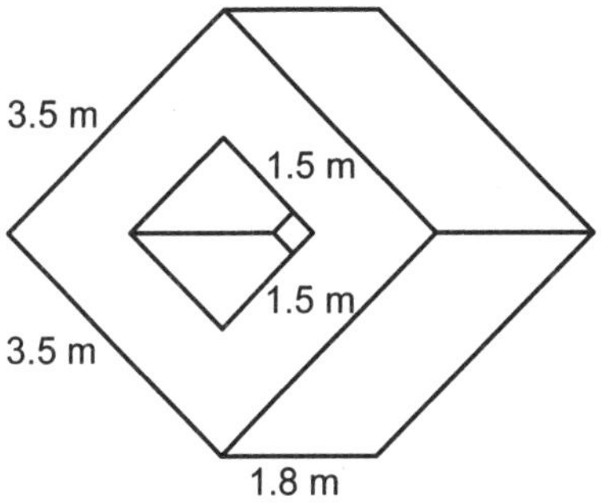

8. Use the objects in Question 7 to answer the question.

a) How much would it cost to make 100 milk cartons if cardboard costs 0.1 cents per square inch?

b) If the cost to clean the exterior of the office building was \$25,518, how much did the cleaning company charge per square foot?

c) How much would it cost to stain the table if wood stain costs \$0.10 per 1,000 cm^2?

Bonus ▶ How much would it cost to paint the sculpture if paint costs \$0.90 per m^2?

Volume and Surface Area

REMINDER: For a rectangular prism with length ℓ, width w, and height h,

Volume $= \ell wh$ and Surface Area $= 2\ell h + 2\ell w + 2wh$

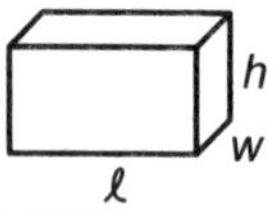

1. Find the volume and the surface area of the rectangular prism. Hint: All measurements must be in the same unit.

a) 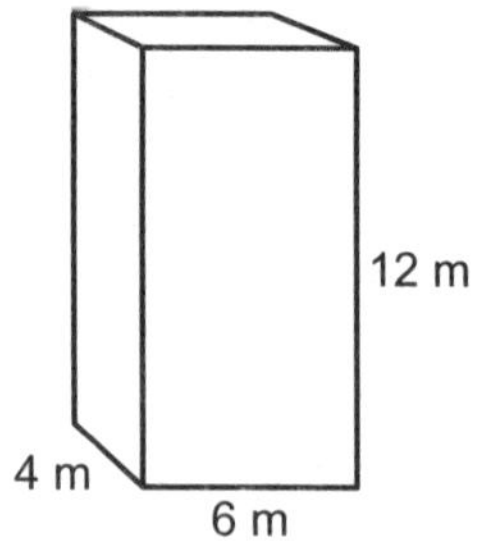

b) 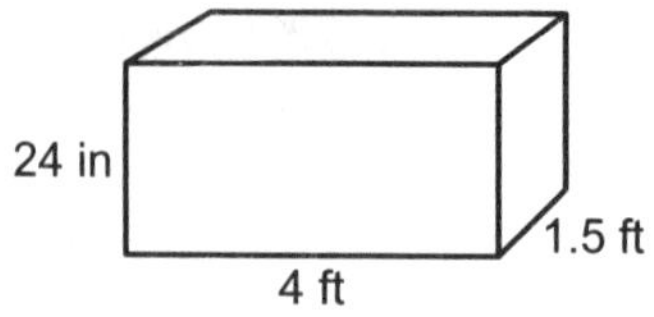

c) 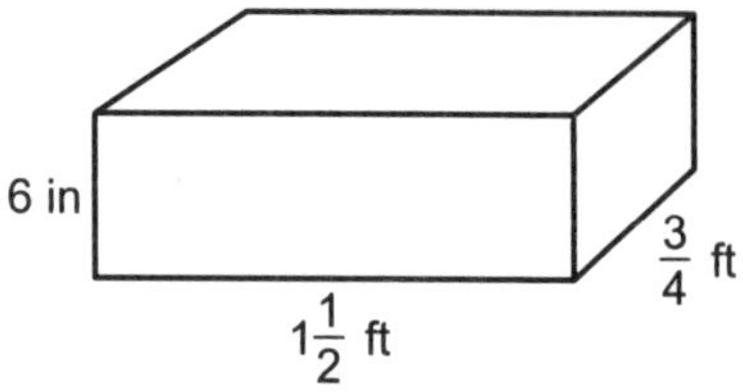

2. A rectangular prism has volume 120 in^3. It is 4 inches long and 6 inches high.
   a) Find the unknown dimension of the prism.
   b) Find the surface area of the prism.

3. A cube is a rectangular prism in which all edges have equal length a.

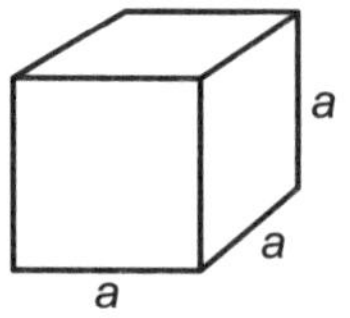

   a) The formula for the volume of a cube is $V = a^3$. Explain why.
   b) The formula for the surface area of a cube is $SA = 6a^2$. Explain why.
   c) Find the volume and the surface area of the cube with edge a.

   i) $a = 5$ in   ii) $a = 12$ cm   iii) $a = \frac{1}{2}$ ft

REMINDER: For a polygonal prism, Volume = (area of base) × height, or $V = B \times h$, and Surface area = the sum of the areas of its faces.

4. Explain why there is no single formula for the surface area of all polygonal prisms.

5. Find the volume and the surface area of the polygonal prism. Hint: All measurements must be in the same unit.

a) 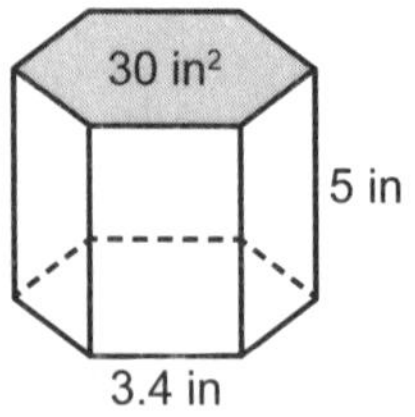

All edges of the hexagon are 3.4 inches.

b) 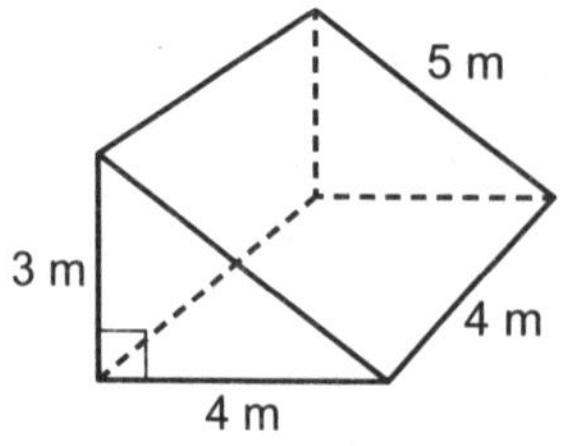

c) 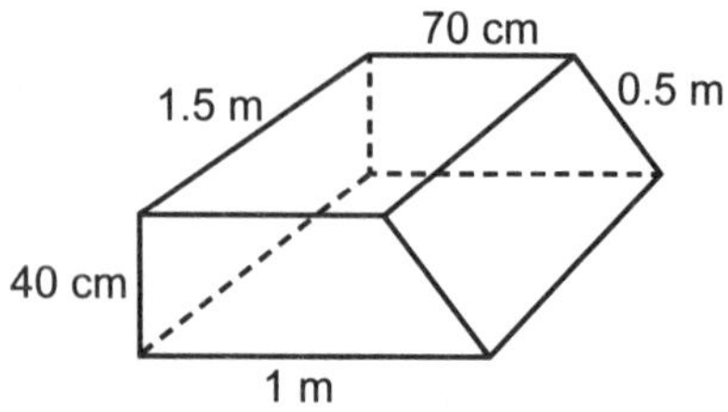

6. a) Each dimension of the larger juice box is twice the corresponding dimension of the smaller juice box. Write the dimensions of the larger box.

b) The small juice box costs $0.50. How much should the large juice box cost, if cost is proportional to volume?

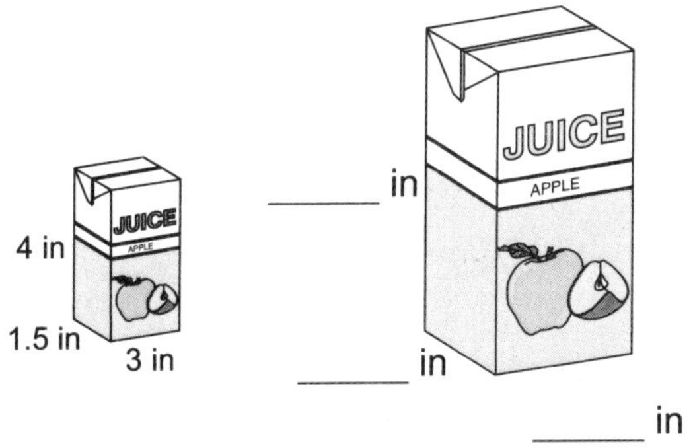

7. a) The boxes each have a volume of 8 in^3. Which box has the least surface area?

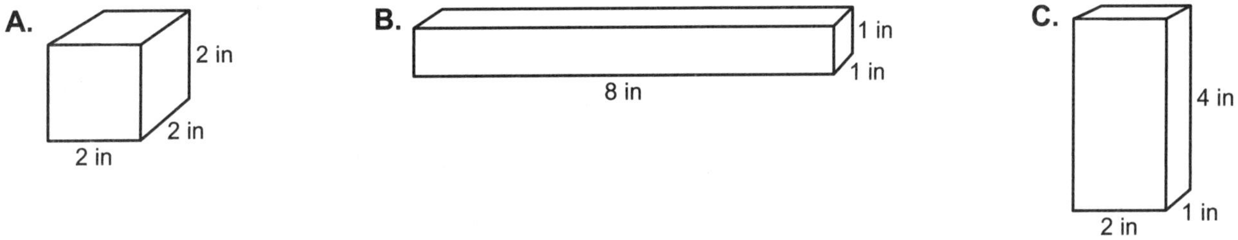

b) Find 3 possible sets of dimensions for a rectangular prism with volume of 24 in^3. Which has the least surface area?

c) Describe the shape of the rectangular prism with the least surface area for a given volume.

8. An A-frame cottage has the dimensions shown on the diagram.

a) Fire regulations allow for 1 person per 500 ft^3. How many people can stay in the cottage?

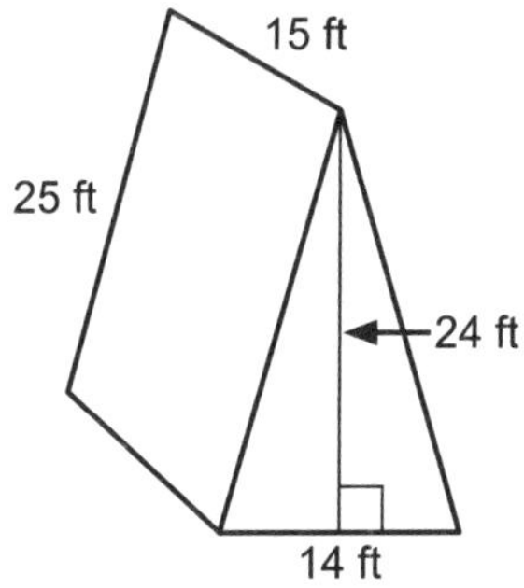

b) How much longer would the cottage need to be to accommodate 12 people?

c) How many shingles do you need to cover the sides, if shingles are 12 inches wide, 36 inches long, and stop 12 inches above the ground?

9. Abdul is installing a pool in his backyard. He has the choice of two designs:

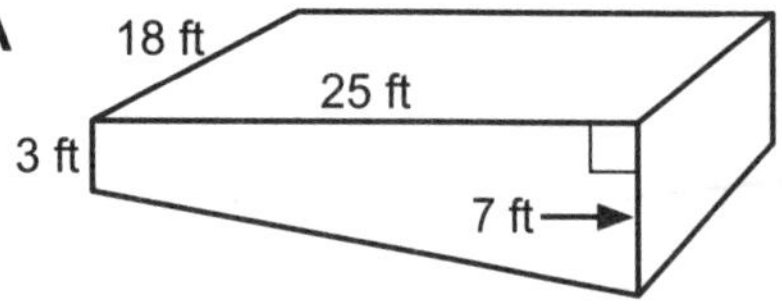

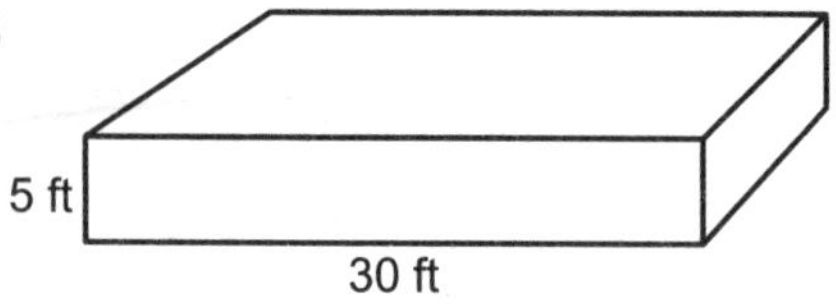

a) Find the volume of Pool A.

b) Pool B has the same volume as Pool A. What is the width of Pool B?

c) Design a new pool with the same volume, but with a different shape.

10. Find the volume and surface area of the 3-D shape. Do your rough work in your notebook.

a)

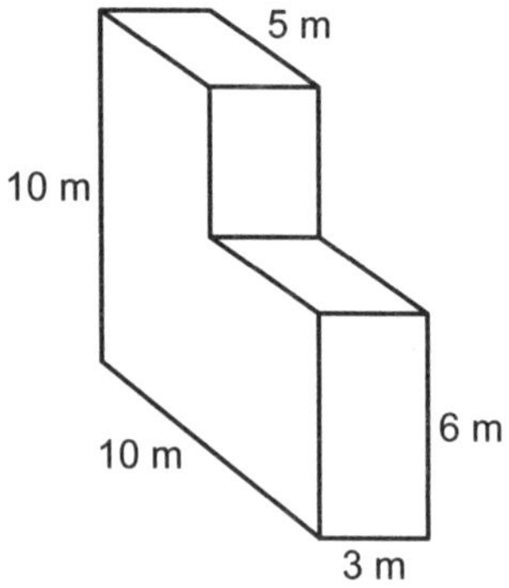

$V =$ ____________

$SA =$ ____________

b)

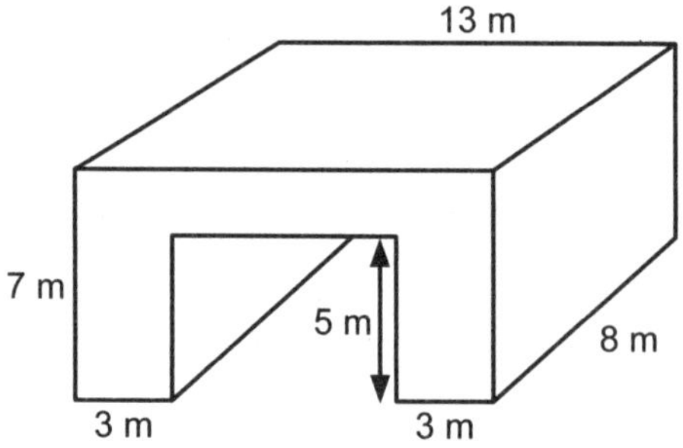

$V =$ ____________

$SA =$ ____________

c)

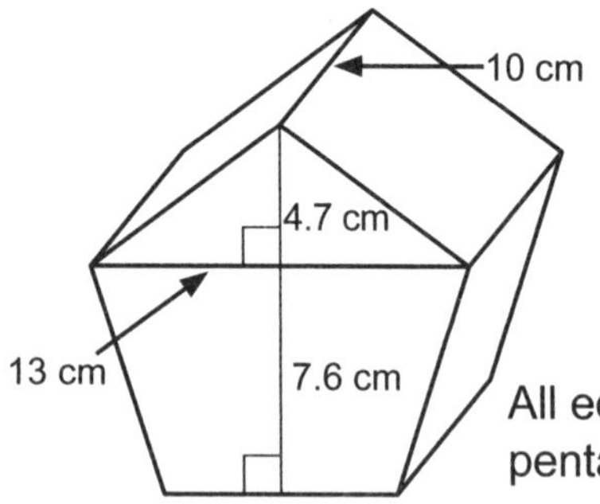

All edges of the pentagon are 8 cm.

$V =$ ____________

$SA =$ ____________

d)

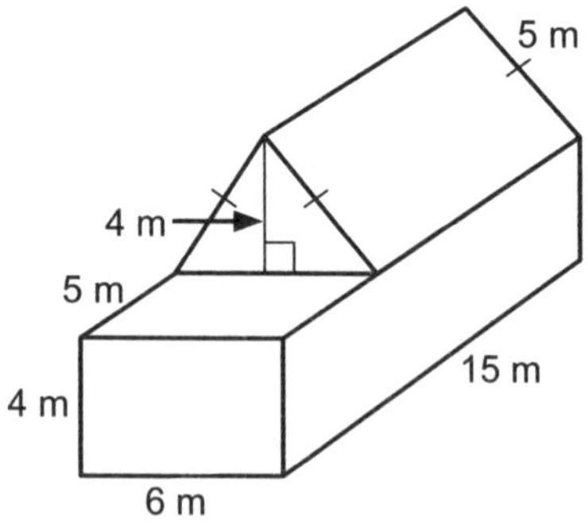

$V =$ ____________

$SA =$ ____________

11. Check your answer to Question 10.b) by calculating the volume and surface area in a different way.

G7-30 Cross Sections of 3-D Shapes (Introduction)

A **plane** is a flat surface that goes on forever in every direction.

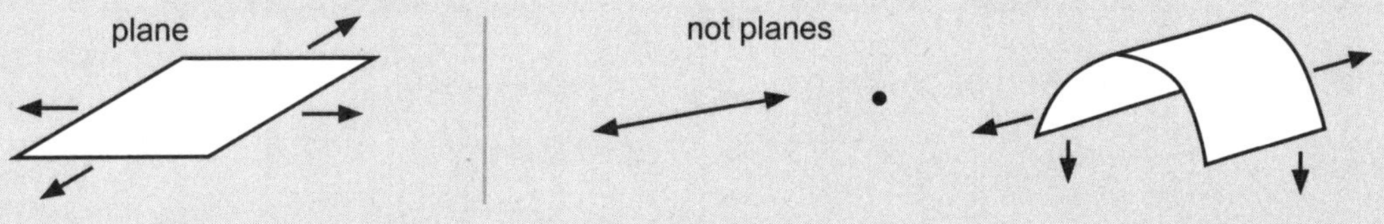

Lines and points are not planes because they are not surfaces. Curved surfaces are not planes because they are not flat.

1. Is the object a part of a plane?

a) a television screen ___________ b) a television ___________

c) a bowl ___________ d) a face of a cube ___________

A **cross section** of a 3-D shape is the intersection of the shape with a plane.

Example: When you cut a sandwich (a rectangular prism) straight through with a knife (a part of a plane), the cut makes a cross section in the shape of a rectangle.

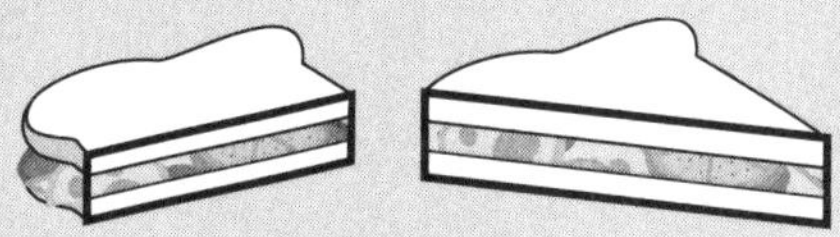

Cross sections can be different shapes, depending on the 3-D shape and the angle the plane cuts it on.

2. The cross section is shown in dark gray. Describe the cross section as a point, a line segment, a triangle, a quadrilateral, a pentagon, or a hexagon.

a) 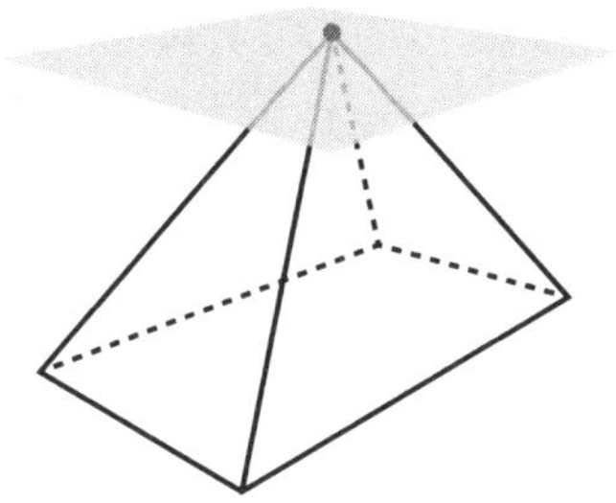

____

b) 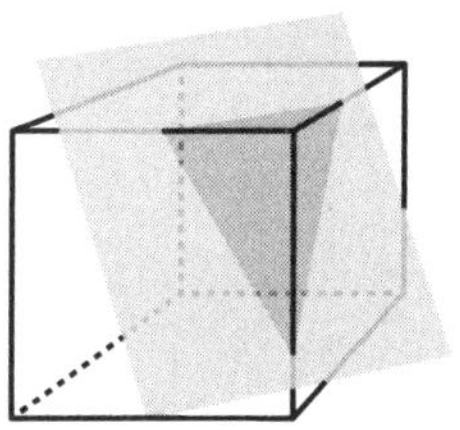

____

c) 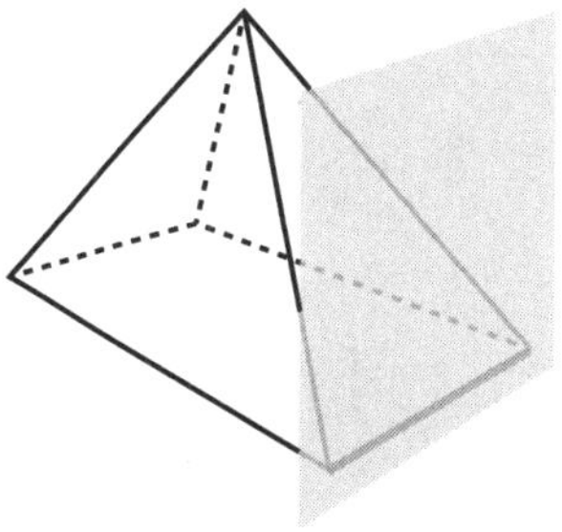

____

d) 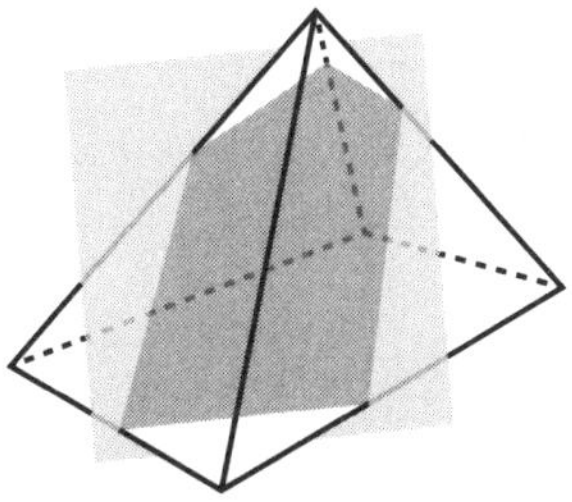

____

e) 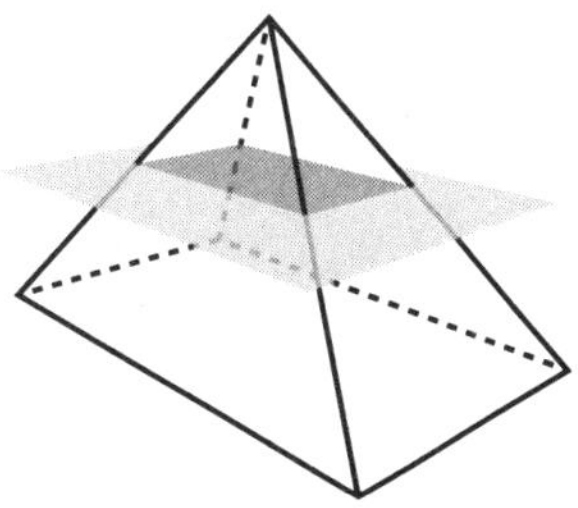

____

f) 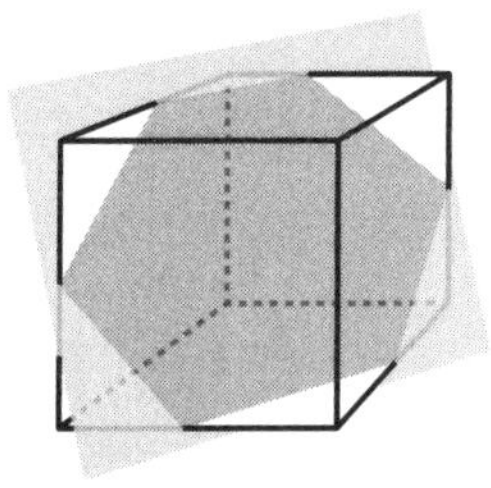

____

3. Can a cross section of a rectangular pyramid be a hexagon? Explain.

Two planes are **parallel** if they never intersect. Two flat surfaces are **parallel** if the planes they are a part of are parallel.

4. Shade the faces that are parallel to the bottom face.

a) 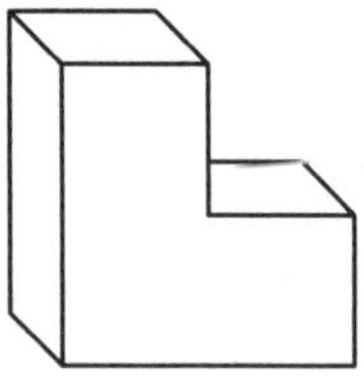

b) 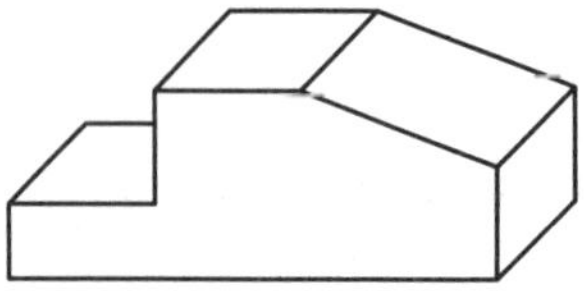

c) 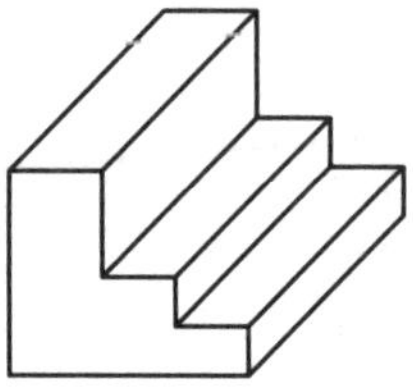

REMINDER: Two shapes are congruent if they are both the same shape and size. Two shapes are similar if they are the same shape but different sizes.

5. The planes are parallel to the base. Are the cross sections similar or congruent?

a) 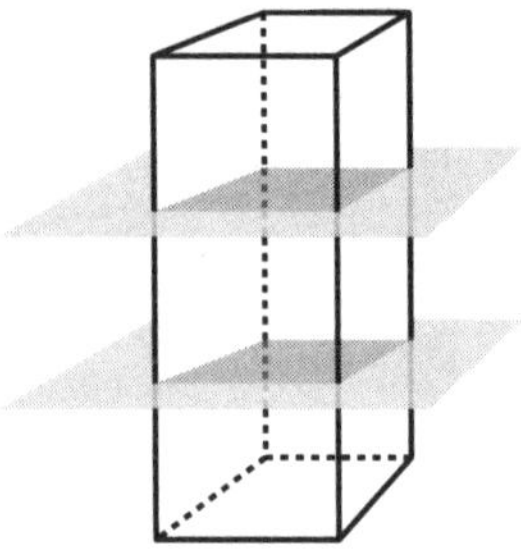
____

b) 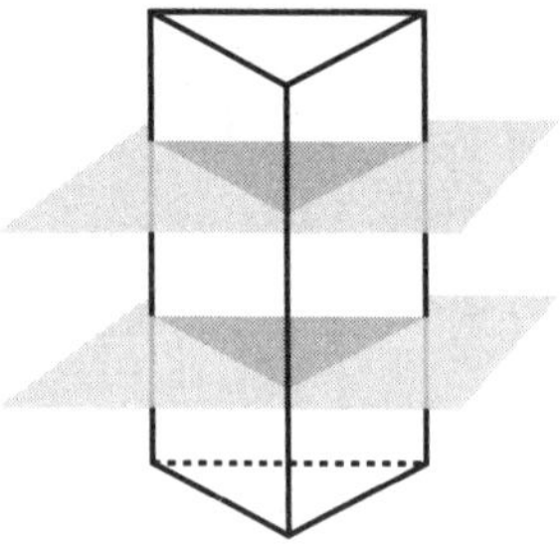
____

c) 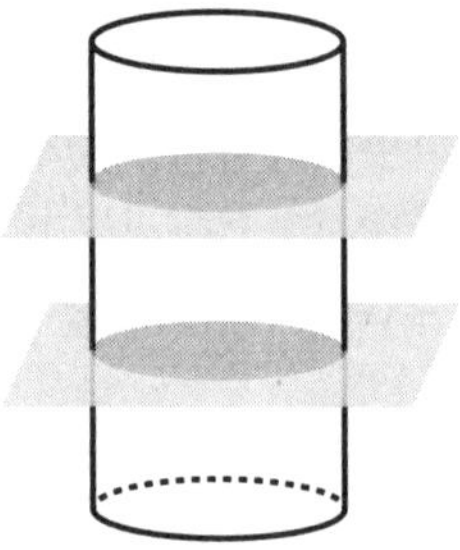
____

d) 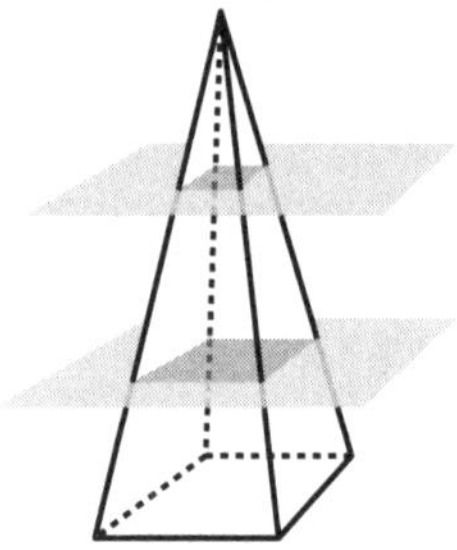
____

e) 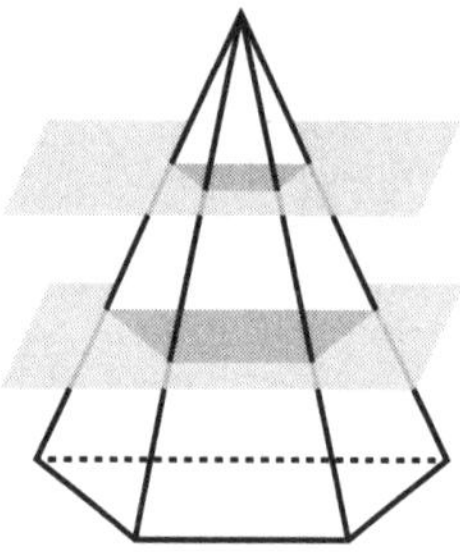
____

f) 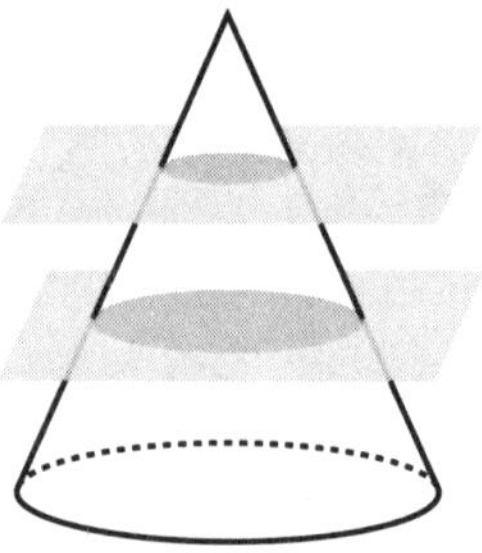
____

6. Write "similar" or "congruent."

a) The cross section parallel to the base of a prism is ____________________ to the base.

b) The cross section parallel to the base of a pyramid is ____________________ to the base when it does not pass through the top vertex.

7. Describe the cross section of a pyramid that is parallel to the base, and passes through the top vertex of the pyramid.

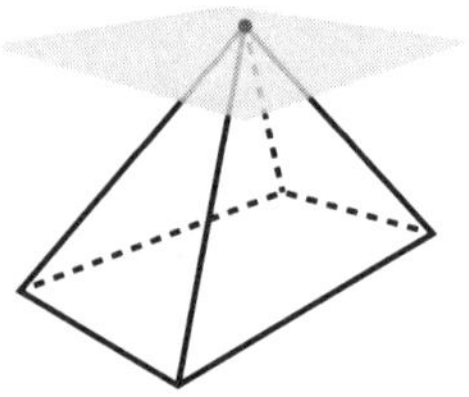

G7-31 Cross Sections of Rectangular Prisms and Rectangular Pyramids

1. Draw vertical lines to complete the vertical cross section of the cube.

a)
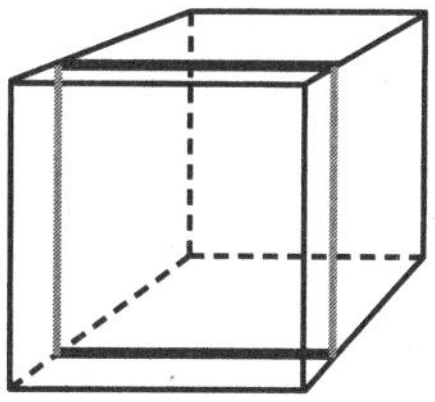
b)
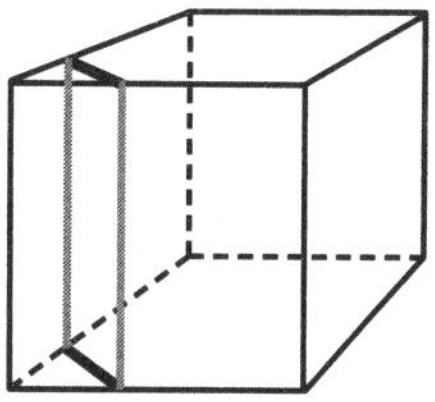
c)
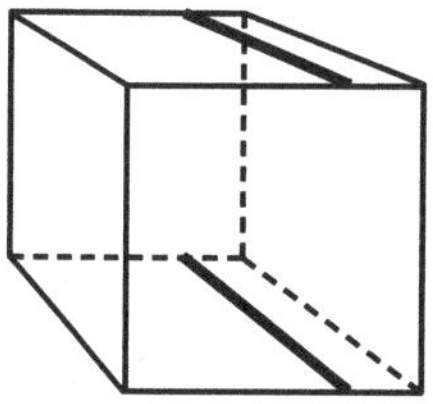
d)
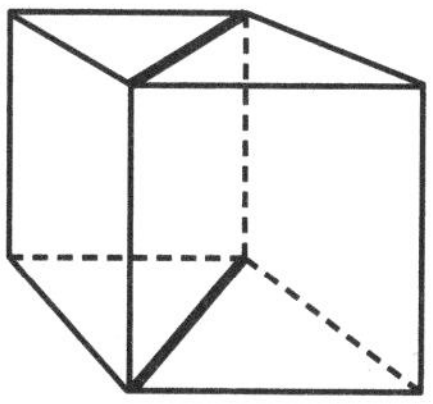
e)
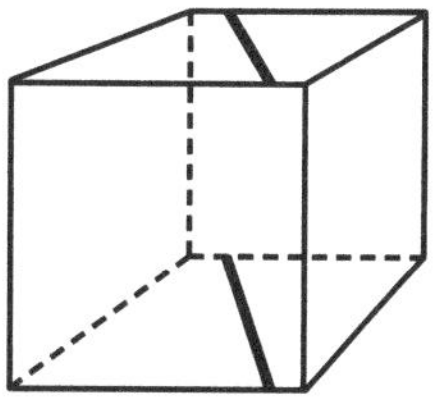
f)
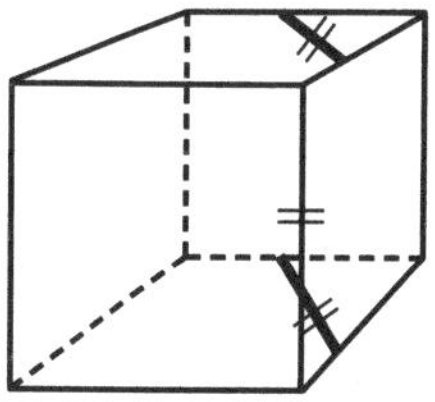

All the lines through a point in the top face are perpendicular to the vertical lines they meet.

Examples:

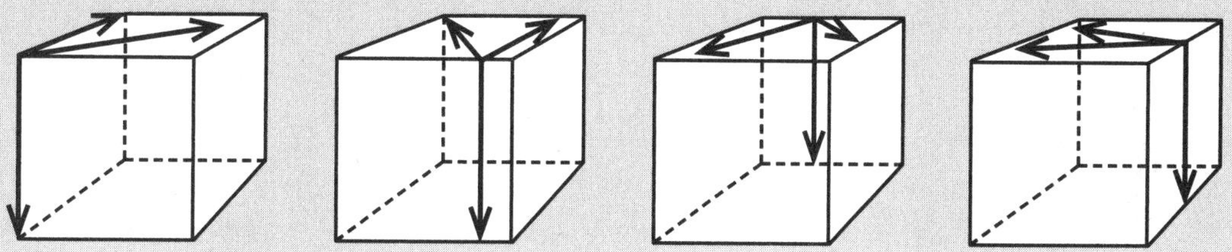

2. Vicky says the cross sections in Question 1 are all rectangles. Is she correct? Explain.

____

____

3. Circle the cross sections in Question 1 that are squares.

Is the thick edge the entire cross section or only part of the cross section?

The plane touches an edge of the cube.

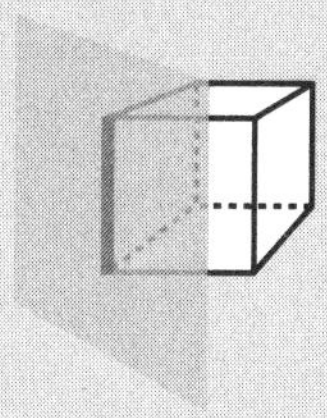

The thick edge is the cross section.

The plane touches a face of the cube.

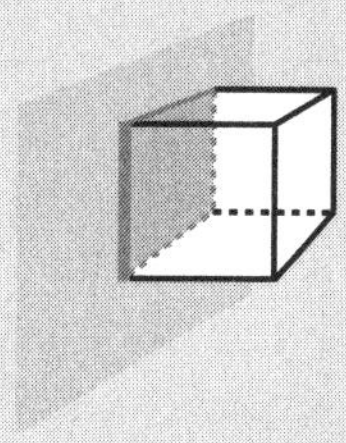

The thick edge is only part of the cross section.

4. Can the thick edge be the cross section of the cube with a **vertical** plane? Explain.

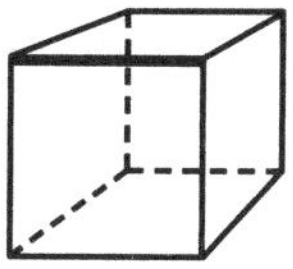

____

____

When two planes are parallel, a plane intersecting them creates parallel lines.

5. Mark the parallel sides of the cross section with the same number of arrows.

a)
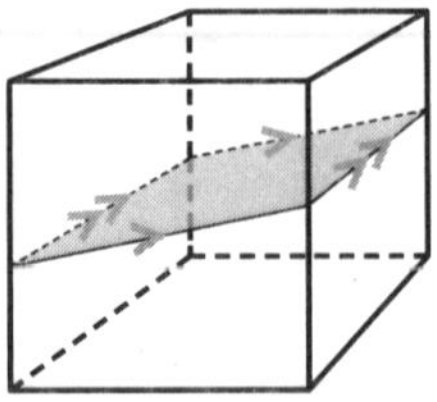

b)
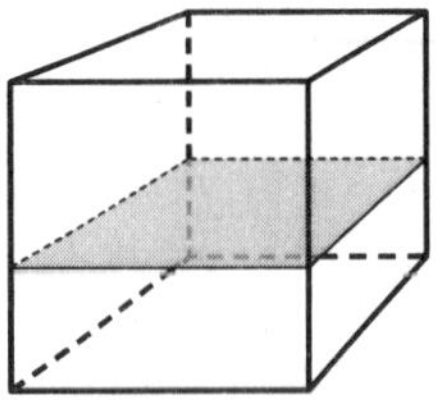

c)
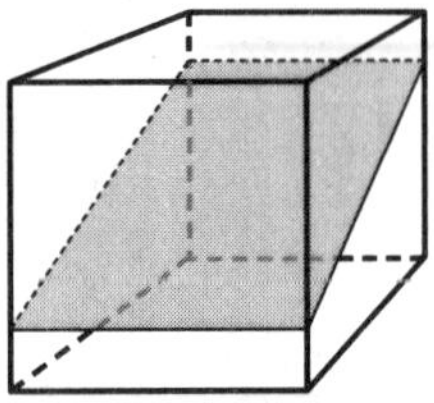

d)
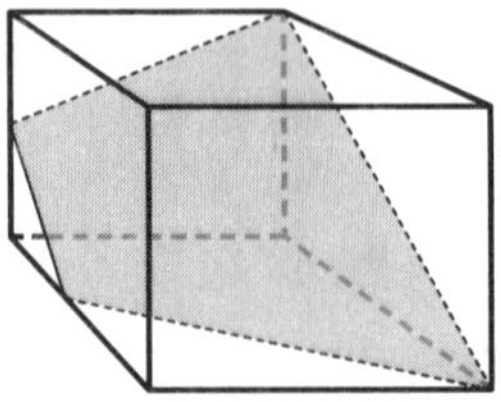

e)
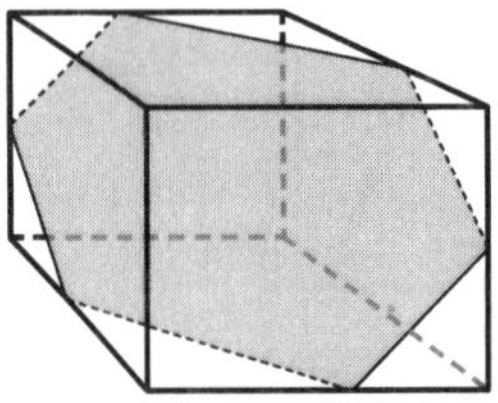

f)
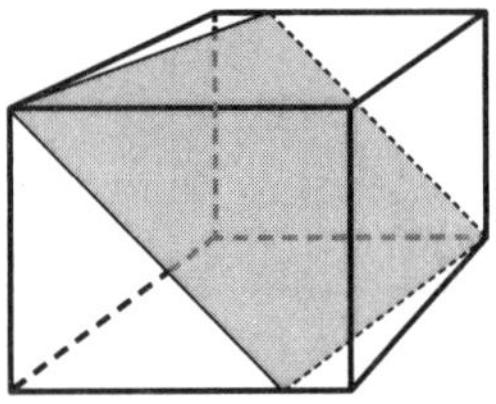

g)
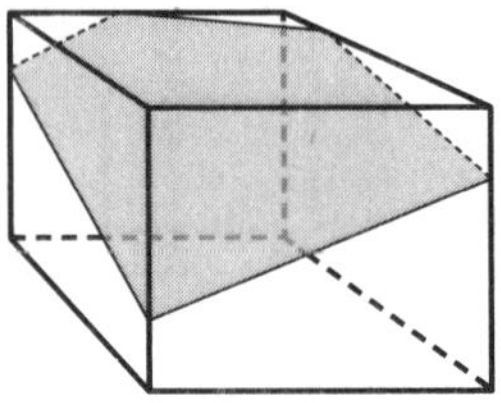

h)
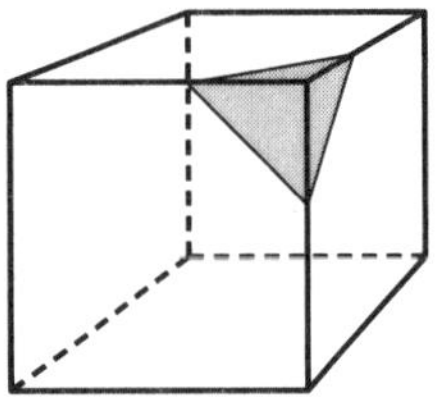

i)
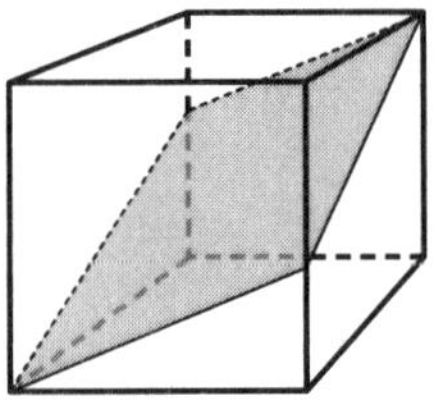

These cross sections have sides that are parallel to an edge of the prism. The cross sections are rectangles.

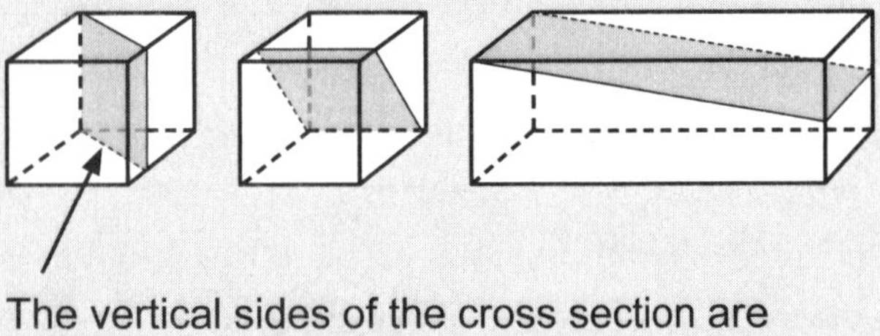

The vertical sides of the cross section are perpendicular to the horizontal sides of the cross section.

These cross sections do not have sides that are parallel to an edge of the prism. The cross sections are not rectangles.

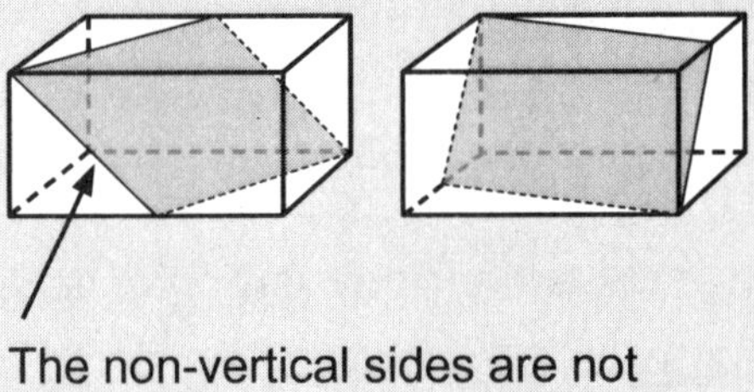

The non-vertical sides are not perpendicular to the horizontal sides.

6. In Question 5, lines that look parallel to an edge are, in fact, parallel. For which part or parts of Question 5 is the cross section …

a) a hexagon? ______

b) a pentagon? ______

c) a trapezoid? ______

d) a triangle? ______

e) a rectangle? ______, ______, ______

f) a parallelogram, but not a rectangle? ______, ______

7. The base of the rectangular pyramid is horizontal. What shape is the cross section? Be as specific as you can.

a) a horizontal plane

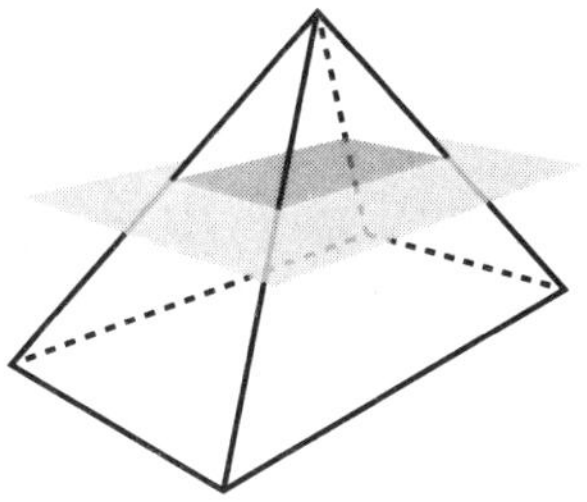

b) a plane that is angled up from the base and cuts the plane parallel to the edge

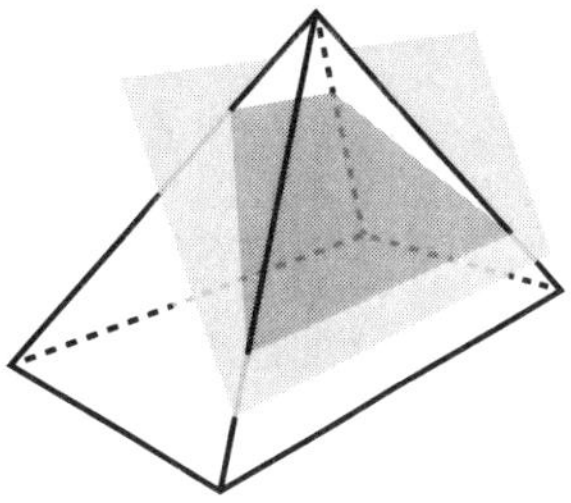

c) a vertical plane that passes through the top vertex of the pyramid

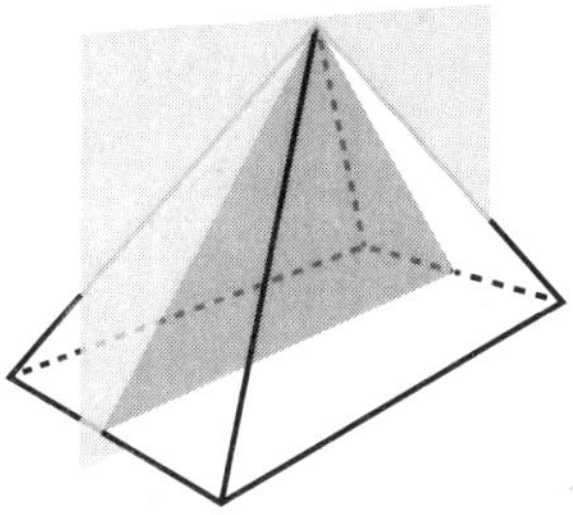

d) a vertical plane that misses the top vertex of the pyramid

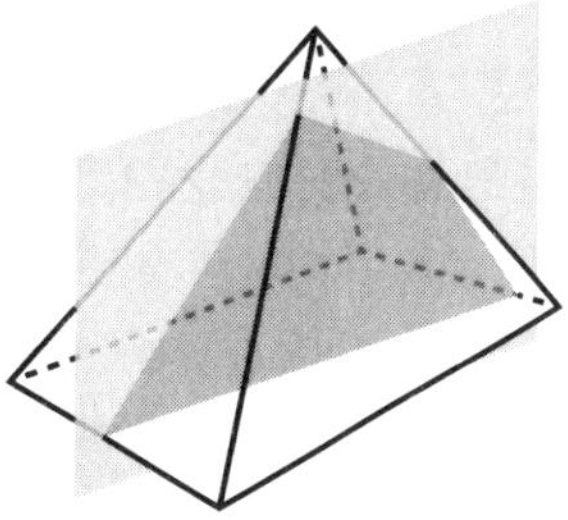

e) another vertical plane that misses the top vertex of the pyramid

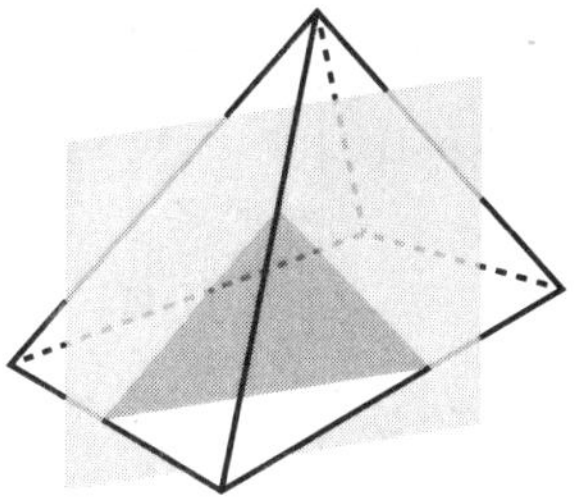

f) a vertical plane that passes through two adjacent base vertices

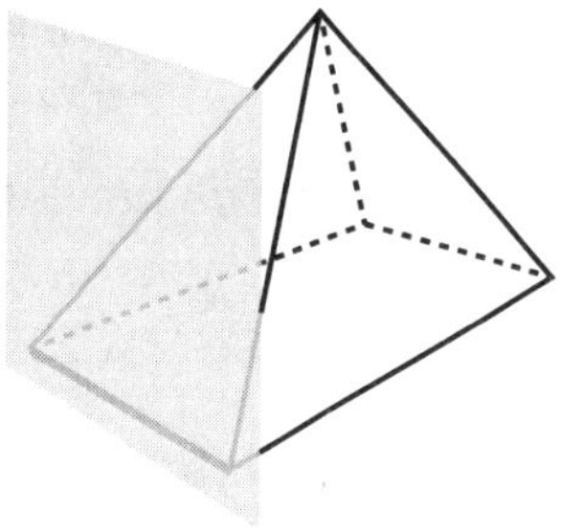

g) a vertical plane that passes through exactly one base vertex

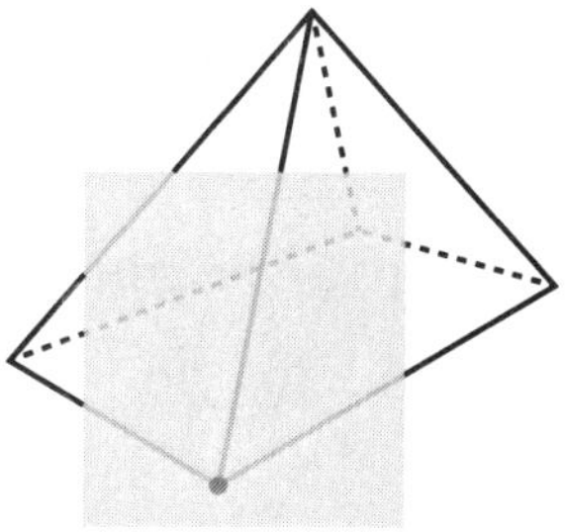

h) another vertical plane that passes through exactly one base vertex

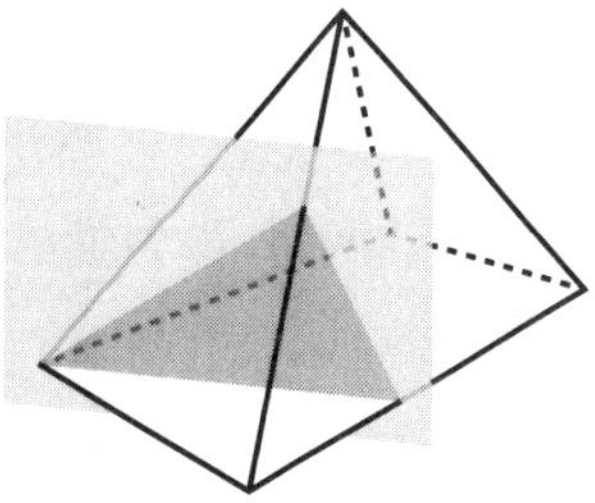

SP7-10 Mean, Median, and Frequency

To find the **mean** of a set of numbers:

Step 1: Add the data values.

Example: For the data set 5, 2, 2, 5, 6:

Sum of data values $= 5 + 2 + 2 + 5 + 6 = 20$

Step 2: Divide the result by the number of data values.

Mean = sum of data values ÷ number of data values $= 20 \div 5 = 4$

1. Find the mean. Some means will not be whole numbers.

a) 3, 4, 4, 8, 8, 9 b) 1, 2, 3, 4, 5, 6, 7 c) 11, 13, 14, 20, 22, 25, 26, 27, 30

2. a) Find the mean of the data set 2, 3, 6, 9.

b) Add 4 to each data value in part a) to get the data set 6, 7, 10, 13. What is the mean of the new data set? How does it compare to the mean of the original data set?

c) Construct a data set that has mean 7.

d) Find the mean of the data set 2, 2, 3, 3, 6, 6, 9, 9. How was this new data set obtained from the original data set? How does the mean of the new data set compare to the mean of the original data set?

e) Predict and check the mean of the data set 2, 2, 2, 3, 3, 3, 6, 6, 6, 9, 9, 9.

To find the **median** of a data set, put the data in order. Count one number at a time from each end until you reach the middle.

4 7 (8) 13 18

The median is 8.

1 3 (4 6) 9 11

When there is an even number of data values, there are two values in the middle. The median is halfway between 4 and 6, so it is 5.

The **range** of a data set is the distance between the highest and the lowest values in the data set.

Range = highest value − lowest value

3. a) Find the mean and the median.

i) 9 20 22

Mean: *(9 + 20 + 22) ÷ 3*

= 51 ÷ 3 = 17

Median: *20*

Range: *13*

ii) 38 39 41 46

Mean: ______

______

Median: ______

Range: ______

iii) 10 15 20 25 30

Mean: ______

______

Median: ______

Range: ______

b) Order the numbers from lowest to highest, then find the mean and the median. Show your work.

i) 15 18 40 32 25 ii) 29 26 16 23 17 15 iii) 40 25 10 15 20

4. When finding the median, does it matter whether you write the data values from lowest to highest or from highest to lowest? Explain.

5. In 2008, the population of the United States was 307 million people, and the country's electricity consumption was 4,401,698 gigawatt-hours per year (GWh/yr). Canada's population in 2008 was 33 million and the country's electricity consumption was 620,684 GWh/yr. Which country used more electricity per person?

The **frequency** of a value is the number of times it occurs in a data set.

Example: 1, 3, 0, 1, 1, 3, 1, 1, 1, 0, 1 ⟶

Data Value	Frequency
0	||
1	~~||||~~ ||
2	
3	||

Record all values within the range, even if they don't occur in the set.

The value that appears most often in a data set is the **mode**. The mode in the example above is 1.

6. a) Transfer the data into the tally chart. Cross out each number as you mark it in the chart.

i) ~~2~~, ~~3~~, ~~2~~, ~~0~~, ~~2~~, ~~2~~, ~~3~~

Data Value	Frequency
0	/
1	
2	////
3	//

ii) ~~4~~, ~~3~~, 1, 4, 3, 4, 1, 3, 4, 3, 4

Data Value	Frequency
1	
2	
3	/
4	/

iii) 2, 5, 5, 5, 2, 2, 2, 2, 2, 5

Data Value	Frequency

b) How many numbers are in each data set? i) 7 ii) ______ iii) ______

c) How many tally marks are in each frequency column? i) 7 ii) ______ iii) ______

d) If your answers to b) and c) are not the same, find your mistake.

e) What is the mode in each data set? i) 2 ii) ______ iii) ______

7. Use the data set 3, 5, 5, 5, 6, 6 to answer the question.

a) Find the sum of the data values. 3 + 5 + ______ + ______ + ______ + ______ = ______

b) Write how many times each data value occurs. Then find the sum.

(______ × 3) + (______ × 5) + (______ × 6) = ______ + ______ + ______ = ______

c) Did you get the same answer in parts a) and b)? If not, find your mistake.

d) Find the mean. ☐ ÷ ☐ = ☐

total of data values ÷ number of data values = mean

8. Use the two methods of finding the sum in Question 7 to find the mean.

a) 2, 1, 5, 2, 3, 8, 6, 6, 5, 2

b) 6, 6, 2, 6, 2, 6, 2, 6, 2, 2

Bonus ▶ Find the mean: 600, 600, 400, 400, 400, 600, 400, 400, 600, 600.

SP7-11 Mean, Median, and Dot Plots

1. Anwar wrote 5 science tests and 8 math tests last year. Here are his results:

   Science: 82, 79, 75, 84, 80 Math: 75, 81, 77, 86, 79, 80, 83, 82

   In which subject did he do better? Hint: Find the mean for each subject.

2. There are 20 employees at XYZ company. One person has a salary of $200,000, two people have salaries of $75,000, and all the rest have salaries of $17,500.

   a) What is the mean salary?

   b) What is the median salary?

   c) Which reflects the salaries in the company better, the mean or the median? Explain.

   ____

3. You work at a clothing store and your manager says that, every week, you need average daily sales of at least $500. Do you think the manager is talking about the mean, median, or mode? Why?

   ____

4. a) The mean of a data set is 10. The data values are 2, 19, 7, 4, 15, and one other number. Let x represent the missing number. Write an expression for the mean, then solve the equation.

   b) If your marks were 80, 93, and 91 on your first three history tests, what do you need to get on the next test to average 90 on the first four history tests?

5. Here are the data values for three data sets:

A:	10	10	10	10	10	10	10	10	10
B:	1	10	10	10	10	10	10	10	19
C:	1	5	8	10	10	10	12	15	19

   a) Find the mean, median, and mode for each data set.

   b) Can you use the mean, median, or mode to show the difference between three data sets? ________

   c) Find the range for each data set. A: ________ B: ________ C: ________

   d) Does the range give you more information to compare data set A and data set B? ________

   e) Does the range give you more information to compare data set B and data set C? ________

All **dot plots** have a group of data points that are represented with a symbol such as • or X.

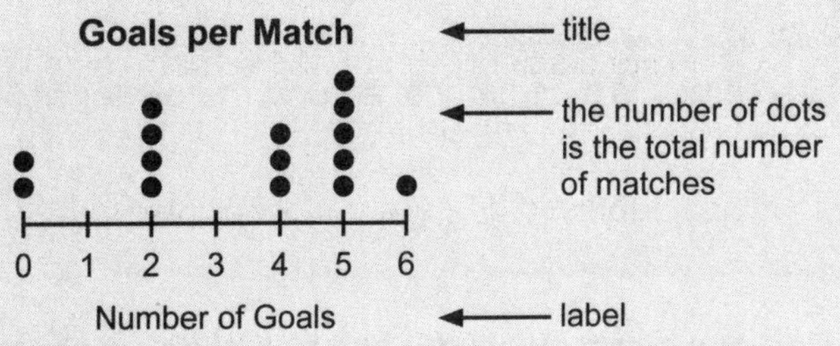

The numbers can start at any value, including 0.

6. The data shows how many books Sandy's class read.

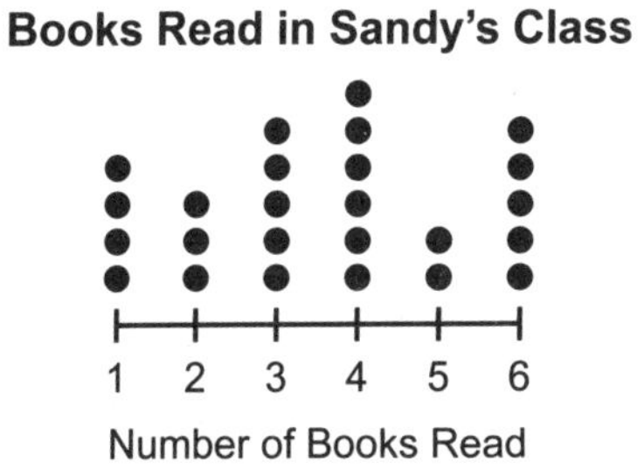

a) The mode is ______.

b) How many students read exactly two books? ______

c) The largest number of students read ______ books.

d) The number of students in Sandy's class is ______.

e) ______ students read either five or six books.

7. The data shows how many miles people walked in a week.

Miles Walked	1	2	3	4
Number of People	𝍸 ||	𝍸 |||	|	||

a) Fill in the missing numbers on the number line.

b) Plot the data.

c) What answer was given most frequently? ______

d) How many people walked at least two miles? ______

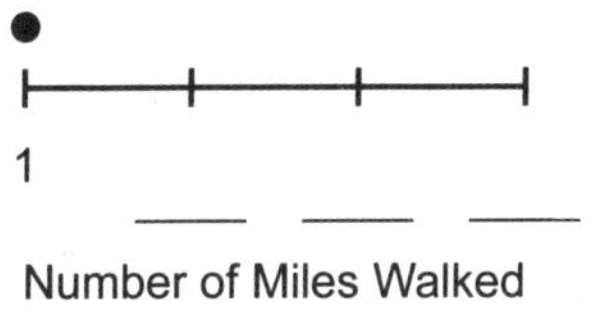

8. Use the dot plot to fill in the tally chart.

10	11	12	13	14	15

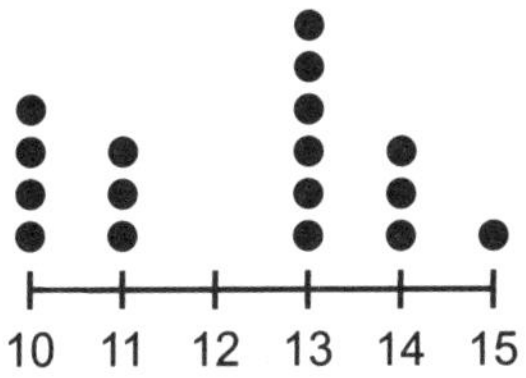

9. You are going on a trip during the March break and you want to decide what clothes to pack. The chart shows the highest daily temperatures at your destination during the March break last year.

Day	1	2	3	4	5	6	7	8	9	10	11	12	13	14	15
°C	23	22	20	21	22	23	23	10	2	2	5	7	8	12	17

a) Find the range, mean, median, and mode.

b) If you looked only at the mean, median, or mode of the temperatures, what mistake might you make in your packing?

SP7-12 Shape and Symmetry of Dot Plots

This dot plot is symmetrical around the center at 5.

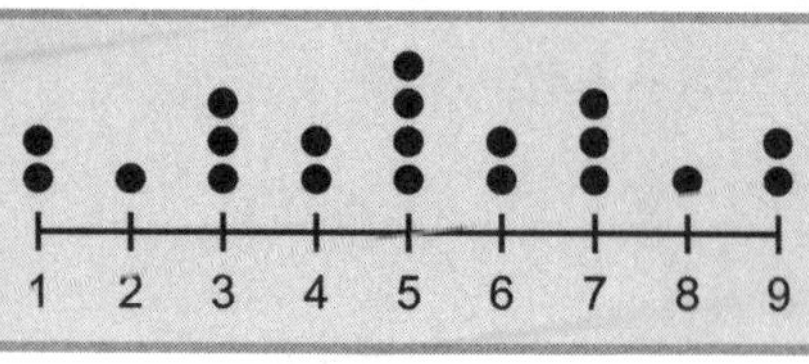

1. Part of a symmetrical dot plot has been graphed around the center at 16. Plot the missing data. Use the fewest number of dots possible.

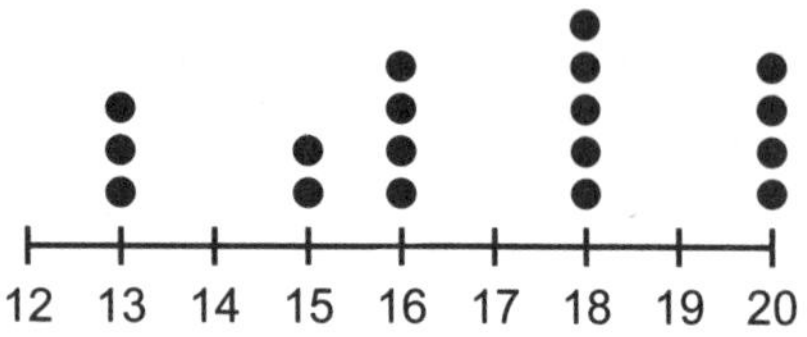

2. a) Plot the data from the tally chart.

b) Is the dot plot symmetrical? ________

c) The center of the dot plot is at ________.

d) Find the mean and median.

Mean: ________ Median: ________

12	||
13	|
14	~~||||~~
15	|
16	||

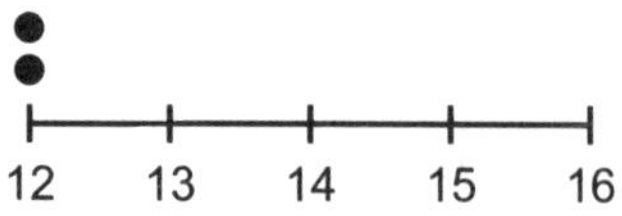

e) What do you notice about the median, the mean, and the center?

____

____

3. a) Use dot plots A, B, C, and D to complete the table.

Dot Plot A

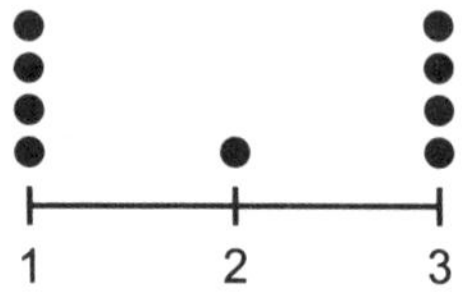

Dot Plot B

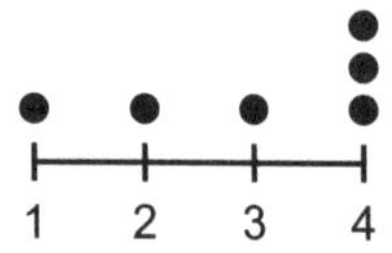

Dot Plot C

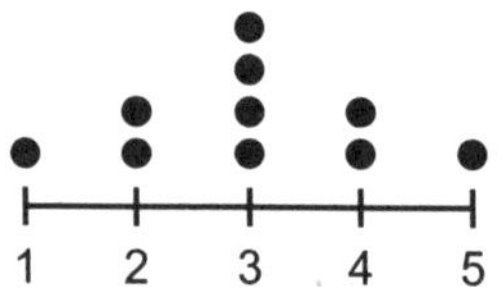

Dot Plot D

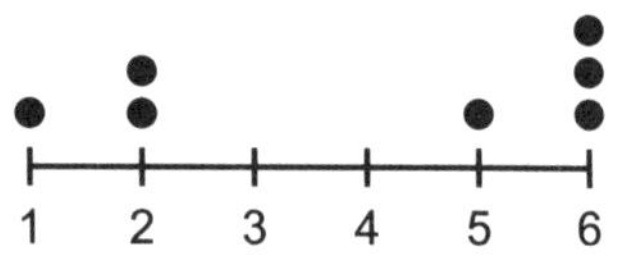

×4 → 4 ×1 → 2 ×4 → 12

Total: 4 + 2 + 12 = 18

Mean: 18 ÷ 9 = 2

Do your rough work like this in your notebook

	Dot Plot A	Dot Plot B	Dot Plot C	Dot Plot D
Mean				
Median				
Is the dot plot symmetrical?				
Does the mean equal the median?				

b) What can you predict about the median and mean of symmetrical dot plots?

____

4. The dotted line represents the mean of a data set and the Xs represent spaces. The number of spaces below the mean is the same as the number of blocks above the mean. Write a number sentence to show this.

a)

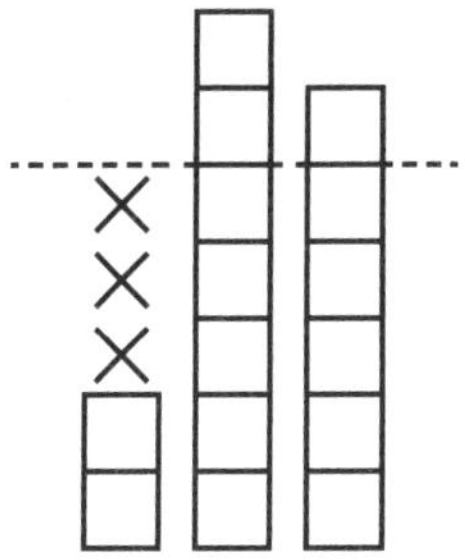

2 7 6

3 = [*2*] + [*1*]

b)

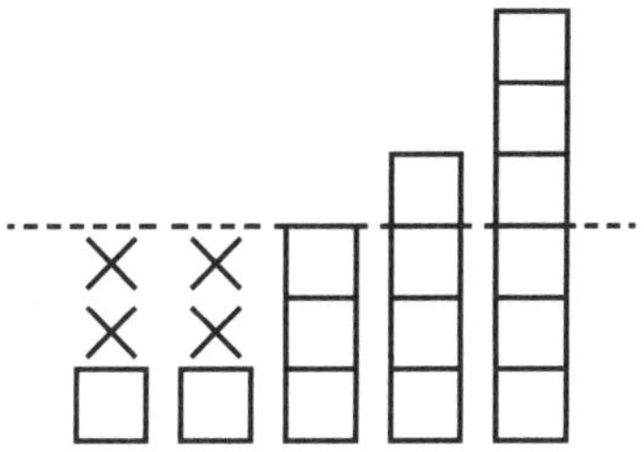

1 3 4 6

2 + 2 + 0 = [ ] + [ ]

c)

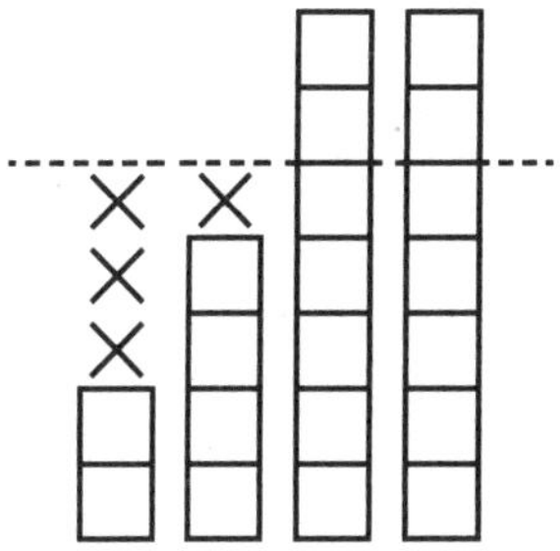

2 4 7 7

[ ] + [ ] = [ ] + [ ]

Now draw the blocks and the mean on grid paper, then write the number sentence.

d) 2 6 7

e) 3 4 8 6 9

f) 2 4 5 5

5. Use the number sentence to find a data set with mean 4. Draw circles to help you.

a)

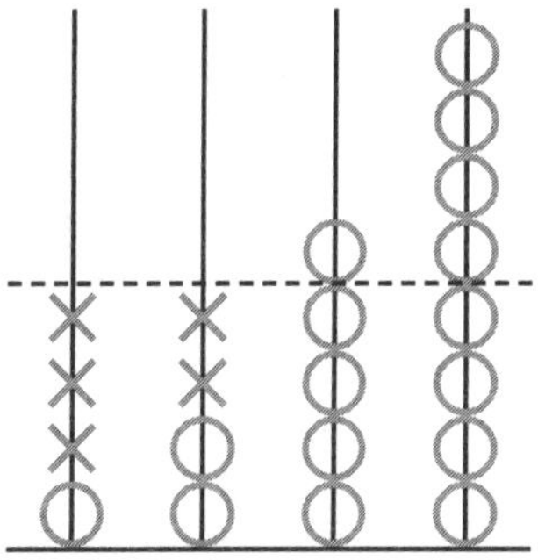

3 + 2 = 1 + 4

Data: *1, 2, 5, 8*

b)

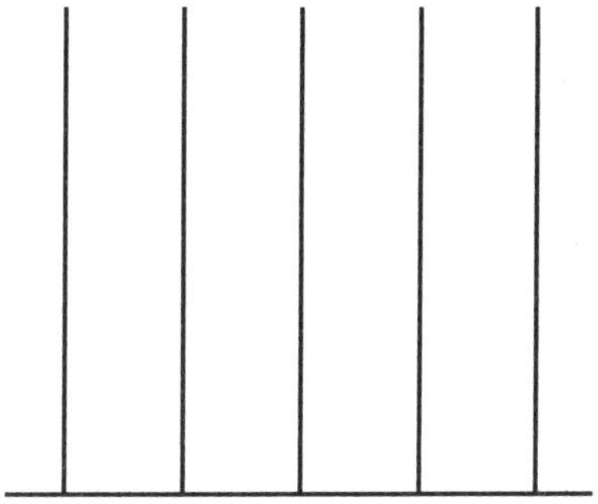

2 + 2 + 1 = 2 + 3

Data: ________

c)

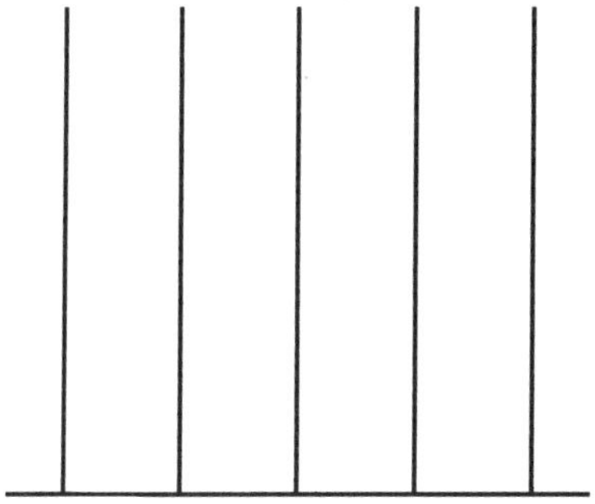

1 + 1 + 1 + 1 = 4

Data: ________

Every data value in a set is a certain distance from the mean of that set. To find the **deviations** from the mean, you can subtract the mean from each data value.

Example: For the data set 2, 5, 6, 7, the mean is 5. So the deviations from the mean are:

2 – 5, 5 – 5, 6 – 5, 7 – 5, or –3, 0, 1, 2.

6. a) Find the deviation of each data value from the mean of each data set in Question 4.d) to f).

i) *–3*, *1*, ____

ii) ____, ____, ____, ____, ____

iii) ____, ____, ____, ____

b) Add the deviations for each data set from part a). If your answers are not zero, find your mistake.

i) –3 + 1 + ____ = ____

ii) ____ + ____ + ____ + ____ + ____ = ____

iii) ____ + ____ + ____ + ____ = ____

Peter wants to guess the mean of these 10 test marks: 1, 5, 5, 6, 6, 6, 6, 7, 8, 10.

His first guess is 5, which gives the following deviations from the mean: −4, 0, 0, 1, 1, 1, 1, 2, 3, 5.

These add to a positive number, so the guess needs to be bigger. Guessing 6 gives the following deviations: −5, −1, −1, 0, 0, 0, 0, 1, 2, 4. These add to a total of 0, so 6 is the mean.

7. Find the mean by guessing and checking.

a) 1, 2, 3, 4, 5, 6, 7, 8, 9

b) 2, 3, 3, 5, 5, 7, 7, 8

c) 3, 5, 10, 11, 13, 17, 18

d) 10, 11, 14, 19, 22, 24, 26, 26, 28

8. Micky collected the following data about birds' eggs.

Bird	**Clutch Size (Number of Eggs)**	**Egg Length (cm)**
Albatross	1	11
Emperor Penguin	1	12
Flamingo	1	9
Ostrich	9	14
Common Loon	2	9
White Stork	3	7
Ibis	3	6
Water Pheasant	4	4

a) What is the mean length of the eggs?

b) What is the mean clutch size (number of eggs)?

c) List the birds with a clutch size below the mean.

d) Do the birds with smaller-than-average clutches have eggs shorter than the mean?

e) Do the birds with the clutch size that is at least the mean size have smaller eggs? Which bird doesn't fit the rule? Why do you think this bird doesn't fit the rule?

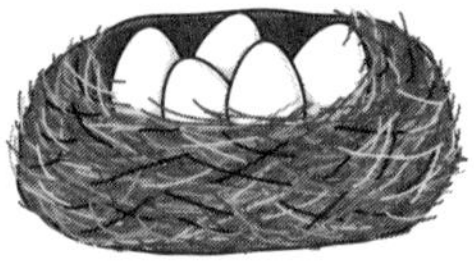

9. a) Jack has 3 apples, Lily has 5 apples, and Ray has 10 apples. How many apples should Ray give Jack and Lily if the they want to share the apples equally?

b) Find the mean of the data set 3, 5, 10. How is your answer related to part a)?

c) Beth has 6 apples. Does she have to give any apples to Ray, Jack, or Lily for the apples to be shared equally among the four people? Do any of the others have to give apples to Beth? Explain.

SP7-13 IQR and Box Plots

The median of an ordered set divides the data into a lower half and an upper half. The median of the lower half is called the **first quartile**, or **Q1**. The median of the upper half is called the **third quartile**, or **Q3**.

median = 9

3 4 6 8 9 13 15 16 21

lower half: 3 4 6 8 — Q1 = 5

upper half: 13 15 16 21 — Q3 = 15.5

1. Label the median (M), the first quartile (Q1), and the third quartile (Q3), and mark each position with an arrow.

a) 3 5 5 11 13 18 22 29

Q1 (between 5 and 5)   *M* (between 11 and 13)   *Q3* (between 18 and 22)

b) 2 4 6 7 11 16 16 22 23 23 24 26

c) 13 19 21 27 30 34 36 41 45 46

d) 0 1 2 3 4 5 5 6 6 7 7 8 8 9

2. Find the median, Q1, and Q3.

a) 1 2 3 4 5 6 7 8 9 10 11 12 13   Median = _____   Q1 = _____   Q3 = _____

b) 15 25 35 45 55 65 75 85   Median = _____   Q1 = _____   Q3 = _____

c) 1 3 5 8 12 16 17 18 21 26 35 45   Median = _____   Q1 = _____   Q3 = _____

d) 7 9 13 14 19 22 27 41 44   Median = _____   Q1 = _____   Q3 = _____

e) 13 20 26 28 36 41 42 45 49 54 72   Median = _____   Q1 = _____   Q3 = _____

Bonus ▶

f) 10   2,341   4,179   15,416   17,803   39,105   44,013   1,312,759

Median = ____________   Q1 = ____________   Q3 = ____________

g) 4,005   6,170   9,000   14,105   32,411   41,712   67,142   92,312   115,741

Median = ____________   Q1 = ____________   Q3 = ____________

The **interquartile range (IQR)** is the difference between Q3 and Q1. It shows how spread out the middle half of the data is around the median. It is a measure of **variability** in a set of data. In some sets, the data points are more tightly clustered around the median than in other sets.

Q1 = 5   M   Q3 = 14

1   4   6   9   11   12   16   23

|← IQR →|

$IQR = Q3 - Q1$

$= 14 - 5$

$= 9$

3. Find Q1, Q3, and the IQR of the data.

a) 6   7   11   15   16   20   23   28

Q1 = *9*   Q3 = *21.5*   IQR = *21.5 − 9 = 12.5*

b) 26   31   51   67   76   81   88   105   112   141   145

Q1 = ______   Q3 = ______   IQR = ______

Bonus ▶ 567   2,935   5,402   23,601   32,145   55,171   82,720   93,111

Q1 = ______   Q3 = ______   IQR = ______

4. a) Circle the median in each set and draw arrows to show Q1 and Q3. Then find the ranges and IQRs.

	Data	**Range**	**IQR**
Set 1	1, 1, 2, 5, 8, 12, 15, 16, 18, 19, 89		
Set 2	1, 8, 9, 11, 13, 15, 17, 17, 19, 27, 89		
Set 3	1, 1, 2, 3, 5, 8, 13, 21, 34, 35, 89		

b) Can you use the range to compare the variability of these data sets? ______

Why or why not? ______

c) In which set are the data points most tightly clustered around the median? ______

How does the IQR tell you this? ______

5. Find the missing values.

	Q1	**Q3**	**IQR**
Set 1	18	31	
Set 2	214	241	
Set 3	0		1,000
Set 4	53		4
Set 5		43	17

Box plots summarize data from sets. Box plots are made on a number line and show five pieces of information about the set.

The box plot and the dot plot on the right represent the same data. The lowest value is 2, Q1 is 4, the median is 8, Q3 is 10, and the highest value is 14.

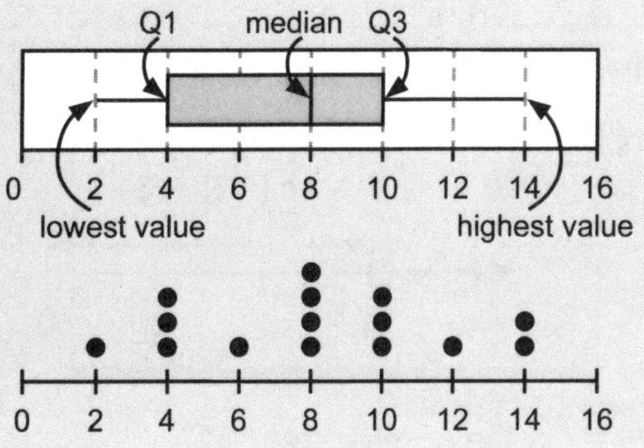

6. Use the box plot to find the median, IQR, and range.

a)

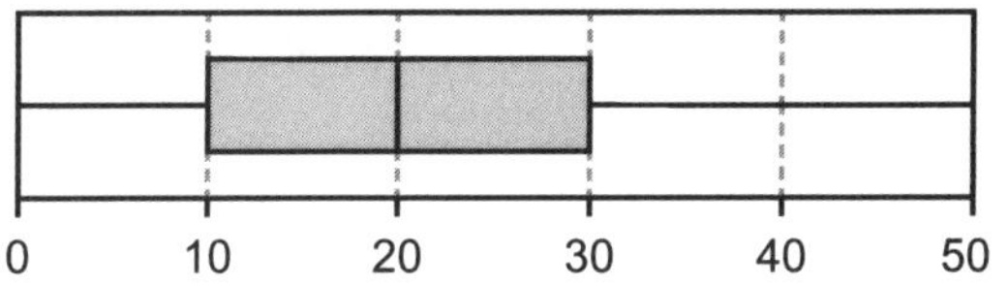

Median = *20* IQR = *30 − 10 = 20*

Range = *50 − 0 = 50*

b)

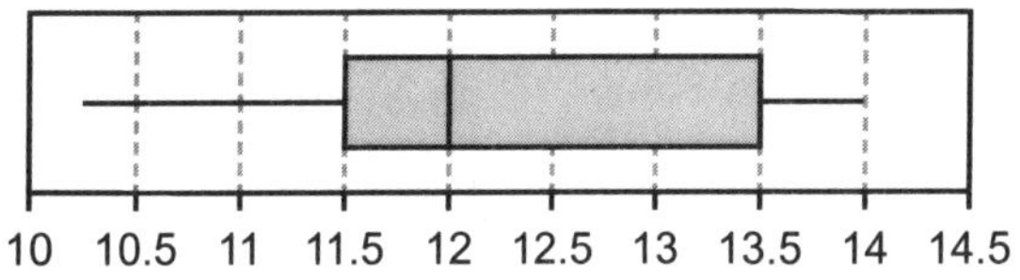

Median = ______ IQR = ________________

Range = ________________

c)

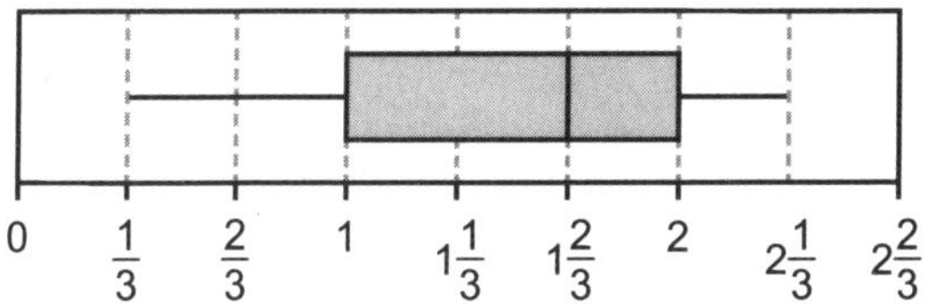

Median = ______ IQR = ________________

Range = ________________

d)

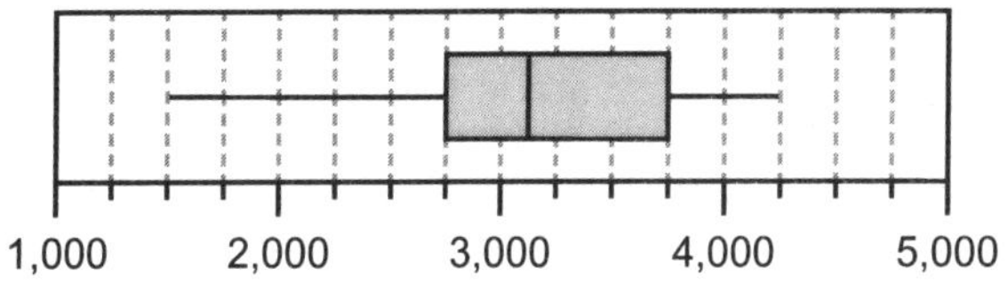

Median = ______ IQR = ________________

Range = ________________

7. Draw a line to match each dot plot with the box plot that shows the same data.

A.

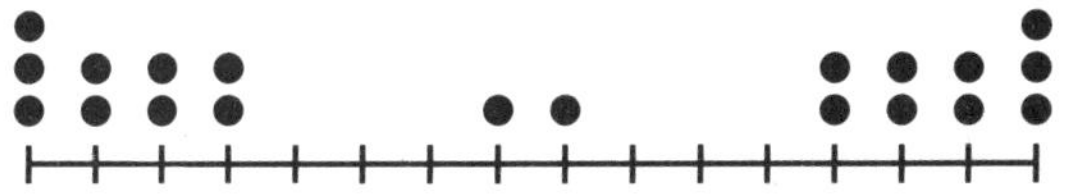

D.

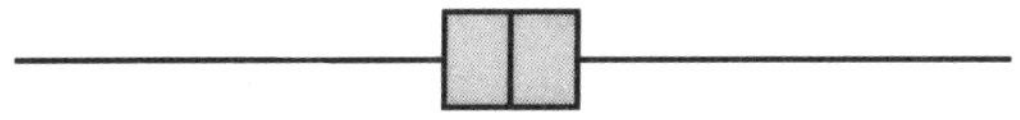

B.

E.

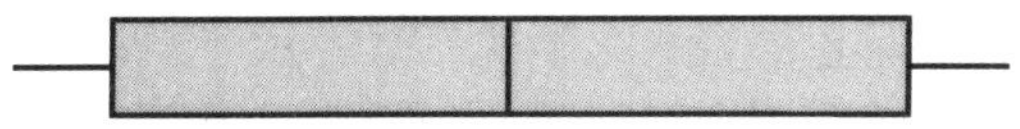

C.

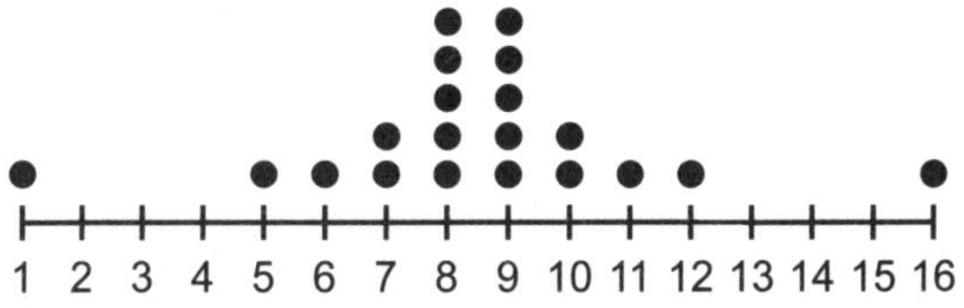

F.

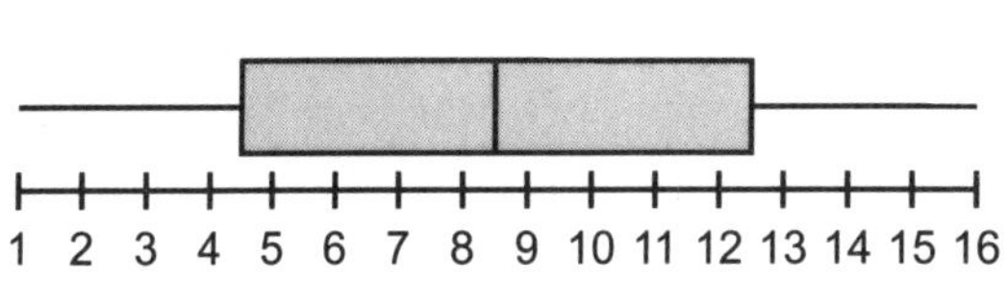

SP7-14 Mean Absolute Deviation (MAD)

REMINDER: The absolute value of a number is its distance from 0.

Examples: The absolute value of −3 is 3.
We write this as $|-3| = 3$.

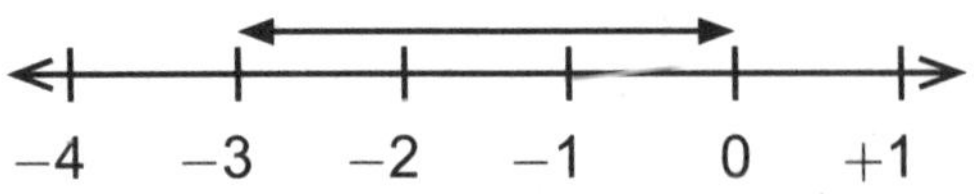

The absolute value of +4 is 4.
We write this as $|+4| = 4$.

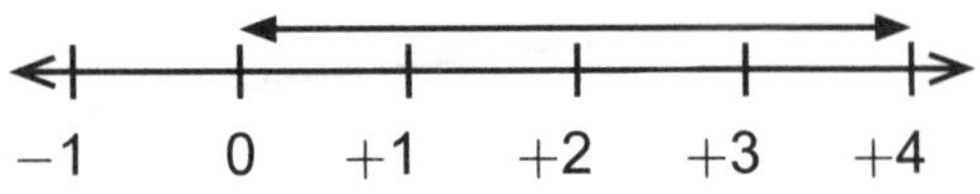

1. How far is the number from 0?

a) −5 is ______ units from 0. b) +7 is ______ units from 0. c) 0 is ______ units from 0.

2. What is the absolute value of the number?

a) $|+2| =$ __2__ b) $|-12| =$ ______ c) $|+5| =$ ______ d) $|-0.5| =$ ______

e) $|2^3| =$ ______ f) $|-2^3| =$ ______ g) $\left|-\frac{-1}{3}\right| =$ ______ h) $|-2{,}125| =$ ______

The **absolute deviation** of a data point is its distance from the mean. It is the absolute value of the deviation.

Example: The data set is 0, 6, 9. The mean is $\frac{0+6+9}{3} = \frac{15}{3} = 5$.

data point mean

$|0 - 5| = 5$, so the absolute deviation of 0 is 5.

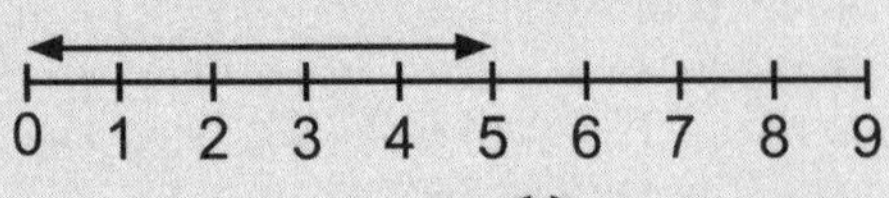

$|6 - 5| = 1$, so the absolute deviation of 6 is 1.

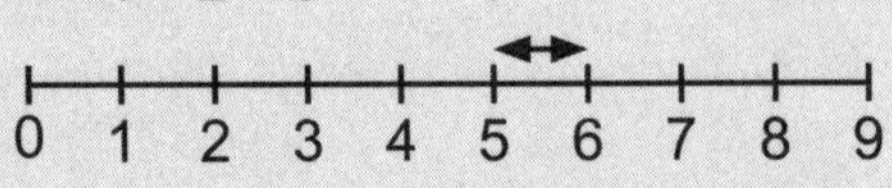

$|9 - 5| = 4$, so the absolute deviation of 9 is 4

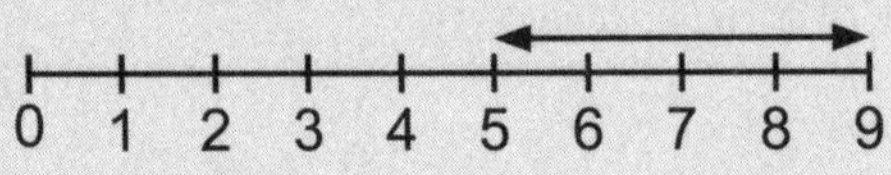

3. The mean of the set 2, 5, 6, 9, 10, 12, 13, 15 is 9.

a) Find the absolute deviation of each data point.

Data Point	2	5	6	9	10	12	13	15
Absolute Deviation	7							

b) What are the minimum and the maximum absolute deviations from the mean?

Minimum absolute deviation: ________ Maximum absolute deviation: ________

c) On average, how far from the mean is each point in the set?

____

____

The **mean absolute deviation**, or **MAD**, of a data set shows how spread out the data points are around the mean. It is the mean of all the absolute deviations of the data points.

Example: To find the MAD of the data set 4, 8, 9:

Step 1: Find the mean. $\frac{4+8+9}{3} = \frac{21}{3} = 7$

Step 2: Find the absolute deviations from the mean 7. $|4-7| = 3$ $|8-7| = 1$ $|9-7| = 2$

Step 3: Find the mean of the absolute deviations. $\frac{3+1+2}{3} = \frac{6}{3} = 2$

4. Set 1 and Set 2 each have three data points as shown on the number lines.

a) Find and circle the mean of each set.

Set 1

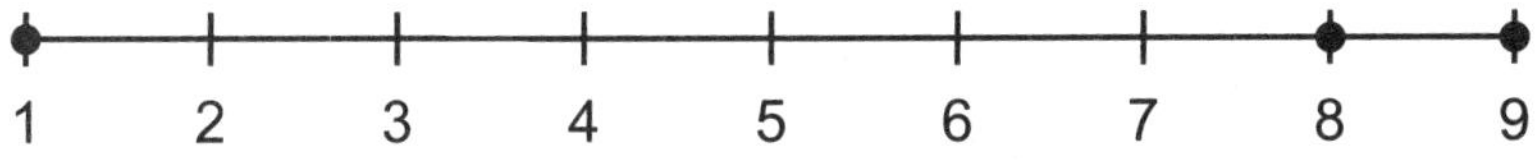

Set 2

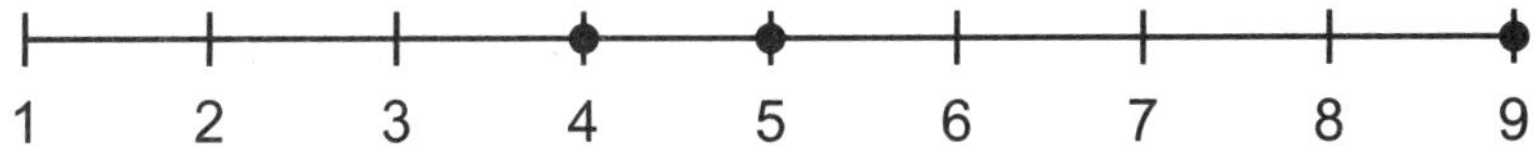

b) In which set do the data points appear to be more tightly clustered around the mean? ________

c) Find the absolute deviations and write them in the table.

Set 1

Data Point	1	8	9
Absolute Deviation			

Set 2

Data Point	4	5	9
Absolute Deviation			

d) Find the mean absolute deviation of each set. Set 1: ________ Set 2: ________

e) For which set is the MAD greater, Set 1 or Set 2? ___________

f) Which data set is more tightly clustered around the mean, the one with the higher MAD or the one with the lower MAD?

____

5. a) Find the mean of the data set from the given dot plot.

i)

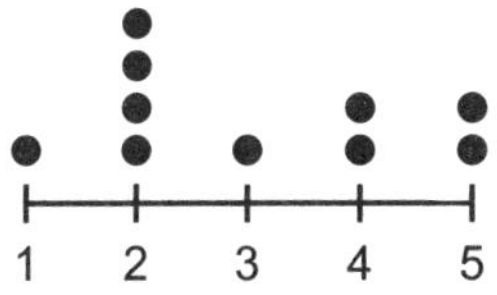

ii)

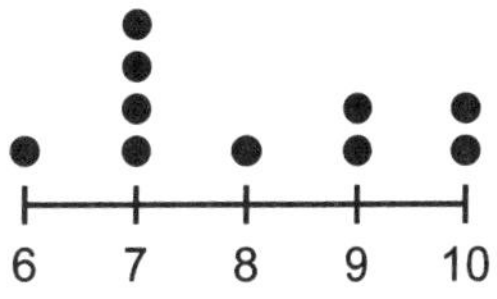

b) Find the MAD of each set in part a).

c) What can you say about the MAD when two dot plots have the same shape, but different means?

6. Consider the set 2, 3, 5, 7, 202.

a) What is the range of the set? ____________________

b) Remove one value from the set and find the range of the new set. Repeat with all other values.

New set: *3*, *5*, *7*, *202* Range: *202 − 3 = 199*

New set: ______, ______, ______, ______ Range: ____________________

New set: ______, ______, ______, ______ Range: ____________________

New set: ______, ______, ______, ______ Range: ____________________

New set: ______, ______, ______, ______ Range: ____________________

An **outlier** is a data value that is far from the rest of the data values in a set. Removing an outlier changes the range of the set a lot.

Examples: In the set 2, 3, 4, 5, 90, the number 90 is an outlier.

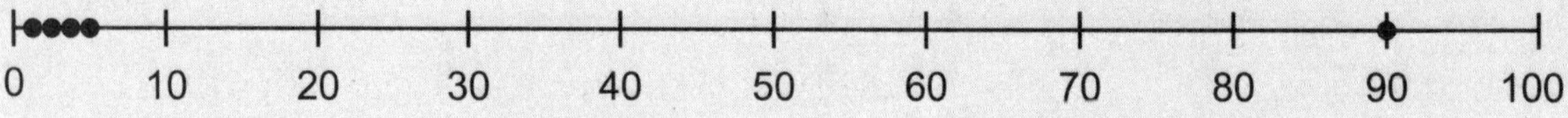

In the set 2, 400, 406, 435, 470, 475, the number 2 is an outlier.

7. Consider the set 2, 2, 3, 4, 5, 74.

a) Circle the outlier.

b) Find the mean, median, IQR, and MAD of the set.

c) Write the set without the outlier: ______, ______, ______, ______, ______. Then find the mean, median, IQR, and MAD of the new set.

d) Which measure of center changed more when you removed the outlier: the mean or the median? ____________________

e) Which measure of variability changed more when you removed the outlier: the IQR or the MAD? __________

f) Choose any value in the original set other than the outlier. Write the set without it. Find the mean, median, IQR, and MAD of the new set.

g) What affects the mean and MAD more: the removal of the outlier or the removal of another value?

____

8. Jenny's math test scores (out of 20) are 16, 17, 17, 5, 19, 18, 17, 20, 19.

a) What is the outlier in this set? ________

b) When Jenny's teacher finds the average for the report, should he include the outlier? Discuss with a partner.

9. The dot plots show the number of snowfall days of 15 different cities in Michigan and in New York in January:

Snowfall Days in Michigan:

Snowfall Days in New York:

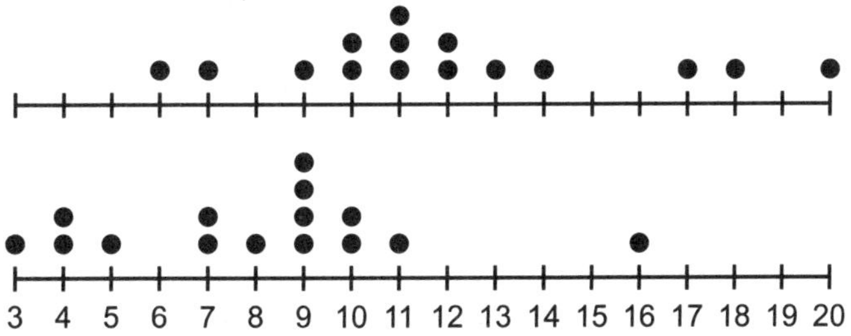

a) Which state has the bigger ...

i) median? __________ ii) mode? __________ iii) range? __________

b) Predict which state has the larger mean and MAD, then check your prediction.

10. The dot plot and the box plot both show the same data.

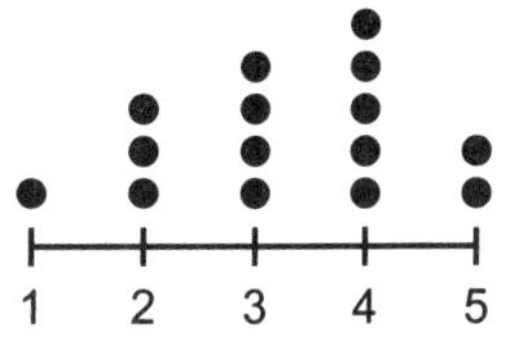

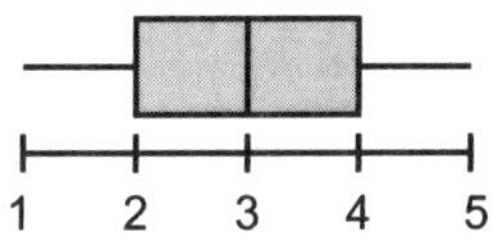

a) Use the box plot to find the median. Check your answer using the dot plot.

b) Which type of graph makes it easier to find the median, the box plot or the dot plot?

c) Find the mean of the data.

d) Which graph did you use to find the mean? Why?

e) Can you tell from the box plot if the data set is symmetric? Check your answer using the dot plot.

11. The box plots represent the waiting time in minutes of 50 random customers at Bank A and Bank B.

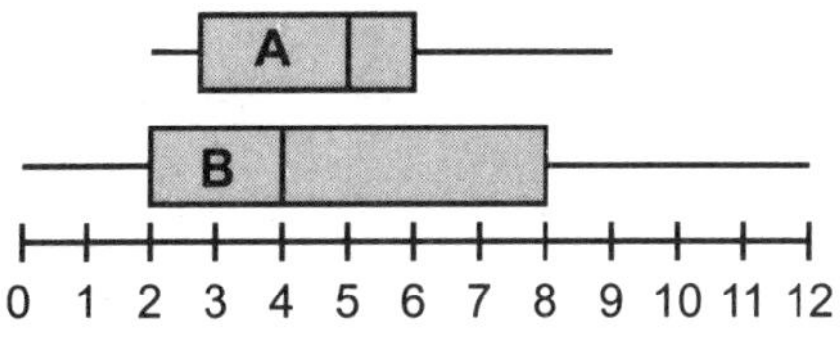

a) Which bank has the lower median waiting time? __________

b) Which bank has the lower IQR? __________

c) Which bank has the lower variability? __________

d) At which bank is there a greater risk of waiting a long time? __________

e) Would you choose the bank with the lower median waiting time? Why or why not?

____

SP7-15 Bias in a Sample or Census

A **population** is the entire group of objects, living things, or people. You can gain information about a population by surveying a **sample**, or a part of the population.

If you collect information by surveying an entire population, you are using a **census**.

If you survey only a part of the population, you are using a **sample**.

1. Would you use a sample or a census to find out …

   a) what movie your five friends want to watch? ________________

   b) who your school thinks should be school president? ________________

   c) how smoking affects people's lungs? ________________

   d) whether people in your home city would support a NBA basketball team? ________________

2. A principal wants to find out if students want school to start and finish half an hour earlier, but she doesn't have time to ask everyone. She surveys two groups, with the following results:

A. The first 50 students who arrive in the morning.	YES 40	NO 10
B. Five students from each of the 10 classrooms.	YES 20	NO 30

   a) Why didn't the two surveys get the same results?

   b) Which group's opinion will be most similar to the whole school's opinion?

   c) If there are 500 students in the school, how many do you think will want school to start and finish half an hour earlier?

A **representative sample** is similar to the whole population. A **biased sample** is not similar to the whole population because some parts are not represented.

3. Which sample in Question 2 is biased: A or B? _____

4. Decide whether each sample is biased or representative. Explain the cause of any bias.

   a) A school that goes from Grades 1 to 8 is planning a party and wants to have board games at the party. To find the most popular board games in the school, they ask …

      A. 40 students from Grades 7 and 8

      B. 5 students from each grade

   b) Scientists are comparing the heart rate of 15 year olds before and after half an hour of exercise. They test the heart rate of …

      A. 25 members of a school track and field team

      B. 25 students from one class

5. A city wants to build a new hockey arena, a new swimming pool, or a new library. Which of the following is the best site for a survey about what to build? Why? What is wrong with the other three options?

A. A beach ______________________________

B. A bookstore ______________________________

C. During a professional hockey game ______________________________

D. A shopping mall ______________________________

6. Eddy and Kim are running in a student election. They want to know how many of the school's 250 students will vote for them.

Eddy asks the 25 students in his class and finds that 15 will vote for him and 10 will not.

Kim gets a student list from the principal and asks every tenth student on the list. She finds that 15 will vote for her and 10 will not.

a) Whose sample is more biased? Why?

b) Who do you think will win the election? Why?

7. Josh wants to know how many hours per day his classmates play video games. He asks the students in his class the following question:

Research shows that certain video games help your brain develop, and the more you play the better. How many hours a day do you play video games?

1 hour a day or less	1–3 hours a day
3–5 hours a day	more than 5 hours a day

Will Josh's survey results be biased? Explain.

8. To find out whether school uniforms should be required, two questions are proposed:

A. Do you think that students should be allowed to express themselves by what they wear?

B. Do you think that equality among students is important enough to require consistent student uniforms?

a) Which question do you think was proposed by someone in favour of school uniforms? ______

Which question was proposed by someone against school uniforms? ______

b) Write a question the school could ask that does not already suggest an answer.

____

____

SP7-16 Using Samples to Draw Inferences

Reasoning from a sample of the population is called making an **inference** about a population.

Example: There are 150 Grade 7 students in the middle school. Marta wants to know how many have cell phones. She randomly selects 30 Grade 7 students and finds that 16 of them have cell phones. Marta uses a proportion to predict how many students in Grade 7 have cell phones:

$\frac{16}{30} = \frac{x}{150}$ Using cross multiplication: $16 \times 150 = 30x$, so $x = \frac{16 \times 150}{30} = 80$

Based on the sample, Marta can predict that 80 Grade 7 students have cell phones.

1. a) Out of every 50 words that Jim types, 3 words have a mistake. His essay is 3,000 words long. How many words have a mistake?

b) Out of the first 50 words that Jim typed, 3 words have a mistake. His essay has 3,000 words. About how many words would you estimate have a mistake?

2. The United States has around 115,000,000 employees. From a random sample of 132,675 workers, 36,095 leave for work between 5:00 a.m. and 7:00 a.m. Estimate how many employees in the United States leave for work between 5:00 a.m. and 7:00 a.m.

3. A shipment from a lamp factory consists of 9,000 lamps.

a) A quality-control technician randomly picks a sample of 15 lamps from the product line and finds that none of them are defective. How many would he estimate are defective in the entire shipment?

b) A quality-control manager randomly picks a sample of 75 lamps from the product line and finds that 2 are defective. How many lamps would he estimate are defective in the entire shipment?

c) Who has the more reliable prediction, the technician or the manager? Explain.

4. Bev wants to know whether the students in her grade want a soda machine at school. She asks everyone to drop a red marble in a jar for "yes" and a blue marble for "no." She counts the marbles and finds 18 blue marbles and 24 red marbles.

a) Imagine a deck of cards with 18 black playing cards and 24 red playing cards that you have shuffled well. What colour of cards represents the blue marbles? __________

b) What is the ratio of red cards to all cards in the set? __________

c) If you pick the top card, what color do you expect it to be? __________

d) How is shuffling the cards similar to picking people at random to survey?

____

5. In a free throw competition, each player is allowed to take 5 shots. Players earn one point for each free throw they make. Here are the points scored by 30 randomly selected players:

2	1	0	0	1	3	2	0	3	1	1	0	4	3	1
0	4	1	3	1	0	5	2	2	1	0	1	2	0	1

Data Value	Frequency
0	
1	
2	
3	
4	
5	

a) Transfer the data into the tally chart and find the frequencies.

b) Estimate the number of players who don't score any points if 1,500 people take part in the competition.

c) Find the range, median, Q1, and Q3 for the data set.

Range = __________ Median = ______ Q1 = ______ Q3 = ______

d) Draw a box plot for the data set.

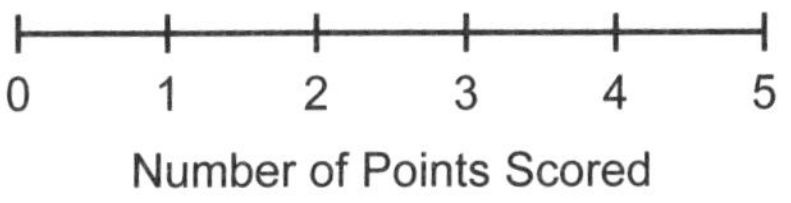

e) Find the mean of the data set.

Bonus ▶ Players win $1 for every point they score, so each player can win from $0 to $5. Based on the sample, what is the fair price for the competition?

6. Last year, Ben bought 30 books for the library. The prices of the books are as shown below:

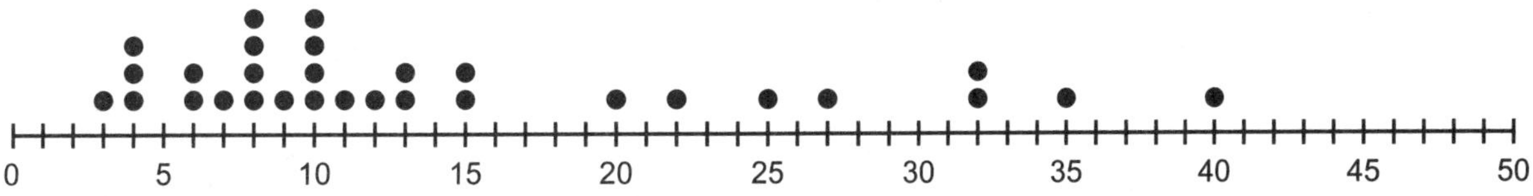

This year, Ben plans to buy 50 books for the library. To prepare his budget for this year, should he be more interested in the median or the mean of the prices from last year's purchases? Explain.

SP7-17 Sampling Variability

1. a) What proportion of the numbers from 1 to 1,000 are multiples of 5?
Remember: A number is divisible by 5 if its ones digit is 0 or 5.

b) Three samples of size 10 were chosen at random from the numbers 1 to 1,000:

Sample	Number of Multiples of 5 in the Random Samples	Fraction of Multiples of 5 in the Random Samples
A. 996, 356, 705, 324, 237, 152, 31, 483, 544, 806	1	$\frac{1}{10}$
B. 455, 70, 458, 203, 192, 367, 364, 296, 905, 135		
C. 86, 231, 394, 978, 313, 94, 527, 375, 893, 732		

c) The three samples come from the same population. Why don't they have the same proportion of multiples of 5? Why are they so different?

d) Here is a dot plot showing the number of multiples of 5 in 30 random samples of size 10. Circle where the number of multiples of 5 in samples A, B, and C are located on the dot plot.

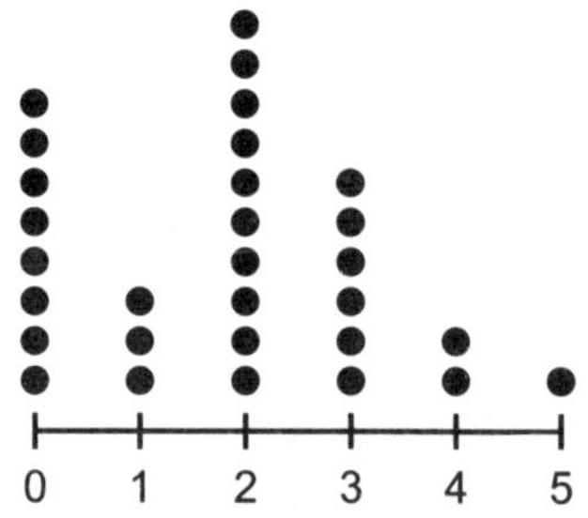

Number of Multiples of 5
in Random Samples of Size 10

e) Find the range, median, Q1, and Q3 for the data set in part d).

Range = ______________ Median = _____

Q1 = _____ Q3 = _____

f) Draw a box plot for the data set.

2. Combine the three samples from Question 1.b) to make a larger sample of size 30.

a) How many multiples of 5 are in the larger sample? _____

b) What proportion of the larger sample are multiples of 5? _____

c) Is the proportion of the larger sample closer to the true proportion? _____

d) Here is a dot plot of 30 random samples of size 30 with the number of multiples of 5 in each sample. Find the median and IQR.

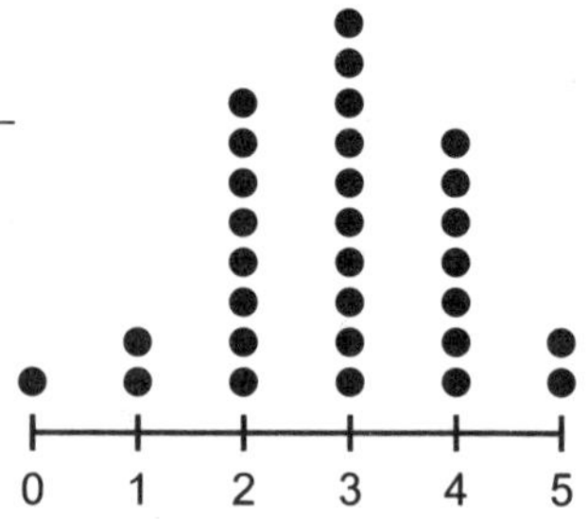

Median = _____ Q1 = _____ Q3 = _____ IQR = _____

e) Compare the IQR of sample size 30 with the IQR of sample size 10.

3. A typical bingo game uses numbers from 1 to 75. Vicky takes a random sample of five numbers from a bingo set and finds the mean of the sample. For example, if she takes 26, 13, 49, 7, 67, the mean is $\frac{26+13+49+7+67}{5}=\frac{162}{5}=32.4$. Vicky rounds the mean to the nearest whole number, which is 32.

a) Vicky does her experiment 20 times. The means are in the table below:

32	42	33	46	49	30	41	38	35	44
43	36	48	36	28	41	40	37	34	47

i) Draw a dot plot for the data set.

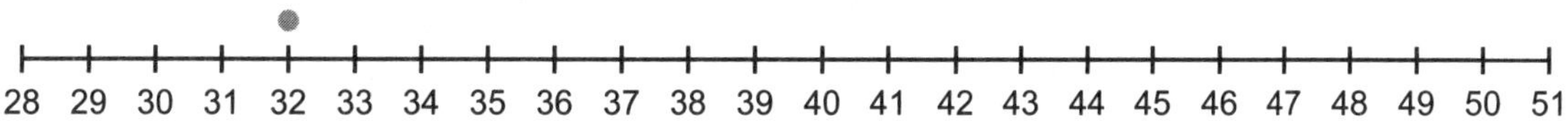

ii) Find the median and mean of the data set (mean of the means).

iii) Find the IQR and MAD for the data set.

b) Tom does the same experiment as Vicky with a sample size 30. He does the experiment 20 times. The means are in the table below:

40	38	35	41	37	36	42	35	36	42
39	36	37	33	38	38	40	44	34	39

i) Draw a dot plot for the data set.

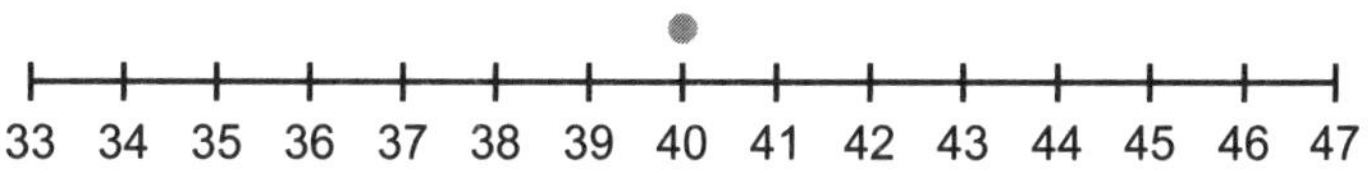

ii) Find the median and mean of the data set (mean of the means).

iii) Find the IQR and MAD for the data set.

____

____

c) The true mean of the population (all numbers from 1 to 75) is 38. Who has a closer mean to the true mean, Vicky or Tom? _______________

d) Which sample size has low variability? Hint: Which one has the smaller IQR and MAD?

____

SP7-18 Degree of Overlap of Two Populations with the Same Variability

1. a) By looking at the box plots, would you describe the medians as being close together or far apart?

i) 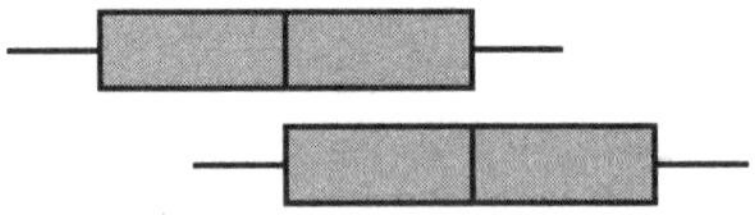

____

ii) 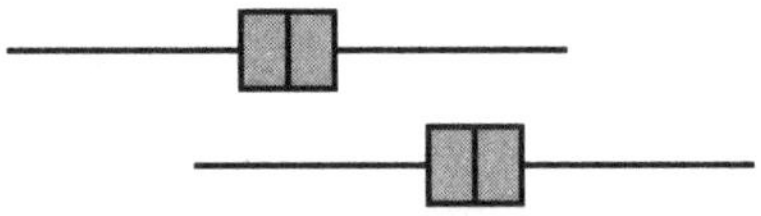

____

b) The medians of the box plots are 2 apart. Find the IQR of both box plots.

i) 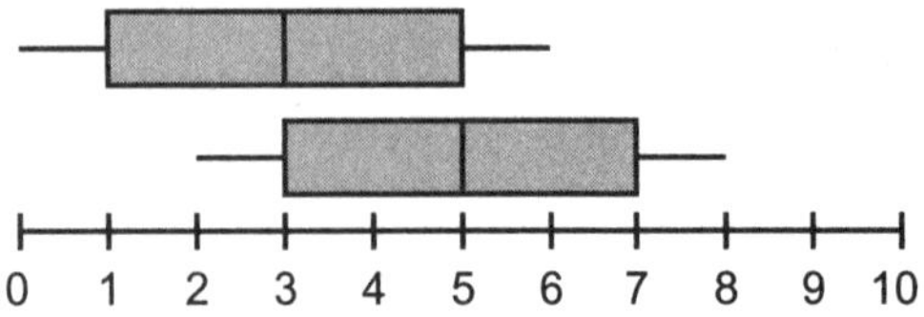

IQR = _______

ii) 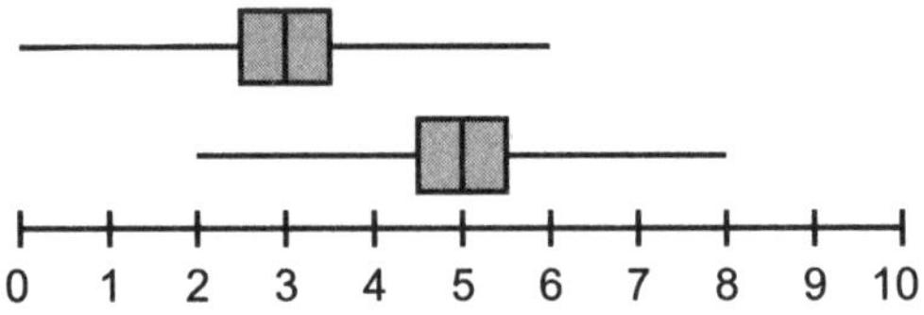

IQR = _______

Jay compares the marks of 15 students in Class A and 15 students in Class B:

Class B marks:

Class A marks:

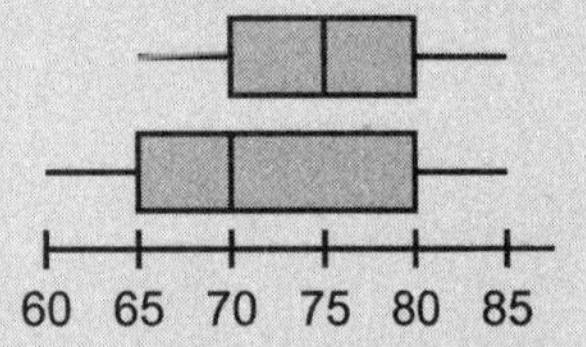

Jay notices that both data sets have very close centers and spreads. Jay puts one box plot over the other one to see the **overlap**. The intersection of the boxes in the box plots is dark gray.

Overlap of Class A and B:

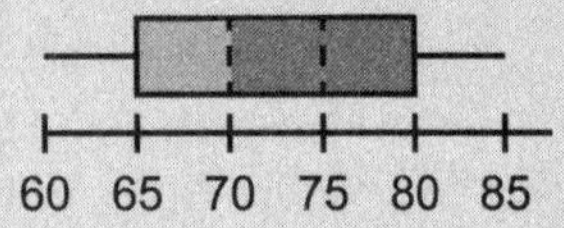

When Jay puts one box plot over the other, most of the boxes turn dark gray. There is high overlap.

2. For each pair of box plots, determine whether there is no overlap, small overlap, or high overlap.

a) Sample B:

Sample A:

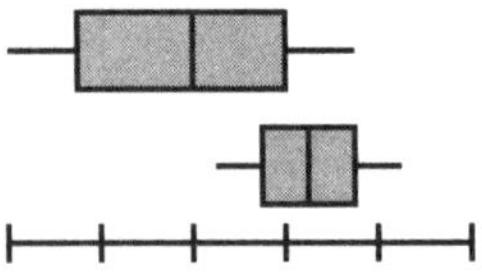

_______________ overlap

b) Sample B:

Sample A:

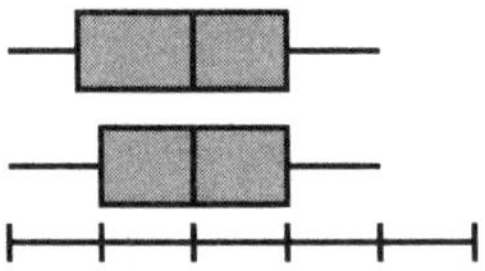

_______________ overlap

c) Sample B:

Sample A:

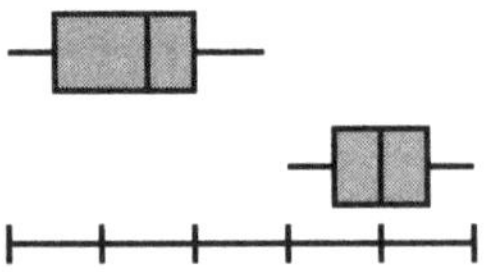

_______________ overlap

d) Sample B:

Sample A:

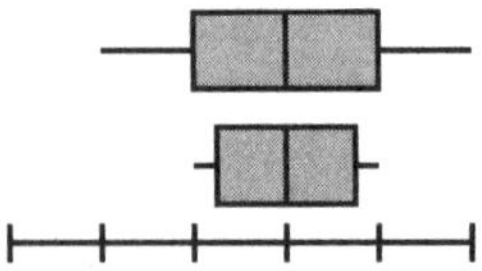

_______________ overlap

e) Sample B:

Sample A:

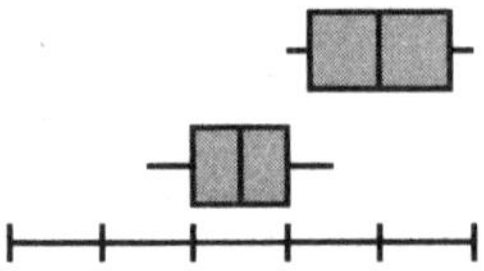

_______________ overlap

f) Sample B:

Sample A:

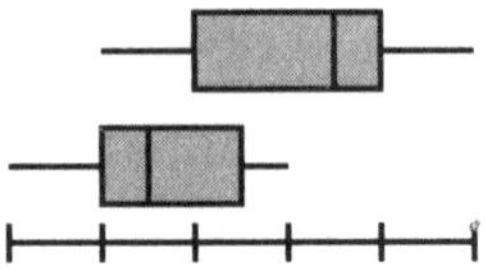

_______________ overlap

3. Look at the pairs of dot plots below.

A. 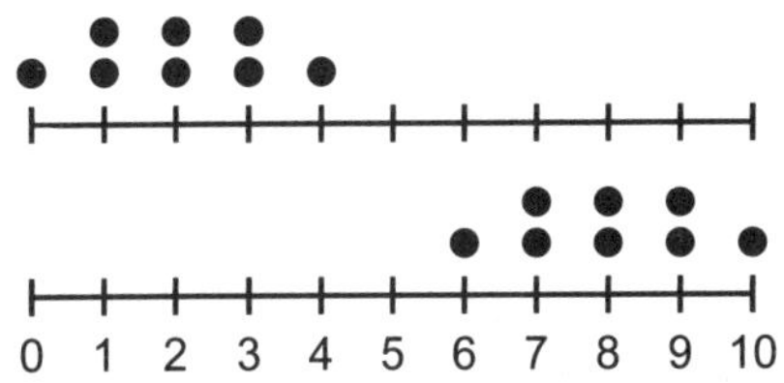

B. 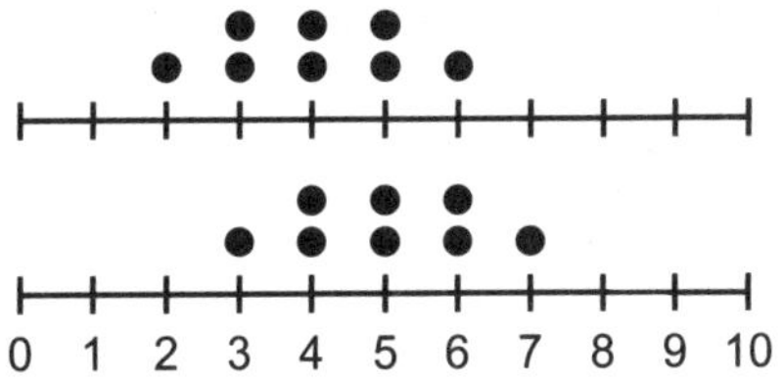

a) How far apart are the means?

In A, the means are ______ and ______, so the means are ______ units apart.

In B, the means are ______ and ______, so the means are ______ units apart.

b) Tessa says that the MADs are all the same and she can tell that without calculating. Is she right? Explain.

____

c) Find the means and MADs of the two data sets in A to show that Tessa is right.

d) Do the data sets appear to overlap?

In A: __________ In B: __________

e) Which is greater, the MAD of both sets, or the difference between the means?

In A: ______________________ In B: ______________________

4. Box plots A and B represent sets that have 100 data values.

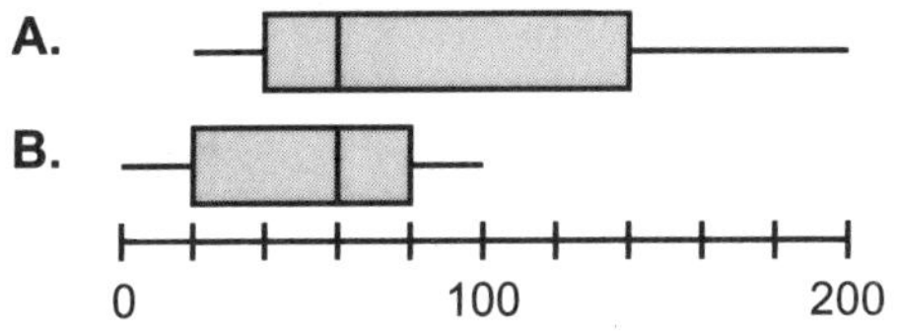

a) Which box plot has the greater range, A or B? ______

b) Which box plot has the greater IQR? ______

c) In which box plot are the data points more tightly clustered around the median? ______

d) Would you describe the degree of overlap between the two data sets as no overlap, small overlap, or high overlap? ______________________

5. Look at your answers to Question 1.

a) Which pair of data sets appears to overlap more: i) or ii)? ______

b) Is the difference between the medians greater than or less than the IQR?

i) ______________________ ii) ______________________

6. The dot plots show the life expectancies for most of the countries in Africa and Europe.

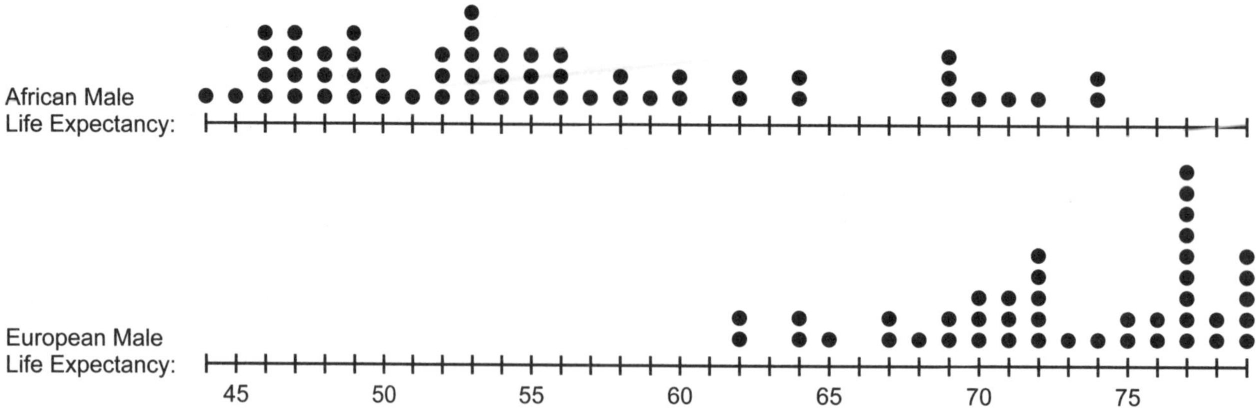

a) Estimate the mean for African and European countries. Africa: ______ Europe: ______

b) Which continent has the higher MAD? ________________ How can you tell from the dot plots? ____

c) Is it rare to see a country in Africa with a male life expectancy at least 7 years away from the mean? ________

d) Is it rare to see a country in Europe with a male life expectancy at least 7 years away from the mean? ________

e) Do any countries in Africa have a life expectancy near the European mean? ________

f) Do any countries in Europe have a life expectancy near the African mean? ________

g) Is the overlap between these two populations high or small? ________

7. The dot plots show the heights of 15 Grade 7 soccer players and the heights of 15 Grade 7 basketball players:

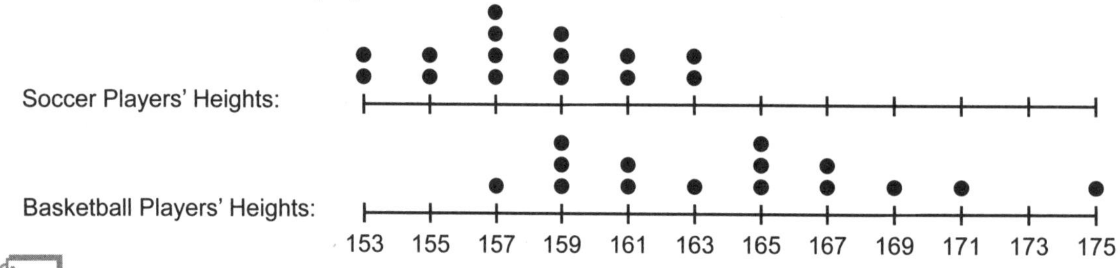

a) Find the range, median, Q1, and Q3 for each set of data.

b) Draw a box plot for each set of data.

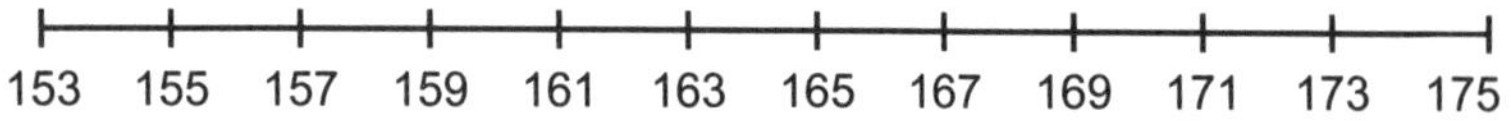

c) Would you describe the degree of overlap between the height of the soccer players and the height of the basketball players as no overlap, a small overlap, or a high overlap?

SP7-19 Using Mean and MAD to Compare Populations

You can express the difference between the centers of two populations using MAD. Find the difference between the mean of two populations and divide it by the greatest MAD. For two populations that have high overlap, this number is less than 1.

1. Alexa randomly sampled 15 girls and 15 boys in Grade 7 who have cell phones and asked them how many minutes per day they spend texting. The data and summary measures are as follows:

Gender	**Texting Time per Day (minutes)**															**Mean**	**MAD**
Girls	34	43	27	51	45	25	30	37	29	44	38	41	31	39	32	36.4	6.24
Boys	23	22	24	21	22	42	35	18	31	36	22	17	14	44	31	26.8	7.76

a) Use the same scale to draw a dot plot for each data set.

Girls:

Boys:

14 16 18 20 22 24 26 28 30 32 34 36 38 40 42 44 46 48 50 52

b) Is there more variability in the girls' texting time or in the boys' texting time? ___________

c) Find the median, Q1, Q3, and range for each set of data (girls and boys).

	Median	**Q1**	**Q3**	**Range**
Girls				
Boys				

d) Draw a box plot for each set of data.

Girls:

Boys:

14 16 18 20 22 24 26 28 30 32 34 36 38 40 42 44 46 48 50 52

e) Is the overlap between these two populations high or small? ___________

f) The difference in the means is: ______ − ______ = ______.

Divide the difference in the means by the greater MAD: ______ ÷ ______ ≈ ______.

The mean of girls' and boys' texting times per day differs by ______ times the variability of the number of minutes spent texting.

2. A bag contains 100 cubes. 55 cubes are blue, and the remaining 45 cubes are of any other color.

a) Thirty Grade 7 students each take one sample of size 20 from the bag. The table below shows the number of blue cubes from each draw and the frequencies:

Number of Blue Cubes	7	8	9	10	11	12	13	14	15
Frequency	2	3	1	6	5	4	5	1	3

i) Divide the number of blue cubes by the size of each sample (20) to find the sample proportion.

Number of Blue Cubes	7	8	9	10	11	12	13	14	15
Sample Proportions	*0.35*	*0.40*							

ii) Draw a dot plot for the data.

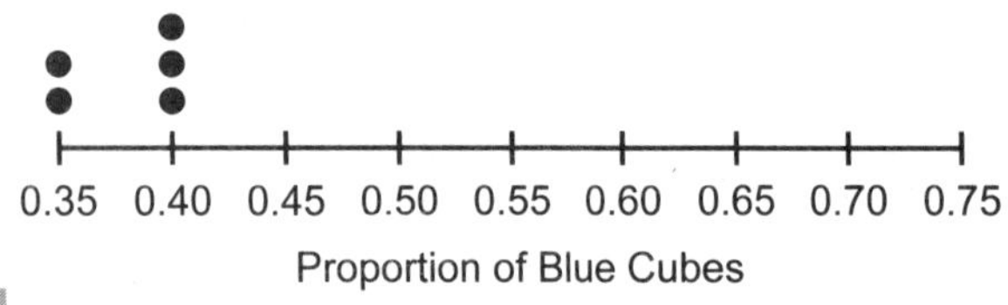

iii) Find the mean and MAD of the sample proportions.

b) Thirty Grade 7 students each take one sample of size 40 from the bag. The results are shown in the table below:

Number of Blue Cubes	18	19	20	21	22	23	24	25	26
Frequency	1	2	3	5	7	7	2	2	1

Answer parts ii) and iii) from part a) using this table.

c) Find the difference between the means from parts a) and b), then divide it by the greatest MAD. Did you get a number less than 1? Is there no overlap, a small overlap, or a high overlap?

3. Groups A and B are compared first by heights and then by ages in the box plots below:

Heights

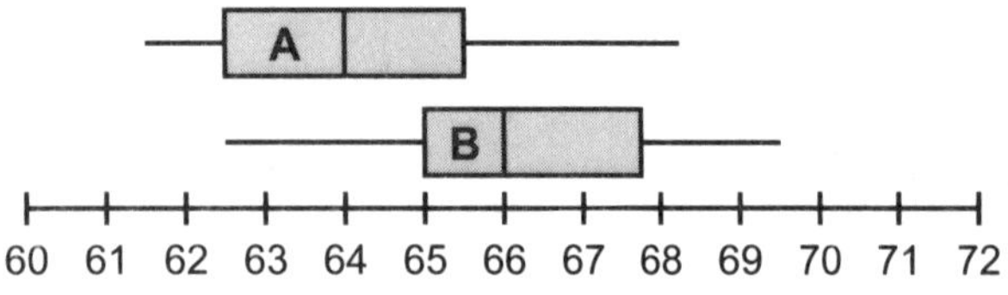

Ages

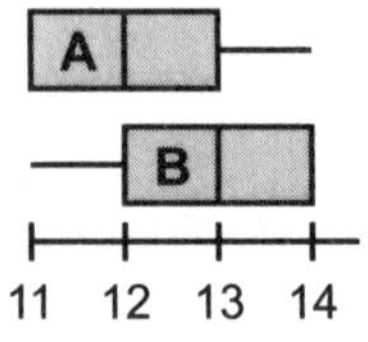

Which is more likely to be a coincidence of the random samples: that the heights are different or that the ages are different?

4. Ivan takes twenty samples of size 20 from a big bag of candies to find what percent of the candies are red. The table below shows the number of red candies:

Number of Red Candies in Sample Size 20	3	0	5	7	4	1	2	3	5	2
	3	5	4	0	6	7	3	2	6	5

a) Draw a dot plot for the data.

b) Find the mean and MAD.

c) Ivan takes twenty samples of size 50. The table below shows the number of red candies:

Number of Red Candies in Sample Size 50	11	8	10	9	10	11	10	12	9	8
	12	10	9	8	8	10	11	9	13	10

Draw a dot plot for the data, then find the mean and MAD.

d) Compare Ivan's results from part b) and part c). What percent of the candies in the bag do you think are red?

5. Twenty-five students were surveyed about how many hours per week they spend watching television and how many hours per week they spend on the Internet. The dot plots represent the results:

Time Spent Watching TV (h):

Time Spent on the Internet (h):

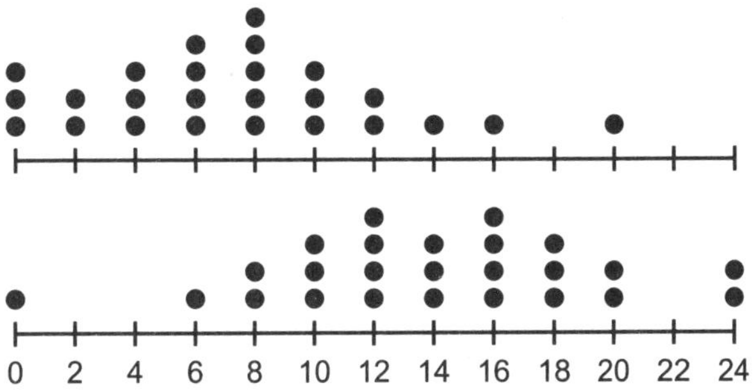

a) Find the range of the two samples. TV: _______ Internet: _______

b) Find the median of the two samples. TV: _______ Internet: _______

c) Draw the box plots. How would you describe the overlap?

Time Spent Watching TV (h):

Time Spent on the Internet (h):

d) Use a calculator to find the mean of the two samples. TV: _______ Internet: _______

e) The difference in the means is ______ − ______ = ______.

Divide the difference in the means by the MAD of hours on the Internet:

______ ÷ ______ ≈ ______, so the mean of Internet hours differs by ______ times the variability of the number of hours on the Internet.